Spirit Mediumship and Society in Africa

Spirit Mediumship and Society in Africa

JOHN BEATTIE ELIZABETH COLSON
M. J. FIELD G. KINGSLEY GARBETT
ROBERT F. GRAY ROBIN HORTON
S. G. LEE I. M. LEWIS
JOHN MIDDLETON AIDAN SOUTHALL
R. E. S. TANNER PIERRE VERGER
F. B. WELBOURN

Edited by
John Beattie and John Middleton

Foreword by Raymond Firth

AFRICANA PUBLISHING CORPORATION · NEW YORK

*Published
in the United States of America 1969
by Africana Publishing Corporation
101 Fifth Avenue
New York, N.Y. 10003
Library of Congress catalog card no. 70–80849*

Printed in Great Britain

CONTENTS

CONTENTS

PLATES

Plate 1 is reproduced by courtesy of the Ghana *Daily Graphic*. Plates 2, 3, 4 and 5 are reproduced from E. L. R. Meyerowitz's *Akan of Ghana*, Faber, by kind permission. Plate 6 is from a photograph by E. L. R. Meyerowitz, by kind permission. Plate 7 is from a photograph by M. J. Field. Plates 8, 9 and 10 are from photographs by S. G. Lee. Plates 11, 12 and 13 are from photographs by R. E. S. Tanner.

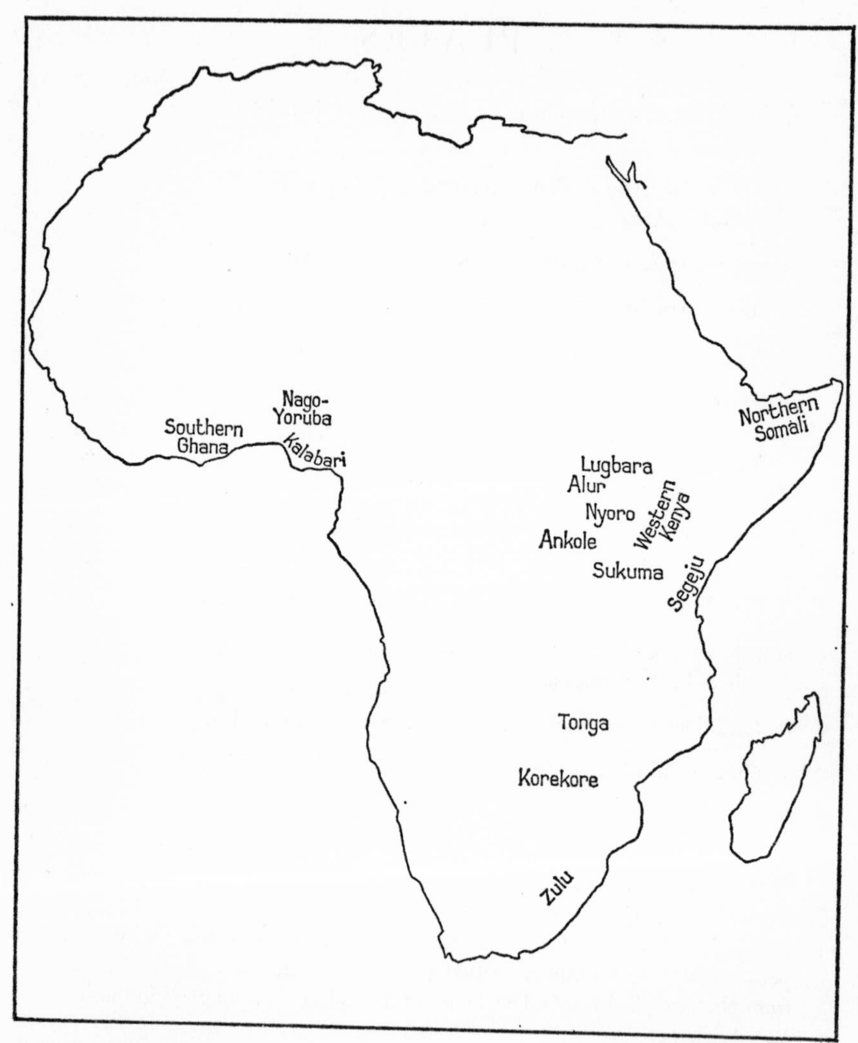

Location of societies discussed

FOREWORD

© *Raymond Firth*

Spirit possession and spirit mediumship are among the most widespread and most intriguing phenomena in the occult field. Under these names, or as ecstasy, pythonism, demon possession, devil-dancing, shamanism, spiritism, spiritualism, they have been the subject of a vast literature extending over at least two thousand years. In the classical Greek period accounts of Dionysiac cults refer to possession by the god in which worshippers saw visions and performed feats of an extraordinary kind. In Christian proselytization in the nineteenth century, possession and mediumship often presented problems for the missionary, who found himself opposed, as he thought, by evil spirits in person.[1] In Britain after the first world war spiritualism responded to a widespread interest of bereaved families wishing to get into touch with their loved sons who had died: more generally, it attracted the attention of the Society for Psychical Research, leaders of the churches, and a host of earnest seekers after evidence of the survival of human personality after bodily death. In such contexts spirit mediumship has been variously described as psychic renewal, discovery and utilization of the miraculous powers of the human mind, irreligious spirit communication, a superstition leading to loss of health, loss of morals and loss of faith.[2]

Social anthropologists too have studied spirit possession and spirit mediumship, but from a different point of view. They have been concerned not with problems of survival of personality of the dead, but with problems of multiple personality of the living. Many of them have been faced in the field by dramatic changes of personality in men or women they were studying – startling yet evidently accustomed alterations of behaviour, with trembling, sweating, groaning, speaking with strange voices, assumption of a different identity, purporting to be a spirit not a human being, giving commands or foretelling the future in a new authoritative way. Sometimes it has been hard for the anthropologist to persuade himself that it is really the same person as before whom he is watching or confronting, so marked is the personality change. Most anthropologists have not been equipped to study the technical physiological and psychological questions involved in such trance or dissociation. But they have been able to focus upon aspects of the phenomena usually neglected by other students of the subject – the social position of the performer, the reactions of the audience, the structural type of personification adopted by the medium, the relation of the seance to events before and after, the general place of the spirit cult in the social and religious system of the people.[3]

I have been interested in the subject of spirit mediumship for forty years, ever since with some surprise I found myself plunged unexpectedly into a succession of mediumistic seances during my first field trip to Tikopia. Long before then, anthropologists such as Rivers and Ling Roth had begun to pay attention to such phenomena, but full-length studies have been rare. I appreciate then the opportunity of contributing a short note of introduction to this volume on spirit possession and spirit medium phenomena in Africa.

This volume is valuable because it gathers together under a single cover material from a wide range of African societies. It allows similarities and differences to be easily perceived and suggests social correlates of these in terms of age, sex, marital status, social grading and wealth. It includes material on both traditional and modern cults. It provides a basis of comparison with analogous material from other areas. By revealing underlying elements in the significance of spirit medium cults for members of various types of society, these studies will help us to understand more clearly how and why such cults can give way before the introduction of medicine and hospitals of Western type or the advance of a new proselytizing religion.

In my own work I have found it convenient to separate the phenomena of spirit mediumship in particular from those of spirit possession in general. In both a person's actions are believed to be dictated by an extra-human entity which has entered his body or otherwise affected him. Both kinds of phenomena may often be regarded as instances of multiple personality, that is the individual concerned assumes another identity, refers to his normal self as 'he' and sincerely differentiates this new identity sharply from his everyday self. But in spirit possession his behaviour does not necessarily convey any particular message to other people. It is primarily regarded as his bodily expression of spirit manifestation. In spirit mediumship the emphasis is upon *communication.* The extra-human entity is not merely expressing himself but is regarded as having something to say to an audience. This implies that the verbal and non-verbal behaviour of a person who, possessed by a spirit, acts as a medium, must be more highly *controlled* than that of a person simply possessed. In some societies possession is a form of collective extravaganza, routinized and tolerated, though not everyday behaviour. By common convention in many other societies a person regarded as possessed tends to be classed as a sick patient for whom treatment is necessary. But a possessed person who acts as a medium tends to be regarded as a hale person who is carrying out a special role. The behaviour of both tends to be largely stereotyped, to conform to a kind of code. But what is particularly interesting here is that in many societies the code of the medium is used to provide an interpretation of the code of the possessed patient. Under pressure of the social conventions, the medium in *his* spirit terms works out the stresses which the patient displays in *his* spirit terms. For societies lacking modern psychological medicine, spirit medium treatment of patients can be an extremely interesting instance of self-help.

What stands out in so much of the material is that spirit mediumship and, in many cases, spirit possession also, is not an isolated individual phenomenon but a cult. It is part of a complex series of ideas and practices of a relatively integrated kind, oriented to the recognition of extra-human powers.

Spirit possession and spirit mediumship have a conceptual field and an operational field. Conceptually, they help to produce evidence in the eyes of other members of the society for the reality of the spirit world in which traditionally these people have been taught to believe. Here and now, as they see it, spirits from an unseen universe take on material shape and communicate with men. But in many societies spirit possession and spirit medium cults offer a field for some degree of individual self-expression, maybe of a fantasy order, going well beyond the conventions of tradition.[4] Spirit mediumship may thus allow of flexibility in the conceptualization of the spirit universe, and presumably thereby offer some possibilities of change in belief.

Operationally, spirit possession allows an individual to throw off ordinary restraints and, in speech or in non-verbal behaviour, to act in ways not sanctioned by his ordinary role in society. Anthropologists as a rule (there are some notable exceptions, as in this volume) know very little about what kinds of person are most liable to act in such ways, or what kinds of circumstance may lead to a person's breaking through the conventional boundaries of social behaviour. Often we can merely speculate as to the forms of suffering (or alternatively, perhaps, of compensation) which such individuals may have in entering and continuing in possession states. Some accounts indicate that physical discomfort and mental pain are definitely involved on some such occasions. Others seem to show that whatever be the physical and psychological difficulties entailed by the 'possession syndrome', some personal benefits may at times accrue. Redress or enhancement of status is one such compensation which is suggested strongly by much of the anthropological evidence. The evidence is not always clear, but it does seem that some readjustment in the relative status of the sexes may be promoted by some of these possession or spirit medium cults.

Unlike many other investigators, anthropologists have not been much interested in the question of truth or fraud in the spirit presentations. They have generally assumed that the 'spirits' were aspects of phases of the medium's personality, produced by stress, or allowed and stimulated to come to the surface by customary forms of conditioning. The anthropological problem of fraud in spirit mediumship lies at the level, not of spiritual *versus* human phenomena, but of unconscious *versus* conscious production of symptoms. For an anthropologist, the phenomena of spirit mediumship are 'genuine' if the performer actually enters the trance state and does not merely simulate it. Trance simulation undoubtedly occurs among peoples who have confidence in spirit medium performances, and is known by them to occur. Though it may invalidate for them the efficacy of an individual performance, such 'faking' is not held to destroy the truth of the spirit cult as a whole. Moreover, in some cases the conscious 'acting out' of the expected mediumistic role, even though recognized as an 'act' by the audience, may be thought to benefit a patient.[5]

But instances of simulation of trance are very significant in throwing light on another set of problems, in the relation between personal predisposition to trance and social demand for it. We may assume that anyone who enters into a state of 'possession' must have some innate tendency to suggestibility. In many forms of spirit mediumship some kind of auto-suggestion is used by the performer to induce his trance state – locking his hands together and tensing his muscles, rhythmic swinging of head, monotonous beating of drum, and so on. But the social pressures on an individual to enter the trance state are often considerable. Even apart from occasions of collective ecstasy, as in the charismatic phases of pentecostal sectarian gatherings, the sheer expectations of an audience often help to provide a situation congenial to the development of trance behaviour in persons in the appropriate social position. But despite the social pressures and despite the individual's own efforts to seek the oblivion of trance, there are occasional failures. If then the practitioner should simulate the disjunction of personality which he normally accomplishes, this is usually less an attempt at trickery than at evasion of embarrassment at not being able to give the public what it wants.

For social benefits too often appear to accrue from spirit mediumship. At a low level, direction of attention, satisfaction of curiosity, and interest in novelty are afforded to an audience observing the behaviour of a possessed person and the practices of a spirit medium attempting to cure him. In sophisticated situations aesthetic elements may be involved in the symbolic behaviour of possessed persons or mediums, especially when the behaviour of the latter takes on rhythmic form, as in song or dance. In some cases spirit medium cult behaviour may assume a succession of formal oppositions to produce a kind of dramatic conflict.[6] Such aesthetic elements may contribute to relaxation of performers and of audience, and serve to some extent in giving relief from stress.

But the most important social function is to provide treatment for sick people. This the cults do by operating a set of extra-normal behaviours in speech and gesture. They offer to the sick person, who is himself behaving in an abnormal way, a framework of ideas and practices which is very different from that of normal, everyday life. For the more purely physical ills the therapeutic effect of spirit medium practices may be no more than reassurance. But for the mentally ill (the 'possessed'), the conceptualization in spirit idiom gives diagnosis and prognosis in terms of the patient's own fantasies. Such a mode of fighting fire with fire often seems to have great stress-reducing effect, for both patient and audience. Such extra-normal behaviour, including verbal statements, is presented with an air of authority which transcends the authority of ordinary human beings. So, since the general intent of the mediumistic performance is to suggest a procedure of recovery to the patient, such suggestion is given with a strength exceeding that which his family, kin and other members of his community could ordinarily give. Studies of this order then can be very significant for psychological medicine. They throw light on explanatory systems of disease and healing in a wide range of societies in which modern medicine is endeavouring to come to terms with traditional therapeutic practices.[7]

London
March 1968

RAYMOND FIRTH

NOTES

[1] For example, see Rev. John L. Nevius, D.D. (for forty years a missionary to the Chinese), *Demon Possession and Allied Themes*, London 1893.

[2] For a set of essays giving very varied opinions see Huntly Carter (ed.), *Spiritualism: Its Present-Day Meaning*, London 1920.

[3] For general references see Marcelle Bouteiller, *Chamanisme et Guerison Magique*, Paris 1950; Mircea Eliade, *Shamanism: Archaic Techniques of Ecstasy* (trans. from French, Willard R. Trask), New York 1964; Hans Findeisen, *Schamentum*, Stuttgart 1957; R. W. Firth, 'Shamanism' in Julius Gould and William L. Kolb (eds.) *A Dictionary of the Social Sciences*, London 1964.

[4] *E.g.* see my 'Individual Fantasy and Social Norms: Seances with Spirit Mediums' in *Tikopia Ritual and Belief*, London 1967, pp. 293–329.

[5] See John Beattie, *Initiation into the Cwezi Spirit Possession Cult in Bunyoro*, African Studies, Vol. 16, 1957, pp. 160–161.

[6] See my 'Ritual and Drama in Malay Spirit Mediumship', *Comparative Studies in Society and History*, Vol. IX, 1967, pp. 190–207.

[7] See *Magic, Faith and Healing: Studies in Primitive Psychiatry Today*, ed. Ari Kiev (with foreword by Jerome D. Frank), New York, London 1964.

ACKNOWLEDGEMENTS

Elizabeth Colson

I worked among Plateau Tonga, September 1946 – September 1947 and June 1948 – September 1950; among Valley Tonga, September 1956 – September 1957 and September 1962 – August 1963 and July–August 1965, with brief visits in June 1949 and January 1960. The work was sponsored by the Rhodes-Livingstone Institute, though the Social Science Research Council financed the 1965 trip. I am indebted to my colleague Dr Thayer Scudder for the use of his field notes on the Valley Tonga and for his criticisms on a draft of this paper. The material on *masabe* possession was first presented at a seminar held at the University of California, Berkeley, 1964. I have to thank the following members of the seminar for their comments and criticisms: B. Blount, W. Curly, L. Kirk, P. Lyon, C. Mitchell, W. Pendleton, and I. Zaretsky. Mr Zaretsky also made a careful critique of an early draft of the completed paper. A grant from the University of California African Studies Program assisted in the analysis of the material.

G. Kingsley Garbett

Fieldwork was made possible first (1960–61) by the award of a Fellowship by the International African Institute and secondly (1963–64) by support from the University College of Rhodesia and Nyasaland. I gratefully acknowledge this assistance. I must also thank numerous colleagues at Manchester University and the University College of Rhodesia and Nyasaland, particularly Dr A. L. Epstein, Professor M. Gluckman, Professor J. C. Mitchell and Dr J. van Velsn who on various occasions have criticized some or all of the arguments advanced above.

ACKNOWLEDGEMENTS

S. G. Lee

I am indebted to the Wenner-Gren Foundation for Anthropological Research, New York, for the fellowship without which my field work would not have been possible. My two Zulu research assistants, the late Charles Mthembu, and Arthur Umlaw, were invaluable as helpers and on their integrity and intelligence the whole validity of the research rests. Drs E. A. and M. Barker of Zululand made available to me all the resources of the Charles Johnson Memorial Hospital and to them I will always be grateful. Mr D. S. Wright and my wife helped greatly with the reading of a first draft, as did Mrs M. Lamb with the final preparation of this paper. To all of these my thanks.

John Beattie

My fieldwork in Bunyoro (1951–53, 1955) was mostly financed by the Treasury Committee for Studentships in Foreign Languages and Cultures, London (the 'Scarbrough' Committee), whose support I gratefully acknowledge.

Robert F. Gray

The field work on which this paper is based extended from February to June, 1956. This research was supported by the Ford Foundation and the Institute of Current World Affairs.

I. M. Lewis

This paper is based principally upon research carried out in Northern Somaliland between 1955 and 1957. For helpful comments on earlier drafts I am especially grateful to Drs B. W. Andrzejewski and Peter Ucko.

John Middleton

I should like to acknowledge the help given to me, in my research and in the initial writing-up of my field material, by the Worshipful Company of Goldsmiths, London; the Colonial Social Science Research Council, London; and the Wenner-Gren Foundation for Anthropological Research, New York. Dr John Beattie has made several helpful comments on the original draft of this paper.

INTRODUCTION

John Beattie and John Middleton

I

There is an immense literature on spirit mediumship, spirit possession, shamanism, and related phenomena. Almost all of it relates to societies outside Africa, particularly to Asia and North America. The most comprehensive account is probably that by Eliade (1951). However it contains relatively little African material, and it is not written from an anthropological or sociological viewpoint but rather from that of the historian of religion concerned with symbolic interpretation and the diffusion of items of culture. Adequate comparative studies of the relationship between forms of mediumship and the social order are lacking. The best account of these phenomena from Africa are those by Leiris (1958) on Ethiopia and by Nadel (1946) on Nuba shamanism. Many monographs and papers on African peoples contain some data, but they are scattered and many are of little value: the most useful bibliography is by Zaretsky (1967). This volume of essays is an attempt to begin to fill this gap in the ethnography of Africa.

Our first task is to ask what we should understand by the terms 'spirit mediumship' and 'spirit possession'. Firth has suggested the following definitions (1959, 141):

> *Spirit possession* is a form of trance in which behaviour actions of a person are interpreted as evidence of a control of his behaviour by a spirit normally external to him. *Spirit mediumship* is normally a form of possession in which the person is conceived as serving as an intermediary between spirits and men. The accent here is on communication; the actions and words of the medium must be translatable, which differentiates them from mere spirit possession or madness. *Shamanism* is a term I prefer to use in the limited North Asiatic sense, of a master of spirits.

We follow Firth's definitions, but should be inclined to add that possession may include both 'real' and 'assumed' trance.

In this book we are concerned with spirit mediumship and spirit possession, but primarily with institutions centring on spirit mediumship. As in the analysis of any social institution, we can study these from three aspects. We can ask what the people who have such institutions think about them; we can ask what they do about them; and we can ask how what they think and what they do relate to other aspects of their cultures. So this brief Introduction has three sections. First we consider the ideological aspects of mediumistic cults: mediumship implies beliefs and values concerning the world, and these must be understood if the behaviour being investigated is to make sense. Next we regard the ways in which the people who have the cults put their ideas and beliefs into action; what is actually done? Here the questions are what kinds of people may become mediums, how they do so, and what actually happens in mediumistic performances? And finally we examine briefly the social and cultural contexts of the cults. We ask how, if at all, they reflect aspects of the kinds of societies and cultures in which they occur, and what kinds of social and psychological implications cult behaviour may have, whether or not the people involved are aware of these implications. Inevitably there is some overlap between these three approaches, but analytically the distinction between them is crucial. For they imply significant differences between the kinds of questions which it is useful to ask (rather than differences between the phenomena themselves), and these questions may be and sometimes are confused.

II

The conception underlying all mediumistic cults is that there is a distinction made between the immediate and ordered realm of the human and social, on the one hand, and a realm of spirit outside and beyond the control and full understanding of men, on the other. The boundaries between them may vary from one culture to another. But in all of them this outside realm is seen as containing spiritual forces of various kinds, and in many cultures it is believed that through spirit mediumship men may, for their own purposes, enter into relationship with some of these forces. The mediumistic relationship is thought to be a particularly direct and close one, more so than can be achieved through such means as sacrifice, prayer, or the observation of omens, all of which may, though they need not, be associated with mediumship.

We need not consider here the large and perhaps unanswerable question, in a sense a question about origins, why men everywhere have peopled their world with a multiplicity of supra-human, or extra-human, gods and spirits. One answer is that where, as is commonly the case in small-scale preliterate societies, there is no sufficient body of empirical knowledge to enable men to cope in practical terms with many of the hazards of life, then these hazards may be, so to speak, personified by being turned into spirits, and then dealt with through ritual and symbolic procedures. If the threatening forces can be represented as somehow like people (though essentially not people), then a kind of social relationship can be entered into with them and their hostility may be averted or mitigated by invocation, prayer and sacrifice. Another answer is that when man became human he was faced with the intellectual problem of understanding and explaining his world; on this view his gods are in effect proto-scientific hypotheses about the nature of the forces which surround and act upon him, and so they go some way to satisfy his need to understand. It seems probable that the evolution of religion, in Sir Edward Tylor's meaning of the term as a belief in spiritual beings, involved both of these concerns, which indeed are still with us. But we would be inclined to give priority to the first (see Horton, 1960; Beattie, 1966).

We can distinguish two broad though not mutually exclusive categories of extra-human powers that may be spiritualized. First, there are those imagined forces which though not themselves human are believed to have been left by once-living people. These are conveniently, and conventionally, called ghosts. In Africa the ghosts of dead kinsmen, often of remoter ancestors in either line of ascent, are believed to exercise powerful effects on the living, acting either individually or as a collectivity. Though 'ancestor worship' is very much a matter of degree, we may note that all the people discussed in this book, except the Islamic or Islamicized Somali and Segeju, are reported to be more or less concerned with ghosts of the dead. But men may be concerned with the ghosts of non-kin as well as with those of actual or putative relatives. In some societies the ghosts of long-dead, sometimes legendary, kings or 'heroes' may be thought important for the living, as among the Baganda, and among the Kalabari and Banyoro described in this book. Often these powers are merged with the spirits of natural, elemental forces, referred to below; this is one case in which the two broad categories here being distinguished are not mutually exclusive. Thirdly, in many societies the ghosts of unrelated persons, recently dead, may be thought to be able to harm persons who caused them offence or injury when they were alive. And lastly, in some societies where hunting is an important activity, the ghosts of slain animals may be believed to be capable of affecting the future success of the huntsman who killed them, and so may have to be dealt with through possession ritual.

The second broad category of extra-human spiritual powers or agents are those gods and spirits which represent certain non-human forces in the environment and which for the most part are not thought to be associated with once-living beings. In many of the societies considered in this book such elemental forces as thunder, lightning, rain, rivers, the bush, are personified as spirits, sometimes as being *sui generis*, sometimes, as we have just noted, as identified with ancient semi-legendary rulers, like the Bacwezi of Bunyoro and Ankole. Frequently, also, such terrifying and uncontrollable events as sudden and disastrous epidemics are similarly spiritualized, like plague and smallpox among the Interlacustrine Bantu and the Zulu. It is not surprising that where well-developed mediumistic cults exist, the new and often disturbing forces of social change are often dealt with in the same way, as among the Tonga, the Banyoro, the Banyankole, and the Lugbara, in whose cultures even the new faith brought by the Christian missionaries has been assimilated to the traditional cults. Finally, in both East and West Africa, it is believed that certain man-made ritual objects or 'fetishes', imbued with a special magical power, can possess their owners.

What is common to all these powers is that they represent forces which, it is believed, can affect living people in important ways. Ancestors, the ghosts of dead neighbours and kin and of ancient kings and hero-gods, powerfully symbolize the essential social forces of familial, neighbourly, and political obligation, and the systems of authority usually associated with them. The spirits of nature, of epidemic diseases and of social change represent formidable and potentially dangerous aspects of the physical and social environment.

A basic feature of the extra- or supra-human domain is that it is conceived of as the realm of Spirit, or Divinity, or whatever term seems the most appropriate for what is often called a High God. In most African religions the High God is thought to be otiose, remote and detached from men; usually there are myths to explain this separation. Spirit, in this sense, is typically the original Creator, and is considered ultimately responsible (although it may act through lesser spirits) for the design and preservation of the universe, as well as, in some of its aspects, for change and destruction. It is noteworthy that although almost all of the peoples discussed in this book have a notion of a High God, in none (with the possible exception of the Yoruba) is it thought that this god can enter into relationship with men through spirit mediumship. Spirit, in this most abstract sense, is not usually identified with any practically important aspect of the social or physical environment, and there would therefore be little point in attempting to communicate directly with the High God. Contact is made with lesser spiritual forces, of the kinds mentioned above, whose power stems ultimately from Spirit. Sometimes these lesser spirits are taken to be 'refractions' of all-embracing Spirit (as among the Nuer; see Evans-Pritchard, 1956); at other times they are regarded as quite separate and distinct powers, subordinate to but not identified with a single High God. Very often, it appears, this may be a matter of degree.

Next we ask how spirits (we use the term generically here, to include ghosts) are regarded, and what they are thought to do; the latter question is of course a question not about behaviour but about belief. First, are they conceived as malevolent or benevolent? From the evidence in this book it is plain that while some spirits (notably and predictably the *shetani* and jinns of the Segeju and Somali) are thought to be wholly malevolent, no spirits are thought to be beneficent all the time, although many, such as ancestral ghosts and the traditional 'white' Cwezi spirits of the Banyoro, are believed to be so as long as they receive the attentions that they need. That spirits should not be thought of as unconditionally well-disposed towards the living is not surprising. Spirit cults provide a means of coping with and explaining actual or anticipated misfortune, not good fortune. If all were for the best in the best of all possible worlds there would be little need of spirits.

Ideally, the thing to do with unambiguously malevolent spirits is to get rid of them. Somali and Segeju adopt this approach, and so do Banyoro with regard to some less important ghosts and spirits. But most spirits are not regarded as wholly bad, even though their beneficent aspect may consist rather in leaving men alone than in conferring positive good on them. Thus in the case of Sukuma ancestral ghosts, and also of some Alur *jok*, the object of men's sacrifice and prayer is to keep the spirits at a distance rather than to enter into closer relations with them. However, most of the peoples discussed in this book do not conceive the relationship between men and at least certain more important spirits in these apotropaic terms. What is sought is a positive, usually enduring, relationship between the inhabitants of the realms both of man and of spirit, a relationship which, it is conceived, will be of lasting benefit to both of the parties to it.

We use the word 'both' advisedly, for usually ancestral and other spirits are thought to be dependent on living people, as well as the other way around. Without its human medium a spirit can have no effective social existence. Thus mediumship is conceived as a kind of exchange, and just as man may be said in a sense to have made the spirits he depends on, so he can, if he so wills, unmake them. Among the Kalabari a rejected *oru* spirit loses its power; Sukuma ancestral ghosts depend on being remembered, and in Bunyoro an *mbandwa* spirit which fails its human client may be abandoned or destroyed. Thus there is an essentially reciprocal element in men's relations with the spirit world; the dependence is conceived as two-way.

The benefits that spirits are believed to bestow have both positive and negative aspects. When properly approached and conciliated, they may, it is believed, withdraw illness or other misfortune which they have caused because of neglect by the living of an obligation either to them or to some other living person. But as well as this, it is believed that they can confer the positive benefits of health, prosperity and, especially, fertility on their adherents. Since, as we have noted, recourse to mediumship is most usually made when misfortune threatens, the former aspect is generally the more conspicuous. Often both occur together. In any event, the maintenance of good relations with the spirits, or at least with the more powerful of them, is usually regarded as of high importance; this is why traditional mediumistic cults, centring on ancestral or other major powers, are usually regarded as basically auspicious. Often, as among the Banyoro, certain spirits are thought to stand in a tutelary or 'guardianship' relation with the members of kinship or other groups; sometimes, as with the Korekore and the Kalabari, there is an association with specified territories.

One of the most important powers often attributed to spirits is the power of divination, of providing, through their mediums, information about future events and of matters removed from ordinary perception. Where 'practical', evidential grounds for decision-making are available, divination (of which divination through spirit mediumship is only one, though a very important, form) may provide an answer (see Park, 1963). Typical situations where divination is resorted to are those in which sorcery or witchcraft is suspected, suspicions which in the nature of the case are unlikely to be backed up by clear and unambiguous evidence (see Middleton and Winter, 1963). But, usually, not all spirits are thought to be able to divine; thus in Bunyoro the traditional Cwezi spirits are said never to do so, only the newer, less reputable, spirits, whose mediums, often suspected sorcerers themselves, may command large fees. But prophet-diviners may and frequently do have a larger social and political importance, especially in the context of rapid social and cultural change, in which the intervention of Spirit is usually represented as especially dangerous. Prophet-diviners have been described for many peoples, as, for example, the Lugbara (Middleton, 1963), the Nuer (Evans-Pritchard, 1940, 1956) and many others. In more recent years these prophets may be associated with separatist churches and sects (for examples, see Sundkler, 1948; Welbourn, 1961), and of course comparable movements have been described from many parts of the world (see, for example, Mair, 1959; Worsley, 1957).

The beneficent aspect of traditional spirit cults, referred to above, has important implications. It means that the cults are very widely regarded as auspicious, very different from the more nefarious activities associated with sorcery and witchcraft, with which all spirit cults have often been indiscriminately classed by Europeans. In fact they often form, as it were, the established religion of the communities which have them, and far from being socially disapproved, participation in the cults is obligatory. There is commonly an explicit association with the notions of purity and whiteness; for example, Banyoro and Alur distinguish the cult of 'white' or traditional spirits from the more recent 'black' ones. Whether or not actual dissociation takes place, mediumship in such contexts is in no sense an aberrant activity, but rather a moral obligation. A point that is brought out again and again in the essays in this book is that generally African mediums are not deviants, homosexuals, epileptics, or otherwise maladjusted; often indeed they are chosen expressly for their moral probity and virtue. Thus in Bunyoro, mediums of the traditional 'group' *mbandwa* cult were required to be young, innocent, and 'well-behaved', usually girls in their early teens. And participants in the Korekore cult were required to have 'white hearts' and to be free of ill-will towards their fellow participants. Traditional African mediums are often priests in a tribal religion rather than magicians, for they are believed to mediate between the spirit world and men, and so to convey to their congregations the beneficent power of the gods.

III

We turn now to consider what people do about spirits rather than how they think about them. We ask who becomes, or may become, mediums, why do they do so, and how do they go about it? We then consider what actually happens in spirit seances.

In 1913, Sir James Frazer wrote:

> Among savages the theory of inspiration and possession is commonly invoked to explain all abnormal mental states, particularly insanity or conditions of mind bordering on it. So these persons more or less crazed in their wits, and particularly hysterical or epileptic patients, are for that very reason thought to be peculiarly favoured by the spirits and are therefore consulted as oracles, their wild and whirling words passing for the revelations of a higher power, whether a god or a ghost, who considerately screens his too dazzling light under a thick veil of dark sayings and mysterious ejaculations. I need hardly point out the very serious dangers which menace any society where such theories are commonly held and acted upon. If the decisions of a whole community in matters of the gravest importance are left to turn on the wayward fancies, the whims and vagaries of the insane or the semi-insane, what are likely to be the consequences to the commonwealth? (*The Belief in Immortality, I, 15*).

Our understanding of spirit mediumship has moved a long way since Frazer wrote these words, and in Africa at any rate mediums are by no means 'crazed in their wits'. On the contrary they are usually shrewd, intelligent, and accepted members of their communities. In most of the societies considered in this book, almost anyone may become a medium if he wants to, though sometimes he must await selection by accredited mediums, and in some cases mediumship or membership in specific cults is restricted to, or forbidden to, members of particular social groups; for example, the ruling Bito clan in Bunyoro is debarred from participation in the Cwezi cult. Where the group or 'guild' aspect of mediumship is stressed, a long and costly initiation ritual may be prescribed.

Sometimes mediums are people who in everyday life occupy positions of relatively low status; for some of the peoples described in this book mediumship is a means to a measure of prestige for persons who would otherwise lack it. It is noteworthy that in several of the societies studied (Alur, Lugbara, Nyoro, Somali, Segeju and Zulu) possession, or some form of it, is thought of as primarily, though not exclusively, the preserve of women, whose participation in positions of high social or political status is in most traditional African societies either non-existent or limited. There is, further, an association in some cultures between male homosexuality, with transvestism, and spirit possession, especially where mediumship is mainly a female concern. We have argued that such an association is rare in Africa, but among the peoples discussed in this book there is a suggestion of it in Zulu *ukuthwasa* possession, as there is also for the Lugbara of Uganda.

Mediumship as a means to high prestige and status may provide a strong motive for cult participation on the part of the under-privileged (Lewis's account in this book provides a vivid illustration of the rewards Somali women may derive from it). But in many, probably most, cases the precipitating cause is some form of illness, which is diagnosed by divination as being due to spirit activity. Sometimes, as we have seen, possession is induced so that the spirit can be compelled to leave its host, and so can be either banished or destroyed. In Bunyoro, Somaliland, and elsewhere, minor spirits may sometimes be thus summarily dealt with. But much more usually (as in Ghana, Dahomey, and Bunyoro) the illness is attributed by the diviner to the neglect of an ancestral or other spirit which has beneficent as well as maleficent aspects, and it is believed that the spirit's goodwill can only be restored if it is enabled, through mediumship, to express itself and say what it wants – for example, a sacrifice, a shrine, or the discharge of a neglected obligation.

Of course people may elect to become mediums for other reasons also, and nowadays not the least important is the consideration of economic gain. We noted above mediumship's importance as a means of divination. When possessed, mediums may determine the nature and causes of a client's illness or other affliction, and advise him what he should do about it (perhaps that he should become a medium himself). Well-known mediums may charge heavily for their services. Also where the necessary rituals of initiation into cult membership are lengthy, expensive and carried out under the direction of established mediums, there are large profits to be made by those skilled in cult activity.

Actual techniques of possession vary widely, as also does the degree of dissociation experienced by the medium. Rhythmic music and movement, sometimes dance, are commonly associated with possession ritual, combined sometimes with the use of medicines, especially inhalants, and all of these may promote dissociation. A question of some comparative interest is whether, in particular cases, mediums are acting a part, rather than being genuinely unconscious of what they are doing. As we should expect, the matter is very much one of degree, and it is significant that the cultures considered in this book range from those in which genuine dissociation is reported (the West African cases, also the Alur, and the Kenya separatist church described by Welbourn) to those in which it is more or less frankly admitted that possession does not or need not really occur, but may often be simulated (Ankole, Bunyoro, Lugbara). But whether or not they report that mediums are really dissociated, and if so in what degree, almost all of our contributors stress the dramatic quality of cult behaviour. Usually it involves dressing in unfamiliar, often striking and colourful, attire, the use of a special spirit language or vocabulary, and the assumption, often with notable histrionic skill, of a pattern of behaviour accepted as appropriate to the spirit supposed to be present. It appears that it is the act, the drama, that is believed to be therapeutically effective; whether there is actual possession or not is not necessarily the major consideration. It is significant that so many of our contributors have stressed the dramatic quality of mediumship, for despite analogous aspects in early Greek religion, with some exceptions most anthropologists have tended to emphasize the instrumental rather than the expressive aspects of spirit mediumship.

IV

Finally we consider in a little more detail the social and cultural contexts of spirit mediumship. First of all, can it be said to reflect any other features of the societies and cultures in which it is found? For many, perhaps all, of the societies discussed here, it certainly can. Thus where social importance attaches to membership in descent groups, we often find mediumship involving possession by ancestral ghosts; this is the case in Dahomey, among the Kalabari, Sukuma, Banyankole, and probably elsewhere. In Bunyoro, also, mediumship in its traditional form was a concern of descent groups, but although it was believed that ancestral ghosts could possess their descendants, the objects of the group cult were former hero-gods, the Cwezi, and not related ghosts. Both here and in nearby Ankole the traditional medium was, as Welbourn says, a kind of household priest.

But cults may reflect a centralized political order as well as a segmentary kin-based one. Thus for the Kalabari the 'hero' cult involves the whole community, not (as other Kalabari cults do) its component divisions, and Alur mediums may be possessed by the ghosts of dead chiefs, so long as these are not genealogically related to their mediums, that is, so long as they are not ancestors. Korekore mediums operate in 'spirit provinces', the guardian spirits being associated with the original invaders and being linked in a complex genealogy. Basangu spirits among the Tonga also reflect social and political aspects of Tonga society.

Associated with these social aspects of mediumistic cults is their moral quality. We noted above that traditional cults are usually thought of as beneficial, and their mediums much respected; we noted also that participants in cult activity are generally required to be pure in heart and on mutually good terms. But, in addition, the spirits themselves are often represented as giving advice, warnings, or directions bearing explicitly on the moral order of the society. Basangu spirits express public opinion; Korekore mediums mediate in disputes and reflect the consensus of the community; possessing spirits in Ghana 'demand goodness'. And it may be argued that an unpopular moral decision, or a rebuke administered to a fellow-member of the local community, may be more acceptable and less resented (at least overtly) when it purports to emanate not from a human but from a spirit.

There is of course an obverse side to this: sometimes cult behaviour may provide a way of 'letting off steam'. Behaviour which would not be tolerated in everyday life may be permitted, even expected, in possessed persons. As we noted earlier, a seance may be what Verger describes as 'a theatrical performance or even an operetta', and there is no doubt that it may perform many of the cathartic and other functions ordinarily attributed to drama. In fact one of the most interesting lines of enquiry suggested by these essays is the degree to which spirit mediumship is, or may be, no more – and no less – than a kind of drama, differing perhaps in the degree of involvement (or dissociation) of the actors, but essentially a theatrical performance. The beginnings of classical drama in the possession rituals of ancient Greece provide some interesting parallels (Harrison, 1903). Certainly there is no doubt of the dramatic quality of many mediumistic cults in Africa, providing as they do both lively entertainment and a means of catharsis. It would appear that the relief of anxiety thus brought about may be definitely therapeutic; certainly it can be felt to be, as Field puts it, 'wholesome and sustaining'.

There is an apparent paradox still to be mentioned. Almost always traditional mediumistic cults are essentially conservative, for they express and help to sustain the traditional standards and values of the society. Yet we have noted that mediumship plays an important role in situations of radical and disturbing social change. The paradox is resolved if we accept that in most traditional societies change is regarded as something unwanted, even as dangerous and evil, And, like other external and uncontrollable forces, it is often regarded as a consequence of the activity of Spirit, in one manifestation or another. Thus the forces of radical change may be spiritualized in order that they can be accommodated and thus in some way controlled.

Social change commonly involves change in the pattern of authority; the introduction of new forms and modes of power involves the need to control or manipulate them. This may be attempted in several ways, but perhaps the most common is through prophet activity. Prophets are typically charismatic leaders whose influence comes from their claim to be mediums in touch with the spiritual source of the external powers which are thought to be adversely affecting the society.

The role of mediumship in situations of rapid social change is twofold. First, it provides a means by which the people concerned can comprehend the agents of change, and can incorporate these and their consequences into their system of mythological beliefs. Secondly it can provide a basis for the legitimization of new patterns of power and authority where they have come into being. These are aspects of a single process but they may conveniently be distinguished.

The theatrical aspects of mediumship cults, of which we spoke above, are especially clear in the context of social change, which in many areas has added a wide range of new and colourful characters to the *dramatis personae* of the cults. Since spirit cults provide, among other things, a way of coping with potentially inimical forces in order to come to terms with them, it should not surprise us that in many areas the new forces of social change have been readily assimilated to the pre-existing cults. Such new spirits are reported for the Tonga, the Alur, the Zulu, the peoples of southern Ghana, and the Banyoro, and many aspects of social and cultural change and of the Western cultures identified with it are represented. These range from symbols like aeroplanes and military tanks to such abstract qualities as 'Europeanness'. Of special interest is the widespread assimilation into the cults of the very force which was dedicated to its destruction, the teaching of the Christian missionaries themselves. Among the Tonga the Christian 'God', as well as Jesus and the angels, may possess mediums, and in Bunyoro what can be called the spirit of Christian worship ('I pray to God every day') is one of the wide range of present-day possessing spirits. Another example is that of the Lugbara spirit called *Balokole* ('the Saved'). Possession by the Holy Spirit is reported from Ghana and Kenya as well as from Zululand, and in all these countries the amalgamation of traditional and Christian practice has led to the emergence of prophet-led separatist churches in which possession plays a major and culminating role.

A great deal more could be written in interpretation and analysis of the material presented in the essays that follow, but our object in this short introduction has simply been to set out, as a kind of guide, a very few of the major themes which run through the essays. As first-hand ethnographic accounts of a widespread but as yet insufficiently described cultural institution, the essays have considerable interest and importance in their own right. We believe also that as far as the interpretation of their material is concerned, our contributors are well able and qualified to speak for themselves.

REFERENCES

BEATTIE, JOHN 1966 'Ritual and social change', *Man* n.s. 1(1): 60–74.

ELIADE, MIRCEA 1951 *Le chamanisme et les techniques archaïques de l'extase.* Paris. English Translation, *Shamanism.* London, Routledge & Kegan Paul, 1964.

EVANS-PRITCHARD, E. E. 1940 *The nuer.* Oxford, Clarendon Press.
1956 *Nuer religion.* Oxford, Clarendon Press.

FIRTH, RAYMOND 1959 'Problems and assumptions in an anthropological study of religion', *Journal of the Royal Anthropological Institute* 89(2):129–148.

FRAZER, SIR JAMES 1913 *The Belief in Immortality, I.* London, Macmillan.

HARRISON, JANE 1903 *Prolegomena to the study of Greek religion.* Cambridge, Cambridge University Press.

HORTON, ROBIN 1960 'A definition of religion, and its uses', *Journal of the Royal Anthropological Institute* 90:201–226.

LEIRIS, M. 1958 *La possession et ses aspects théâtraux chez les Ethiopiens de Gondar.* Paris, Plon.

MAIR, L. P. 1959 'Independent religious movements in three continents', *Comparative Studies in Society and History* 1(2):113–136.

MIDDLETON, JOHN 1963 'The Yakan or Allah Water cult among the Lugbara', *Journal of the Royal Anthropological Institute* 93(1):80–108.

MIDDLETON, J.; WINTER, E. H. (editors) 1963 *Witchcraft and sorcery in East Africa.* London, Routledge & Kegan Paul.

NADEL, S. F. 1946 'A study of shamanism in the Nuba mountains', *Journal of the Royal Anthropological Institute* 76:25–37.

PARK, GEORGE K. 1963 'Divination and its social contexts', *Journal of the Royal Anthropological Institute* 93(2):195–209.

SUNDKLER, B. G. M. 1948 *Bantu prophets in South Africa.* London, Lutterworth Press.

WELBOURN, F. B. 1961 *East African rebels.* London, S.C.M. Press.

WORSLEY, PETER 1957 *The trumpet shall sound.* London, MacGibbon and Kee.

ZARETSKY, IRVING 1967 *Bibliography on spirit possession and spirit mediumship.* Evanston, Northwestern University Press.

WEST AFRICA

SPIRIT POSSESSION IN GHANA

© *M. J. Field*

THE NATURE OF SPIRIT POSSESSION

In Southern Ghana the phenomenon of spirit possession (as I have witnessed it on many diverse occasions during thirty-five years) always follows well-defined lines.

The possessed person is in a state of dissociated personality whereby a split-off part of the mind possesses the whole field of consciousness, the rest being in complete abeyance. Splitting of the stream of consciousness into parallel streams is familiar to anyone who can 'do two things at once' such as playing the piano and simultaneously planning a summer holiday, or driving a car 'automatically' while thinking about something quite different. It is the total banishment of all but one stream which is the essential feature of dissociation. It is not true of the possessed person that, as Africans have it, 'something has come to him'; rather is it that something has *gone* from him.

In the classic cases of 'loss of memory' the dissociation differs from that of spirit possession mainly in its duration.

The dissociated state in spirit-possession (often called 'trance') is of brief duration, usually an hour or two, very seldom as long as a whole day. When normal consciousness is regained the subject has no recollection of what he did, said, observed or felt while possessed. The dissociation closely resembles that which operates in sleep-walking and hypnotism. Even the normal sleep of ordinary people carries a small quota of dissociated consciousness, as anyone may observe by gently pulling away the blankets from a sleeping person: the sleeper will, without waking, intelligently pull them back, but will not, in the morning, remember the episode.

The possession fit, or trance, exhibits two distinct phases. There is a short opening phase of dazed, mute inaccessibility and a second, longer phase of excitement with great activity – dancing, singing, leaping, running, miming, 'prophesying' and so on. The second phase is conspicuous and dramatic and is a favourite subject for travel films, but I have never known a sight-seer to photograph or even notice the inconspicuous first phase. To observe this it is necessary to know who is likely to become possessed and to watch him closely, though it sometimes happens that the trance aborts in the dazed phase and the subject remains slumped in his seat or huddled on the ground, whence, if he is obstructing the dancers, he is carried, feebly wriggling, from the scene. This first phase is not unlike an insulin sopor.

It does of course often happen that the spirit comes upon someone in the act of dancing, and that there is no cessation of this activity. The dreamy first phase of possession is, however, never absent, but is represented by a marked slowing down. Then suddenly comes a burst of energy.

It is sometimes asked, how much control has the subject, whether novice or expert, over the onset of his trance? The answer is, about the same control as ordinary people have over falling asleep. Most of us are conditioned to fall asleep regularly in accustomed circumstances, though sometimes sleep may fail to come. At times of extreme boredom or fatigue sleep may overcome us anywhere but we need not, as a rule, fall asleep if determined against it. Educated Africans are less often possessed than illiterates and probably for the reason that they are unwilling to exhibit themselves in this 'heathen' capacity.

Most possessed persons appear to have some control over the duration of their trances and to come out of them conveniently at dinnertime or just before the passenger-lorry departs. This has been wrongly taken as evidence of faked possession, but it merely adds another similarity between trance and sleep.

Both the beginning and the end of the excited phase are abrupt. At the beginning, the dazed and oppressed subject suddenly leaps to his feet with flailing arms and if he is a 'strongly' possessed novice, unconditioned by training, is liable to dash off into the bush so fleetly that he may outrun pursuers, get lost and perish of hunger and thirst. At the end of the excited phase he usually flings himself violently against a wall and slides limply to the ground or throws himself into the supporting arms of friends. A moment later his face loses the abstracted, often mask-like, expression that characterizes trance and regains awareness as does the face of any person awaking from sleep or hypnosis. If, during the excited phase, he has squandered much energy, he is naturally tired, even exhausted, and may drop into normal sleep then and there but usually he is able to walk home. In William Sargant's book, *Battle for the Mind,* picture no. 5 shows a woman, not necessarily exhausted as Sargant supposes, in whom the excited phase is abruptly terminating in the customary manner: 'the spirit is leaving her'. Probably this woman, one moment after the photograph was taken opened her eyes, looked bewildered, then became aware of her thirst and her aching limbs and limped quietly home to drink copious draughts of water, wash off her sweat, take her supper and sleep quietly.

Many subjects describe an aftermath of quiet, blissful euphoria after possession. This, as we shall see later, is of some importance in therapeutic procedures and in the new 'spiritual' churches.

The excitement of the second phase is mainly motor. The subject is literally 'moved' by the spirit, sometimes to be driven into the wilderness but more often to be thrown into hours of ceaseless jigging and dancing. Even when he is sedately divining and answering supplicants' questions, a close inspection reveals that his fingers and toes are finely trembling.

At times the possessed person performs incredible feats of strength and endurance. Probably the explanation of this is that, among ourselves, not even the few highly-trained athletes ever exert themselves to the last reserves of their energy. We are all restrained, a long way short of total exhaustion, by self-observation and self-concern. The possessed person has no more self-observation than has the sleep-walker who climbs without falling a roof where he could never venture when awake. It is not surprising that reliable witnesses narrate accounts of persons who have died of post-possession exhaustion and of others who have dropped dead at the height of their excitement. More astonishing were the accounts which I heard from good witnesses of an old priest who, when gasping out the last days of his life with pulmonary tuberculosis, still became from time to time furiously possessed, rose from his bed and danced with incredible violence. Had this man been laid, in a comatose state, in a sepulchre and got out, his friends would not have asked who rolled away the stone from the door: they would have known that he did it himself.

Possessed people in Ghana do not cut themselves with knives, walk on hot cinders, gouge out their eyeballs or inflict on themselves any of the other physical outrages described in different parts of the world. Whether they feel pain in their trances we do not know as they have no recollection afterwards of their feelings. But they do not appear to feel hunger, fatigue and appropriate discomfort. Signs of these returning sensations are among the first changes that come over the face when the 'spirit' abruptly departs. If an onlooker holds a long drink to the lips of a perspiring possessed dancer, he will usually swallow it greedily but no gratification appears in his face.

The excited phase of possession is capable, when habitually practised by dedicated persons, of much conditioning and modification. The untrained novice is prone to rush off into the bush, to his own danger, but the habituated trained subject is not. Another important difference between the novice and the adept is that the former is usually incapable of any speech except perhaps a meaningless babble often taken to be a foreign language. After weeks, months, or even years of mute trances, the power of speech gradually arrives. The subject is then regarded as the mouthpiece of unseen powers. When he becomes capable of answering questions he is the channel of communication with the divine.

There seems no reason to doubt that the utterances of a possessed person, concentrating on a narrowed field, may exceed in wisdom those he can achieve when exposed to all the distractions of normal consciousness, though of course no amount of dissociation can make a poor intelligence into a rich one. Many ordinary people have solved problems – problems on which they have competently pondered already – in their sleep. A few (such as J. W. Dunne) have undoubtedly foreseen the future in sleep. Hypnotized persons have performed unwonted feats of memory. A friend of mine who had resisted years of earnest effort to learn French spoke it excellently in the delirium of a febrile illness. The mind has undoubtedly recesses of memory and judgment which, closed to normal consciousness, may be accessible in sleep, hypnotism, dissociation and other states. It seems to be true in Ghana that a possessed person often understands and speaks a language of which he has no normal knowledge, but investigation of his life-history always reveals that at some time in childhood he was exposed to that language and subsequently forgot it.

INDUCTION OF DISSOCIATION

Most Africans who hope to be possessed on any given occasion are careful to fast. No doubt the low level of blood sugar so induced helps dissociation. Many rural people go off to their farms or to hunt in the early morning without breakfasting and if some distraction occurs they may go foodless all day. Such conditions often provide the first occasion of possession. 'On the way home from the farm in the evening he began shaking and soon we saw that something had come to him.'

Drumming, singing, clapping and the rhythmic beating of gong-gongs and rattles, alone or all together, are the commonest inducers of possession. The drumming is exciting, the clanging iron is a harsh monotony from which consciousness readily recoils. More possessed people are likely to be seen at a well-orchestrated dance than on any other occasion.

Most people who are possessed as a part of their profession – priests, diviners, priestly auxiliaries, and medicine-men's auxiliaries – are conditioned to become possessed when they place themselves suitably, just as most of us were conditioned to fall asleep in a comfortable bed in a dark, quiet room. Some priests have only to enter the sanctuary when the drums and gongs are beating and the flute wailing. Some diviners gaze into a black liquid to the sound of gongs. Another may have to hold upon his head, again to the sound of gongs, a weight heavy enough to make his neck ache. But there are occasions when 'the spirit', like sleep, is wooed in vain.

Induction of dissociation by the inhalation of fumes, as was practised by Moses and the Delphic soothsayers, is not, so far as I know, practised in Southern Ghana but I believe it is by the Dagomba of Northern Ghana whose diviners, I am told, sprinkle certain dried herbs into a charcoal fire and breathe the fumes.

Substances taken by mouth are not among the usual methods of inducing possession, though I have seen priests chewing secret 'medicine' said to help them in their work. No priest or diviner takes alcohol on ceremonial days but laymen sometimes complain that they cannot take a thimbleful of drink without becoming possessed. They distinguish sharply between a large intoxicating dose and a small dissociating dose.

Last but not least among the precipitants of possession is unwonted strong emotion. Fear, rage, grief, awe, wonder and what may best be called 'religious emotion' have all been known to throw people, often for the first time, into dissociation.

THE POSSESSING SPIRIT

West African theology postulates one supreme Sky-god or Rain-god and a multitude of lesser deities who are all 'sons' or 'fragments' of the supreme god and partake of all his attributes except aloof indifference. The most ancient gods are the works of Nature – rivers, lagoons, lakes, hills, the sea, trees and wild animals. There are also war-gods, fertility goddesses and others having no particular association with Nature. Alongside of these are the Dead – both the long dead and the recently dead – who are all able to bestow both bane and blessing and are therefore virtually deities.

Perhaps the mythical forest dwarfs, who are everywhere recognized and in some places worshipped, should be put among the long dead, as it may be that they represent a lingering tradition of an extinct pygmy race. Every god, though he may rank as a very small god, is thought of by his worshippers as omnipotent, omniscient, omnipresent and accessible. He also demands goodness.

In addition to all these, some 'medicines' or magical apparatus, originally designed for one circumscribed purpose, have gathered so much veneration that they have all the attributes of discerning deity.

All these spirits are capable of possessing people though they do not all habitually do so.

When anyone is 'strongly' possessed for the first time, or so often possessed that he is suspected of being called to a dedicated career – 'a god wants to come to him and work' – efforts are made to find out what spirit is possessing him. He consults an established diviner, who becomes himself possessed by his own deity and answers the question. He gives the name of the intrusive deity and perhaps tells the suppli-cant that he must train as a full-time priest and set up his own shrine. Or he may say, 'A family god feels slighted because you have become a Christian without arranging for his future annual rites. You must do this or he will follow you and bring misfortune throughout your life'. Again he may say, 'An ancestor is annoyed because you have neglected him for several years. Kill a sheep for him and he will let you alone'. Or again (among the Ga) 'Such-and-such a big god wants you to become one of his priestly auxiliaries and every year at the annual festival he will possess you and speak through your mouth'. Or yet again, 'You must go into training as a medium and then you must marry a herbalist – you know that there is one who wants you. You must then help him in his diagnoses and treatments by consulting your familiar spirit'.

Sometimes at a festival dance a number of different spirits will possess a medium in succession, imposing on her a variety of miming. The medium may announce, 'I am such-and-such a venerated ancestress'. The attendants will then array her in rich silks and jewellery, fan her, powder her, perfume her and place white goat-skins for her to walk upon. She will then sail graciously round greeting the most eminent members of the assembly. A few minutes later she may be possessed by a dead and gone warrior: she will call for a sword and stride about ferociously brandishing it, uttering war-like shouts and singing war-songs. Then an animal-god, say a leopard, may come upon her and she will go on all fours, snarling, snapping, scratching and biting pieces out of live fowls. On one occasion at a herbalist's annual festival the possessed medium doubled herself up in agony and uttered groans and cries of pain: she was possessed by all the herbs that the herbalist had used throughout the year and had crushed, pounded, boiled, and made to suffer in the service of man. During this possession by herbs various patients came and consulted her about herbal remedies.

I have not heard of anyone practising an indigenous West African cult who was possessed by Almighty God, but I heard of a Moslem in the far north who became possessed and was driven for a very long sojourn into the bush: of him it was said 'God took him'.

Perhaps at the present day the most active possessing spirit is 'The Holy Ghost'. The numerous shrine cults, privately owned and profit-making, which sprang into existence during the cocoa boom after the First World War, swept the country like a bush-fire; they reached their zenith in the nineteen-thirties and have now died down with the same suddenness that they flared up. They have been displaced by the 'apostolic' or 'spiritual' Christian communities, mostly led by self-appointed 'prophets'. These draw converts equally from the long-established Christian churches and from the shrine cults and they are multiplying every day. They probably represent a revolt on the one hand against the joylessness of what missionaries call 'the atmosphere of Christian worship' and on the other against the extortionate money-making of the shrines. At any rate their members seem, in all the perplexity and insecurity of emergent Ghana, happier, more generous and more unafraid than other people. They claim that their worship is in the manner of the Christian communities described in the Acts of the Apostles and that they are possessed and moved by the same spirit in the same way and in the same large numbers. Anyone who has attended their meetings and also reads the Acts with an open mind, remembering that the general level of Galilean credulity of the period was about that often met in Ghana today, can have little doubt that he is reading about something he has seen. The worshippers attend the meetings with ardour and regularity, they dress in white and wash in holy water, they make a joyful noise unto the Lord and come before his presence with singing, drumming, dancing and clapping, they practise the laying on of hands and claim miracles of healing, and above all they are possessed in large numbers. There is no doubt that the peaceful euphoria that follows possession plays a large part in maintaining enthusiasm and good temper.

But occasional possession by 'The Holy Ghost' is not new to Ghana. Ever since Christianity came to West Africa converts have embraced it from a variety of motives, some more creditable than others. It has often happened that a convert was faced with pros and cons and joined the church with these unresolved. Then one Sunday in church 'something' would 'come to him' and he would be possessed. Then arose the questions. Was this the Holy Ghost? Or was it, in missionary idiom, 'the power of the devil'? Or was it a native deity 'calling' the convert back from his mistaken allegiance? Often he would visit a soothsayer who would only prescribe a sheep to propitiate the deity. Then perhaps the same scene in church would occur again and yet again till over-much money had been spent on sheep. Then at last it would be decided that the deity had called the convert back to be a special servant. He would then accept his calling, go and train as a medium and be at peace.

THE POSSESSED PERSON

As the reader will already have gathered, any layman can be casually possessed at an exciting dance or on an emotional occasion without causing comment, but if he is so 'strongly' or so frequently possessed as to endanger his life or upset his routine he is believed to have been called by a deity to a dedicated career.

He may then go into training as a priest-diviner of the kind common in Ashanti. Or, among the Ga and Adangme, whose traditional priests are never themselves possessed, he (or, more often, she) may become a priestly auxiliary, possessed only when the deity holds one of his annual festival dances. These posts are official appointments but the medium is appointed only after the deity has spontaneously indicated that he has chosen her. Unlike the unpossessed priest she has no authority and 'no mouth' except when she is possessed. A traditional tribal deity may have half-a-dozen or more of these women.

Again, a gifted medium may go into private practice as a soothsayer. She does not operate a shrine with a quorum of elders, an orchestra and all the insignia of a god, but she runs a little practice entirely alone and shares her profits with no-one. Sometimes she marries a herbalist and they run a profitable business together, she diagnosing and prescribing, he adminstering treatment.

An emotional occasion on which non-professionals are possessed is the ceremony of 'carrying the coffin'. If it is suspected that a death is the result of malicious sorcery, the deceased is carried in his coffin (in earlier days it was a basket) all round the town on the pall-bearers' heads. These bearers become possessed by the spirit of the dead man and this controls their movements. The coffin appears to buck and shy and, taking the bit between its teeth, charges madly off, compelling the bewildered sweating bearers without any apparent volition of their own. If the coffin stops at any one house and plunges about before its door, this house is taken to be the dwelling of the sorcerer. The explanation of this is that the bearers, like all possessed persons, are merely expressing strongly held but quietly whispered public opinion.

It is not often in Ghana that possession is induced for therapeutic reasons, but this is sometimes seen in the Ga ceremony of 'driving away a bad *gbeshi*'. A bad *gbeshi* is thought of as an influence of ill-luck inhabiting a person and bringing him misfortune and unprosperity when circumstances appear propitious. For the expulsion procedure he is taken by the medicine-man and his apprentices to the outskirts of the town and the bad *gbeshi* driven out of him into the bush or perhaps tied to a post or even induced to enter a fowl which is then driven away. The patient is made to hold on his head either a big bowl of water-and-herbs or a fowl. The assistants stand around beating gongs, singing, clapping and urging the *gbeshi* with threatening shouts to 'come out'. The patient goes first into the sopor stage of possession, looks dazed and dreamy and sways drowsily. Then suddenly 'the *gbeshi* gets up' and the patient dashes wildly off into the bush still carrying his head-load and pursued by the assistants, all reviling the *gbeshi* and commanding it never to return. When the patient's excitement leaves him he is brought back well content. He has no recollection of any part of the episode except the beginning, but he feels the contented euphoria of post-possession and is convinced that the evil thing has left him and that the future is bright.

In the days of warfare it was not only the fighting men who went on military campaigns. Each man's own little party of camp followers – boys and women – carried his provisions and sometimes went into the firing-line to re-load his guns. If he was killed these supporters would often fight in his stead. Occasionally a woman under stress of grief and despair would become possessed and charge into the enemy's lines, terrifying the warriors not only by the horrible ferocity and strength of her onslaught, but by the conviction that supernatural powers were driving her. In the nineteen-thirties I attended the funerals of several old women who were given full military honours and was told of the parts they had played.

THE 'SOCIAL FUNCTION' OF POSSESSION

The utterances of the possessed prophet, priest or soothsayer are seldom original or startling. They are usually the enunciation of public opinion, often in its most traditional and conservative mood. Immorality is reproved, innovation is denounced and the scandals that everyone knows of but does not mention are brought into the open and condemned. The anxious and the innocent are encouraged and consoled.

Possession endows the speaker with authority and this makes his utterances acceptable. A supplicant will accept at the shrine the same advice that he has rejected from his parents or his wife and he suffers thereby no loss of face.

Furthermore, the possessed medium is exonerated from all personal responsibility for his utterances. It is not he but a deity who has spoken. An obscure little rural priest was moved by his spirit to travel a hundred miles to Kumasi where, endowed with the authority of possession, he forced his way into the presence of the Ashantihene and told him some unpalatable truths. He was listened to with respect and treated with reverence.

The medium who becomes a professional priest or diviner is supplying a demand. He will not succeed unless he gives good value and inspires confidence. During his training he submits to much discipline and hardship – such as fasting and chastity. When fully established he may, if he is lucky, get rich, but he must order his life more strictly and diligently than do most other rural people. He must, in short, be 'a good personality'. His calling is not (contrary to popular belief) the resort of inadequate maladjusted neurotics and hysterics.

Most mental phenomena are capable of both healthy and morbid use. There is no more reason to label all dissociation as 'hysterical' than there is so to label all laughter and weeping. 'By their fruits ye shall know them.' And the fruits of most spirit possession in Ghana are wholesome and sustaining.

TYPES OF SPIRIT POSSESSION IN KALABARI RELIGION

© *Robin Horton*

This essay is deliberately concerned with 'traditional' as opposed to 'modern' forms of behaviour. That is, it is concerned with forms which, if the recollections of older people are to be trusted, are the survivals of a system of beliefs and practices that reigned unchallenged in the latter part of the nineteenth century. It is this system that the present essay aims to outline.

Judging from what old men say, the last seventy years of rapid change have been kind to some forms of possession and hard on others. Thus for certain forms, the earlier situation as conveyed in reminiscence tallies closely with present-day observation. But other forms, which reminiscence asserts were once to be found in most Kalabari communities, can now only be seen in one or two out-of-the-way villages. And yet others live on in reminiscence alone.

Our reconstruction of the 'traditional system', then, will have to be based on a judicious combination of first-hand observation and oral testimony; and inevitably, our description and analysis will lack the certainty of work done in a more contemporary frame of reference. The task, however, is still worth-while. For, as will become evident, it is only by considering the 'traditional system' against the background of pre-colonial conditions that we can start to understand present-day forms of possession behaviour.

In Kalabari communities today, one can see several kinds of possession behaviour in addition to the 'traditional' ones I shall describe here – notably the various kinds associated with the powerful and ever-proliferating separatist churches. Elsewhere, I hope to deal with 'traditional' and 'church' possession as co-existing twins, in a more contemporary frame of reference. But the present task, logically speaking, comes first.

I have sketched Kalabari traditional cosmology and its general social background in several previous publications.[1] But it will be as well to start off with a reminder of some Kalabari beliefs relevant to the theme of possession.

For Kalabari, every person, animal, plant and thing has a guiding spirit which controls its behaviour 'as a steersman controls his canoe'. Then, over and above such spirits associated with particular material objects, there are three great categories of free spirits who influence whole constellations of events, and whose generic label is *oru*.

First of these categories is that of the dead (*duen*). These are the spiritual portions of human beings, that leave their bodies when they die. In the after life, the dead continue to hold much the same values as they held in life: thus they look after their real or fictional descendants as fathers look after their sons, and they demand respect from their descendants just as fathers demand respect from their sons. The power and influence of every descent group is underpinned by the spirits of its deceased heads, or is diminished by the anger of these spirits at breaches of the code of solidarity among fellow members.

Second come the heroes (*am'oru*). These are beings who formerly lived among the people of New Calabar and other Kalabari communities, and who founded the various communal institutions. Instead of dying, however, the heroes disappeared without leaving any descendants. As the dead underpin the strength of their descent groups, so the heroes underpin the strength of the total community and of its institutions.

Third come the water spirits (*owuamapu*). These own the various rivers and creeks which surround the community. Whereas dead and heroes are guardians of the established social order, water spirits are first and foremost forces of the extra-social. Thus they control the waters with which Kalabari have to struggle in gaining a living as traders and fishermen. They are also the forces behind such human activity as is individualistic or deviates from the social norm: they are held responsible both for individual acquisition of abnormal wealth and power, and for the actions of innovators.

The premise which guides all human intercourse with the *oru* is that this intercourse involves beings of the same kind. Granted that the spiritual portion of the individual human being is far less powerful than even a small *oru*: it is nevertheless something enjoying the same order of existence as the *oru*.

One consequence of this premise is the very general idea that *oru* can be made or unmade by the concerted action of their human congregations. The more people lavish invocations, offerings and festivals upon any *oru*, the more powerful it becomes both to reward and to punish them. And the less they attend to it, the less powerful it becomes. Unanimous rejection of an *oru* leads to complete loss of power; and there are some well-attested cases of Kalabari communities throwing out unsatisfactory *oru* with impunity.

Other consequences of the premise are to be found in the ways in which Kalabari use sculpture and possession in ritual directed to the spirits. Both sculpture and possession are devices which, by associating *oru* with material bodies, bring them down temporarily to the same level as the spirits of men. In the case of sculpture, the aim of the exercise is to secure control over *oru* by fixing them during the process of invocation and offering; and this is done by associating them with inert, immobile wood.[2] In the case of possession, the aim is that of encouraging *oru* to make their attributes and wishes known to men; and this is done by inducing them to enter living, mobile human bodies. Both of these complementary ritual devices pre-suppose a fundamental equivalence between *oru* and human spirits.

Ultimately, all spirits operate under the aegis of the supreme being, Tamuno. Tamuno is conceived in a complex manner: on the one hand as a unity, and on the other hand as having special manifestations concerned with the community, with the various descent groups, and with individuals. There is no need to elaborate here on the ways in which the supreme being and her[3] manifestations are brought into the interpretation of everyday events. Suffice it to say that the guiding premise of human intercourse with her is the very opposite of that which orders human intercourse with the spirits. Tamuno is a being of a different order of existence from the spirits, whose every doing she controls. Hence she cannot be made or unmade by any human congregation. 'Tamuno's case is never lost', as they say. Since she controls the spirits of her invokers as she controls the spirits generally, ritual approaches to her manifestations contrast sharply with approaches to the spirits. Praise songs and any other than token offerings are absent, since persuasion and flattery would be absurd in this context. Again, both sculptural representation and possession are absent, since here the object of ritual cannot be put into a position analogous to that of a human guiding spirit vis-à-vis its body.

TYPES OF SPIRIT POSSESSION IN KALABARI RELIGION

The basic ideas of Kalabari cosmology thus make possession of human beings by spirits a perfectly understandable phenomenon. Equally, they make possession by the supreme being or by any of her manifestations unthinkable.

Kalabari conversation about the spirits refers to four 'traditional' categories of possession; and these provide convenient headings for description and analysis. In what follows, I shall deal with each category in turn, outlining first the kinds of spirit involved, then the characteristic features and setting of possession behaviour, and finally the typical pattern of recruitment to the possession role.

ORU SEKI ('SPIRIT DANCING')

This type of possession is associated with the founding heroes of the community, and with the big water spirits that control its surrounding creeks. In certain special situations, it is sometimes also found associated with the dead.

The recollections of elderly people make it clear that, in pre-colonial times, most Kalabari communities staged elaborate calendrical festivals for the heads of their founding heroes – festivals in which *oru seki* was the culminating event. Since the advent of Pax Britannica, however, the community has gradually lost its former overwhelming importance in the life of its individual member. And with this loss of importance, there has been a decline in the enthusiasm with which communal cults are kept up. In most communities, the great festivals have been severely truncated. Days of elaborate ritual have been reduced to hours or minutes of perfunctory action. *Oru seki* has dropped from the proceedings. Nevertheless, there are one or two places where special circumstances have allowed community life a continuing vitality no longer seen elsewhere; and here the great festivals still continue.

One such place is Soku, a small village tucked away in the creeks in the north-west corner of Kalabari territory. Here, the community maintains an elaborate annual festival for Fenibaso, head of its heroes and patron of head-hunting and war, and, with somewhat less regularity, a complementary festival for Duminea, head of the local water spirits.[4]

In what follows, I shall give an outline description of possession and its setting in the Fenibaso festival.[5] Characteristically, the Soku people insist that their 'big festival' is quite different from its equivalents in other villages. But the testimony of older people and my own limited observations of other festivals suggest that much of what happens in the Fenibaso festival exemplifies a pattern once common to all Kalabari communities. And in drawing attention to what seem to me to be the highlights of the occasion, I shall try to pick out those aspects that best illustrate this pattern.

The celebrations for Fenibaso take place at the beginning of the rainy season. They start on a *keke*, the day of the week consecrated to the spirits. On the appointed day, the head priest and a number of helpers assemble in Fenibaso's cult-house – a large corrugated-iron structure in the centre of the village. They spend some hours washing and repainting the hero's altar. Then, with the village head and elders in support, the head priest presents an offering of *agbara*[6] fish and plantain, telling the spirit to accept it happily, to bring 'coolness', children and good things to the community, and to come and play with his people on the morrow.

In actual fact, the first phase of the festival is dominated not by Fenibaso himself, but by a violent and ferocious minion known as 'Head-of-the-Canoe-Prow'. On the morning after the first offering, the priest of this junior spirit bathes and purifies himself in readiness for the ordeal ahead of him. Soon, he is called out by representatives of the young men's age grade, and is taken to the house of Duminea, head of the local water-spirits and 'friend' of Fenibaso, to be dressed in the garb of his possessor. His dress includes a length of Real India covered by one of White Baft, tied about the waist and belted with a strip of Ikaki[7]; a brass chain round the neck; a live chick looped about his torso on a length of fresh palm-frond; a red woollen cap with two fishing-eagle feathers projecting downward over the eyes; three manillas on his right wrist, and kaolin rubbed down both his arms and across his chest. Most of these items are typical of priestly dress generally. They are at once the garb of the spirits and the symbols of their presence. As for the live chick, this is a decoy for evil spirits who may come to worry the priest whilst he is possessed.

After having these things put on him, the priest is taken to Fenibaso's cult-house, where they complete his dress by covering his face with kaolin. Finally, he takes Fenibaso's sword from the altar, and comes out to stand in front of the cult-house door.

Plate 1 Scene of excitement in Ghana with possessed medium in left foreground

Plate 2 Possessed priestly auxiliary (stooping) and possessed girl, Southern Ghana

Plate 3 Possessed priest and priestly auxiliaries, Southern Ghana

By this time, a crowd of women and older men has gathered in the square at the side of the cult-house, eagerly awaiting events. Members of the young men's age grade appear with matchets, and form a line behind the waiting priest. Then the *iju* drummer and his assistants start to beat out an urgent rhythm, calling the praise-names of the spirit. The young men start to strike each others' matchets in a rhythmic accompaniment to the drumming. All watch the priest expectantly for signs that the spirit is about to 'enter his head'.

After some minutes of this deafening build-up, the priest starts to tremble, and the young men cheer frantically to encourage the spirit. The trembling stops, starts, stops. Then a huge convulsion shakes the priest's body and he rushes headlong into the dancing square. He slashes wildly at the attendant young men, who scatter in all directions. But he leaves the spectators unmolested.

When 'Head-of-the-Canoe-Prow's' first violence has moderated, the young men form a half-circle round him in preparation for his war-play. The idea of the play is that one should muster the nerve to stand with matchet on guard until the spirit has drawn near enough to bring down his sword upon it. The resulting blow constitutes a point of honour. The complication of the game is that the spirit may either approach to administer an honourable rat-a-tat on one's matchet, or may end with a fearful lunge or slash which can cause serious injury; and the secret of successful play is to be able to take to one's heels when, and only when, the vertical weaving of the sword gives place to a horizontal sweep. Every move of the game is followed with delight by the spectators – especially by the women, who taunt the young men that they should give place to the elders.

At intervals during the war-game, the drummers change their rhythms, and the spirit abandons his swordplay to dance. Altogether, the drummers play three or four distinct rhythms; and as they switch from one to the other, so the spirit changes his step.

After the final bout of swordplay, the drummers work up to a climax and the spirit rushes headlong into the cult-house. In a few minutes the priest emerges, dressed once more in his everyday clothes, no longer possessed, and looking exhausted. He goes home to rest.

On the evening of the same day, the young men call for the priest once again, and the whole sequence is repeated. Again on the next day, the priest is called out once in the morning and once in the evening.

On the third day, the sequence of events changes a little. In the morning, there is the usual swordplay in the square. In the evening, however, there is what is known as the 'town running'. In this, the spirit, summoned to the priest's head by drums and singing, chases the young men headlong four times round the town. After this, he plays a brief tableau with two men who impersonate rival headhunters and ambush him. Having thrown them off, he is grabbed by two more young men, who calm him down. Finally he leads the young men in procession, first to the house of the village head, and then to the houses of the various other priests involved in the festival. As he reaches each house, the young men set up the chorus, 'Chief, mean one, truly mean one! One whom hunger is killing, one of no account, truly mean one!' The owner of the house comes out with a show of being stung by this address. Then he places a few coins on the spirit's outstretched sword, making a short prayer for life and prosperity. After this, the young men escort the spirit back to the cult-house, where he leaves.

On the morning of the fourth day, 'Head-of-the-Canoe-Prow' is called out for the last time. After a final war-game, he retires to the cult-house, leaves his priest, and does not appear again.

At dusk the same evening, preparations are made for the culmination of the festival: the appearance of Fenibaso himself. Offerings of *agbara* fish and plantain are first made at the altar of the deceased heads of the village, with an invocation for prosperity, peace, children, money. Next, a representative of the village head presents a ram to Fenibaso on behalf of the community. Fenibaso's priest cuts its throat and drops the corpse on the altar. Vigorous kicking from the corpse signifies the spirit's acceptance. All present raise the ritual cheer: 'Ye-asukpe! Ya! Ye-asukpe! Ya! Ye-ende! Yefa! Ye-ende! Yefa! Shall we take it? We shall take it'. Afterwards, the meat is divided and sent for cooking.

At this stage, everyone retires for a brief rest. About an hour later, the three priests involved in the final possession dance go out to the cult-house to dress. These are the priests of Fenibaso himself, of one of his followers known as 'Helmsman', and of Duminea, head of the local water-spirits. All three have their limbs and torsos painted with white kaolin spots on a background of reddish rust mixture. Then they are girded with White Baft on Real India, and belted with Ikaki cloth and bells.

When the dressing is finished, Fenibaso's priest pours a libation at the altar, with the invocation: 'We are about to do the last thing of the festival, so let it bring to the village peace, prosperity, children, money'. He shares the remainder of the gin with the village head and with the other two priests. Then the village head picks up an immense feathered head-dress which has been placed ready on the altar, repeats the invocation, and puts it on Fenibaso's priest's head. Finally an attendant, picking up Fenibaso's sword, raises it four times to the altar and puts it in the priest's right hand.

Outside in the square, hurricane lanterns reveal most of the village waiting. Young boys, white handkerchiefs tied round their heads in imitation of war-dress, circle the arena with horrific grunting cries. They are joined by the young men, who swell the noise with their ritual cheers of 'Ye-asukpe!' As the drummer starts to call the names of Fenibaso, the three priests come out and form a line at the door of the cult-house. Clashing their swords, they set up a deafening counterpoint to the drums. Before long, the priest of Fenibaso trembles violently and rushes out in front of the drums, possessed. The two other priests, also mounted by their spirits, follow him out into the square. As Fenibaso cavorts around, 'Helmsman' and Duminea act as foils to him – crossing swords when he turns on them, jumping aside when he lunges. Around the three spirits circle the young men, some of them cartwheeling joyously with burning brands which they knock together to send up fountains of sparks.

At the end of the dance, the three spirits retire. The drum-rhythm changes and Fenibaso comes out alone, holding in front of him a basketwork tray. As he circles the square, onlookers rush out to put a few pennies in the tray, begging him: 'Peace, prosperity, children in our house!' He turns back for the last time to the cult-house, with the voices of the women rising to a final unison: 'Peace, strength, children, life!' Then he disappears and the drums are cut. Everyone runs off the square to avoid having his spirit abducted by the unseen guests who now start to leave the village.

Later that night the priests, now their everyday selves, share out the cooked meat of the offering amongst the men of the village. Still later, they perform a rite designed to dismiss all alien spirit guests who have come to watch the spectacle.

Two mornings later, all the priests involved in the festival go out to gather a bundle of mangrove suckers from a nearby creek. The priests formally cut and chew some of the suckers on the spot. Then they bring the rest back to the village head's house. The village head presents the suckers to his ancestors, saying: 'Well, these are the chewing sticks, which we have cut and chewed. A man who has finished his chewing, that man will eat. The festival is finished, and we are going out to look for our livelihood. Man, woman, worker in the forest, worker in the swamp, let it go well with them. Ourselves, we are no traders. Fish, that is what we kill. We are going to put out the fishing fences. Let all be well with us'. After this, Fenibaso's priest takes the suckers to the hero's cult-house, where he repeats the invocation. Then he puts them back in the village head's house, where people come in to chew them throughout the morning. At mid-day, the village head delegates a young relative to open a new fishing season in his name by putting out 'the fishing fences of the *oru*'. That night, the young man goes out again to collect the catch; and in the morning the latter is divided amongst all those who have taken active part in the festival. The celebrations are now over for the year.

I have here been able to give only the bare bones of a long and elaborate festival. Nevertheless, many of the features which emerge from this description can be taken as fairly typical of *oru seki* festivals generally.

First of all, the festival is staged expressly to enable Fenibaso to appear before his worshippers and receive their adulation. The greater the adulation, the greater the pleasure of the spirit, and the greater his power to promote the community's welfare. Equally expressly, it is an occasion to be frankly enjoyed by the worshippers. And since enjoyment and adulation here go hand in hand, so too do recreation and promotion of communal welfare.

Secondly, the performance of the festival is a question put to the spirit about his continued concern for the community. And the very fact that he consents to enter his priest's head is a positive answer to this question.

Thirdly, the content of the possession behaviour which occurs during the festival provides a dramatic reminder of Fenibaso's attributes and of his place in the total cosmology. It reminds the congregation of his concern for the communal welfare and of his patronage of the arts of headhunting and war. It reminds them of the complementary relation between the forces of youth ('Head-of-the-Canoe-Prow') and the forces of maturity (Fenibaso himself). Again, it reminds them of the relation between Fenibaso, master of the community's characteristic means of gaining a livelihood, and Duminea, controller of the waters in which these techniques have to be used.

Something that emerges very clearly from a study of this and other festivals is how closely the '*oru* dancing' is controlled by traditional prescriptions. The exact stage of the proceedings at which each spirit will 'climb on' his priest, as well as the pattern of behaviour the latter will display once possessed, is laid down in such prescriptions. The main instrument for enforcing them appears to be the drum orchestra. This is used not only to induce possession, but also to guide the possessed person's every step. In this and other '*oru* dancing' festivals, it is common to hear people talking of the drummers as 'inflaming' or 'cooling' the spirits, and as 'putting them up to' their various moves.

A final point worth noting about the Soku festival is the obvious and at the same time apparently genuine reluctance with which 'Head-of-the-Canoe-Prow's' priest submits to his part in the proceedings. My feeling is that here is a man genuinely frightened by what may happen at a time when he is no longer in control of his body. That this is a genuine fear with a good cause is strongly suggested by my own observations on the two occasions when I attended the festival. On the first of these occasions, the priest got a severely strained ankle tendon during the course of the war-play – a wound which had no effect on his performance during the play itself, but which lamed him for weeks afterward. And on the second occasion, a cut which he incurred when his own sword slipped led to a tetanus infection that nearly killed him. All this would suggest a fair degree of dissociation.

In all types of possession, indeed, Kalabari insist rather strongly on the reality of dissociation and on the inability of the priest to remember what happens to him during possession. Although I know several *oru seki* priests rather well, I have not yet had any of them admit to an element of acting in their behaviour. If acting there is on these occasions, it has to be kept very quiet.

With the decline of the communal cults, many of the priesthoods associated with *oru seki* possession have fallen vacant. So, in forming an idea of the general conditions of recruitment to these offices, we have once again to depend largely on the recollections of old people rather than on first-hand reports. Once again, however, the recollections or elders in places where there are no longer any active possession priests are fairly well substantiated by the testimonies of the three main performers in the Fenibaso festival.

Three important priests are involved in this festival: the priest of Fenibaso himself, the priest of 'Head-of-the-Canoe-Prow', and the priest of Duminea. All three of these men hail from Bokiame, the particular section of Soku charged with supplying priests for Fenibaso and Duminea. All three report on their recruitment in much the same terms.

In each case, things started with the death of the old priest. Members of Bokiame went to consult diviners, who told them to bring out the present holder of the office as the dead man's successor. Up to this point, the man chosen had had no sickness or other symptoms indicating that he might be called to a special office. And when the news of his selection came, he greeted it with dismay. He was put off by the thought of the many irksome prohibitions which the priest of a big spirit has to observe, and was frightened by all he had heard of the consequences of breaking such prohibitions. (Two of these men, it seems, made serious attempts to dodge the draft altogether, and were only brought into line by illness and by reminders of relatives who had died after trying the same thing).

Once the new priest had been named by the diviners, and had agreed to fill the vacant office, he was taken before his spirit, and introduced by the elders as the latter's servant. Installation ceremonies seem to have been simple, and formal training for the priestly role absent. The new man was simply expected to carry out invocations and offerings from that day onward, and to submit to possession when next the festival calendar required it.

In summarizing the salient features of this type of possession, the main point to be made is that this is more a matter of society imposing its will on an individual, than of an individual using peculiar behaviour to adjust to society. The community demands intermittent dramatic appearances of its guardian spirits as a reassurance of their continued presence and power; and in order to secure these appearances it commandeers the bodies of certain of its members. It does so without any obvious reference to the psychic suitability of the individuals concerned, and certainly with no reference to their conscious likes and dislikes in the matter. What is remarkable here is that in some cases at least it seems able, despite these apparently unpropitious conditions, to force genuine dissociation upon those whom it selects.

ORU BIBI N'EKWEN
('SPEAKING WITH THE MOUTH OF THE ORU')

This type of possession, like *oru seki*, is associated with the founding heroes of the community, and with the big local water-spirits. It is associated with the dead only in a few communities and there only in very special situations.[8]

Since *oru seki* and *oru bibi n'ekwen* are associated with much the same range of cults, it is hardly surprising that much of what was said about the decline of *oru seki* is true of *oru bibi n'ekwen*. In all the communities where I have so far worked, indeed, the offices connected with this type of possession have been vacant for some time. Here, then, we have to rely almost exclusively on the memories of older people.

As in the case of *oru seki*, such memories suggest a fairly uniform pattern. Formerly, it seems, most communal cults that had an '*oru* dancing' priest also had a second figure known as the 'speaker with the mouth of the *oru*'. This figure appears to have fulfilled his (or her) role in two ways. First, he became possessed at the request of people who came to consult his spirit about the causes of their misfortunes. The clients called up the spirit with an invocation and a libation of gin, and when it came upon him it answered their questions, diagnosing the spiritual causes of their troubles and suggesting appropriate remedies. More important, perhaps, the 'speaker' was apt to become spontaneously possessed at times of communal crisis, whereupon his spirit would deliver a judgment on the situation. A 'speaker' attached to any cult could become possessed and give judgment in this way; but such judgment carried most weight when it came from the head of the community's founding heroes. What the latter said at such times, indeed, is supposed to have been binding on the community.

In the village communities generally, I found it difficult to get any case material on crisis appearances of the 'speaker' and his spirit. Requests for such material were invariably answered by the vague reply that these appearances 'helped the town when there was big trouble and people were about to fight'. In the off-shoots of the Owame (New Calabar) trading state, however, I fared rather better. Here, for structural reasons,[9] people have a longer and more detailed memory for social crisis; and I was able to collect traditions relating to four specific crisis appearances of Owamekaso, head of the New Calabar heroes.

The first of these appearances was when two dynasties were contesting the kingship in 1863, with a violence bordering on civil war. Owamekaso mounted her[10] 'speaker' and told both parties that they should cease quarrelling forthwith and take their dispute before the Aro oracle. They promptly did as they were told. The Aro oracle said that their dispute would be resolved by war against another nation, and that they should await this war without further struggles. Soon, indeed, war came. The nominee of one of the dynasties proved unable to take effective command; whilst Abbi, nominee of the other dynasty, gathered his reluctant townsmen, led them to victory, and was promptly installed.

The second appearance was on the eve of a battle between Owame and Bonny (probably in the 1870s). Owamekaso again came out, and told everyone that they should forget their quarrels and all pull together if they wanted to resist the onslaught that was coming.

The third appearance was after the civil war of 1879–1883, when the dissidents, who had fled to found a new town, sent representatives to talk reunification. Owamekaso came out and spoke against it, saying that the dissidents had broken her laws by making war upon their own people, and so should not be readmitted to the community.

The fourth appearance was at the time of the early Christian conversions in the 1890s, when Owamekaso came out and demanded that the Christians should be put to death for 'spoiling the town'. (Owing largely to outside intervention, this last request was not complied with).

In all these crisis appearances of Owamekaso, we can see a dramatic restatement of the ultimate values of community life, and a demand for immediate compliance with them. This demand was particularly effective in situations of communal strife, since, coming from a spirit revered on all sides, it enabled parties who had taken up extreme positions to climb down and compromise without loss of face. (Occasions 1 and 2). Note, however, that the basis of this appeal was to traditionally established values rather than to compromise for its own sake. Where a compromise between disputing factions would have interfered with the upholding of these values, it was the compromise rather than the values that went by the board. (Occasions 3 and 4). Finally, it seems that where the appeal to established values was not clearly relevant, Owamekaso was loth to pronounce. This is suggested by Occasion 1. Here we see her pronouncing against the fighting, but passing the question of succession to an outside agency.

Of late, much has been said about the role of spirit mediums as catalysts of social change. But in so far as the New Calabar case material gives us any clue as to the traditional role of the 'speaker' in Kalabari communities generally, it points to this role as essentially conservative, directed to the prevention of change and the upholding of tradition.

If we are to believe the testimony of older people, the general pattern of recruitment of 'speakers' contrasted rather strongly with the pattern of recruitment of 'dancers'. First of all, recruitment was more open. Whereas an '*oru* dancing' priesthood was usually vested in a particular lineage and restricted to people of a specified sex (generally male but sometimes female), a 'speaking' priesthood was usually open to any member of the community, and often was not restricted to people of a specified sex. Secondly, the processes that led to someone becoming a 'speaker' originated in the person involved rather than in the congregation at large. Thus the first intimations that someone was to be called came from that person's own behaviour. He became mentally disturbed, and sooner or later showed signs of a secondary personality. It was only when his family had consulted diviners about these symptoms, and had begun to tell people about the verdict, that the community took notice and made its own enquiries about the matter. At this stage, however, the community did assume control. If it had reason to doubt the genuineness of the claim being made, it was liable to arraign the would-be 'speaker' for fraud. This happened a few years ago, to a New Calabar woman who claimed that Owamekaso was worrying her to become her 'speaker'. The chiefs of the town made their own consultations with diviners, found her guilty of deception, and fined her heavily. The community could also dethrone an established 'speaker' if his utterances seemed to be getting wild. This happened to a famous nineteenth-century 'speaker' of Owamekaso, who was dethroned on a charge of trying to pass off drunken utterances as those of the spirit. Significantly, this man continued to enjoy great influence as a seer acting in a private capacity.

From the fragmentary information we have, then, it would seem that a 'speaker' of the head of the community's heroes enjoyed a brief but crucial influence at times of crisis. Equally, however, it would seem that this influence was subjected to close control by those over whom it was exerted. If his utterances deviated far from the required statement of traditional values, he was in danger of losing his position.

Since 'speakers' were not forced to take up their roles as were 'dancers', it is relevant to enquire into their motivations. Unfortunately, however, we do not have sufficient material to reach any firm conclusion about these. We can only speculate that the role of 'speaker' may have represented an alternative path to influence for people of ability somehow debarred from more orthodox paths.

'Speaking with the mouth of the *oru*' seems to have differed from '*oru* dancing' in several important respects. Both kinds of possession, it is true, were triggered off by external events. But whereas in 'dancing' the public determined what these events were to be, in 'speaking' some part of the individual's psyche took the initiative in reacting to them. Again, whereas 'dancing' typically involved a more or less stereotyped motor response, 'speaking' involved a much more flexible, more reasoned response.

These differences may help to explain why, in cults that featured both kinds of possession, the 'dancing' and 'speaking' roles were nearly always allocated to different people. They may also help to explain why, although the community controlled both kinds of possession in their fully-developed forms, it imposed 'dancing' upon a nominee, but allowed the would-be 'speaker' to select himself. Perhaps there was an intuitive recognition that these different types of possession behaviour were best performed by different kinds of people requiring different means for their selection.

Despite the differences, however, it is important to stress once again a feature in respect of which both 'dancing' and 'speaking' contrast strongly with the next form of possession to be discussed: once fully developed, both are subject to close control by the community at large.

EREMIN' ORU KURO (POSSESSION BY 'WOMEN'S ORU')

This category of possession is typically associated with the minor water spirits that inhabit the remoter creeks or have no special domain of their own. As the label frequently given to it suggests, it nearly always affects women. Such women are known as *oru kuro ereme*: '*oru*-carrying women'.

Whereas 'dancing' and 'speaking' for the great public cults are in serious decline, possession by 'women's *oru*' continues to flourish. Indeed, one gets the impression from older people that this type of possession is much what it was in pre-colonial times.[11] Both by virtue of the number of those affected (estimates suggest that in some communities this can be up to five per cent of all adult women), and by virtue of the large part that possession plays in their lives, this type is perhaps the most interesting of all.

Whereas the types of possession so far considered are generally manifested in one or two rather specific roles, 'women's *oru*' possession tends to be manifested in a complex of interrelated roles, some of them diffuse rather than specific.

First in this complex is a role akin to that of the 'speakers' of the major community cults – the role of diviner/prophet/social critic. People possessed by 'women's *oru*' play a very important part in divination. To secure the services of an *oru kuro* woman, one goes to her house and tells her that one wants to talk to her spirit. She then takes a bottle of palm gin and a shilling or two, goes to the spirit's shrine, and calls upon it to mount her. After a while she goes into the shrine, puts on special clothes associated with the spirit,[12] and sits down. Before long, she becomes drowsy. Then the spirit mounts her, jumps up, and comes to confront its client.

The spirit, when it comes, behaves in a calm, coherent way. The most obvious index of its presence is not any violent or frenetic behaviour, but the speaking of an alien tongue. There is a fairly standard 'water-people's language' spoken by most of these possessing spirits. Samples of it suggest that many of its words are formed by substitution of syllables in ordinary Kalabari words, by use of lengthened forms from the drum-language, and so on. Alternatively, some spirits speak in a neighbouring tongue such as Saka, which their carriers generally purport not to understand. Some, again, speak a stuttering form of ordinary Kalabari.

Another common index of spirit presence is a restless striding up and down which goes on whilst the spirit is talking and listening. Yet another index, though by no means a universal one, is a fine body tremor.

Apart from the alien tongue, which usually requires an interpreter, a session with an *oru kuro* woman's spirit much resembles a session with any other type of clairvoyant diviner.[13] Being a spirit, the woman's possessor is credited with an ability to 'see' directly the spiritual causes of any affliction. In fact, the possessing spirit usually feels after the causes of the trouble by careful suggestion and observation of the client's reactions, though some element of visionary experience may be involved as well.

Diagnoses by 'women's *oru*' run the gamut of the various invisible agencies postulated by Kalabari religious theory. One common type of diagnosis, however, is of especial interest. In this, the spirit tells an afflicted client that his troubles stem from failure to acknowledge a relationship with one of the water people. Moreover, says the spirit, the afflicting water-man is his own junior relative (or his houseboy, or his child). From such a diagnosis, it follows that the afflicted person has kinship obligations for the rest of his life, not only toward the spirit actually worrying him, but also, on the latter's behalf, toward the possessor of the *oru kuro* diviner, who is revealed as his own spirit's senior kinsman or parent. These obligations lie largely in attending and helping to organise festivals for the diviner's spirit, and in coming to any important rites that may be done for the spirit in response to some special situation. We shall say more of them anon.

Alongside the possessing spirit principally concerned with divination, it is common to find a sort of junior side-kick known as *owu biribo* – 'Water Doctor'. This character commonly bears an Ibo name, speaks Ibo, and is credited with the knowledge of herbs and other pharmacopoeia popularly associated with Ibo doctors. His role partly overlaps that of the principal spirit; but whereas the latter is chiefly concerned with diagnosis, *owu biribo* is chiefly concerned with treatment, and especially with such things as herbal remedies and the extraction of noxious charms. Often the principal spirit makes a diagnosis, then commits the client to *owu biribo* for appropriate treatment.

When one of the water spirits has been summoned to the head of an *oru kuro* woman for a divining session, it often departs again at the end of the business for which it was summoned. But at other times, it turns its attention to bystanders, making unsolicited observations on their condition, on their relations with the spirits, and on misfortunes and afflictions liable to overtake them. It may even parade about on the street, accosting passers-by and telling them of unseen agencies with which they have become embroiled. A common reaction to such scattering of diagnoses is one of bored amusement. However, as my assistant pointed out, one may be amused at the time if one is enjoying good health and prospects, but more seriously inclined if one subsequently develops the sort of affliction predicted.

Often, the *oru kuro* woman's spirit arrives spontaneously – to tell someone of an affliction, to warn an individual or a group of impending trouble, or to criticise some laxity of morals or neglect of custom. Kalabari say that before a war or similar crisis, many *oru kuro* women become possessed and prophesy in this way. Though here they resemble the 'speakers' of the big communal cults, my impression is that their spirits tend to be freer and more adventurous in their utterances. It is perhaps not a coincidence that when Owamekaso was possessing her 'speaker' and demanding the deaths of the first Christian converts, the spirit of one of the best-known *oru kuro* women of the times was telling people that they should all join the church, since the *oru* were weak and their day was over.

Mingled with the divining and prophesying is a good deal of boasting about the power and fearfulness of the water-spirits, and a good deal of propaganda about the splendours of their home beneath the rivers. At this point, the role of diviner/prophet passes over into that of myth-spinner/storyteller. In some cases, the possessing spirit comes expressly to tell a story of happenings in his town; and this story may be a saga which goes on night after night for a month – the *oru kuro* woman becoming possessed anew for each instalment. Such sagas have two levels of impact on the audience. On the surface, they are a sort of advertisement for the water-spirits. At a deeper level, their *dramatis personae* provide a cover for real-life characters and their escapades, thus lifting gossip to the level of art tinged with social criticism.

Yet again, we sometimes find the possessor of an *oru kuro* woman appearing in the role of member of the prestigious masquerading society – *ekine*. Normally in Kalabari communities, *ekine* membership is confined to men. Sometimes, however, the male spirit possessor of a woman demands membership in virtue of his sex; and this may be granted. I have not heard of any cases where the spirit actually takes part in masquerades; but he does have the privilege of sitting with *ekine* members in their meeting house, of singing with them, and of taking part in their deliberations.

Finally in this inventory of roles played by the possessors of *oru kuro* women comes that of 'Big Man' or 'Chief'. This role, in a sense, takes in all of the others so far discussed; but it is also at times played out apart from them. Perhaps it is best seen during the periodic festivals which these spirits demand from their carriers. Such festivals often involve expense and spectacle equivalent to what is found in the big group cults; and in the case of successful *oru kuro* diviners the congregation may be nearly as large.

A good example here is the festival given annually by Oruba Horsfall of Abalama for her spirit Owuala. Oruba is one of the more famous among Kalabari *oru kuro* women; and the celebrations are correspondingly lavish. In November 1957 I was staying in the village next door to Abalama, and I saw something of the preparations for the festival as well as of the celebrations themselves. Proceedings started with Owuala possessing Oruba and ordering that she should go into the fatting room for a month to prepare herself for the festival. During this time, Oruba stayed in the house most of the day, being waited upon by a number of women whom Owuala had diagnosed as being 'worried' by his children or kinsmen, and who were therefore under pressure to attend at such a juncture. Though she spent most of the time eating and sleeping luxuriously, she also came out daily to dance and sing the praises of her spirit. Her women attendants formed an enthusiastic chorus, and a man who had been pointed out as a junior brother to Owuala in the world of the water-spirits discharged his kinship obligations by providing a free accompaniment on a battery of pot-drums. Throughout this period in the fatting room, Owuala came from time to time to deal with the troubles and complaints of the visiting women, to issue instructions about the forthcoming festival, and to sing his own praises.

On the eve of the festival, a host of people arrived from villages near and far. Owuala came on Oruba's head, marshalled the visitors, and set them to work sweeping the dancing arena, repairing the house, painting the cult-objects, and cooking. All that night the guests kept wake, singing the praises of Owuala and other water-spirits. Owuala came and danced before them for several hours. Later in the night, some of his sons and junior kinsmen mounted other women present and danced around him.

At dawn, one of the men of the village was appointed by Oruba to make the invocation and offering to Owuala. Two cocks and a fine ram were offered, slaughtered, sent to the pot, and later shared and eaten by those present. After the main offering, a procession of people came up to the shrine, each one making his own private requests and giving a few small coins.

In the afternoon, the drummers got to work again. Owuala soon reappeared, and led out all the young men in a running, serpentining dance round the village, with the women cheering him on enthusiastically. He continued his dance till nightfall, then dismissed everyone until the morrow.

The next afternoon, Owuala came out once more to lead the young men in the dance. Then he declared the festival at an end, and the following morning most of the guests departed.

Superficially, all this looks much like one of the festivals given for the big spirits whose cults are a community concern. But the resemblance does not go deep. In the first place Owuala, and not the community, is the ultimate arbiter of the form the festival should take. There is no question of the community taking action against his carrier if the proceedings deviate from its expectations. Secondly, Owuala himself organizes the festival, directs his worshippers as to their various parts in it, supplies their food and accommodation, and generally lords it over them. Thirdly, the worshippers come as individuals, and from many different communities. Most of them, it seems, come because of relationships between their own water-spirit familiars and Owuala – relationships that in many cases turn out to have been diagnosed by Owuala himself.

During the 1957 festival, I managed to interview fifteen of the fifty odd people who were attending. Of these fifteen, three men were attending because their own spirits had come out of the world of the water-people, where they were sons of Owuala. One man was attending because his spirit was junior brother to Owuala. One was attending because his spirit was a friend to Owuala. And one was attending because he was the acting priest of one of his village heroes, whose daughter Owuala claimed to have married. Four women were attending because their spirit possessors were sons of Owuala. One woman was attending because her possessor was junior brother to Owuala. And one was attending because her own spirit was the daughter of

Owuala. Apart from these people, there was one man who had come to petition for the spirit's aid in getting promotion in his job, and two women who were relatives of Oruba the carrier. Nine of those who were there in virtue of their spiritual kinship with Owuala had definitely had this kinship diagnosed by Owuala. Since the fifteen people interviewed were a random sample of the festival congregation, it is probable that thirty or forty of those in attendance were there in virtue of such spiritual kinship.

It is not for nothing that *oru kuro* women say of one of their number whose spirit has such a following at its beck and call: 'She has become a chief in water-spirit country'. For the effective result of building up a congregation of this sort is that the possessor of an established female medium, who is usually male, becomes the head of a sort of 'shadow descent-group' composed of both men and women and numbering anything up to fifty souls. Over this group, the possessor himself exercises authority on the pattern of a human house head or chief. And his carrier, even when she is not possessed, takes on much of the same authority as his agent. The parallel with the normal pattern of male leadership in fact extends further still. For in the terrible jealousy that often exists amongst *oru kuro* women, in their attempts to denigrate one another and so lure each others' clients away, and in their ever-present fear that rivals will use medicine to drive their possessors away from their heads, we can see a reflection of the tensions and struggles of the harsh world of male politics.

In dealing with recruitment, it will be useful to refer to a sample of 34 *oru kuro* women and 2 men whose life-histories I have taken down in some detail. As the sample would appear to be random in all relevant respects as regards both individuals and communities, I think it can fairly be taken as representative of Kalabari *oru kuro* carriers generally.[14] If there is anything unrepresentative here, it is probably the proportion of women to men. Since in all my enquiries I only ever heard of one more man carrying a 'woman's *oru*', the proportion in the sample would appear somewhat overgenerous to men.

Let me deal first of all with the women. All but one of them reported their call to mediumship as beginning with an unpleasant disturbance of health or fortune. Many reported what are usually called 'psychological' symptoms: e.g. fugues, withdrawals, ungovernable temper tantrums, persecution feelings, migraines, and apparent schizophrenic

Plate 4 Possessed priestly auxiliary, Southern Ghana

Plate 5 Priest and possessed priestly auxiliary, Southern Ghana

Plate 6 Possessed priestly auxiliary, Southern Ghana

Plate 7 Possessed mediums at a festival dance, Southern Ghana

episodes. Many reported physical symptoms, occurring either alongside the psychological disturbances or by themselves: e.g. recurrent miscarriages, chronic limb pains and swellings, abdominal pains, tropical ulcers, and general debility. As regards age of onset of these troubles, 17 reported this within the years 0–14, 17 reported it within the years 15–29, whilst none reported from 30 onward.

Most of the carriers claimed that these troubles were the spirits' way of drawing attention to themselves, and that relief only came when they finally submitted to possession. But it should be noted that troubles of the kinds reported often do not lead to possession, and that they may be dealt with by a variety of other means. Thus although the women in our sample appear to have found relief from their troubles through acceptance of marital relationships with water-spirits and subsequent submission to being possessed by them, other women appear to have found equal relief through acceptance of such marital relationships without submission to being possessed. Others again have had such marital relationships diagnosed, but have rejected them and gone through elaborate rituals designed to sever them. Yet others have had much the same troubles diagnosed in terms that do not refer to water-spirit partners at all, and have had them dealt with in quite other ways. Many of the women in our sample, indeed, seem to have had other diagnoses of their troubles and to have tried other remedies before finally opting for water-spirit husbands and obtaining relief through possession.

There seems no reason to doubt that the kinds of trouble reported here often are relieved by the various ritual techniques available to Kalabari. Equally, it seems clear that a technique which relieves a symptom in some women may have no effect on the same symptom in others. What it is about some women that makes possession an effective way out of their troubles will perhaps become clearer when we look at later stages of the carrier's career.

In our sample of *oru kuro* women, circumstances surrounding the actual onset of possession seem to have varied quite widely. In 5 cases, possession appears to have been deliberately provoked. In each of these cases, the woman's troubles were diagnosed as coming from a water-spirit husband, and she agreed to accept possession by him. But she was so seriously sick that the established *oru kuro* woman in charge of her case decided to bring matters to a head as soon as possible by calling the spirit to mount her. This she did by summoning a pot-drummer and a chorus of other *oru kuro* women to sing the songs appropriate to the spirit suspected to be the victim's 'husband in the water'. The spirit duly entered the victim's head, sang, and danced. The officiating *oru kuro* woman then questioned it as to what it wanted with the victim, how it should be called, and what rites should be done to appease it.

In the rest of the cases in the sample, the initial possession seems to have been more spontaneous. At the time of onset, the women had already agreed in principle to accept possession, but no attempt had been made to force the spirits to come upon them. In several cases the spirit came whilst the woman was attending a dance. In several others, it came when she was in another *oru kuro* woman's house, consulting the latter's spirit about her troubles. In yet others, it came when she was simply walking in the street or sitting down at home.

Following upon this initial possession was a period of months or even years when the spirit settled down. Victims seemed to agree that when it first came, it was apt to be violent, unamenable to human entreaty, and unpredictable in its habits. How did it become the relatively disciplined, socialized being that one is accustomed to see in the house of an established carrier? In 14 cases, the women reported a period of months or even years spent in the house of another *oru kuro* woman. At the beginning of this period, the spirit would come and go in a capricious way, showing no sense of when it was welcome and when not. It would also make extravagant demands on its audience, some inconvenient, some impossible to satisfy. At this stage, the supervising *oru kuro* woman would try, by coaxing and cajoling, to make it come and go to order. She would also reason with it whenever it appeared, gently pointing out which of its demands were socially acceptable and which were not. After some time of this, the appearances of the new spirit were under control. It came when invoked by its carrier, stayed a reasonable time, and behaved in a generally tractable way. One medium summed up the whole thing nicely when she said: 'I went away for training, just as they send schoolboys to school'.

The other 20 cases in our sample denied spending a training period in another carrier's house. Nevertheless, most of them seem to have had help from neighbouring, established carriers in bringing the initial unruliness of their spirits under control.

As regards the time of onset of actual possession behaviour, 3 women reported this in the years 0–14, 25 reported in the years 15–29, 5 reported in the years 30 onward, and 1 gave no definite answer.

In relation to marriage, 18 women reported reasonable marriage relationships both before and after the onset of possession; 8 women reported reasonable relationships before the onset, but not afterwards; 6 women reported reasonable relationships after the onset, but not before; and 2 reported never having been married.

In relation to childbearing, 1 woman reported giving birth successfully both before and after the onset of possession; 16 women reported giving birth successfully before the onset but not afterwards; 9 women reported giving birth successfully after the onset but not before; and 8 said they had never given birth successfully.

Before commenting on these figures, it is worth taking a closer look at the 'after-but-not-before' figures for marriages and births. In the case of marriages, of the 6 women reporting in this category, 5 were probably too young at the onset to have had husbands before it anyway. In the case of births, of the 9 women reporting in this category, 5 were probably too young at the onset to have given birth before it anyway. If, then, we confine our attention to those whose reported age of onset indicates that they definitely could, other things being equal, have married and given birth both before and after possession, we get the following figures:

18 women reasonably married before and after possession; 8 women reasonably married before possession but not afterwards; 1 woman reasonably married after possession but not before; and 2 never married. 1 woman giving birth successfully both before and after possession; 16 women giving birth successfully before possession but not after; 4 women giving birth successfully after possession but not before; and 8 women childless.

As regards childlessness, I have no accurate statistics relating to Kalabari women generally; but my impression is that the proportion of chronically childless women in our sample is not startlingly greater than the proportion in the population at large.

From our figures, then, it appears that possession by 'women's *oru*' typically starts in early womanhood, and after marriage. There is little evidence that such possession is a *response* to childlessness, the great obstacle in the way of women who are trying to fulfil the expectations associated with their main roles as mothers and wives. On the other hand possession, or the psychological condition of which it is a symptom, does appear to have an adverse effect on women's capacity to fulfil these expectations. Thus our sample provides some indication that it may work against its victims' successful functioning as wives, and particularly against their ability to bear children.

In this last respect, our findings accord with popular beliefs that the spirits tend to stop *oru kuro* women from having children, and that such women are difficult to control, unamenable to household routine, and so make bad wives. They also accord with statements by the *oru kuro* women themselves. Thus most of those who stopped giving birth after they had become possessed attributed this to the spirit. Some simply said, 'He doesn't allow me to give birth any more'. One said, 'My water-husband and I married in the land of the *owu*, and I bore for him there. So he doesn't want me to give birth here'. Again with husbands, a typical remark is, 'Men come for me; but my husband in the water will not agree'. Rather revealingly, one woman said: 'My husband in the water tells me to marry a man without half a penny, and to give him all the orders. But I want to marry a man who is somebody, a man who will command me. That is why I do not marry again'.

Even one of the women who had succeeded in remaining happily married after possession told me that her spirit was often peevish about her earthly husband. When he came on her head, he was wont to amuse everyone by singing:

> Every day, day, day, *kumba, kumba, kumba.*
> Even on a *keke* day there is no end to it.
> Every day, day, day, *wele, wele, wele.*
> Even on a *keke* day there is no end to it.

Kumba and *wele* are water-spirit words for sexual intercourse; and the spirit is complaining in the song that his carrier spends so much time sleeping with her earthly husband that she does not even stop to think of him on the *keke* day of the week that is his by right.

All this notwithstanding, it is clear from our sample that a considerable proportion of *oru kuro* women do stay married after possession, even though many of them bear no more children. In some cases they manage this by teaming up with the type of man referred to in the complaint quoted earlier: the type with not a halfpenny in his pocket who is content to be given orders, to act as interpreter and general factotum in his wife's shrine, and to live off the earnings of her spirit. In other cases they team up with a more positive, more virile sort of man who is willing to compromise with their eccentricities because he values their personal divining services. In earlier days, indeed, many successful *oru kuro* diviners ended up married to important chiefs in the New Calabar trading state. Many of the great chiefs of the nineteenth century set a high value on their *oru kuro* wives, whose spirits provided a sort of early-warning system vis-à-vis the machinations of their political rivals. They lavished money and goods on them, and generally set them up in great magnificence. With a large number of more orthodox wives at their disposal, they were able to allow these women to go very much their own unwifely ways.

Before discussing the two men in our sample, one thing should be noted. It is that a great many men go to diviners with troubles much the same as those reported by women in the sample. And a great many of these men also receive the diagnosis that a water-spouse or water-friend is worrying them for recognition and for fulfilment of obligations. But whereas in women such a diagnosis is very frequently followed by possession, in men this sequel is very rare. As I said earlier, I heard of only three men possessed by minor water-spirits of the 'women's *oru*' type during two years' stay in Kalabari.

One of the two men in our sample was possessed by a male 'water-friend' whose divining prowess was known all over the Kalabari area. He had a large 'shadow descent-group' which attended on his spirit at festivals of great magnificence. He seems to have been called to mediumship in much the same way as many of the women: through sickness, followed by diagnosis of an unacknowledged relationship with a water-spirit, followed by a sojourn in the house of an established *oru kuro* woman while his possession was being brought under control. He was a pleasant though forceful personality, married to one wife, with several children. If there was something that made him an exceptional person, it was the fact that he was one of the first twin-babies to be rescued from death in an era when twins were still an abomination marked down to be thrown away in the 'bad bush'. The case of the second man was somewhat different. He was possessed by a female 'water-wife', whose divination activities were not very successful. He too seems to have been called to mediumship in much the same way as many of the women. He was a little ashamed of being possessed by his female spirit, saying that such a thing did not become a man. He was a gentle person, married but childless.

We shall say more about these two men when we come to consider what the causal background of this kind of possession may be.

Before closing this section on recruitment, I should perhaps say something about the formal rites which acknowledge a carrier's relationship with her water-spirit partner. These rites tend to vary a great deal according to the whim of the supervising *oru kuro* woman who prescribes them. At their core, however, they always include what is known as *efere gbana* – 'laying the plate on the table'. In this rite, the carrier invites a number of friendly *oru kuro* women as witnesses, entertains them lavishly with food and drink, and makes them presents of Real India cloth. Then she brings out a small stool, covers it with a white cloth, and lays on it various objects of which the following are usual: a white plate, a manilla, a gob of kaolin, a pod of alligator pepper, a piece of kola, a bottle of Krola[15], a bottle of palm gin, a bottle of perfume, a tin of powder, and a length of Ikaki cloth. There is no space here to go into detail about the significance of these various objects. Suffice it to say that the 'laying of the table' is for the spirit, and is a domestic gesture which signifies the carrier's willingness to care for her partner.

Note that this is not a rite of marriage. In Kalabari thinking, the marriage has been contracted in the world of the water-people before birth, between the carrier's own guiding spirit and her water-spirit partner. What *efere gbana* does is acknowledge the tie and the obligations that go with it.

I did not say anything about this rite earlier on, because it is not done at any specific stage in the development of possession. Some of the carriers in our sample reported having done it before they became possessed. Others reported doing it afterwards. Yet others said they were still waiting to get together enough money do to it. What everyone agrees is that it must be done sooner or later if one is to enjoy a quiet life with one's spirit partner.

Traditional prescription and public control play a far smaller part in possession by 'women's *oru*' than they do in either of the first two types described. The initial development of possession is largely spontaneous. True, the first suggestion about relationship with a water-spirit and the possibility of possession usually comes from another person – a diviner. But this diagnosis is often one among several offered in a situation of misfortune; and in the last analysis it is the would-be carrier who acts on it. Again, the 'training' of the newly-arrived spirit by an established carrier is not so much an attempt to determine the positive content of possession behaviour as an attempt to discourage antisocial extremes and to make the behaviour more amenable to control by the carrier herself. And once possession is fully developed, there is no attempt by the community to impose any sort of restriction on its content. Finally, while it is true that in their broad outlines, the principal roles played by 'women's *oru*' are fairly standardized, within these outlines there is still an enormous individual variation.

Since the individual looms so large in possession by 'women's *oru*', it is legitimate to ask what kind of personal predicament leads someone into this kind of behaviour. It is also legitimate to ask the closely-related question as to why such behaviour should be overwhelmingly associated with women.

Here, I think, we should pause to consider the general position of women in Kalabari communities. Though women exert a great deal of influence through their relations with husbands, children and kinsmen in the domestic sphere, their participation in the wider political and status system is very restricted. Though they sometimes participate in lineage or 'house' assemblies, they hold no offices in such assemblies. They are excluded from active membership of the community council, from the *ekine* society, and from the occupation of *biribo* (diviner/herbalist) which is one of the few rewarding specialist pursuits. Again, though in most communities there are pressure groups drawn from among the older women, they have little in the way of formal organization. Thus there is no system of office and authority running parallel with that of the male world.

Far, indeed, from being provided with their own parallel world of power and authority, women are encouraged to spend much of their lives in an intense, vicarious participation in all male pursuits. When men bring out the masquerades that absorb so much of their time and energy, a chorus of older women cheers the maskers on with exuberant praise songs, whilst an audience of younger women watches every move with rapt attention. When men marry or accede to office, the same exuberant female chorus praises them by chanting the great deeds of their ancestors. When prominent men quarrel over matters of power and position, it is often their female relatives or wives who egg them on. Women, rather than men, are the ultimate custodians of the great male deeds of the past. Often, in fact, it is they rather than the men who know just how some contemporary male activity should be carried out.

Now vicarious participation seems rather an unsatisfactory solution to the problem posed by female aspirations toward power and status. True, it provides a kind of opportunity to deal with these aspirations – i.e. by identifying with men. But this is a pale and unsatisfactory thing when set against the bitter fact that it continually serves to rub in – the fact that the male world is the only worth-while one.

I think it is as a response to this situation that possession by 'women's *oru*' can best be understood. First of all, the fully-developed complex of possession roles typically figures a man: not just an ordinary man, but a man of wealth, power, and status. In adopting this complex of roles a woman is enabled, from time to time, really to 'be' what she has always yearned to be but never can be in ordinary, normal life. The salient features of the recruitment process do much to support this interpretation. Thus the onset of possession, as we have seen, is typically in early womanhood and after marriage: at the time, that is, when the frustrations inherent in the female role-complex have become maximally apparent. Again, onset of possession appears to be associated with a definite trend toward cessation of childbirth and withdrawal from the married state – signs, perhaps, of a deep-seated rejection of woman's basic roles.

A look at the two males in our sample confirms rather than throws doubt on this interpretation. The first of the two, as we noted, was a rescued twin. As such, he grew up under a certain stigma – an ascribed status barrier to some extent akin to that affecting women. In carrying a spirit, he was able to transcend this barrier in much the same way as an *oru kuro* woman transcends the sex barrier. The second of the two is not so readily classified. Perhaps, with his gentle, ineffectual nature and his rather shamefaced association with a female possessor, he was jumping the sex barrier in the opposite direction.

Broadly viewed, then, possession by 'women's *oru*' would seem to provide a means whereby people miscast in their social roles on criteria beyond their power to change can get themselves to some extent properly cast again.[16]

But there is another aspect of 'women's *oru*' possession which we should keep in mind. In the prophetic and myth-spinning activities of these spirits, it will be remembered, we found interesting hints of innovation. It may be that the adoption of the *oru kuro* role offers not only a loophole for the socially miscast, but also a suitable platform for introducing innovations into a highly conservative culture.

POSSESSION DURING MASQUERADE DANCING

The spirits involved in this category are again typically minor water-spirits. They are often distinguished from other kinds of such spirits by the label 'playing *oru*'.

As I have already written at some length about the masquerade[17], I shall merely present a brief outline here, for the sake of completeness.

In an '*oru* dancing' festival such as the one described at the beginning of this essay, a phase of invocation and offering is followed by a phase of dramatic presentation during which the invoker becomes possessed by the spirit invoked. The two phases are seen as jointly instrumental in securing ulterior benefits from the spirit. In a masquerade festival, there are the same two phases, and the same occurrence of possession in the second phase. The important difference is that here the invocation and offering has as its main object the securing, not of ulterior benefits, but of an intrinsically enjoyable dramatic phase.

In the typical masquerade festival, proceedings start with invocation and offering addressed to the wooden headpiece which is believed to be the temporary seat of the masquerade's water-spirit 'owner'. The invocation asks that the dancer be given clear ears to hear the drum, and smart feet to follow it. The offering is generally of a fowl. On the morrow, the dancer is dressed in the masquerade costume and capped with the headpiece. He is led out before the drums, and dances to their dictation. He may dance through the performance without the spirit coming upon him. But if he is a good dancer, he should feel the drums 'pushing' him and taking charge, until he no longer moves under his own command. And at this stage, he is said to be possessed. A dancer is praised for his performance under possession because, although he is not strictly accountable for his actions at this time, he has to dance with some competence before the spirit of the masquerade will deign to mount him.

In the usual masquerade performance, the dancer is to be seen carrying out a closely-prescribed series of steps and tableaux. And as in '*oru* dancing', it seems to be the drum that keeps him in line with the prescription. Sometimes, however, a possessed masquerader will create a new variant of one of the standard traditional dance sequences, and this will be remembered by his name when he is dead and gone. Sometimes, again, a man will import a new masquerade into the community, and work out his own interpretation of it in concert with the drummers. Here, then, there is an element of individual creation and choice which would be unheard of in the context of '*oru dancing*'.

To perform a masquerade, one must enter the *ekine* society. Anyone who wishes to do so must obtain a sponsor from among established members of the society. Approval of the sponsor ideally depends only on dancing ability. Entrance payment is small. Although rights to dance many of the plays are vested in particular descent-groups, an equal number of plays are open to any member of the society who can convince his fellow-members of his suitability for the part. Hence even if one does not rise to the heights of creating a new variant or of importing and reinterpreting a foreign masquerade, one has considerable scope for personal choice as regards what to play.

In some ways, as we have seen, the masquerade resembles the '*oru* dancing' festival. In both cases, the core of the possession behaviour is dance sequence. And in both cases, the drums play a crucial part not only in inducing possession but also in controlling its course. But whereas the aim of inducing possession in an '*oru* dancing' festival is that of pleasing the spirit and securing his continued benevolence, the aim of inducing possession in a masquerade is basically an aesthetic one. Again, whereas there is virtually no room for an individual contribution to the content of '*oru* dancing' behaviour, such a contribution is much appreciated in masquerading.

CONCLUSION

From this inventory of Kalabari possession behaviour, it should be clear that the four main types discussed have widely differing significances both for the actors involved and for their audiences. I can think of no single line of interpretation, either sociological or psychological, which could possibly do justice to the diversity of these phenomena.[18]

Before closing, however, I should like to draw attention to an interesting correlation which emerges from this diversity: a correlation between the kind of spirit to which possession is attributed, and the form and setting of the possession behaviour.

Possession, the reader will have noted, involves spirits of varying degrees of importance to the community. On the one hand, there are the 'big' spirits – the founding heroes and those water-spirits that control the neighbouring creeks. On the other hand, there are the minor spirits – the host of water-people vaguely associated with the more distant creeks, or with nowhere in particular. Now there are certain interesting differences between possession by the big spirits and possession by the minor ones. Possession by the big spirits is subjected to a public scrutiny and control which discourages any departure from a traditionally-prescribed content. Its principal significance is that it reminds people, sometimes at recurrent intervals and sometimes at times of communal crisis, of the presence and attributes of the spirits, and of the values they support. Its general setting leaves very little room for individual innovation on the part of the medium. Possession by the minor water-spirits, on the other hand, is virtually free from public scrutiny and control. Although it too serves to remind people of the presence and attributes of the spirits, it has a much wider range of significance. Thus it provides a means of personal adjustment for those whose ascribed position in society is excessively irksome to them. It also provides the occasion for both narrative and dramatic art. Finally, it provides a means for the propagation of new ideas about the world. In all these contexts, the impress of individual innovation is very evident.

These differences are, I think, fairly readily explained. First of all, doctrines relating to the founding heroes and the big local water-spirits occupy a crucial place in the community's world-view. They both interpret, validate and indicate means for the perpetuation of the established order of society and ecology. Any change in such doctrines is potentially a grave threat to the established order of things. Hence there is continual public scrutiny to ensure that no such change takes place. Since possession by the big spirits gives dramatic reminders and illustrations of these doctrines, it must be included in the scrutiny.

Doctrines relating to the minor water-spirits are, by contrast, rather marginal to the community's world-view. Collectively, it is true, these minor spirits have an important part to play in the explanation of the peculiarities of individual life-courses. But no one spirit is involved with more than a few individuals. Again, these minor spirits are by definition the owners of distant creeks with which the community is not practically concerned. Particular spirits of this class, then, are important neither to the community as a whole nor to any considerable section of it. Hence doctrines concerning them are free from the scrutiny and control applied to doctrines concerning the big spirits. And this freedom extends to possession by them.

One consequence is that possession by the minor water-spirits comes readily under the influence of a variety of desires and needs other than those concerned with the explanation, prediction and control of the world. Thus it becomes caught up in the struggle to find a way round uncongenial ascriptions of status, and again in the struggle to elaborate forms of both narrative and dramatic art. Another consequence is that the individual 'carrier' is free to make his personal contribution to the content of possession: a freedom which has been amply exploited in both of these contexts.

This freedom also makes possession by the minor water-spirits a promising channel for innovations in belief and doctrine which may eventually come to assume importance in the community at large. Since the utterances of these spirits on the heads of their carriers are virtually free from public scrutiny and control, they can serve as vehicles of new ideas which would be scotched at birth if they came from one of the big spirits. Remember how, during the time of the first Christian conversions, it was a minor water-spirit that went about telling people to join the churches since the day of the *oru* was over.

Through the same freedom, it is even possible that these marginal spirits may provide the material for renewing and readapting the very core of the community's world-view. We don't have much evidence on this; but one case is suggestive. This is the case of the spirit carried by one of the two men in our sample of people possessed by 'women's *oru*'. This spirit was first announced as the owner of a distant creek, far away from the community's own sphere of interest and operations. Later, it came to announce itself as a controller of local waters who acted together with the established big water-spirit Duminea. During a visit by a Shell prospecting party, it assumed responsibility for the oil resources of the neighbouring creeks; and when oil was found, the community gave it the credit for the discovery. For some time now, the community has been on the brink of treating it as an object of public cult.

With this case in mind, we may look again at some of the myths which tell how village heroes originally came out of the world of the water-people to live with men. I have already offered an intellectualist interpretation of such myths.[19] But it would seem possible to supplement this with a more historical (though highly speculative) interpretation. It is that the heroes, and other big spirits, were originally introduced to the community as minor water-spirits on the heads of *oru kuro* people; and that they stayed incubating on the sidelines until, at some time of social upheaval and change requiring new interpretative concepts, they came out to make grander claims for themselves.

Elsewhere, I have described how in former times Kalabari got rid of spirits who seemed to have no further usefulness to the community.[20] We may have a clue here as to how they got themselves new spirits to meet new challenges to their way of life.

NOTES

[1]Longer expositions will be found in Horton, 1962 and Horton, 1965a.

[2]For a detailed analysis of the ritual context of sculpture see Horton, 1965a.

[3]Note that Tamuno is a woman, as also are the heads of the heroes in several Kalabari communities, e.g. Owemekaso of New Calabar. In a society where women occupy a markedly subordinate position. this may seem a little odd. In fact, however, it is quite consistent with Kalabari ideas about the relationship between the sexes.

Women, it is true, are subordinate to men. But it is women who bring into society its most important assets – people – and men who only subsequently take over control of these assets. Again, women are stereotyped as gentle and productive; men as violent and destructive. These latter aspects of femininity outweigh the fact of subordination when it comes to defining many of the gods.

[4]For an illustrated account of the Duminea festival, see Horton, 1965b.

[5]I hope to give a blow-by-blow description of this and other festivals in a future book on Kalabari religion. Since there is no space for such detail here, I am merely giving the highlights of the proceedings, especially those immediately relating to possession.

[6]Niger perch.

[7]Real India: a cloth formerly brought from Madras, now mostly from England: reminiscent of Tartan. Ikaki: a cloth woven in the southern Ibo town of Akwete, named after its conventionalized tortoise motif.

[8]As yet, I am not certain why both '*oru* dancing' and 'speaking' are less well developed in connexion with the dead. It may be that the head of a descent-group, because he occupies the status-position filled earlier by his ancestors, provides in his own person a dramatic reminder of the ancestral presence – a reminder which obviates the need for possession. This explanation gains some support from the fact that in one or two communities where 'dancing' and 'speaking' by the dead are well developed, their principal occasion is after the burial of a prominent man and before any successor has assumed his status-position in the descent-group or family. In this interim period, a daughter or sister of the deceased characteristically acts as his vehicle.

[9]Though there are important continuities of social structure as between villages and trading state, there are also considerable contrasts. One of these contrasts concerns the prevalent type of political conflict. In the villages, this tends to be between transient followings, gathered round individuals and dissolving when the latter die or are discredited. In the trading state, it tends to be between enduring corporate groups, the 'houses' or pseudo-lineages. This means that whilst long-distant episodes of conflict are irrelevant to the understanding of present-day conflict in the villages, they are very relevant to such understanding in the trading state. Hence in the latter, traditions of such long-distant episodes are far better preserved.

[10]Owamekaso was one of several female heads of founding heroes. For a note on female gods in a male-dominated community, refer to Note 3.

[11]After what has been said about the declining importance of his home community in the life of the individual, this contrast should not be surprising. For while the heroes and the big water-spirits that own the local creeks are concerned above all with communal welfare, the minor water-spirits that play such an important part in 'women's *oru*' possession are concerned above all with individual fortunes.

[12]Such clothes vary considerably from spirit to spirit. Several of the items of the Fenibaso 'dancer's' dress are very commonly seen in this context too.

[13]See Horton 1964a.

[14]All but one member of the sample hail from the town of Buguma (17), and from the villages of Abalama (2), Teinma (2), Soku (4), Orusangama (7), Kula (3). At a rough estimate the sample probably represents 30 per cent of the people carrying 'women's *oru*' in these six communities. And these six communities, in turn, are drawn from a total of eighteen 'true' Kalabari communities.

[15]A Coca-Cola type of drink made in Nigeria.

[16]I think the extension of the 'role' metaphor by the use of 'miscast' and 'recasting' brings out rather nicely the function of *oru kuro* possession in ensuring the use of individual talents that would otherwise be wasted. It also pinpoints

the much-discussed relationship between this type of possession and psychopathological behaviour: briefly, whilst the *oru kuro* woman is merely miscast, the psychopathological deviant is uncastable.

[17]Horton, 1963: Horton, 1966.

[18]I stress this point because many previous discussions of spirit possession seem to assume that it is a unitary phenomenon susceptible of a unitary explanation: one thinks in particular of discussions of the relation of spirit possession to psychopathology.

[19]Horton, 1962, 202.

[20]Horton, 1964b.

REFERENCES

W. R. G. HORTON 1962 'The Kalabari world-view: an outline and interpretation', *Africa* 32, (3), 197–220.

1963 'The Kalabari *Ekine* society: a borderline of religion and art', *Africa* 33, (2), 94–114.

1964a 'Kalabari diviners and oracles', *Odu* 1 (1).

1964b 'A hundred years of change in Kalabari religion', paper given at conference on The High God in Africa, University of Ife, December.

1965a *Kalabari sculpture*, Lagos. Nigerian National Press for Department of Antiquities.

1965b 'Duminea: a Festival for the Water-Spirits', *Nigeria Magazine*, No. 86, September.

1966 'Igbo: an ordeal for aristocrats', *Nigeria Magazine*, No. 90, September.

TRANCE AND CONVENTION IN NAGO-YORUBA SPIRIT MEDIUMSHIP

© *Pierre Verger*

Possession trances occur regularly among the Nago-Yoruba and Fon people of Dahomey during rites for *orisha* and *vodun*.[1] These deities are seen on the one hand as founders of descent-groups, and on the other hand as forces of nature.

Despite all the transformations that have taken place in these parts over the last century – the weakening of ancient institutions and the partial replacement of traditional beliefs by Christianity and Islam – the cults of *orisha* and *vodun* have, in certain of the villages, retained much of their former vitality. A great part of the population of these communities still participates in their rites, whose aim is the periodic reactualization of the ties that bind living people and their ancestors.

Possession trances form only a part of the typical festival celebrated for the *orisha* and the *vodun*. They are the culmination of an elaborate ritual sequence. Seen from the participant's point of view, such trances are the reincarnations of family deities in the bodies of their descendants – reincarnations which have taken place in response to the offerings, prayers, and wishes of their worshippers.

The mediums of the gods are called *iyaworisha* or *vodunsi* – 'wife of the *orisha*' or 'wife of the *vodun*'. This name does not imply anything as to the sex of the person concerned, who may be a man or woman. Rather, it indicates a subordination to the god. A medium may also be called *elegun orisha* ('the one climbed on by the *orisha*'), *eshin orisha* ('horse of the *orisha*'), *adoshu orisha* ('the one whose head is the bearer of the *orisha's oshu*'),[2] or more generally *olorisha* ('owner of the *orisha*').[3]

People who become possessed by *orisha* or *vodun* in the course of a ritual show behaviour of a very disciplined kind. Such behaviour is modelled on the traditional picture of the personality of the being who is supposed to be incarnated in them.

Ogun (Yoruba) or *Gun* (Fon), god of blacksmiths, warriors, hunters, and all who use iron, is characterized by coarse and energetic manners; *Shango* (Yoruba) or *Hevioso* (Fon), god of thunder, by manly and jolly dances; *Orishala* (Yoruba), or *Lisa* (Fon), the creator god, by calm and serene behaviour; *Shapana* (Yoruba) or *Sapata* (Fon), god of smallpox and the contagious diseases, by restless agitation; *Eshu Elegba* (Yoruba) or *Legba* (Fon), messenger of the other gods, by cynical and abusive attitudes. These examples show just a part of the total range of behaviour which the 'horse of the gods' may adopt.

The first possession fits, which come before initiation, are often wild and violent; but under the supervision of the head priest of the god, they become calm and settled after a short period in his temple. Believers, putting a religious interpretation upon the passage from the first undisciplined fits to the more controlled ones that follow after the initiation, do not see it as a kind of therapeutic system or as the cure of some disease by shamanic treatment. Rather, if the future *olorisha* suffers some illness, it is apt to be considered as an omen from the god, a punishment for failing to observe the obligation to consecrate someone to him.

Manifestations of nervous disease, persistent bad luck, barrenness or a series of abortions in a woman: all of these are typical signs of a god's anger. People who suffer these misfortunes generally go to consult a *babalawo* (Yoruba) or a *bokonon* (Fon), who by consulting the *Ifa* (Yoruba) or *Fa* (Fon) divination apparatus tries to find out the reasons for them. If the enquirer's troubles are found not to be caused by the malevolence of a jealous neighbour or by the spirit of a departed member of the family, but are seen as a sign that an *orisha* or *vodun* wishes to have him consecrated as a medium, he usually agrees to initiation as *olorisha* or *vodunsi.*

This is only one of the ways in which priests are recruited. Sometimes the will of the god is expressed in a dream; or, more spectacularly, a chosen person may succumb to fits of dizziness and fainting in the middle of a public ceremony, and may even rush to prostrate himself in front of an *orisha* or *vodun* 'mounting his horse'.

More generally, however, initiation is performed without waiting till the *orisha* or *vodun* has claimed and called to order the person that must serve him. A person is often initiated as *olorisha* or *vodunsi* when the oracle, consulted at the time of his birth, has indicated that this is his destiny.

At Sakete, I was once witness of a rather impressive ceremony in which the *egun* or ghost of a dead *olorisha* was consulted, in the dark of the night, on a little-frequented road at the edge of the town, to get from him confirmation of his willingness to pass on to one of his daughters the position that he had filled when on earth.

I want to show here that Nago-Yoruba possession behaviour, considered in its religious setting, is an integral part of the culture and has a well-defined meaning within it. I also want to show that there is social pressure on the individual to follow tradition in these matters; and that possession is not a hysterical fit that a doctor is asked to calm down, but is rather seen as an obligation to society on the part of those whom the gods elect to submit to it.[4]

At Sakete and Ifanhim in the Nago region of south-east Dahomey, I have had the opportunity of being present at several rites during which annual offerings of rams were made to *Shango*, the thunder god. In these two neighbouring towns, there are numerous *Shango* worshippers, and many more come in from the farm settlements nearby. Several hundred worshippers congregate at the time of one of these rites. Among them are from one hundred to two hundred and fifty *elegun Shango* (*elegun* is a priest able to become the medium of an *orisha*), all potential 'horses of the god'. During the rite, however, *Shango* 'mounts' only one of them.

The ritual dances are performed with perfect co-ordination by all of the *elegun*, who are accompanied for several hours by the drums, known as *bata*. Possession takes place at the very moment when the ram is sacrificed and offered to *Shango*. The one amongst the host of *elegun* who gets possessed rushes toward the slaughtered body of the animal and takes it in his arms, to show that *Shango* has accepted his offering. At once, the members of the *Shango* group show a general elation; the rhythm of the *bata* drums becomes faster; and while the chosen *elegun Shango* is driven toward the temple where lies the *ashe*[5] of the god, the other dancers whirl faster and faster to joyous shouts of '*Shango* has come!'

The possessed *elegun* is to be the incarnation of *Shango* for seventeen days. His hair is plaited in the shape of a crest, and his body is powdered with red camwood. He is dressed in an *iyeri*, a circle of scarves tied to a belt and swinging to the least movement, and a *bante*, an apron made of ram leather completely covered by cowrie shells sewn side by side. Brandishing an *oshe* or double axe, which symbolizes the action of thunder, he is brought back to the *Shango* worshippers and dances among them for several hours. From time to time he cries with a shrill, tremulous voice. He wears a strange expression, half cunning, half benevolent. But when the orchestra is silent and his actions are no longer sustained by the *bata* drums, he reverts to a blank, stupefied expression.

In fact, *Shango* is not thought to remain in the body of his *elegun* during the whole of the seventeen days. He mounts his medium only when he appears in public, and when he walks through the streets and markets of the town at the head of his worshippers. During rest periods, the *elegun* is possessed by a secondary spirit who accompanies the *orisha*. This secondary spirit makes the *elegun* behave like a little child or simpleton who smiles foolishly at every turn. When the man is in this state the worshippers treat him with a familiarity and amusement very different from the respectful attitude they adopt when he is possessed by *Shango* himself.

In Brazil, among the descendants of Nago-Yoruba people who have remained faithful to the cult of their ancestors' *orisha*, the *elegun* in this kind of resting state is said to be possessed by *ere* or *ashere*. Among the Nago-Yoruba this being is addressed as *inu eru de* – 'the one who arrives with the luggage'. This label indicates his position as associate of the *orisha* himself. It is in this state that the *elegun* is given food and drink and is allowed to sleep and answer nature's calls. When he is possessed by the *orisha* himself, his body must be completely insulated from these prosaic needs.

In Nigeria, the possession behaviour of *elegun Shango* is marked by spectacular demonstrations of the god's power. Often, for instance, he transfixes his tongue with a rod of iron, walks along with it in a leisurely fashion, and later takes it out without seeming to be inconvenienced by the experience. He seems unworried by what has happened even after possession is over.

In the little village of Ishede, I have been able to watch several offerings of food to *Ogun Igbo-igbo*. These are made once in the Nago-Yoruba four-day week, on *ose*, the holiday of the *orisha*. Once in every two weeks, on *ose kekere* (the little holiday), a minor rite is performed; and once in every two weeks, on *ose nla* (the big holiday), a more elaborate rite is performed. In another study,[6] I have already given a detailed description of the *ose nla* rite; but I here summarize its principal features in order to provide a further example of the setting and content of Nago possession.

In the nineteen-fifties, Ishede had around two thousand inhabitants. Some forty of these were Muslims, twenty-five Catholics, twenty Protestants. The others were animist, and with the exception of one dedicated to *Shango* and one to *Oshun*, all of them were under the protection of *Ogun Igbo-igbo*.[7]

Ishede provides a useful indication of what Nago-Yoruba villages were like before the arrival of the Europeans. A long time ago the inhabitants came from Ire, the place of origin of *Ogun*, their *orisha*. They remained for a long time in a neighbouring region called Holli, and finally settled at Ishede during the last century.

In Ishede, the *alashe* (*ashe* keeper) of *Ogun Igbo-igbo* has the role of chief of the community, and is helped in this by a council of elders. His authority is based on the power of the *orisha*, who is a remote and deified ancestor. The *alashe* is addressed as '*Kabiyesi*' by those who speak to him, and he is saluted by prostration. Both of these salutations are reserved for *Obas* (kings). It is as representative of the god *Ogun* that he receives such respect. We have here a true theocracy.

During the weekly rite for *Ogun*, the *alashe* is accompanied and surrounded by: *Saba* (his assistant), *Okere* (Saba's assistant), *Ashogun* (in charge of the *orisha Ode*, a hunter), *Oluponan* (in charge of *Eshu Elegba*) *Iyafero* (a woman charged with calming *Ogun* down when he becomes too violent), *Alaposi* (drummer), the *Elegbenla* (soldiers of the *orisha*) the *Ishoro* (who interprets the will of the *orisha*), *Arosheku* (who in special circumstances bears on his head the *ashe* of the *orisha*), and the *iyaworisha* (women dedicated to the *orisha* who sing for him).

On the holiday of the *orisha*, all of these dignitaries gather in a forest glade in front of the temple of *Ogun*. They bring offerings of food, part of which is laid in front of the *ashe* – the seat of the power of *Ogun* which is kept inside the temple – and part distributed and shared among the various groups of worshippers in a series of very formal gifts and counter-gifts. This distribution is followed by a communal meal. Every participant is seated in a place determined by his position in the cult organization.

At the door of the temple, there is an orchestra composed of three drums: an *aposi* (a little drum with an earthenware body), an *ogidan* (an elongated drum), a *kele* (a little drum raised on legs), accompanied by an *agogo* (an iron bell).

The periods of drumming are broken by silences at moments of adoration of *Ogun* by the priests within the temple. The rest of the congregation remain outside, prostrate on the ground, hearing from time to time a faint bell-ringing coming from the sanctuary – a noise that is accompanied by a few short and sonorous strokes on the *aposi* drum.

After a while, the dignitaries come out of the temple and return to their respective places. The orchestra starts its drumming again, calling the names of the gods with a frenzied beat.

Sometimes, it happens that *Ogun* does not answer the call; and if this is so, the ceremony comes to an end. But if he does answer, *Saba* utters a shout, and is followed by *Okere, Ashogun, Oluponan* and *Iyafero.* All five go into possession.

Alashe himself does not participate in this possession, though it is he who presides over the celebration of *Ogun's* holiday. The group of *iyaworisha* chant acclamations and sing the praises of *Ogun Igbo-igbo* with solemn, fervent voices.[8]

The five priests now appear wearing pointed caps, fully possessed. The first three hold bells and cutlasses. *Iyafero* holds a fan, and *Oluponan* a cudgel, the *ogo* of *Eshu.*

Shaken by sudden leaps, they get up with angular gestures, meet in front of the temple, and together dance a kind of quadrille to the beat of the drums. One after the other, they go to salute the audience and the various consecrated places in the glade. All the while, the *iyaworisha* sing and shout the praises of *Ogun.*

These dances and songs last about an hour. Afterward, the *Alashe* holds a meeting with the still-possessed *olorisha* under the awning of the temple. Then *Saba* shouts again, and everybody goes to sit down once more in his own appointed place. There is a long pause. Little by little the *olorisha* return to their normal state. The rite comes to an end. The audience returns to the village, and is soon followed by the dignitaries, who prostrate a last time in front of the temple.

I have often seen a very similar rite, again performed once every four days, in honour of an *orisha* called *Ondo* at Pobe.

Here, too, food is offered to the *orisha* and distributed among the worshippers. The subsequent trances follow a highly standardized scheme. During seven consecutive calls by the orchestra, one sees a progressive modification in the facial expressions of the various *olorisha*, who sit bareheaded and composed, awaiting possession. Their features stiffen more and more; they swallow their saliva; their bodies sway slightly and are overrun by tremors; their eyes are shut; their hands contracted. At the seventh call there is a shout from *Oluponan*, who is possessed by *Eshu* – a shout upon which the other *olorisha* leap up, put on their pointed caps, seize their *adja* and cutlasses, and go to salute their *Kabiyesi*, shaking left hands with him and touching the ground three times with their bells.

They walk bent forward and with large paces, raising their feet very high. They show signs of great agitation. Their faces are contracted and their mouths open. They pull their tongues and shake them. They open their eyes wide. They take on a patriarchal expression, blinking their eyelids continuously and speaking tremulously, like comedy grey-beards, very old and slightly gaga. In this style, they express wishes of happiness, longevity, fecundity and wealth for their audience.

In a village of the same region, Ilodo, I was able to attend a rite marking the first public appearance of a new initiate of *Ogun Edeyi*. A detailed description will show how the possession behaviour of the various priests conformed to the personalities of the *orisha* they were incarnating.[9] Some of the chants recorded are a constant feature of the rites held on each *ose* of the *orisha*. At other moments, the action was more spontaneous and the dialogues the fruit of passing inspiration; but both still conformed closely to the traditionally prescribed characters of the *orisha* involved.

This rite was held in front of the temple of *Ogun Edeyi*. Its general organization was similar to that described for *Ogun Igbo-igbo*. But in this case, a character called *Fashina* played an important role. *Okere* also bore the title of *Ijishe*. And *Oga Onsa*, chief of the *egbenla*, interfered frequently in the dialogues between the various *orisha*.

Since the beginning of the *ose nla* was similar to that of *Ogun Igbo-igbo*, we shall start at the point when the drums are calling the *orisha* with accelerated rhythms.

Ijishe, who is the first to appear in possession, utters a loud shout and goes inside the temple, leaving *Iyafero* for some time dancing alone. After a while *Ijishe* comes out of the temple. He walks restlessly here and there, shaking left hands with the audience. He walks with stiff legs, hopping from one to the other, looking at the sky. As he shakes hands, he says '*asheun*' ('thank you', 'so be it'). He follows the orchestra's changes of rhythm, and from time to time makes violent shoulder movements known as *ijika*.

At this point, *Iyafero* enters into trance and begins to dance calmly.

Oga Onsa comes, cuts the head off a fowl, and pours the blood on a place called *idomosun* where the *osun* irons representing the dead ancestors are planted. Later, he pours water on the place.

After this the *iyaworisha* dance, then they prostrate in front of the temple where *Alashe* shakes his bell to salute them.

While all this is going on, the inhabitants of Ilodo and neighbouring villages arrive in little groups, in spite of rain which continues throughout the ceremony. People have come in greater numbers than usual because this is the first appearance of an *iyaworisha* of *Ogun Edeyi*, a woman who is going to be consecrated to him for ever.

The woman's own family has brought many calabashes containing offerings of food and money.

All the children of this woman have died, one after the other, a few days after their birth. According to the belief of this region, she has been the victim of an *abiku*, a supernatural being that comes to earth for a few days at a time in the bodies of a succession of children.

Ogun is said to have chosen this woman and taken her under his protection three weeks ago. On the day in question, she stopped in the street, made disturbed gestures, and went to the front of the *orisha* temple where she fell stiffly to the ground. She was taken inside a nearby building, where she is now in the process of being initiated.

Before long the three drums start to beat, and the established *iyawo* of *Ogun* come out leading the novice who is in a state of trance. She is dressed in a white cloth, has her head shaved, and bears a fan. Guided by the *iyawo*, she goes to the house of *Eshu Elegba*, followed by the entire congregation. Here she witnesses the sacrifice of a rooster and offerings of food and money.

After this, everyone returns to the front of the temple to watch the dance of the *iyawo* and the novice. They dance, retire into the temple and come out again twice. Then the drums stop beating, and there is complete silence. In violent trance, the novice shouts her new name: '*Pete di oisha, Ori kuti*'. People in the crowd shout and snap their fingers. This is the name the woman will be called by from now on.

Once more there is silence as people await a manifestation, a message, some extraordinary deed by the new *iyaworisha*. After some time, she shouts: 'There is a man called *Sumamu*, a muslim, who in Ramadan fast time stole a sheep, killed it and ate it. *Ogun Edeyi* killed him'. Everybody laughs and rejoices.

Now the drums beat again, and the *iyaworisha* dances and sings[10]:

I have come, we say, I have come.
Ori kuti has come now.
I have come, I have come today.
Pete di Oisha has come now.
I have come to see the one who has a title now.
I have come; may the unbeliever disappear.
I have come, I have brought the passer-by, see the holiday.
I have come *Tomula*, see the holiday.
I have come, wife of the king, I have come today.
The *ishoro* has come.
I have come *Torojo*, see the holiday.

After a time, the drums stop, and the novice stumbles and falls to the ground. She is revived and brought into the temple.

In spite of the rain which falls harder than ever, the drums start to beat again with a rapid rhythm; the *egbenla* dance in an agitated way, and the *olorisha* join in, shaking their *aja* bells.

Fashina now comes out of the temple in a state of trance, goes to salute the house of *Eshu* and comes back to sing:

What do you want to do?

The chorus of *iyaworisha* answers:

We worship the *orisha*.
If we worship the *orisha*
We will always have money,
We will always have children.
Our little children will not die in youth.
We shall be standing for the *orisha*.

Fashina Ogun sings:

Hear!
If the country does not fare well,
It would be advisable to make sacrifices;
If there are death and illness,
Make sacrifices.
If somebody wants to harm the village,

I shall kill him . . . (*he dances*).

Oga Egbenla sings:

If I kill someone, it is because he has done something wrong.
I shall say to my soldiers to go and fetch his corpse
As an example to other malefactors.

The chorus of *egbenla* sings insistently with a swift rhythm. *Okere* falls into trance; the audience snaps fingers; *Okere* shouts, goes to the house of *Eshu* and comes back.

The rhythm of the drumming remains swift for a while, but changes; an *elegun* of *Shango* falls into trance. An *oshe* is given to the man, and his cloth is bound over one of his shoulders.

The rhythm of the drums changes again, and new trances appear among the *olorisha* of *Ode* (god of the hunters), *Oya* (wife of *Shango* and goddess of the tempest and of the Niger river), *Odua* (name given in this region to *Obatala*, god of the creation of human beings), *Omolu* (one of the names of *Shapannan*, god of smallpox).

The role played by the drums in the incitement of possession is a vital one; but it is not the mere mechanical action of an overwhelming rhythm, thousands of times repeated, that causes the trance. Each *orisha* or *vodun* has his own rhythm to which the *elegun* or *vodunsi* is sensitized in the course of initiation; and it is only the hearing of this particular rhythm at the stage of the feast when the god is called that incites the trance of his medium. What we appear to have here is a kind of conditioned reflex, created in the unconscious mind of the medium during the course of his initiation.

The drums enjoy great respect because they are not merely musical instruments. They are considered as the voice of the gods themselves; through them, the gods are called and answer at the same time. The sound of the drums is vital in building up the atmosphere of the ceremony, and is particularly impressive in a civilization based on spoken words and not on written ones.

As new *orisha* appear, the audience utters their praises. Symbolic objects are distributed to the various *olorisha* as follows:

Ogun Fashina: a pointed cap, two *aja* (hand bells) and a cutlass.
Shango: a double axe or *oshe*.
Oya: a fan.
Ode: a cutlass and two hunting sticks.
Odua: a tin stick.

Oluponan: a cudgel, the *ogo*[11] of *Eshu Elegba*, and a cutlass.
Iyafero: a fan and two *aja*.
Ogun Fashina sings:

If we see *Ogun* what do we ask him for?

The iyaworisha chorus:

We ask him for everything.
We do not know what is going to happen tomorrow.
We do not know who is going to be taken by *Ogun*.

Shango asks for money from someone in the audience, gives it to *Oya* and sings:

Shango is married.
May everybody be happy.

While *Shango* is dancing, the chorus of *iyaworisha* sings:

If we see *Shango*, what are we going to do?
We his children are going to dance.
We his children are going to rejoice.
Shango carry me on your back.
Man as powerful as an *oshe*.
We salute *Shango*.
He dances as he fights.
Let me go out with *Woru*.
With him I go, with him I come back.
He makes the old man marry again.

Shango thanks the drummers and expresses wishes for happiness:

Everything is going to be right.
They are going to get wealth.

Iyafero sings:

I direct all the priests of the *orisha*.
I am stronger than them all. (*She dances.*)

Ashogun sings:

I am afraid of everybody.
But if anybody claims to be higher than *Ogun*.
I shall lower him down. (*He dances.*)

Oluponan sings and goes away.
Shango sings:

If the rain does not fall,
People say it is because of *Shango*.
The day that a woman gives birth to seven children together,

People say that *Obatala*[12] has done it for the good of the country.
If there is selling on credit without payment, it is because of *Elegba*.

Ode sings:

If you do not knock at the door before entering a house,
You risk finding a man and his wife on the bed.

Omolu sings:

People of Popo do not eat leaves.
Ashogun says that somebody must not walk alone at mid-day.

Odua sings:

If there is yam in the fields,
I shall give some to *Obatala*.
If there are beans in the fields,
I shall give some to *Obatala*.
Obatala who leans on a stick of tin.

Okere Ogun sings:

You will not meet death on your road.
No sudden death, the country will be full of people.
There will not be enemies.
I am the enemy of everybody.
I kill everyone the *orisha* tells me to. (*He dances.*)
Nothing bad will happen.
Happiness, long life to everybody.
(*Looking in the direction of the temple.*)
Be careful; the dreadful one is coming.
The bush birds remain in the bush;
The house birds remain in the house.
If they do not see each other for a long time,
One will visit the other.

Saba Ogun comes out of the temple. He walks with bent knees, sword in hand. He shouts before the audience. He goes to salute the drummers.

Okere Ogun is still singing:

I hear noise in the bush.
When I arrive there, I see the death of an evil-doer.
I am satisfied. (*He dances.*)

Shango sings:

I want to go, I want to go, I want to go.
I want to say goodbye to the king.

My people, I return to the house of my *ashe*.
Dance with me.

Saba Ogun says:

I am glad that all the *orisha* have gone.
I have room to dance. (*He dances with Iyafero.*)
See the new *iyaworisha*, it is *Ogun* that chose her.
Is it not good? It is because I have seen the death on her that I took her.
Now she is not going to die; no more danger for her;
She is going to have a lot of children; boys and girls.
I am going to tell her father and her husband what they must do now.
Because she is not the same any more; the husband must not beat her any more,
He must leave her in peace.
If the husband has something to say, he must tell it to me.
It is *Ogun* now who is the father. Everybody must hear, men and women.
I choose even people in the north, the Gun people, the Mina people.
I have chosen a woman here and I do not see the husband.

Oga, the chief of the soldiers, tries to calm him, saying:

Be calm, do not look at the question of the children now, do your work.

Saba Ogun:

I have chosen somebody's wife, and the husband is not here.

Oga Egbenla:

Take care of the wife; do not take care of the husband.

Saba Ogun:

The woman is going to have a lot of children.
She had a lot of stillborn children before.
That is finished. Now she will get a lot of living children.
If someone wants to harm the woman, I am ready to kill.
Let everybody be careful. Happiness, long life.

Oga Egbenla:

If she has children and they do not die any more, *Ogun* will be more glorious. (*Arrival of the father of the new iyaworisha.*)

Saba Ogun:

Do you give me your daughter; yes or no?

The father:

I give her completely. *Ogun* may take her and leave her in the bush or in the water; wherever he wishes.

Saba Ogun:

Is that said with a good heart?

The father:

Yes, it is with a good heart. I am too young to say no in front of the *orisha*. The *orisha* is my father.

Saba Ogun:

I knew before choosing her that it would be for her happiness.

The father:

Yes, it is *Ogun* who knows the good and the evil. May he save my daughter for me. I shall do whatever *Ogun* may ask me. If necessary, I shall give him all my children and myself.

Saba Ogun:

If you are always at my side, I shall do everything that you ask me for your happiness. Your daughter will be in good health. She will have a lot of children, boys and girls, and all will live.

The father:

Please give me a young girl to bring me water to drink.

Saba Ogun:

If you are obedient, you will have all this. But if you are not obedient, I shall know it.

The father:

I am in a hurry.

Saba Ogun:

If you come here regularly, you will have all you want; the daughter I have taken from you is too young to help you.

An uncle of the *iyaworisha:*

Keep my brother's daughter well; she is young; find happiness for her, because she has lost lots of children. Now that you have taken my brother's daughter, I want to see a lot of her children. No more *abiku*[13], they bother me too much. You are our saviour. May nothing happen in the house of her father and mother. I trust in *Ogun*, I and all my family.

Saba Ogun:

It is I who have chosen her. I have not asked anything for her.

I lead her feet and her head.

The father of the *iyaworisha*'s husband:

I have come.

Saba Ogun:

The father of the *iyaworisha*'s husband is a little drunk; you must not appear so in front of me.

(*The father of the husband kneels and talks wildly.*)

The husband's brother:

My name is *Awa*. I am very glad of the choice of the *orisha*. When I heard it, I went to the father's house to ask if it was true; and he answered me, 'Yes, it is *Ogun* the *orisha*, and it is mine too.' I myself worship him too.

Saba Ogun:

The woman came out today.

Husband's brother:

Ogun has come. We are very happy. The *orisha* has given a name to the girl. I do not want her children to die when she comes home again. If she has children, may they live, may she have money. If somebody wants to harm her, may the *orisha* kill that person. I worship the *orisha*.

Saba Ogun expresses wishes of happiness for the family, and the family takes its leave from *Ogun*. *Saba* and *Iyafero* enter the temple. The crowd disperses.

These festivals give the impression of a theatrical performance or even an operetta. Their cast, costume, orchestral accompaniment, solo and chorus differ little in spirit from the Mystery and Passion Plays enacted in medieval Europe in the forecourts of the cathedrals. The salient difference is that in the present case the actors, if we may so call them, are in a state of trance.

The conventional character of each *orisha* was respected even in the spontaneous parts of the ceremonies which I witnessed.

The great part played by convention in trance behaviour has already attracted the attention of Michel Leiris, who has written of it in his study of possession in Ethiopia.[14] It also attracted the attention of the late Alfred Métraux, who suggested the term 'ritual comedy' for rites performed by *voodoo* followers in Haiti.[15]

In this article, I have not tried to indicate the part played by the simulation or fraud which seem likely affect this and other forms of possession behaviour. It is enough for us to realize that some of the trances are real, and that people in trance have acquired their conventional behaviour through the application of certain techniques during the course of a more or less lengthy initiation.

NOTES

[1]*Orisha* and *vodun* are the general names given by the Yoruba and Dahomean people respectively to the deities worshipped by them. They are generally considered to be the very remote ancestors who dealt during their lifetime with some force of nature, and who can still do so on behalf of their worshippers.
[2]The *oshu* is a little ball the size of a nut, made of several ingredients (leaves, blood of sacrificed animals, and minerals). It is thought of as fixing and stimulating the *ashe* or power of the *orisha*. The *oshu* is placed on the shaven head of a new initiate, as a consecration to a particular *orisha*.
[3]It is not the idea of ownership that is intended in this expression, but that of the interdependence of the *orisha* and his medium.
[4]Roger Bastide develops this point of view in his book. He observes that trances among African descendants in South America are not nervous phenomena, but the outcome of social pressures.
[5]*Ashe* is the vital power of the *orisha*. The same word covers some of the things serving as the supports of this power: e.g. *Shango's* thunderstones (neolithic axes), *Ogun's* symbolic iron tools, and river stones for water *orisha*.
[6]See Verger, 1957.
[7]In this region, *Ogun* bears several different names; such as *Ogun Igbo-igbo* at Ishede, *Ogun Edeyi* at Ilodo, *Ogun Igiri* at Fasha, *Ogun Elenjo* at Ibanion on the Nigerian border. Anyhow, he is the same as the *Ogun Onire* of Ire Ekiti in eastern Yoruba country. The second names are added for further identification, just as people leaving the family compound to settle in a new place get a new compound and a new name, and are the starting point of a new descent-group.
[8]A recording of this ceremony has been made by Gilbert Rouget of the Musée de l'Homme of Paris. (L.D. 12 longue durée 30 cm., 33 t./m).
[9]Notes on, and pictures of, this ceremony were given in Verger, 1951.
[10]The Yoruba texts of these songs were published in Verger, 1957.
[11]*Ogo* is a carved cudgel used by Eshu, messenger of the other *orisha*.
[12]*Obatala* is the *orisha* of the creation of the body of human beings. He is also called *oshala* or *orishala*.
[13]*Abiku* is a supernatural being supposed to come to earth and return to heaven several times through a series of abortions of the same woman.
[14]Michel Leiris, 1958.
[15]Alfred Métraux, 1955.

REFERENCES

BASTIDE, ROGER 1951 *Sociologie et psychanalyse*. Paris, Presses Universitaires de France.

LEIRIS, MICHEL 1958 *La possession et ses aspects théâtraux chez les Ethiopiens de Gondar*. Paris.

MÉTRAUX, A. 1955 'La comédie rituelle dans la possession', *Diogene*, 11.

VERGER, PIERRE 1951 'Une sortie de lyawo dans un village Nago au Dahomey', *Etudes dahoméennes*, 6, 11–26.

1957 *Notes sur le culte des Orisa et Vodun à Bahia, la Baie de tous les Saints, au Bresil et à l'ancienne Côte des Efclaves en Afrique*. Dakar, IFAN, Memoire No. 51.

CENTRAL AND SOUTH AFRICA

SPIRIT POSSESSION AMONG THE TONGA OF ZAMBIA

Elizabeth Colson

Some 300,000 Tonga inhabit the Southern Province of Zambia and adjacent provinces of Rhodesia. In the hills of the Rhodesian escarpment and in the Zambezi Valley near the Kafue River entrance, Tonga and Shona villages are intermixed. Major differences in language and custom distinguish the two peoples, but in their spirit cults, Tonga and Shona (especially Korekore and Zezuru) show many resemblances. The Tonga have probably borrowed much from the Shona, though their closest linguistic and cultural affiliations are with fellow Zambians of Southern and Central Provinces.

Zambian Tonga today form three administrative divisions: Toka-Leya of Kalomo and Livingstone Districts, Plateau Tonga of Mazabuka and Choma Districts, and Valley Tonga of Gwembe District. The international boundary, the Zambezi River prior to 1958 and now the Zambezi and Lake Kariba, separates the last from nearby Rhodesian Valley Tonga. Valley Tonga were formerly concentrated on the banks of the Zambezi. Since 1958 much of their country has been flooded by the formation of Lake Kariba. They now live either in the Zambian and Rhodesian hills above the lake or in the Lusitu area in the Zambezi Valley below Kariba Dam.

I have not worked among Toka-Leya and know little of the extent to which they resemble other Tonga. This paper therefore is concerned with Plateau and Valley Tonga alone and more specifically with the latter among whom I have worked most recently. Valley Tonga are still active participants in various spirit possession cults. In the late 1940s the cults vanished from many Plateau neighbourhoods. I do not know how prevalent they may be on the Plateau at the present time though in 1965 possession still occurred and possession dances were still held.[1]

THE POSSESSING SPIRITS

Tonga recognize three varieties of possession, each due to a particular class of spirit. These are treated in different fashions and have different consequences for the one possessed and for the public. In each variety, a spirit is said to enter (*kunjila*) the body of the one possessed; during periods of active possession the vehicle is addressed as the spirit and treated in ways regarded as appropriate for that spirit. During inactive periods it is common to speak of a spirit as being on the body of its vehicle, or perhaps near the body. Its presence is then disregarded. When the spirit departs, abandoning its vehicle entirely, the latter becomes cool (*tontolo*).

Basangu possession is the most important variety of possession as far as public consequences are concerned. It provides the inspiration for public ritual and is linked closely with social and political life. Perhaps *basangu* were once men, earlier prophets and community leaders. Perhaps they have always been spirits who have gone from one human vehicle to another. Tonga may disagree on this point without feeling it important. It is what a *basangu* does, not where it came from, that interests people.

Some Tonga use *basangu* as a term for any spirit, though its specific meaning seems to be that which I have adopted in this paper – spirits concerned with community welfare. Plateau Tonga may distinguish between singular (*musangu*) spirit and plural (*basangu*) spirits. Valley Tonga use the plural form. I shall follow this usage.

Basangu mediums, called prophets in earlier publications which dealt with their social role rather than the circumstances of possession, are also called *basangu*. Some but not all mediums, especially among Valley Tonga, and some early men of note are thought to continue in death as in life in their roles of leadership. Shrines built at their graves form focal points for neighbourhood rituals relating to the rains, the harvests, and the warding off of disasters. Each Tonga neighbourhood has at least one such shrine. The custodian is a member of the lineage or matrilineal group of the dead who has inherited his personal spirit (*muzimu*). On ritual occasions involving the shrine, the custodian is referred to as *basangu* even though he is very rarely a medium. He carries out the regular routine but has no new inspiration. Meantime the *basangu* spirit which may have possessed the dead either vanishes completely or reappears in a medium in some distant neighbourhood, or chooses a new local medium who need not be of the same lineage or clan as the dead. The same *basangu* may be in several unrelated mediums; a medium usually has only one *basangu* but he may occasionally be visited by a great number.

Basangu mediums are true mediums; for they are intermediaries between the spirits and the world of the living. Their messages are almost always of public import, the medium being only the vehicle through which they are transmitted.

The second form of possession, by *masabe,* is the most common and most spectacular. *Masabe* is a word used for both spirits and their associated dances. *Masabe* though sometimes originating in human dead are anonymous, unlike *basangu* who have individual names. If of human origin, *masabe* represent alien humanity and are known by tribal rather than by personal names. There are also animal *masabe,* spirit *masabe,* and *masabe* which seem to represent a summing up of new experiences symbolized through some one identifying feature as Airplane, Dance, and Guitar *masabe.* Whereas *basangu* possess their mediums because they seek to control or help the public, *masabe* seek vehicles through whom they can express their own desires and essential natures. The *masabe* medium is no medium at all in the sense of being an intermediary. The possession experience is of private import; it is addressed to the one possessed. It has its public aspects only because treatment involves the performance of a dance ceremony in which others must participate. Failure to carry out the instructions of the *basangu* can react upon the public rather than upon the medium who is only a vehicle of the command. Failure to carry out the orders of *masabe* reacts upon those possessed; for *masabe* affect only their own vehicle, unlike *basangu* who influence the world of nature, especially weather.

The third type of possession is ghost possession involving spirits known as *zilube, zelo, basikazwa,* and sometimes *basangu.* Ghosts originate in the forgotten local dead or are spirits who have fallen into the control of sorcerers, or perhaps they are a spirit remnant created at each death. Informants differ. A ghost enters its victim for the purpose of killing. Sudden violent illnesses are therefore attributed to ghost possession. Treatment is carried out in private and involves fumigation and the clanging of iron implements in an attempt to force the ghost to leave its victim. Before it flees it should call out its own name and perhaps the name of the directing sorcerer. The released victim should show immediate improvement.

Ghost possession differs from *basangu* and *masabe* possession in being wholly undesirable. Victim and helpers seek only to expel a ghost and prevent its re-entry, whereas *basangu* and *masabe* mediums expect a long-term association with their spirits and some personal benefits from being possessed. The ghost has no message to give, either public or private; it has no desires to be appeased. Ghosts have no mediums, only victims, and these must be short-term ones; either a ghost is expelled or the victim dies.

The Tonga identify the various types of spirits by the circumstances in which they manifest themselves. Indeed perhaps there is but one class of spirits and the various names refer only to the different ways in which this impinges upon men. A request for a description of any category of spirit usually brings the information that any and all may be called wind (*luwo*), 'because we do not see them. We know what they are by what they do, just as we do not see the wind but know that it is present by what it does'. If you ask what is *basangu*, you are told that *basangu* is spirit (*muuya*) which speaks through mediums on matters of public concern. If you ask what is *masabe*, you are told that *masabe* is spirit (*muuya*) which enters people to make them ill and force them to dance *masabe*. If you ask what is *zilube* or *zelo* or *basikazwa* you are told that these are spirit (*muuya*) which comes only to kill. All differ from *mizimu*, shades or ancestral spirits, who are also spirit (*muuya*), but who do not possess the living and who send illness and misfortune only to their own kin when they wish to be remembered or to call attention to some wrong.

Muuya, translated above as spirit, has a primary meaning, air, or breath; it also means essence or whatever it is that endows a phenomenon with its essential nature. A human being has *muuya*, connected with breath but capable of moving about independently as in dreams, trances and after death. Animals also have *muuya*. So do bicycles, cars, tractors, trains, motor boats, airplanes, and various disembodied creatures of the bush. In describing possession by Dance and Guitar *masabe*, informants still speak of the medium being entered by *muuya*, but they are no longer certain that this *muuya* can be likened to breath or how it emanates from 'Dance' or 'Guitar'. There is something which projects itself into humans and makes them behave in characteristic fashion, and this is called *muuya*.

In this paper I shall be concerned only with *basangu* and *masabe* possession. Ghost possession is best dealt with in a discussion of sorcery. Shades, who have their own cult (see Colson, 1960, 122–161; and Colson, 1962, 1–65) do not deal in possession. Nor does God, at least in the past. Mediums if possessed must be possessed by *basangu* or *masabe*.

BASANGU AND THEIR MEDIUMS

A *basangu* medium enters upon his vocation after an experience which he interprets as evidence that a spirit has chosen him as its vehicle. What this experience is varies from medium to medium.

No-one becomes a medium solely of his own volition. A few aspirants attach themselves to active mediums as occasional attendants hoping thereby to catch the attention of a spirit. Sometimes one does become possessed, but there is no surety that this will happen. A medium may be indicated in childhood, the diagnosis being made through a diviner who attributes some illness or abnormal behaviour to the entry of *basangu*. Parents may have such a child observe taboos associated with the *basangu*, but it is recognized that the *basangu* may desert before the child becomes a true medium. For this there must be active possession which usually takes place only after maturity. Most mediums are first indicated as young adults or in middle age, only occasionally later in life. Recurrent dreams in which *basangu* appear are a frequent symptom of future possession. Another manifestation may be a prolonged illness unresponsive to other diagnosis and treatment. I know of no standard procedure for confirming a diagnosis. In some instances, a patient is brought to an established medium who may recognize the signs of a spirit's presence and perhaps recommend ways of dealing with it.

Finally the spirit is expected to take full control of its vehicle who may be seized with convulsive tremblings, cry out in a strange manner, rush from the homestead and be found wandering in a dazed condition, or drop to the ground unconscious. The spirit then speaks through the medium to announce its arrival. Members of the homestead report the coming, usually by clapping, in the characteristic rhythm used in greeting and thanking a *basangu*. Neighbours may gather to greet the spirit with clapping and songs associated with *basangu*. These deal mainly with the desire for rain and emphasize the *basangu's* association with weather.

In this first greeting, people thank the spirit for visiting them and ask what it wishes. It is expected to announce its name and history and why it has chosen to reveal itself. It may predict epidemics, drought, or other misfortune, or demand that old rituals be observed or new ones instituted; it may complain that shrine custodians are lax in their duties; it may call attention to the breaking of taboos or changes in custom. After this the new medium has provisional acceptance as a possible resource in times of trouble, though real acceptance must wait upon events which will test the validity of the message. Meantime people clap and offer thanks to be on the safe side if in fact a spirit has visited them.

Since each *basangu* has a name and should be able to tell something of its former history when it speaks through a new medium, it is possible to know whether a new or well-known spirit has arrived. This is of little moment to the Tonga who judge by results rather than by repute. One spirit is as good as another so long as it gives effective help when this is needed. Still, a few spirits are famous and these are claimed by a number of living mediums. They also reappear over the years. The *basangu* Monze which still possesses a number of mediums was known at least by the middle of the nineteenth century when it possessed the famous rainmaker Monze.

Where a number of different mediums claim the same spirit this does not create a cult in the sense of an organized group of mediums and followers. Each medium is independent. When several mediums live in the same neighbourhood, they co-operate occasionally although almost certainly each claims a different spirit. Their concerted effort takes place only in times of great stress when they seek to persuade the spirits to break a prolonged drought or to bind up continuing rains. Usually mediums ignore one another's activities or view one another as rivals. Neighbourhood people consult any local medium. If the first consultation proves ineffective they either return to the same medium or ask another for help. If they have no local medium or have little faith in him, they turn to mediums in any nearby area. Exceptionally, in times of real disaster, they send to custodians of distant shrines or to famous mediums outside their own region. *Basangu* therefore do not have jurisdiction over limited areas of land, and their mediums are thought to be able to influence events in any part of the country. Though they are consulted on behalf of neighbourhoods and their message is usually either to a neighbourhood or to the whole countryside, their powers are unrestricted by regional boundaries.

Mediums are said to vary in ability. Most claim to be able to obtain occasional messages when the spirits themselves are willing. They then tell of coming events or explain why the spirits are angry or inform the public that they have been told to make certain demands. A few claim constant inspiration with continuous knowledge of what their possessing spirits know. They claim clairvoyance, foreknowledge of events, the ability to know everything in the minds of those who come to consult them, and all that has happened while they were *en route* and what is going on at their homes, a knowledge of all languages, and any number of other qualities. A medium may therefore be recognized as having extraordinary powers, but outward physical manifestations of power are usually anything but colourful. I have heard tales of mediums who danced about the countryside on their heads while in a state of possession, of others who balanced objects at impossible angles, of others who carried impossible loads with no sign of strain. I have known mediums who claimed to have done such things in the past when they were first learning to cope with their power. I have never seen any such demonstrations when a medium faces the public in a consultation.

At such times, people take little interest in any physical manifestations which might signify that the medium is possessed. They concentrate rather on what he has to tell them. Usually the medium does not go into a public trance. If he summons people because his spirit has communicated a message for them, he claims to tell them what he has already learned in dreams or in trance. He does not then and there demonstrate how he obtained his information. His voice is likely to deepen, break into a falsetto, or come in deep panting breaths, but other manifestations do not occur. He sits in his doorway; the public stand or sit facing him; they clap; he makes his pronouncement ; they clap. Sometimes they argue with him and demand that he obtain a new message, saying they will not accept the first one in which he is undoubtedly mistaken.

If people on their own initiative visit a medium to seek information, he must induce possession. Occasionally entry of the spirit takes place publicly. While the public claps and calls out to the spirit, the medium drops in a rigid trance from which he is revived after being carried inside his hut. Usually the medium enters his hut before the trance begins. Two or three men regarded as able negotiators enter for the consultation. They demand; they shout; they plead; they threaten violence. The medium moans and cries out. Aromatic smoke fills the hut as medicine is burned or smoked to force the spirit to speak out. Fumigation is a common means of forcing an alien presence which has seized upon a body to rouse itself to proclaim its wishes. When the medium falls, he is said to die or faint (*ku-fwa*); in this trance, the spirit takes control and is then said to have arisen (*ku-buka*). It now has free control of its medium for a short space. Then it is said to depart (*ku-unka*). The medium sits dazed, the face changes expression, the voice changes quality. Some mediums deny memory of what they have said or done during the course of the trance and rely upon those who were present to inform them of what has happened.

Despite everything, the medium may not be able to invoke the spirit. Sometimes, the spirit gives indication of its presence but will not speak or if it speaks refuses to help. When it does speak, the medium's voice is usually staccato and the words are abbreviated and cryptic, but apparently he always speaks in Tonga. At the end of the consultation, the men who have been questioning the medium emerge to report to those assembled outside. The people discuss the message, seeking to interpret its meaning, canvassing whether the medium has been genuinely inspired, self-deceived, or deliberately deceiving. A polite clapping and calling of thanks ends the meeting.

Nothing in the consultation is structured to encourage any possibility of trance among participants other than the medium. There is no expectation that anyone other than the medium will be possessed, and to the best of my knowledge this never happens.

Gifts are made to either spirit or medium; it is not always clear who is thought of as the recipient. Those who are concerned about rain take bead wristlets to tie about the wrist of the medium; blue or black beads signify a request for rain, white beads a request for a dry spell. When the request is granted, further payment is expected. A black cloth is almost invariably included in the rain fee which may also include money and grain. Such payments are delivered by one or two representatives who clap before the house of the medium. Usually the fees are the perquisites of the medium, though he may send a portion to a shrine associated with his spirit.

Mediums say their spirits are with them even when they are not active, but this does not entitle a medium to special treatment at all times. Mediums are treated with respect only when people wish to consult them, or when there is overt evidence that a spirit is active. Most mediums wear wristlets of bright or dark blue beads as an external mark of their vocation. Some Plateau mediums build tiny hut shrines beside their own huts for offerings to their *basangu*. Valley mediums usually have no special shrines. In both areas the medium is commonly treated with the same lack of ceremony as other members of the community. He leads the normal life of other Tonga though he observes special taboos laid down by his spirit. Both men and women mediums marry and have children, quarrel and become involved in law suits, fall ill and have divinations, make offerings to the shades of their ancestors, die and are mourned in normal funeral rites. People are very clear that they respect spirit rather than medium. It is only when they are concerned with the former that they are prepared to clap before the latter.

Even then they are not overly humble or reverent. The Tonga are notable for their lack of concern with office or rank or the elaborations of social organization. Chieftaincy was introduced by European officials who needed local administrative agents; even village headmanship has been formalized for the same reason. Until an alien administration created chieftaincies and then the Tonga divisions, the largest political units were small neighbourhoods. Kinship organization does not encourage the build-up of large-scale associations. Age groupings were and are embryonic and informal. In the past people tended to be parochial and to value individual independence. Each household has been expected to provide for itself and to look to kin, neighbours, and bond friends only in emergencies. Leadership has been situational and occasional: any concept of an unequivocal leader to whom one could and should turn on all occasions is lacking.

Basangu and their mediums fit into this general pattern. All *basangu* are regarded as in some way in communication and interchangeable. An appeal to one implies a request that it mobilize its fellows. Nevertheless no one spirit has power over others, just as no medium controls another. People pick and choose among spirits and mediums when they need assistance as they pick and choose among human helpers. Spirits and mediums may move and are not bound to local areas, just as most Tonga are free to shift about. Men turn to *basangu* and their mediums only in emergencies and for the most part expect to handle their own affairs. They no more welcome the idea of continuous supervision and interference by *basangu* than they welcome the idea of continuous supervision by human officials.

The Tonga regard the *basangu* as indigenous features of their life. Much of what little legend they cherish deals with the exploits of former mediums or prophets. At the same time they recognize that *basangu* have their parallels elsewhere. Valley Tonga connect them with the *mhondoro* or tribal spirits of the Shona of Rhodesia (see Gelfand, 1959, 13–66; and Gelfand, 1962, 5–50). Some local mediums are said to be possessed by spirits which also possess *mhondoro* mediums in Rhodesia. Possessing spirits of other mediums are said to stand in a kinship relationship, usually that of sister's child, to particular *mhondoro* spirits. On occasion Valley Tonga neighbourhoods send representatives to consult *mhondoro* mediums on the Rhodesian Plateau, just as other neighbourhoods send to consult *basangu* shrines or mediums on the Zambian Plateau. General pronouncements made by *mhondoro* mediums may be quoted and accepted. Thursday is a day of rest for some Tonga neighbourhoods because a *mhondoro* has so ordered. Those who visit *mhondoro* mediums are impressed with the elaboration of their rituals and seem to consider this as reflecting the power of their possessing spirits. Yet this has not led them to elaborate their own cult or to attempt to organize the various *basangu* and their mediums into some orderly array in imitation of the linkages among *mhondoro* mediums. I do not know if western Plateau Tonga are equally willing to rely upon Ila and Sala mediums. Certainly Ila in the past have consulted Plateau Tonga mediums and sent delegations to their shrines. (For further information on the organizational role of *basangu* see Colson, 1962, 84–101; Colson, 1960, 162–169; and Scudder, 1962, 119–129).

MASABE POSSESSION

Masabe and *basangu* possession are demonstrated in very different circumstances. Instead of the solitary medium facing the public and empowered to make a pronouncement, the *masabe* medium performs in association with others in a dance ceremony whose purpose is the cure of a particular patient struck down by the *masabe*. The ceremony permits the *masabe* to manifest itself in such a way that its chosen vehicle can learn its desires and by meeting these control future manifestations. During the course of the ceremony, one *masabe* such as Airplane may enter any number of mediums, and any one medium may be entered consecutively by different *masabe*, signalling each new arrival by some characteristic action. Drummers and chorus then shift to the appropriate music. The medium begins the associated dance. Others join and in turn may be possessed.

Each spirit has its appropriate dance, and dance and spirit are called by the same name. Some Tonga say that *masabe*, the general term used for any possession dance and its spirit, should properly be used only for dances introduced prior to about 1940, not for more recent dances. The distinction may be based on a difference in drum style. If so it is too subtle for my ear. Three drums provide the basic accompaniment for all possession dances save Guitar which is accompanied only by the instrument of its name. All possession drumming has the same general pattern though each dance has its characteristic variations. The drum rhythms are regarded as intimately related to the development of full possession in the medium.

Initial *masabe* possession occurs in various ways.

Possession can occur spontaneously from contact with the possessing phenomenon. The first Valley Tonga entered by Airplane is reputed to have become possessed about 1954 when a plane flew over her village. Dazed she fled to the bush, and had to be brought back to the village. She learned the demands of the spirit either in vision or in dreams: drum rhythms, songs, dance steps, the drama incorporated in phases of the dance, the articles desired by the spirit, and the plants required for treatment. At the first Airplane dance she was both patient and instructor, teaching drummers, chorus and attendants. After this the dance spread to other people, first in her own village and neighbourhood and then to others in the same vicinage, flowing along the path she had made. Some were possessed when planes flew over but apparently received no new revelations that radically altered the form of the dance. This had been created and standardized by the first woman possessed. Others began to dream of planes and this was interpreted as a sign of possible Airplane possession. Others became ill and diviners suggested the new spirit might be at work. If treatment with Airplane medicine gave relief, this was proof that the spirit was indeed present and that the full-scale curing dance must be performed. During the course of the first dance, the spirit was expected to impel the patient to dance in its characteristic style and thus to confirm its presence. Full recovery gave the final proof that Airplane spirit had been seeking to express itself through the patient who had now learned to cope with it.

At early Airplane dances the original medium served as instructor. When Airplane was danced in nearby neighbourhoods, she was summoned to direct the treatment and to teach the people her songs. Her drummers accompanied her since local men had not yet learned the new rhythms. After the first few cases of possession and cure, her presence was no longer required. Local mediums and drummers could now carry out the ceremony without further reference to her. At this point, with knowledge of Airplane widely spread, the number of possessions increased rapidly until eventually the popularity of Airplane as a possessing spirit began to wane with the appearance of new dances attributed to other spirits.

Other dances have much the same history, though most of them originated outside Tonga country. They either spread in across the borders, or they are introduced into the heart of the country by foreigners who work in the railway hamlets, the farms, and the administrative and other centres which attract labour. Each person possessed becomes a possible focus for the further spread of a dance; each dance performance is an occasion for instructing onlookers in what is expected of the one possessed by this spirit.

Tonga do not think that *masabe* possession is solely due to chance or to the inherent qualities of the one possessed, though some today classify it as a contagious disease. Those already possessed are said to have the power to direct their *masabe* into other people. The breath or essence (*muuya*) of the medium goes with and directs the essence of the *masabe* to its victim. This may either be a conscious projection or be the result of angry thought or speech. The sender is identified by the *masabe* itself which speaks out through its victim during one stage of the dance to announce who it is and who has sent it. Usually the victim has little trouble then in supplying a motive to the sender. The latter is asked to take part in the last dance of the series required for a cure and is given a gift of a chicken or a few shillings to wipe out any remaining hostility.

The sending of *masabe* is a minor form of sorcery since it implies illness for the one to whom it is sent, but as *masabe* does not kill this is a venial matter even when it arises from malice. Valley men say that women are more prone to *masabe* possession than men because women are full of malice (*munyono*) and inclined to brood over petty grievances. Men can protect themselves against the consequences of such brooding by their medicines; other women – who are usually the ones to arouse the anger in any event – are more vulnerable. Usually it is a close kinswoman who is named as the *masabe* sender, and her ascribed motives are petty ones: the victim has refused assistance, food, or clothing, or perhaps has spoken disrespectfully. Those named as *masabe* senders include mothers, sisters, father's sisters, grandmothers, husband's sisters and brother's wives, fellow clanswomen, and close friends. Sometimes the act is attributed to love rather than malice, the sender desiring to share her experience with her kinswoman or friend. Whatever the ascribed motive, those who have to pay for the curing dance and care for the patient are unlikely to see this as a friendly action, even though the victim herself, who is the centre of attention, may feel gratitude.

I have no evidence that Tonga in fact attempt to send *masabe* into others. They do use the threat, 'Perhaps you wish to dance'. I have not heard of an accused refusing to admit responsibility. A few mediums may find in their reputed ability to direct their *masabe* into others a source of satisfaction and a feeling of power, though in the nature of the case each *masabe* can be directed only once to a particular person. Most people concern themselves little about the matter and neither fear nor respect *masabe* mediums for their power, though they may admire them for their dancing ability or their ability to dramatize their roles during possession. People also acquire a reputation for knowing *masabe* medicines, but this need not involve possession. The originator of a dance learns the appropriate medicines in dreams or visions, but can then give or sell this knowledge independently of any transfer of the spirit. Most mediums do not buy a knowledge of their dance medicines; many who know the medicines are not mediums. They have sought the knowledge as they have sought knowledge of other medicines, because they thought it might be useful.

Any illness may be attributed to *masabe*. No association exists between types of illness and particular *masabe*. In diagnosing the presence of a particular spirit, the only relevant symptom is in the patient's dreams. I have known dances performed as tentative cures for a badly infected tooth, an eye infection, an ear condition which may have been mastoid, a severe concussion due to a fall, a badly infected and swollen breast, mental disturbance after childbirth, general debility diagnosed at hospital as due to cancer of the throat, and a large number of conditions where it was not clear what ailment was involved. Possession also takes place spontaneously during the course of a dance among onlookers with no immediate history of illness. Some women refuse to go near the dances for fear that they will be seized by *masabe*. Once a woman has been possessed and cured, she is drawn to the dance where repossession is common. If she attempts to resist the drums and stay away, she feels a physical excitement associated with a rapid throbbing of the pulse. Until she joins the dance she can expect this to become increasingly uncomfortable.

Those who have been possessed speak of a preliminary tingling in their limbs, the rapid beat of the pulse and the throbbing of the heart. Then comes blackness just before they lose consciousness in the trance, at which point they fall, the body completely rigid as it drops. Onlookers call out that the person is dead or unconscious, medicine is given, the spirit then emerges in control (having arisen). Finally it departs and the dancer returns to normal.

TYPES OF MASABE

It is probably impossible to construct a list which would show all *masabe* known to the Tonga; for such a list would always be in a state of flux. Dances known in one part of the country may be unknown elsewhere. Old dances regarded as extinct are occasionally revived during the course of an evening's performance; others are now only names and those once possessed say that the spirits have departed. Dances are awaited which are known to exist but whose spirits have not yet entered local people.

Such information as I have is summarized in Table I. Starred names are old *masabe*, introduced before 1940. Names indicated with a plus are dances seen either by Scudder or myself. The list may involve some duplication since alternative names may exist for the same dance. Some Valley informants class Mangoni, Mazulu, and Mazezulu together; others separate them. Valley Tonga from Chipepo Chieftaincy (Middle River) classed the Impande dance of Mwemba Chieftaincy (Upper River) with Mazulu or Mangoni, basing their identification upon the drumming. I doubt this particular identification and suspect that Impande is in some way connected with the Shona Mhondoro cult. Both words refer to the large shell ornament once worn by those of wealth and authority. In 1957 an Impande dance was held for a woman said to be possessed by *basangu*; spectators at Impande dances clap as for a *basangu*; *basangu* songs may be sung for Impande. Nevertheless, most informants in Mwemba deny that Impande has anything to do with *basangu*. For them it is simply a possession dance and the only contemporary dance of this type present in the southern part of the chieftaincy. In the past a number of old *masabe* possessions took place; today anyone who is possessed by *masabe* is possessed by Impande. In all other parts of Tonga country known to me, a variety of dances are present at any one time, though one or two dances may have most popularity.

TABLE I

VARIETIES OF MASABE POSSESSION

NAME	IDENTIFICATION	OLD MASABE	OBSERVED
Animals			
cisimbwe	mongoose?	★	
sokwe	baboon	★	+
ceta	monkey	★	
inzovu	elephant	★	+
suntwe	hyena	★	
mwaba	jackal	★	
silue	leopard	★	
bashumbwa	lion	★	+
ingulube	pig	★	+
basikompoli	crane	★	+
induba	lourie	★	
madada	duck		+
Tribal			
Makolekole	Korekore	★	
Manyai	Banyai	★	

Mangoni	Ndebele	★	
Mazulu	Ndebele		+
Mazezulu	Zezuru		
Masala	Sala	★	
Mazungu	Europeans	★	+
Statuses			
Mapolis	The Police	★	+
Matingatinga	The Carrier	★	+
Matobela Injanji	Railroad followers	★	+
Maregimenti	Soldiers		
Madyabantu	Cannibal		
Vehicles			
Citima	train	★	+
Incinga	bicycle	★	
Indeki	airplane		+
Kanamenda	motor boat		
Siacilipwe	bush clearer		
Kandimu	boat engine		
Symbolic Actions			
Impande	shell ornament		+
Ketani	chain – ox chain		
Pumpi	pump	★	+
Guitar	guitar		
Madance	European dancing		
Cilimba	accordion		
Spirits			
Bamooba	Bush spirit		+
Madilidili	?		+
Mangelo	Angel		+
Mauba	?		

Unidentified: Malula (★), Mahia (★), Manyeli (★), Naanea (★), Cimbwasa (★), Cisongo (said to have arrived in 1949 from Balovale), Bashanabule (+).

Recent dances are of varied origins. Bamooba spread to Tonga country from the west in the late 1940s coming from either Barotseland or Balovale. Cisongo was introduced about 1949 by Lovale workers on the railway line, but it reached Valley Tonga in the 1960s. Guitar, Cilimba, and Madance originated between 1956 and 1960 near the railway line and then spread to Valley Tonga. Airplane began in Chipepo, in the Valley, about 1954. Kanamenda, Siacilipwe, Kandimu and Mangelo originated in different Valley Tonga neighbourhoods during the period of upheaval associated with the Kariba resettlement. Between 1963 and 1965 Mangelo spread widely and proliferated into a number of different aspects all of which were said to be European in origin: Negro, American, Japanese. Ketani, Mangoni, Mazezulu and Mazulu arrived from Rhodesia in the later 1940s or early 1950s before the resettlement. Informants deny that they learn new dances in the cities of Rhodesia or that possession dances are performed in Rhodesian towns. Occasionally someone is possessed while living in the towns or on farms in Zambia, though again most informants regard the dances as things of the countryside which are not known in town. Perhaps this is because a possession dance is rarely held in the immediate environs of a town. One diagnosed as possessed is taken to a nearby rural area where treatment is given. Today some people claim that first infection took place in town, but that full possession by the spirit occurred only upon return home. In 1965 Valley Tonga attributed a number of *masabe* to contact with Lusaka. Maregimenti came from Lusaka about 1960, perhaps in the wake of the build-up of the army and its deployment against rioters. Madyabantu is said to have originated from visitors to Kenya who encountered cannibal people with big bellies. They brought the associated *masabe* back with them to Lusaka and then it spread to Tonga country.

Each dance should have its diagnostic dream. One entered by Airplane dreams of being carried by an airplane to the sky and then thrown into water. A Dance dreamer is dancing European dances in a European setting. Siacilipwe arrived in 1957 when bush clearing was in progress in the future Kariba Lake basin. One clearing device was a large iron ball attached to a chain dragged between two tractors. The Siacilipwe dreamer is being dragged about on a chain in a similar manner. In Kanamenda, another new dance associated with the formation of Lake Kariba and the development of its fishing industry, the dreamer is dragged through water by a motor boat. The Guitar dreamer is dancing to the constant thrum of a guitar.

The desires of the *masabe* are adumbrated in the dream but usually go beyond it. They include dress, food, special luxury goods, status symbols, and ceremonious forms of address. The song used for Mangelo reflects the desire for luxury: 'The Americans sent the drum. My blouse and skirt are very expensive. They come from England. Go!

America! Go!' Recent dances have emphasized the demand for soap and water; earlier dances had a strong element of transvestism, the *masabe* demanding men's clothing and characteristic tools.

The Airplane medium must be dressed in leg rattles and a man's hat, and usually a black cloth. During the course of the dance, in which she is now a whirling propeller and then a district officer arriving by plane to hold a village meeting, she must be brought water and scented soap in which to wash. Tobacco must be provided for drummers and dancers during intermission. During active dancing no fire or light may be seen at the dance place. The Kanamenda medium who has dreamed of being dragged through water is treated by being doused with buckets of cold water until the ground is a mud wallow in which she rolls. Scented soap must be provided for her washing. The Bush-clearing dancer is bound with an ox chain which she drags with her as she dances. Her body is anointed with diesel oil. The Dance medium receives soap and water for washing and lathery water to drink to ensure cleanliness inside and out. She is also supplied with bread and tea served if possible in cup and saucer. The Guitar medium should be dressed in fine clothing and provided with bread, biscuits, sweets, and commercial cigarettes. She also receives water and scented soap in which to wash.

Animal *masabe* may only involve impersonation of the animal; for some, appropriate food is provided. Maize cobs and other delicacies are thrown on the ground before the Baboon dancer, who mouths them and eats in baboon fashion.

Clothing is important in most dances. Different coloured cloths become general props to help in impersonation – being tied to this or that part of the body, or held in the hand, or waved aloft according to the nature of the possessing spirit. Police dancers are dressed in the red fez characteristic of the old district messengers, and wearing this they parade in drill fashion. In many dances, women dancers must be supplied with men's hats, shirts, and coats, and they dance with clubs and axes, or sometimes with spears and shield. A few dances require specially constructed costumes: seed leg rattles are common to a number of different dances. Madilidili uses a belt of maize tassels, Bamooba requires a belt or skirt of reeds usually ornamented with metal bottle-tops.

Those who have animal *masabe* imitate the call of the animal; Train dancers whistle and clank like a locomotive; Police dancers use a whistle to give drill orders; Foreign dancers speak in the language of their spirit's homeland. Other dancers may need only to use a falsetto when they call out or address an onlooker.

The pattern of events at any dance is similar, but the style of dancing differs. Some dances are for the most part a simple shuffle with little animation or variety. Cranes wave their arms in graceful flourishes. Elephants lumber on all fours swaying from side to side. In one or two dances which I have not seen, dancers are said to play with fire, running a lighted brand over their bodies and their heads. In another, a dancer is said to gash the body with a knife. The Impande dancer who begins by dancing backward in a rapid shuffle, finally falls to the ground and rolls about with great abandon, swings heels over head, goes rigid, with the body a curve supported only by heels and crown of head. The majority of dances, no matter how sedate, climax in a period of violent action, the rhythm of the drums forcing a faster and faster pace, the feet moving at incredible speeds, arms shaking, head shaking, whole body in vibrant motion. This period occurs after the spirit has taken control of the dancers.

The spirit's emergence is signalled in various ways. Usually the dancer stands or kneels, body rigid, eyes staring straight ahead. Occasionally the first indication is a characteristic cry given as the dancer falls rigid to the ground. If notice is given other performers gather round to arrange the garments so that the fall and subsequent writhings will lead to no immodest exposure of the body. They also attempt to break the fall, lowering the rigid dancer to the ground. If possession and fall are almost simultaneous, the dancer drops with a resounding noise and next day complains of bruising. At the time, there is no indication that pain is felt. From the time that the dancer falls, his or her own personality is thought to be in abeyance until the final departure of the spirit who has now risen to take control. The first portion of the trance is spent in trying to induce the spirit to express itself. Assistants administer the medicines appropriate to the dance – these may be flicked on the body, placed on coals and brought near arms and legs and head in turn, or sometimes placed in the patient's mouth. Next the dancer is expected to begin a rolling and twisting; the assistants bring her to her feet and dance a few steps still supporting her body. Then she dances on her own, with others joining in. Assistants bring clothing in which to array her and produce water or other things she may require. If a rule associated with the dance is broken, as by the bringing of fire, the dancer reels and may fall and need to be treated a second time. The dancing develops into the violent stage, rising towards a final spurt of rhythm. This ends abruptly with the departure of the spirit, indicated in a number of ways. The dancer may bow to the drummers, drop her arms and stand in a relaxed position, leave the circle and the dance ground. With this the drumming stops and the other performers sit back to smoke and recuperate along with the spectators who have been providing a chorus, clapping, singing, swaying, and calling out. Some dancers find it difficult to recover immediately. Those sit for some time staring vacantly in front of them and ignoring those around them. Others, especially those who have been possessed before, seem to pass easily from one stage to another.

Dancing can be enjoyed by both mediums and spectators. Occasionally a dance is held simply for entertainment. It is at these dances that perhaps the greatest amount of dramatic improvisation takes place and the greatest number of *masabe* appear.

The amount of preparation necessary for a performance varies with the type of spirit expected to arrive; some preparation is always necessary. Items of costuming must be available, as also food, soap, and tobacco of various kinds. A drum team must be assembled including men capable of drumming a variety of rhythms. If a new dance is to be tried, a medium may have to be invited from another neighbourhood. Medicines must be obtained from those who know how to collect and prepare the plants. Finally word must be sent out to round up enough spectators to provide a chorus and encourage the drummers and induce the excited atmosphere conducive to the appearance of the spirit.

When a *masabe* medium is first possessed, the full treatment to ensure her control over the spirit involves a series of three dances to be held in different homesteads: the patient's own homestead, the homestead of some other member of his or her lineage, and the homestead of a member of the father's lineage. Each dance must be held specifically for the patient. She may be possessed any number of times at dances held for other people, but this will not ensure her own cure. The possessing spirit is demanding specific recognition by the medium's kin and neighbours, and this can only be satisfied in dances in which the new medium is the focus of attention. Other mediums even then may take the centre of the stage, drawing attention by their spectacular dancing and their dramatic falls, but everyone knows for whom the dance is held and it is to this person that recognition is given. The morning after each dance the patient is feasted, usually with a chicken provided by the owner of the homestead. During the second dance, the spirit announces the name of the kinsman or friend who directed it to the new medium. That person should attend the third and final dance. It is at this time that the new medium appears in full costume, to be given all the spirit desires. During the course of the dance, the medium also receives a bead wristlet of the colour associated with the spirit: white for Airplane, dark blue for Bush Clearer, black for Angel, red for Baboon, and so on for each spirit. The medium's husband or wife should tie the wristlet in place, and this remains as a permanent sign of the spirit's claim upon the medium.

If future illness is attributed to a quickening of the same spirit, a single dance should be enough to quiet it, though sometimes two are held.

The costs of the performance fall upon the kin of the one possessed, more particularly upon the hosts. They pay instructing medium and drummers if these come from outside the village – those who are helping their village mates do not expect payment. The one who sent the spirit receives a small gift. There is the provision of food, soaps, tobacco. A costume may need to be purchased or constructed. Arranging and financing a performance is therefore a matter that implies active concern upon the part of the co-operating kinsmen. In return for their expenditure, they have the knowledge that they have done their best to assist the recovery of their kinsman. They also have the dubious pleasure of playing host to those who come to watch the performance.

The *masabe* medium also has her gains: health, for the possessing spirit is now under control and can be expected to remain quiescent except when the drums beat out its rhythms at another dance; assurance of the concern of friends and neighbours who have worked to restore her to health; the privilege of behaving in a fashion outside the normal behaviour open to her. Few receive any material advantage. The first to introduce a new dance may be paid for serving as an instructor to others. The one named as responsible for the entry of a spirit into a new victim receives a gift. A few mediums become notorious for sending *masabe* to others in their vicinity and they receive a fair number of small gifts as each new victim calls out the name of the popular sender. Most mediums are accused but once or perhaps never. A good dancer is urged to attend other dances where she has a stellar role. This is the most easily available way for a woman to obtain favourable recognition for her artistic talents, at least among Valley Tonga. Plateau Tonga women attend beer drinks along with the men and take part in the dancing and singing that make these gay social occasions. Valley women do not have much opportunity to take part in beer drinks, nor do they frequent the young people's dances after their first child or two. Possession dancing, with its imperative demands for the attendance of the woman when the drums beat, provides an excuse recognized by all as justifying her attendance at the dance. The imperatives, however, operate only when the dancing relates to spirits by which she herself has been possessed, though it is a kindly act to attend the other dances and help in the chorus. Soon the appearance of new spirits and their dances outmode the old. A woman can maintain her role as a dancer only by being repossessed by the new arrivals. When this happens she is again the centre of attention during the original cure, and she retains her prominence in the new dances as she did in the old. Many women are possessed at least once. A few seem to regard possession as a career, and as each new dance appears they are to be found among those who first are seized upon by the new spirit.

FREQUENCY OF POSSESSION

Basangu possession is rare; *masabe* possession, common.

Men and women are subject to both types of possession. Tonga regard them as equally liable to *basangu* possession, and particular *basangu* have had both men and women mediums. Plateau Tonga seemed to think men and women equally likely to be possessed by *masabe*; Valley Tonga in 1956–57 and 1962–63 said that men were unlikely candidates while women were only too prone to possession. In 1965 possession among men showed a significant increase in at least one neighbourhood.

I have no quantitative data on possession for the Plateau people. I know only that both men and women claimed to have been possessed by *masabe* and that both appeared as performers in the few *masabe* dances I saw. At least one of these was held over a man patient. I also know both men and women *basangu* mediums. I have much better information for the Valley Tonga. In 1962 I questioned Valley Tonga in the course of a village census on whether or not they had ever been possessed by *masabe*. The data come from four villages in Old Chipepo (Middle River), one village formerly in the hills but now in the Lusitu, and a portion of one large village in Mwemba (Upper River).[2] Informants sometimes lied about possession, as is evidenced by the fact that the frequencies for the two villages I knew best are far higher than for the sample as a whole. I have therefore not attempted any rigorous examination of the data for patterns that might show associations with age, kin group, education, or other characteristics.

TABLE II

FREQUENCY OF MASABE POSSESSION

AREA	INFORMANTS[3]	NO INFORMATION	POSSESSED	NOT POSSESSED
Old Chipepo				
Females	420	98	96	266
Males	244	90	3	151
Lusitu				
Females	135	8	52	75
Males	90	20	3	67
Mwemba				
Females	163	10	32	121
Males	96	4	8	84
Total				
Females	718	116	180	422
Males	430	114	14	302

Neither an increase nor a decrease in possession seems to have taken place between 1956 and 1962, a time of considerable turmoil for the Valley Tonga. The next two years, which were marked by the political upheaval which led to Zambia's independence, did show an increase in possession in Old Chipepo though not in the other areas of the census. In 1965, I collected information on the same populations questioned in 1962–63 with regard to the number of cases of possession between 1963 and 1965, approximately two and a quarter years. Neither in Lusitu nor Mwemba had there been any significant increase in number of possessions. In Old Chipepo, new instances of possession were common, with Mangelo the most popular spirit, the number of Mangelo possessions having risen from two to twenty-one.

TABLE III
NEW INSTANCES OF POSSESSION IN OLD CHIPEPO POPULATION 1963–65

TYPE OF POSSESSION	NUMBER OF MALES	NUMBER OF FEMALES
Mangelo	5	14
Mauba	–	1
Cisongo	2	1
Bamooba	–	1
Kanamenda	–	1
Maregimenti	–	1
Madyabantu	–	1
Guitar	–	1
Cilimba	–	1
Total	7	22

Instances of possession occur through the whole age range. In 1962–63 the youngest person in any area said to be possessed by *masabe* was approximately two years old. In 1965 I watched Mangelo danced for a baby of one month and was told that it had been tried for a new-born child still in birth seclusion. I have never seen a child under about ten demonstrate possession during a dance. Women beyond sixty usually say their *masabe* have departed though they sometimes take part in dancing when younger people are being treated. Men may become possessed at any age – as children, as adolescents, in early manhood, in middle-age, as elders.

Other information on susceptibility to possession is impressionistic. Adolescent girls are probably highly susceptible. Some informants claimed to have been possessed only as young girls. If one girl in a village claimed a dance, it usually turned out that her close friends also had this dance, and they cited one another as the sender. An epidemic of possession, allegedly Madance, broke out in one of the girls' boarding schools in 1962, with girl after girl falling, writhing, and then demanding soapy water to drink. It is probable that a dancer's daughters are likely to be dancers, but because of the inadequacy of the data this cannot be checked. Women under stress seem likely to be possessed. We noted a number of instances of barren wives, or wives whose children had died, who were treated for possession shortly after the successful delivery of a co-wife. A dance might also follow a period of quarrelling between spouses. Several outstanding dancers possessed by many different spirits are regarded by kin and neighbours as easily excited over trifles, forever running to diviners when others are prepared to wait on further events. Among the few men dancers are some who would be considered neurotics. The great majority of those possessed seem no different from the even greater number who deny possession. Epilepsy though common in some parts of the country is not regarded as an indication of possession, by either *masabe* or *basangu*.

Table II shows that of some 1148 informants questioned in 1962 at least 194 have been possessed by *masabe* at some time during their lives. In this same population there are six *basangu* mediums and one child, a boy of six, said to have been chosen by a *basangu* as its future vehicle. Of the six mediums, five are women. This, however, may not represent a common pattern for the Valley. In other neighbourhoods mediums are men. Informants say that recent mediums are likely to be women because men now refuse to acknowledge their vocation. Education and other experiences lead them to disregard the spirits. Women whose lives are still closely bound to local interests are the ones most concerned with the spirits and the ones most likely to be entered by them.

Although some *basangu* mediums are also *masabe* dancers, the two forms of possession may well appeal to different types of people. I suspect that *basangu* mediums are susceptible to weather changes since they speak of knowing about the possibility of rain or drought, winds or calm, from reactions within their bodies. Successful mediums must also be of some intelligence, skilful students of men and events. No such demands are made on the *masabe* medium. She on the other hand frequently performs physical feats requiring great strength and endurance. The violent gymnastics of some of the dances involve the expenditure of enormous amounts of energy and an indifference to pain and discomfort beyond the ordinary. Each type of medium demonstrates possession in a different fashion, though some stages of the actual trance may appear to be the same. The *basangu* medium is seen as truly one with the spirit when he is able to prophesy and advise correctly. The *masabe* medium's claim to possession is validated in the violence of the dance. The *basangu* medium works isolated from his fellow mediums. He feels no urge to share his possession experience with other men nor does he receive stimulation from the presence and support of other mediums. The *masabe* medium performs best in the company of fellows and finds an excuse for possession only through the recruitment of new victims who form the occasion on which his or her own skill is displayed. Finally the public is restrictive to *basangu* possession, casual about *masabe* possession, reflecting the difference in their consequences for the community. No matter how many mediums fall possessed during a *masabe* performance nothing will happen or can happen to change the ways of the community. The only innovation ever attributed to a *masabe* medium is the introduction of yet another dance. When a *basangu* medium becomes possessed, anything may result. It is vital to know just what message has been sent and what will be its consequences. One medium is all that is required and all that is desired. Unrestricted access to the spirit world would only confuse the issue, introducing contradictory messages. In the consultation with *basangu*, only the one medium is encouraged to show contact with the spirits. If other mediums are present at the consultation they are there as consultants along with the rest of the community.

THE HISTORY OF POSSESSION

The Tonga say they have always had *basangu* and *basangu* mediums. *Masabe* are something new, appearing within living memory. Most believe the *masabe* came originally from Shona-speaking areas of Rhodesia. The very name is probably derived from the Shona *mashave* spirits and mediums (see Gelfand, 1959, 121–153; and Gelfand, 1962, 84–105, 165, 170). Some Tonga, however, derive the name from the *masabasaba*, leg rattles of large seeds used in some of the dances and said to be named from their characteristic sound, *saba-saba-saba*. Jesuit missionaries at Chikuni Mission on the Plateau reported the *masabe* cult as newly introduced in 1918 (Jaspan, 1953, 61, 68). It would therefore have arrived in the period after the establishment of police and administrative posts, the first missions, the building of the railway, and the arrival of the first European farming settlers. Perhaps the *masabe* represent a reaction to the many new contacts with foreigners and with new material phenomena which were already disrupting the old life of the villages.

If the Tonga did adopt a Shona cult at this time, they made radical alterations within it. Gelfand describes the Shona *mashave* as spirits of aliens who die far from home. Other than alien human spirits, the Shona have only baboon *mashave*. They apparently do not contend with the spirits of other animals or with spirits associated with railways, boats, bicycles, or any of the other new experiences incorporated into the Tonga *masabe* dances from the beginning.

In the late 1940s some older Plateau Tonga said that animal dances similar to *masabe* had preceded the arrival of *masabe*, and that such dances had been used primarily by hunters. The hunter danced the day before the hunt and again on his return, and his dancing involved animal imitations. They thought some of the older dances usually classified as old *masabe* might be survivals from the earlier era. This was all they could remember but it suggests that the Tonga may have had dances linked with the hunting cults as did Lamba and other Zambians to the north and west. Doke indeed records that *mashyabe* was the old Lamba name for dances which after 1915 came to be called Wamowa (See Doke, 1931, 251–259). In Tonga this would be Bamooba, but Bamooba reached the Tonga only in the 1940s when it came from the west.

Dances associated with a belief in possession by an alien spirit or entity may therefore have been widely spread within this general region, and the Shona *mashave* only one variation on a common pattern. Yet the immediate neighbours of the Tonga to the west do not seem to have had many dances of the *masabe* type in early years of the century. Smith and Dale (1920, vol. ii, 137–140) who worked among the Ila between 1904 and 1914 do not mention *masabe* by name though they describe one dance, apparently regarded as unusual, in which the drumming pattern, the violent dancing, the use of the axe, and the fact that the dance was being held to cure a woman possessed by the spirit of a Sala alien all show that it belongs to the *masabe* type. Melland who worked with the Kaonde prior to 1921 makes no certain reference to the presence of possession dances (Melland, 1923, 286–287). In the 1920s and 1930s possession dancing became common in many parts of Zambia though all writers imply that locally it was of recent introduction. The possessing spirits are much the same as those recognized among the Tonga, and no doubt many have spread from one group to another. (See Brelsford, 1948, 22–24; Stefaniszyn, 1964, 156–162; White, 1961, 49–52). White, who gives an extensive description of the alien Mahamba cults of the Luvale of western Zambia, makes the only serious attempt to deal with the history of such cults. He derives the Luvale dances from the Congo and Angola, where similar dances had an earlier history. The Luvale cults waxed and waned within a period of perhaps four decades, being already on the decline in the 1950s with the increasing sophistication and experience of the Luvale. White attributes the popularity of spirit dances, such as Airplane and Railroad, to the early stages of contact with a new world of strange, threatening, and attractive phenomena.

The history of possession dancing in this part of Africa is therefore still obscure. The pattern of thinking basic to the dances has been widespread through Zambia and Rhodesia in recent decades. Given the common basis of ideas, it is not strange that similar dances apparently originate in different parts of the country independently of one another. Thus the appearances of Airplane possession among Luvale and Valley Tonga seem unconnected with one another and to have been spontaneous improvisations by people who were prepared to believe that the plane could project something of itself into human beings and who had the common pattern of possession dancing within which to develop the new dance.

A number of features in the history of Tonga *masabe* cults require some comment: the types of spirits represented, the difference in sex ratio between Plateau and Valley, and the general popularity of possession dancing in the Valley to the present time.

In the early years of *masabe*, possessing spirits were drawn primarily from the animal world, almost always representing species which are dangerous or frightening. It is notable for instance that no antelopes figure in the dances, nor any animal commonly hunted as game. If animal *masabe* represent anything, they represent the dangers of the bush, the threat from beyond the human community. Later the animal cults lost their popularity as larger game and more dangerous animals disappeared from much of the countryside and fields replaced most of the waste-land. The village where I have seen most animal impersonation dances performed is one which was isolated in the hills until 1958 when encounters with dangerous animals were still commonplace, and which then moved to the Lusitu where people had to pioneer thickets from which they drove elephant, lion, and leopard. In large villages of the Zambezi plain or in villages of the thickly settled Plateau, people have been little involved in hunting for a long time and are less conscious of the presence of large animals. In these villages, the popular dances over many years have played on other themes, the presence of aliens and the new marvels seen in town or introduced along the railway.

It has already been noted that possession dancing was rare by the 1940s on the Plateau while it has continued to be common in the Valley, but that Plateau men may be as likely to be possessed as are women, whereas few Valley men were possessed prior to the very recent spread of Mangelo and one or two other new dances. This is probably due to the difference in the recent histories of the two people.

In the late nineteenth century Tonga men began to migrate to work. On the Plateau, the building of the railway and the development of a market for farm produce put an end to large-scale labour migration by the 1930s. Men stayed home, farmed, and hoped to sell enough produce to see them through the year on what became a slowly rising standard of living. The Plateau also attracted outside settlers since it was both accessible and healthy. Missionaries built a number of stations and opened schools in the villages which began the battle to attract old and young to the ideas associated with the missions. It was also in this region that European farmers began to settle from about 1913. They provided a source of wages, a school in farming methods, and a model for a European manner of life not represented by the missionary. Indian traders opened shops, and small towns grew up along the railway line which attracted people from many parts of Central Africa. Superficially the Plateau people became much more sophisticated than their Valley Tonga kinsmen whom they tended to despise as backwoodsmen. They had better clothes, they farmed with plough and oxen, they had more schooling and literacy, they had access to trading stores and a range of goods. They became, they said, something like Europeans, and they sought to introduce European standards of housing and clothing. On the other hand, since most of them lived at home throughout the year, their knowledge of life beyond the village was not extensive. What there was did not belong to the men alone. Men and women shared much the same experience, and Plateau women lagged little behind their men in their acquaintance with the manners and customs of other people or in their experience of the mechanical and other wonders associated with the towns. Perhaps this explains why women are no more likely than men to seek an outlet through *masabe*.

It has been quite different for Valley Tonga whose country is isolated from the Plateaux of Zambia and Rhodesia by the rugged hills of the Zambezi escarpments. Until the early 1950s no roads reached their villages. It was impossible to export very much in the way of a cash crop when it had to be carried some fifty miles or more through rugged hills before the nearest trading store was reached. Instead the Valley exported its men who have continued until the present to go out to work on a large scale. They go as youths, return to marry, and then expect to spend the years until middle age alternating between village and town. Most men have spent extended periods in towns or mining compounds. They have made long journeys and know something of Africans of other regions and a good deal about Europeans. Still, it is difficult to assess the extent to which this experience alters them. Their homeland had few schools until the 1950s. Very few have had more than a most elementary schooling, if they have that. In the towns they find only unskilled work and they have no fellows who can act as educated intermediaries between them and other Africans who look down upon them for their lack of education and for the types of work they do. Where they are present in large enough numbers, they form their own communities and spend their time at work and play with other men from the Valley. They know the towns but few regard themselves as town people. When they are ready they come home. Until the early 1950s this meant a walk of some days carrying their possessions once they left the railway. They brought little with them save for a few luxuries now regarded as essentials. In the large Zambezi villages they found vigorous, compact populations ready to absorb them back into the even flow of village life. The villages were large enough to provide a range of amusement. Young people's dances, dance competitions between villages, the prideful performance of the neighbourhood drum team on ceremonial occasions with the mimic war-dances which sometimes merged into armed clashes all gave local life a vitality not to be found in the small villages of the hills or Plateau. The returned migrant talked a good deal about the world outside the Valley and the other men understood and shared his experiences. Nevertheless that world did not become a positive reference point against which all life at home was judged and found wanting.

Valley women did not share this knowledge of the towns and the things of the town. Few before 1962 accompanied their men when they went out to work. Occasionally they visited the railway line when a hunger year drove them to seek food among kin settled on the Plateau. Otherwise towns, foreigners, mechanical equipment, and many of the common experiences of their men were outside their ken. They accepted the towns as a good thing because towns gave men work and from work came cloth, blankets and other things they wanted. But they also regarded the towns and all associated with the towns as rivals for their men who might be induced to stay away for good and thus become lost. In census work, it was strikingly evident that most women had lost a man to the towns – a fiancé, a husband, a son, a brother, a father. Some men say that it used to be difficult to contemplate returning home since Valley standards were so different from those of the town. Valley women continued until 1957 to remove the upper front teeth which made them grotesque to those accustomed to other ways. Perhaps more serious, from what young men say, were standards of cleanliness. Housekeeping is not one of the Valley woman's interests. Though for those who lived near the Zambezi, the daily bath was a commonplace, the bath was likely to be followed with anointment with oil and red ochre. This gave a beautiful sheen but it also rubbed against anything the woman touched. Men objected to the result and called it dirt. They also objected to the smell of the oil used by the women. Trading stores were miles away. Soap was a luxury which men brought back in small quantities and then usually monopolized. Since I have known the Valley people, soap has been one of the most desired articles and it is one of the first items to go on a shopping list when a trading store is available and there is money for a purchase.

Until the 1950s Valley men and women had quite different experiences of the world beyond the Valley. For men it was a well-known world with both its attractions and its dangers. For women it was an unknown region full of desirable things, desirable both in their own right and because they made a woman into the kind of person who could draw men to her. It also held inexplicable equipment, and a multitude of foreigners with strange customs who might well be dangerous.

Roads were built into the Valley in the early 1950s and trading stores and other amenities followed in their wake. These had an immediate impact on Valley life. The old dress began to vanish. By 1962 it was seldom seen anywhere. Small shops proliferated. Money was sufficiently common so that even children could obtain soap and soap powder. Where bicycles were rarely seen in 1949, now a few men had lorries and land-rovers. By 1962 everyone had seen cars, and most had had at least one motor-ride. Planes they had seen for a very long time in the air but now regular plane routes crossed over the Valley. One or two men, but no women, claimed to have had a flight in a plane. Schools were common, and a few girls were already going on to boarding school. A local fishing industry was developing, which brought foreigners into Valley villages, as traders, shop-keepers, and craftsmen, as well as labourers on the roads and in the building of schools and dispensaries.

The old way of life was changing rapidly, but still many women had never reached the railway or seen a town. They were becoming familiar with mechanical devices; with pump engines drawing the village water supply, motor engines labouring along bush paths and installed in the fishing boats the men were buying. Few women as yet felt at home with such things. Very few could ride a bicycle, many could not strike a match. So far the new luxuries had done little to lighten their working lives.

My general impression is that Valley women have less outlet than do the women of the Plateau, despite the gaiety of life in large Valley villages. Possession dances are therefore a welcome escape from the daily round. Active possession requires that her kin provide a woman with the luxuries usually pre-empted by the men who get the great proportion of clothing, soap, tea, biscuits, sweets, cigarettes and other good things.

Among the Plateau people, possession dancing and the resort to possession as an explanation for illness have faded away in many neighbourhoods. The drums in the distance are almost invariably beating *indikiti*, the drumming associated with social dancing at beer drinks. Neither men nor women are likely to see themselves as affected by contact with strange phenomena. *Basangu* mediums persist, though most of the younger people would deny that the present mediums have the powers of those in the past. In the Valley, men who know the life of the towns rarely admit to dance possession, which after all usually reflects only the things which they themselves purport to know, foreign people, machinery, the lure of the towns. It is Valley women who maintain *masabe* possession. Its patterns today most commonly reflect their interests and their desires. The older dances involved the wearing of men's clothing, the use of their implements, the imitation of their occupations. Newer dances have no such stress. Instead they emphasize either the uncertainties of the period when the Valley people were torn from their old neighbourhoods and thrust to pioneer the hills and thickets above the newly created lake, and the appearance of a new way of life centred on the fishing industry and the fishing camps which are growing up about the lake shore, or they stress the desire for the luxuries and gaieties of the town: cleanliness, luxury foods, and the dance associated with fine clothes and the sophisticated women of the towns. Most recently the Mangelo seems to reflect a renewed widening of experience with a body of dangerous foreigners known largely through wireless report and rumour, though perhaps occasionally seen in the new capital city Lusaka.

Until recently both *basangu* possession and the *masabe* cults existed without acknowledgement of the presence of Christianity, and Christianity has not as yet given rise to any separatist movement in this region which admits of possession. Recently, a few mediums have appeared who incorporate aspects of Christianity into their cults. Since the Tonga classify mediums as being either *basangu* or *masabe,* a valiant attempt is being made to force the development of the new cults into one or the other pattern.

In the Lusitu area recently settled by Tonga removed from the Kariba Lake basin, the man who announced himself in 1959 or 1960 as a *Mangelo,* that is 'angel', was coping in some measure with Christianity. He claims to have received his mission from a Mangelo living in Rhodesia who confirmed him in his knowledge of the Mangelo. He himself practises as a healer who drives out ghosts sent by sorcerers. Soon after he began to practise, others announced that they too were possessed by Mangelo, and typically they have developed a Mangelo dance along the lines of other *masabe*. Later it emphasized its origin from 'European spirits', but in 1963 people were still content to be entered by 'angels'. Mangelo has its drum rhythm, its bead wristlets, its songs, its medicines, as does any possession dance, and it is spreading in the same fashion that other *masabe* spread. The various activities of the original Mangelo impinge, however, upon another field – that of communal rituals. As such he becomes associated with *basangu* mediums. Many *basangu* mediums ceased to practise after the people were resettled in a strange land and some claimed to have been deserted by their spirits who were angry at the move. Some Lusitu villagers hoped for a revival of *basangu* guidance through the Mangelo and attributed to him the power to speak about the rain and other matters reserved to *basangu* mediums. Despite this the Mangelo movement is being assimilated to the *masabe* pattern, with men and women made ill by the spirit or essence of angels instead of by the spirit or essence of the airplane or the dance.

In a portion of Mwemba chieftaincy, where again the old *basangu* mediums abandoned their work after resettlement, a woman was introduced as the new *basangu* of the area. Her possession had taken place when she lived at the District headquarters where her husband had been head messenger. Her possessing spirit was God or Jesus or the angels, it was not quite clear which, and she used the sign of the cross and Christian tags freely as she prophesied and related her experiences. After she had first become conscious of her vocation she had visited the most powerful Tonga *basangu* medium of recent years. This medium ultimately agreed that she had been entered by a very powerful spirit. When the woman returned to live in Mwemba, the local people accepted her as a *basangu* medium and consulted her at a time of little rain, using the same procedure as in consulting other *basangu*. Whatever the spirit she announces as working through her, the Tonga accept it as but another *basangu* and she herself as yet another medium through whom the spirit speaks. Since the people of this general area have only Impande as a possession dance and do not lend themselves to the idea of expanding their repertoire, they have only one way to handle her. She is a *basangu* medium, and therefore she is unique. No-one else in the vicinage has shown any indication of becoming possessed by God, Jesus, or the angels.

NOTES

[1]General descriptions of Tonga life are to be found in Colson 1958 and 1962 (Plateau Tonga) and in Colson 1960 and Scudder 1962 (Valley Tonga).

Until late 1964 Zambia was known as Northern Rhodesia; the present Rhodesia was then Southern Rhodesia.

[2]See Colson 1960, 4, 13–17 for definition of these terms.

[3]Information was sought on those born before 1957. The majority of those for whom there is no information were children about whom the question was not asked. A few were absent from the area.

REFERENCES

BRELSFORD, W. V. 1948 *African dances of Northern Rhodesia.* Livingstone, Rhodes-Livingstone Museum.

COLSON, E. 1958 *Marriage and the family among the Plateau Tonga of Northern Rhodesia.* Manchester University Press.

1960 *Social organization of the Gwembe Tonga.* Manchester University Press.

1962 *The Plateau Tonga.* Manchester University Press.

DOKE, C. M. 1931 *The Lambas of Northern Rhodesia.* London, Harrap.

GELFAND, M. 1959 *Shona ritual.* Cape Town, Juta.

1962 *Shona religion.* Cape Town, Juta.

JASPAN, M. 1953 *The Ila-Tonga peoples of Northern Rhodesia.* London, International African Institute.

MELLAND, F. 1923 *In witch-bound Africa.* London, Seeley, Service.

SCUDDER, T. 1962 *Ecology of the Gwembe Tonga.* Manchester University Press.

SMITH, E.; DALE, A. M. 1921 *The Ila-speaking peoples of Northern Rhodesia.* London, Macmillan.

STEFANISZYN, B. 1964 *Social and ritual life of the Ambo of Norhtern Rhodesia.* London, Oxford University Press.

WHITE, C. 1961 *Elements in Luvale beliefs and rituals.* (Rhodes-Livingstone Papers No. 32). Lusaka, Rhodes-Livingstone Institute.

SPIRIT MEDIUMS AS MEDIATORS IN KOREKORE SOCIETY

© *G. Kingsley Garbett*

In an earlier account (1963) I drew attention to the political role of spirit mediums in succession disputes among the Valley Korekore, a northern Shona people. Here I examine the mediatory role of mediums in disputes in land-shrine neighbourhoods.

The Korekore of the Zambezi Valley inhabit a region which is economically undeveloped and where both climate and soils are poor. The population is sparse and widely scattered.

Politically the Valley Korekore are organized into small, autonomous chiefdoms which are only loosely structured. Within a chiefdom people live in tiny hamlets scattered along the major water courses. Descent groups are shallow and dispersed save that royal descent groups have a degree of internal cohesion and provide the kinship framework of a chiefdom to which commoners are attached by multifarious ties. In the past chiefdoms were unstable and fragmented as dissident factions broke away to found new chiefdoms. The creation of the Tribal Trust Lands and the enforcement of the Land Apportionment Act by the European administration nowadays prevent the formation of new chiefdoms. Hamlets, however, are still unstable and have only an ephemeral existence as some of their members break away from time to time to found new ones. For modern administrative purposes a number of chiefdoms have been grouped together and placed under salaried senior chiefs. These in turn are grouped under District Commissioners.

In the remote past Korekore royals appear to have formed the political core of the now defunct kingdom of Monomotapa. The original Korekore appear to have been a band of Karanga invaders who entered the Zambezi Valley in the fifteenth century overrunning the Tonga and Tavara peoples whom they found there. Mutota, who according to oral traditions led the Karanga invasion, is now considered to be the 'father' of the 'real' Korekore – his patrilineal descendants. Abraham (1959, 71) has identified Mutota as Monomotapa. Many present-day Korekore chiefs claim patrilineal descent from Mutota, or from one of his 'brothers', though they do not now all belong to one clan with praise names in common. Mutota, and many of his deceased descendants, are represented by spirit mediums.

Among Valley Korekore spirit possession is a common phenomenon. Many adult men and women, and even some children belong to one or more of the numerous cult-groups which gather periodically to 'dance out' their possessing spirits. Spirit mediumship, on the other hand, in which a person acts as an intermediary between man and spirit (see Firth, 1959, 141) is comparatively rare. Except for those, mostly women, who act as mediums for malevolent ancestral spirits (*ngozi*) believed to have been grossly offended by some misdemeanour of their living descendants, spirit mediumship is confined to a few men and a very few women. These mediums are believed to speak when possessed with the voices of long-dead spirits whose influence is now manifested among the living by their supposed control over the rainfall and fertility of particular pieces of land. Unlike a member of one of the possession cults, who, if he leaves a neighbourhood, can join another cult-group elsewhere, a spirit medium ought only to operate in a particular area, the land of his possessing spirit. Here, through him, the spirit may be consulted about such matters as incest, sorcery and homicide which are believed to affect the fertility of the earth. Some spirits associated with particular areas of land are also ancestors with living descendants. Such an ancestor may be consulted through his medium by his patrilineal descendants about such matters as inheritance, succession, and spirit affliction.

To Korekore, mediums are essentially religious figures clearly distinguishable in function from secular chiefs. Mediums are seen as concerned with the moral order and the relation of men to the earth. Natural disasters such as famine or drought are believed to be due to the anger of the spirit 'owners of the earth', who must be contacted and appeased through their mediums. Nevertheless, though to Korekore themselves this role of mediums as intermediaries between man and spirits is seen as paramount, mediums do perform important political functions. Among other things, they act as mediators not only in certain types of dispute at the level of hamlet and neighbourhood, but also in chiefly succession disputes and in disputes among neighbouring chiefs.

Mediums are peculiarly suited for this role of mediators for when 'possessed' they speak as long-dead spirits. Thus, in a sense, they are translated to a level 'outside' the contemporary social system and so can be called upon to act as unbiased intermediaries.

Frankenberg (1957, 18) in his analysis of a Welsh village drew attention to the role of persons who, because of their position in a particular social situation – a churchman among chapelmen, a man among women – can be regarded as 'strangers' and used as intermediaries by disputing parties. As he points out, in Africa similar principles operate but here 'the stranger . . . whether human or spirit, acts through mystical sanctions to prevent the divisions inherent in a formal structure from breaking into open conflict' (Frankenberg, 1957, 156). Korekore mediums when 'possessed' and speaking as long-dead spirits removed from the contemporary affairs of men, fall into this category of strangers. Their pronouncements are supported by mystical sanctions which are not only believed to operate against the parties to a broken agreement in which they acted as mediators, but against the whole community as well.

Korekore mediums do not mediate just any spirit haphazard. They are organized into a system which, in part, serves to support their role as mediators. For purposes of analysis we may take the present tribal system as composed of two major components: one, the political organization of the chiefdoms; the other, the politico-religious system associated with the spirit mediums. Each component has its own sphere of activity, one largely secular, the other largely religious, though they intersect at certain points. The component in which the spirit mediums are involved has two aspects: a territorial and a lineal. In both aspects mediums have, in addition to other functions, a role as mediators in disputes. Here we shall be concerned almost entirely with the territorial aspect of the system. I have discussed elsewhere (1963) the lineal aspect and the role of mediums in it.

THE TERRITORIAL ASPECT

Among Valley Korekore all land, whether now occupied or not, is divided into areas which I term spirit-provinces. Each is named after, and associated with, the spirit of a man who is thought to have been one of the original Karanga invaders, a descendant of an invader, or, less commonly, an autochthon. Some spirit-provinces are very large, of several hundred square miles in extent, others are only a few acres. Generally the men after whom the spirit-provinces are named are supposed to have been the first occupiers or users of the land. Their spirits are believed to control the rainfall and the fertility of the land in the spirit-province with which each is associated. These spirits I term spirit-guardians (*mhondoro*). *Mhondoro* is a special term for lion; the usual word is *shumba*. But in rituals spirit-guardians are often addressed as 'keepers' or 'guardians' (*vachengeti*).

The spirit-provinces (*nyika ye mhondoro*) are articulated into a single system, which I term a spirit-realm, by a long genealogy which shows the relations among spirit-guardians. In the case of Mutota's spirit-realm the genealogy is some 15 generations in depth. Autochthons are usually fitted into this, where exact genealogical connections cannot be recalled, by placing them in a broad cognatic category as classificatory sister's sons (*vazukuru*). Spirit-realms may be very large. Mutota's spirit-realm, for example, is over 3,000 square miles in extent and includes much of the Zambezi Valley east of the Angwa River, parts of the plateau to the south of the Zambezi escarpment, and extends into Portuguese East Africa.

Formerly, according to Korekore, each spirit-province had a medium associated with it through whom the spirit-guardian would speak on occasions. Today not all spirit-provinces have mediums. Within a spirit-realm the mediums are arranged into a hierarchy which corresponds to a genealogical hierarchy, since they become identified with, and named after, the spirit-guardians whom they represent. At the apex stands a person representing 'the founder' whom I term the senior spirit medium. Mutota's medium, for example, is at the head of a hierarchy of mediums in Mutota's spirit-realm. All other mediums within the spirit-realm are under his authority and are initially tested and installed by him.

Consider Diagram I which represents a hypothetical spirit-realm divided into spirit-provinces of various sizes. The diagram should be read in conjunction with Genealogy I. The founding ancestor, A, has two sons, B and C who in turn have further descendants, D, E, F, etc. Each of A's descendants to the fourth descending generation has a spirit-province named after him, represented on Diagram I, of which

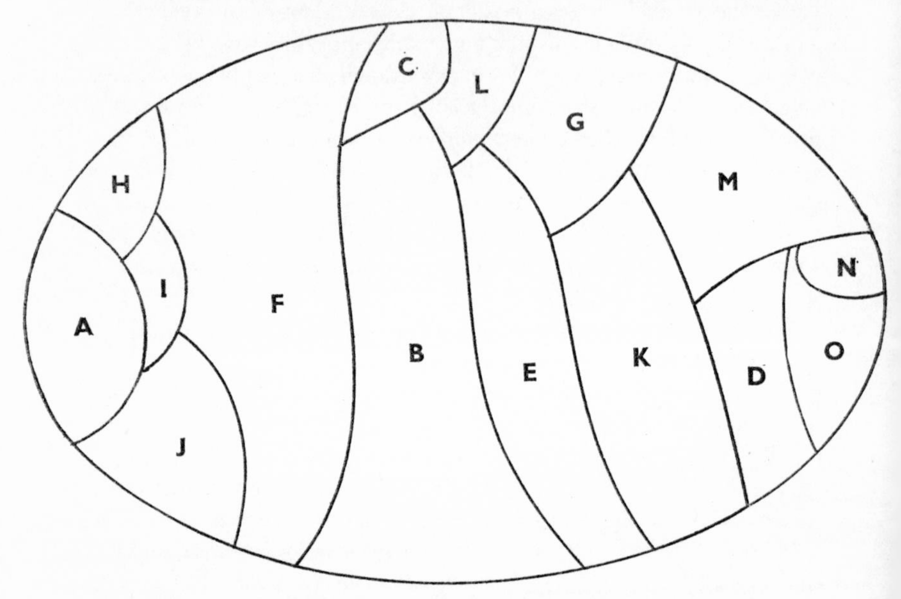

Diagram I. Hypothetical spirit-realm divided into spirit-provinces

he is considered to be the guardian. Assuming that each spirit-guardian is represented by a medium, then the mediums will be ranked according to the positions that the spirit-guardians whom they represent occupy on Genealogy I; thus the medium of H will be inferior to the medium of D since D was the father of H. Similarly the medium of D will be considered inferior to the medium of B. All mediums are inferior to the medium of A, the senior spirit medium representing the founding ancestor. In the case of mediums representing brothers such as B and C the medium representing the elder is considered senior. Thus a spirit-realm consists of a series of spirit-provinces articulated into a single system by the genealogical connections believed to have existed between spirit-guardians.

The model I have presented is a simplified one: genealogies are often much longer and there may be many more spirit-provinces. I have omitted a number of other complicating factors. One of these, however ought to be mentioned. Spirit-provinces can be sub-divided. This happens when a new medium is installed to represent a spirit-guardian

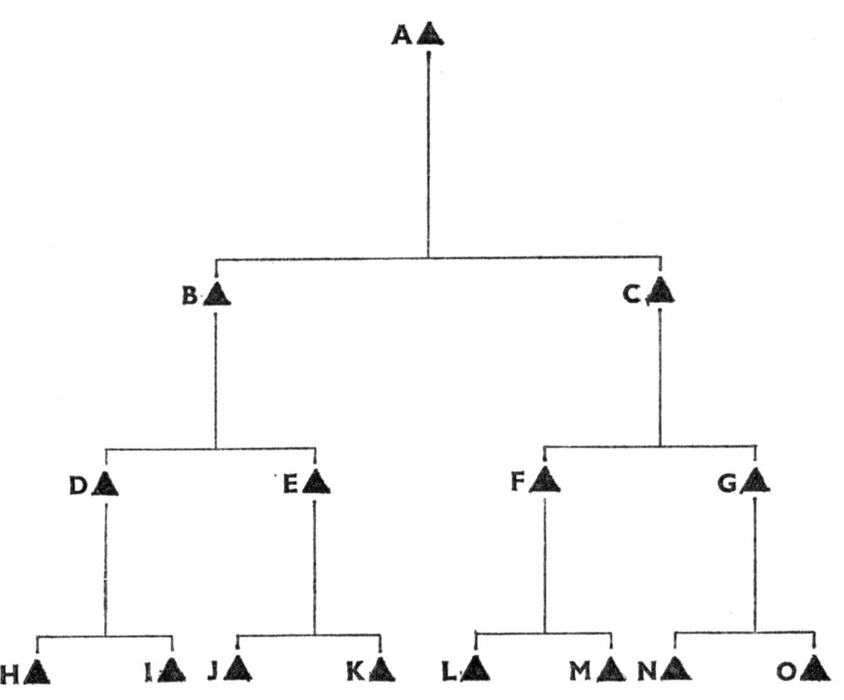

Genealogy I. Hypothetical Genealogy to show relationship between spirit-guardians

who has not 'spoken' before. The new medium will be given a portion of a spirit-province by its medium. (Korekore, of course, see this land as being given by one *spirit-guardian* to another.) The mediums of D, E, and K (Diagram I) might well have been given land when first installed from the once larger province of B. Similarly the mediums of I, G, and M might once have received land from the medium of C. The giving of spirit-provinces in this way conveys to the mediums of B and C a degree of additional authority over the recipients and introduces a measure of decentralization into the system. Routine minor problems, for example, which arise among the mediums of D, E, and K will be dealt with by the medium of B and not referred directly to the senior spirit medium. The authority of the givers of spirit-provinces over the recipients stems from their representing the original 'owners of the earth' who are believed to be ultimately responsible for the fertility of the earth in the whole of their original spirit-provinces. There is in fact a kind of spiritual 'estates of holding' (cf. Gluckman, 1945) though there appear to be only three 'estates' from 'founder' to 'junior' spirit-guardian. It is possible that further sub-divisions might occur, though this has not happened yet.

Boundaries of spirit-provinces do not necessarily coincide with those of chiefdoms (or of modern administrative or international divisions): one spirit-province may cut across the boundaries of two or more chiefdoms. Indeed, when considering spirit-provinces one has to put aside notions of political units since the spirit-provinces are concerned with a different order of social relations. Boundaries, and hence the regularity of the territorial aspect of the system, are maintained in two ways. First, by the extensive knowledge of the senior medium, other mediums, and some elders, of the various boundaries – usually prominent natural features – of spirit-provinces. This wide knowledge of boundaries makes it difficult for one medium to argue that his territory ought to be more extensive than it is. Secondly spirit-guardians are believed to invoke mystical sanctions which may involve death, madness and famine, against any medium (and the community to which he belongs) who attempts to enter the territory of another. One medium may visit another only on very special occasions and then only after he has taken ritual precautions. The most elaborate precautions have to be taken by a senior spirit-medium. Mutota's medium may not cross spirit boundaries without first being blindfolded and then carried over. Korekore say 'We fear that the great spirit may come and eat all the lesser ones'. Thus the mystical sanctions appear to operate to discourage a medium with territorial ambitions from usurping another's territory.

If, after the annual rain ritual has been performed, the main rains do not begin in a spirit-province, a delegation is sent to the spirit-medium representing the spirit-guardian of that province. If after the delegation has carried out the medium's instructions, paid fines, or performed the rituals he has advised, the main rains still do not begin, then a delegation is sent to the senior spirit-medium of the spirit-realm in which the province lies. In the cases where a spirit-province has been formed by a gift of land from a more senior medium to a recently possessed junior medium representing a 'new' spirit-guardian, delegates will proceed from the junior medium to the medium from whom he (or one of his predecessors) received his land before consulting the senior spirit medium. In the territorial aspect of the system, when consultations occur, at the most three, but generally only two, spirit-mediums are involved out of the total hierarchy. In all cases where no spirit-medium is active in a province, then problems are raised directly with the senior spirit medium.

Spirit-mediums are also consulted when a man first opens up new gardens unworked in living memory, to see if the spirit-guardian is favourably disposed to the land being worked. When a man enters a chiefdom and seeks land he pays his respects to the chief and also to the spirit-medium in whose province he eventually decides to make his gardens. In recent years store-keepers, traders and bus-owners have also taken to making yearly gifts to spirit-mediums to ensure that their businesses prosper. Traders and store-keepers often give extensive credit against the promise of grain at the next harvest. The failure of the rains, and hence the failure of their customers' grain crops, can often be disastrous for them. Bus-owners, on the other hand, cannot operate effectively if the rains are very heavy: roads become flooded and mechanical failures and accidents frequent.

In the territorial aspect of the system mediums are primarily concerned with factors affecting the fertility of the earth. As I have indicated, Korekore themselves see the mediums as being concerned with the moral order and with the relationships between men and the earth. Breaches of the moral order are believed to produce disturbances in the natural order and it is only through the spirit-mediums that these can be corrected. The territorial aspect is independent of the political organization of the chiefdoms. A chief does not co-ordinate or initiate rain rituals within his chiefdom, and the spirit-guardian a person propitiates depends upon the spirit-province in which he happens to be living and not upon the chiefdom.

THE LINEAL ASPECT

I outline briefly here only the principal features of the lineal aspect of spirit mediumship. Unlike the territorial aspect of spirit mediumship which involves people because they happen to be living on a particular piece of land which falls in the province of a particular spirit-guardian, the lineal aspect involves people who are members of widely dispersed agnatic descent groups believed to have been founded by certain spirit-guardians. The lineal aspect only concerns those spirit-guardians who are also ancestors with living patrilineal descendants and who are represented by mediums.

Chiefs may be linked directly with the lineal aspect of the system, for many spirit-guardians are also royal ancestors. Some of the patrilineal descendants of Mutota, for example, are royals in several chiefdoms in the Zambezi Valley. Others, of course, are scattered over adjacent areas in other chiefdoms, whilst a few are dispersed in other parts of Rhodesia. In the lineal aspect, patrilineal descendants of an ancestor may come to consult the medium of his spirit from wheresoever they may be living about such matters as the inheritance of wives and property, succession to family titles, and deaths and sicknesses attributed to the malevolence of ancestral spirits. Among royals, mediums play a particularly important role during succession disputes, which occur fairly frequently, because they are supposed to choose from a number of competing candidates the one to succeed a dead chief and, in the past, to install him as the one true chief by conferring spiritual legitimacy upon him. In the lineal aspect of the system the total hierarchy of mediums may be utilized, for should people not get satisfaction from one medium they go to another more senior in the hierarchy and so on until the senior medium is reached. His decision is considered final.

The lineal and territorial aspects of the system in which mediums are involved only completely merge in the office of the senior spirit-medium, for though as one ascends the hierarchy of mediums larger and larger numbers of people are involved in the lineal aspect, it is only the senior spirit-medium who may be consulted by all the patrilineal descendants of the spirit he represents as well as by any of the people living in the spirit-provinces of which his spirit-realm is composed.

LINKS WITH OTHER SPIRIT-REALMS

The senior spirit-medium is important in other respects because it is through his office that links are provided with other spirit-realms. There are several hierarchies of spirit-guardians among Korekore as a whole. Other hierarchies have been reported for neighbouring Shona-speaking peoples, notably the Zezuru cluster (Gelfand, 1959, 5). These various hierarchies are interconnected by a form of perpetual kinship which exists between the offices of mediums who represent certain spirit-guardians. Mutota, for example, is said to have had two 'brothers' and to have had numerous affinal and cognatic kin. These relationships are now perpetuated in the mediumships which represent Mutota's various relatives. Thus whoever succeeds to the mediumship of Mutota becomes 'brother', 'father-in-law', 'mother's brother', and so on, to different sets of mediums occupying the corresponding mediumships in other spirit-realms. Since mediumships in each hierarchy are perpetually linked in this way with mediumships in other hierarchies, these connections spread outwards to include a large proportion of the Shona-speaking peoples.

These links appear to have served to bring different chiefdoms, peoples and tribes, into some kind of wider polity. Ranger (1963a, 1963b) and Abraham (1963), in preliminary accounts, have shown the significance of the role of mediums in organizing political activities among the Shona-speaking peoples on a scale wider than chiefdom or tribe, both in the recent past – during the 'rebellion' of 1896 and its aftermath – and in the earlier period of Portuguese contact. Both present evidence which suggests that in times of stress when secular authority was being undermined, or when chiefdoms could not stand alone against invaders, then links within and between spirit-realms were activated to provide a framework for political and, sometimes, military activity on a wide scale. However, a full sociological analysis of the role of spirit-mediums in the political history of the Shona-speaking peoples will have to await the publication of more detailed evidence. What must be stressed is that whilst Korekore, and this is true also of other Shona-speaking peoples, see the mediums as being religious figures, they do have in fact important political functions.

SPIRIT MEDIUMSHIP

Having considered the system of which mediums are a part I now consider briefly the process by which a man becomes a medium, before turning to discuss the mediatory role of mediums in land-shrine neighbourhoods.

Korekore believe that the few spirit-guardians who return and speak through human mediums do so because when alive they ate special medicines to ensure that their spirits would return. Spirits which speak through mediums are termed *mhondoro* ('lion') and are believed to possess much greater powers and concern themselves with a wider range of human activities than ordinary ancestral spirits (*midzimu*). The latter concern themselves only with the activities of their immediate descendants, providing a measure of protection against sorcery if pleased, and causing illness and misfortune when angered or forgotten. *Mhondoro* spirits, however, are believed to be able to control, among other things, wind, rain, clouds, and lightning. They are supposed to be able to manifest themselves in any shape they choose by using animals or humans as hosts. Lions and humans are considered to be the hosts most commonly chosen by male spirit-guardians though, among Korekore, the very few female spirit-guardians are supposed to favour the python.

After the death of a man (or woman) who has eaten the special medicines, Korekore believe that his spirit seeks out a lion host in the forest. After a period of dwelling in this host and wandering in the forest the spirit-guardian is believed to become restless and desires to speak through a human host. The spirit-guardian then leaves the lion host and travels to a distant land where he seeks out a devout man. The spirit-guardian is then supposed to enter the man and cause him to behave strangely as if he were mad, to eat raw meat like an animal and to wander in the forest. Eventually through dreams the spirit-guardian reveals who he is and then guides the afflicted man back to the spirit-province to be installed as the guardian's medium.

Korekore say that about three generations elapse before a medium appears to represent a spirit-guardian and about five years from the death of one medium until his successor appears. During these periods, and in between periods of 'possession', the spirit-guardian dwells in his lion host in the forest.

This account of how a man becomes a medium is a stereotype which both ordinary Korekore and spirit-mediums relate if asked how possession first occurs. Actual case histories, whilst obviously adapted by the tellers to conform to the stereotype, generally reveal the following pattern. In many cases 'possession' followed a series of illnesses which were at first attributed by diviners to one or other of the *shave* spirits (see Gelfand, 1962, 84ff). After the failure of rituals designed to 'bring out' these afflicting spirits, further divination revealed that it was probably a spirit-guardian who was responsible for the trouble. The patient was then sent to an accredited medium for prolonged observation. If he behaved according to the stereotyped pattern – complaining of strange dreams and wandering in the forest – the medium then sent him to the senior spirit-medium for final tests.

Korekore stress that a medium ought to be a stranger to the area in which he operates and that he ought not to be a patrilineal descendant of the spirit he represents. In practice both of these conditions are not always fulfilled. Korekore also regard favourably a man possessed in adolescence, since they argue that he could not possibly have acquired by learning the esoteric knowledge of traditional history and genealogies which distinguishes a medium from others. Teen-age mediums are very rare, but not unknown. Most mediums appear to become active in their early twenties. In the normal course of events they can look forward to a long period in office, unless discredited, which is rare. This contrasts markedly with secular chiefs who, succeeding to office as old men, rarely reign for longer than ten years, and in many cases for much shorter periods.

The tests arranged for a candidate to a mediumship, beginning first with the preliminary tests prescribed by some accredited medium, and ending with the more searching tests conducted by a senior medium, may take place over a number of years. During this period the candidate is considered as on probation and his utterances, unless they help to establish the genuineness of his possession, may not be taken very seriously. It is accepted that all mediums in these preliminary stages 'make mistakes' in their reciting of genealogies and traditions, until they are 'possessed' strongly. During the probationary period the candidate may be told to let his hair grow, to refrain from sexual congress with women and to avoid eating 'hot' (strong tasting) food. Medicines are mixed with his food to 'bring out' the spirit and he is advised to take large quantities of snuff. This period comes to an end either with the candidate's acceptance or with his rejection by the senior spirit-medium.

The tests conducted by the senior spirit-medium may be very searching. The candidate is supposed to fall possessed in the presence of the senior medium and the possessing spirit-guardian should answer questions about his (i.e. the spirit-guardian's) past life, the site of his grave, the boundaries of his spirit-province and, most importantly, the genealogy which connects him to the possessing spirit of the senior medium. As a final test the candidate has to select, from a number of such objects kept by the senior medium, the ritual staff (*mwangato*) used by the previous medium of the spirit-guardian concerned. These staffs are used extensively in ritual, have individual names of historical significance and are supposed to possess healing properties. When a medium dies his staff is returned to the senior medium. A junior medium, representing a spirit-guardian who has not 'possessed' anyone before, is given a new staff. When the medium has chosen or been given his staff, his head is shaved.

Not all candidates pass their tests. Most are told that they are not possessed by a *mhondoro* spirit but by a *shave*. In this case the senior medium will outline rituals and prescribe medicines designed to exorcise the spirit. A few candidates will be told to go away for a while and return when they are 'possessed' strongly. Persons who just arrive and announce that they are possessed by a particular spirit are unlikely to be accepted. It is only those mediums who are sponsored by important mediums in the system, and who have successfully passed the preliminary tests, who appear to stand any chance of acceptance. Thus recruitment to the system is controlled by the senior spirit-medium in conjunction with the other mediums.

One aspect of recruitment remains to be considered. How do mediums acquire the esoteric knowledge of traditional history and genealogies which is so important for their acceptance and for the maintenance of their postion?

Except in the case of senior mediums, succession to mediumship is not hereditary. The senior mediumship of Mutota is transmitted in alternate generations from grandfather to grandson, the specific heir being nominated during the life-time of the senior medium (though this is kept secret and not known to Korekore in general). This exception serves again to emphasize the key nature of the senior mediumship for the co-ordination of the total system. Succession to other mediumships appears to be haphazard though occasionally one finds that a certain descent group, over time, has provided two or three mediums, though not always to represent the same spirit-guardian. It is this apparent haphazard nature of succession to mediumships which enables Korekore to maintain that a spirit-guardian possesses whomsoever he pleases. Furthermore, there is a sufficient number of cases where mediums were genuine strangers to the spirit-provinces in which they began to operate to give credibility to the accepted view that *all* mediums are strangers.

Close investigation of the backgrounds of a number of mediums revealed that all appeared to have had long periods of direct association with other mediums prior to their possession. Subsequently they had further periods of contact either with the same mediums, or with others during the preliminary tests of the probationary period. It is during these periods both prior and subsequent to possession that mediums appear to acquire the skills and esoteric knowledge which enable them to become established mediums.

Korekore insistence that mediums ought to be strangers, without kinsmen or local interests, and the stringent tests which are administered by the senior medium, can be related directly to the role of mediums as mediators. The resolution of many of the disputes with which mediums deal is vital for the harmonious, ongoing life of a community. To have a medium who is suspected of making pronouncements which obviously favour his own descent group, or a particular faction, destroys his value as a mediator. The whole procedure by which a candidate for a mediumship is selected, observed, tested and retested before he is installed, together with the mystical sanctions believed to operate against a 'false' medium, serve to establish the 'genuineness' of those few mediums who are accepted.

Nevertheless, whilst Korekore are not sceptical of mediums in general, or of the spirit-guardians believed to possess them, they do believe that on certain occasions particular mediums cheat their clients by conducting seances when they are not properly 'possessed'. Scepticism of this type is most frequently found among a medium's kin, close friends and neighbours, who have frequent opportunities of witnessing seances as well as being involved in every-day life with the medium as an ordinary, fallible mortal. Whilst a medium will often claim that he is just an ordinary man like anyone else and will deny all knowledge of what occurs during seances, he attempts to deal with the sceptism of his close associates by a withdrawal from informal contacts as far as possible, and by insisting upon being treated as the spirit-guardian personified. Since it is difficult for a medium's close associates to accept him both as a 'spirit-guardian' and as an ordinary person like themselves, this situation is resolved by a mild form of joking behaviour. It is noticeable that a medium's neighbours, friends and kin more often address him as '*aSekuru*' ('Honoured Grandfather') a form of address which allows of mild joking behaviour whilst still conveying a measure of respect, rather than as '*aMvura*' ('Lord Rain'), the formal and very respectful title frequently accorded him by strangers.

Frankenberg (1957, 19) describes how in a Welsh village, the stranger 'is forced to shoulder the responsibility for decisions when they prove unpopular with dissident groups of villagers'. Among Korekore the spirit-guardian-ancestor ('the stranger') is not always held responsible for a decision which later proves unpopular; on occasions it is the medium. Who is blamed depends upon the particular situation. Widespread natural disaster, such as a general failure of the rains in which every neighbourhood suffers equally, or a decision which later proves unpopular in a community where the interests of no dominant faction are involved, are blamed upon the spirit-guardian-ancestor. This is clearly revealed at land-shrine rituals following an unsuccessful agricultural season. During prayers at the shrine the spirit-guardian may be subjected to considerable abuse. However, when strong factional interests are involved the medium is usually blamed for decisions which, in certain quarters, prove unpopular. For example when a chief who has been selected by a senior medium later proves unpopular with the majority of the people, or with a strong and important faction, people begin to say that the senior medium was 'bribed' and not properly possessed when he made his choice. People argue that the medium falsified, or did not properly communicate, the wishes of the spirit. Thus, they argue, the spirit-guardian-ancestor cannot possibly be annoyed if an attempt is made to depose the chief. Blame in this case is not projected upon the guardian-ancestor for the deposed chief's successor is believed to receive his spiritual legitimacy and power to rule from the very same ancestor: to direct blame upon the latter would undermine important beliefs which support the political system.

A medium's denial of awareness of what takes place during seances and his (usual) extreme reluctance to discuss aspects of his esoteric knowledge, or decisions reached by 'the spirit' outside of the seance situation, are devices to separate his two roles of normal person and possessed medium. By these means the medium attempts to avoid personal blame for unpopular decisions though, as I have indicated, he is not always successful.

When a possessed medium mediates in a dispute, the decision which he makes is in fact arrived at by the people through discussions among themselves and at seances, though they will always say that it was the decision of the spirit. This is why a medium sometimes delays making a decision for as long as possible whilst he waits for public opinion to crystallize on the issue. (Garbett 1963, 11). Colson (1962, 165) makes a similar point when discussing the role of prophets among the Gwembe Tonga. She writes, 'The prophet thus serves to canalize and crystallize public opinion; he cannot introduce a new course contrary to the general sentiment'. The possessed medium, as 'the stranger', is in fact led by the people and not the leader of public opinion (cf. Frankenberg 1957, 18). To illustrate and develop some of these theoretical points I now consider the role of mediums in land-shrine neighbourhoods, which are the basic units in the territorial system in which spirit-mediums are involved.

MEDIUMS AND LAND-SHRINE NEIGHBOURHOODS

Each inhabited spirit-province contains one or more land-shrines depending upon its size and the distribution of its population. Baobab trees are usually selected as shrines though sometimes other large trees are chosen. The shrines are named after the spirit-guardian in whose province they stand. Hamlets which habitually associate to perform an annual ritual at a shrine, I term a land-shrine neighbourhood. Despite the high degree of individual and hamlet mobility land-shrine neighbourhoods have a greater degree of permanence than the individual hamlets of which they are composed. Usually the headman of the hamlet longest established in the neighbourhood is responsible for arranging the ritual though the actual officiants are the oldest living men.

The offerings of beer, snuff and cold gruel (*bota*) made at the shrine are ritually prepared by old women assisted by young virgins and a few little boys. Sexually active persons are believed to pollute the offering during its preparation and must keep away. When they have been prepared, the offerings are made to the spirit-guardian and also to some of his deceased kin – mother, father, paternal grandfather – and possibly to some of his friends who were supposed to have lived with him. Sometimes an additional offering is made to 'the unknown spirit' in case, as Korekore put it, 'we have forgotten someone and he is offended'.

The spirit-guardian and his patrilineal kin are exhorted to bring the rain and make the crops grow whilst other spirits are asked to keep insect and animal pests from the fields: a kind of spiritual 'division of labour'. Prayers are made directly to the spirits, who are not asked, either implicitly or explicitly, to mediate between *Mwari,* the remote High God, and man, as they are among the neighbouring Zezuru (Gelfand, 1959, 13).

In a neighbourhood where a spirit-medium lives, the ritual conducted at the land-shrine is followed in the evening by a dance attended by members of the local neighbourhood and representatives from other neighbourhoods in the spirit-province. During the dance, after much drumming and the singing of special songs favoured by the spirit, the medium falls possessed and receives gifts of black cloth and money provided by members of the province. During the course of the public seance the medium, speaking as the spirit-guardian, will urge the congregation to uphold the laws of the forefathers. He tells them to refrain from sorcery and from committing incest and adultery. Anger with one's neighbours leads to sorcery, which enrages the spirit-guardian, and possibly to homicide, which in addition pollutes the earth. He may also order the congregation to keep the twice-monthly rest days set aside in honour of the spirit.

One of the most important aspects of the land-shrine ritual is that everyone ought to take part in it and contribute grain for the preparation of the beer. In the large spirit-provinces containing several land-shrines there is no overall co-ordination of the rituals either by a chief or by anyone else, but it is felt strongly that rituals will not be efficacious unless conducted at all shrines. In recent years Korekore have attributed the failure of the rains in some localities to the refusal of certain separatist sects to take part in the rituals or contribute towards them. In other areas white missionaries and their Christian converts are similarly blamed. It is felt strongly that everyone ought to come together at the yearly ritual in amity, for the good of the community. At the ritual itself all spears and axes must be laid aside and not brought near the shrine. A man should approach the shrine with a 'white heart' bearing no ill-will towards his neighbours. At the shrine, talking must be subdued and no uncouth behaviour ought to occur, particularly behaviour which might provoke a quarrel. Should a quarrel occur this is regarded as a serious offence which endangers the efficacy of the ritual and hence the well-being of the whole community. Failure to observe ritual injunctions will result in a fine being demanded by the hamlet heads and elders who officiate at the ritual. Formerly this was paid in the form of a hoe left at the shrine but nowadays it consists of money paid to a spirit-medium. Though there are obvious parallels here with rain-shrine communities among the Plateau Tonga (Colson, 1962, 84 ff) there is no general 'peace of the neighbourhood' during the period when rituals are being performed: the 'peace' only operates at the shrine itself.

When a land-shrine is torn by dissension and it is impossible to conduct a joint ritual in amity, then a neighbourhood splits and two or more new shrines are created. The position is similar to that described by Colson (1962) for rain-shrine communities among the Tonga, except that among Korekore a new shrine may only be created after permission has been received from the spirit-medium of the province concerned. He may attempt to resolve the dispute, particularly if it is cast in the idiom of sorcery or of 'spirit affliction' and cannot be resolved in the local secular courts. In this way spirit-mediums are important in the maintenance of community values at the local level since they speak out strongly against sorcery, adultery and homicide and, in certain circumstances, may act as arbiters in some types of dispute.

A DISPUTE IN A LAND-SHRINE NEIGHBOURHOOD

I now consider aspects of a dispute in a land-shrine neighbourhood in which a medium was involved as a mediator.

Colson (1962, 102 ff) has indicated how a degree of social control is maintained in Plateau Tonga local communities by the multiple bonds of kinship, clanship and friendship which criss-cross one another. She shows that in disputes between two parties, third parties sooner or later become involved because they have effective bonds of a similar order with both disputing parties. I could demonstrate this clearly for the members of the hamlets involved in the following case. However, here I have assumed Colson's analysis and only concentrate on the general mobilization of public opinion brought about by a series of natural calamities attributed to the intervention of the spirits.

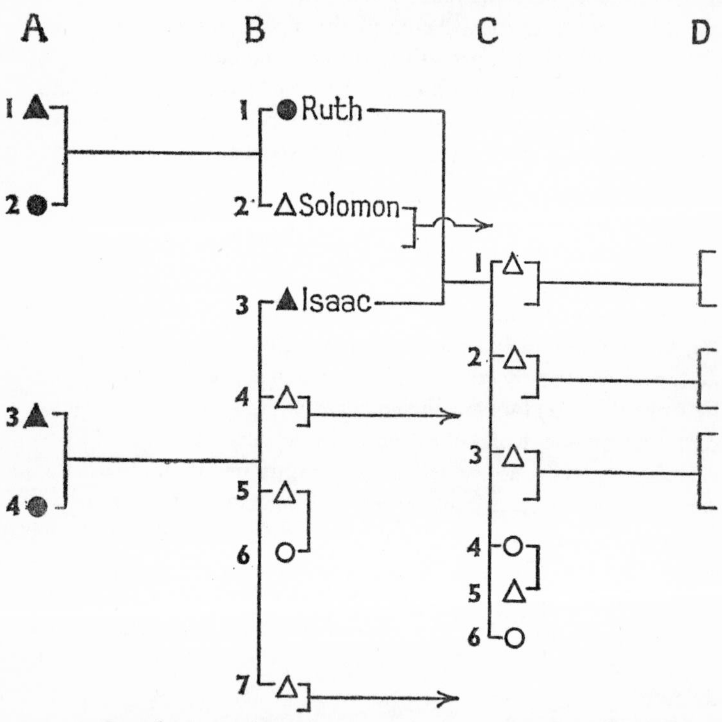

Genealogy II. The case of Solomon and Isaac's brothers

The neighbourhood in which the dispute occurred consisted of 7 hamlets with a population of 127 of which about one third were adults. All save two of the hamlets were offshoots from the oldest established hamlet of which Solomon,[2] the offended party in the dispute, had become headman. All except one hamlet head were commoners. None of the disputants was considered to be descended from the spirit-guardian concerned.

Solomon (B2 in Genealogy II), a hamlet head, had a sister Ruth (B1) who had married Isaac (B3), a man who lived in the neighbourhood. Apparently the marriage was not properly contracted and no bridewealth was transferred. Isaac then left the neighbourhood with his wife and returned many years later. Shortly after his return he died. Ruth, his wife, who had borne him a number of children, died shortly afterwards. Meanwhile, Solomon's father (A1) and Isaac's father (A3), the original parties to the marriage agreement, had both died. Solomon urged Isaac's three brothers (A4, 5, 7) to pay bridewealth to him, as successor to his father, but they declined to do so. The dispute lingered on for a number of years with occasional eruptions until it finally came to a head when one of Ruth's daughters (C4) married. Solomon had really been waiting for this and he claimed the bridewealth coming from the marriage. He argued that as mother's brother this was his right since his sister's marriage had not been properly contracted and her children should therefore be under his guardianship. This claim was strongly resisted by Isaac's brothers. Solomon then considered taking the matter to court but he knew, as did Isaac's brothers, that without the witnesses to the original marriage contract, he might not succeed with his case. There were others, too, who, because of their connections with both Solomon and Isaac's brothers, urged Solomon not to precipitate an open breach.

Whilst Solomon was considering what to do next a number of Ruth's grandchildren, some living in the neighbourhood, others elsewhere, began to fall sick. One of them died. Divination attributed the cause of the sickness to a malevolent ancestral spirit (*ngozi*). Shortly afterwards a woman (B6) married to one of Isaac's brothers was possessed by an *ngozi* which, during a seance, revealed itself as Solomon's father's spirit, angered because the bridewealth had not been transferred.[3] He threatened to continue to afflict his great-grandchildren unless the dispute was resolved.

Tension began to mount in the neighbourhood. Solomon and Isaac's brothers quarrelled at a beer drink and almost came to blows and there was a general feeling among people that the dispute ought to be resolved, particularly as the time for the rain-ritual was approaching. Solomon avoided Isaac's brothers for a time and when the land-shrine ritual, of which he was the organizer, was due to be performed, he failed to notify the three brothers although they had provided grain for the beer. They arrived in any case and a quarrel broke out between them and Solomon at the shrine. Solomon lost his temper and Isaac's brothers, feeling that the congregation gathered at the shrine was generally hostile towards them, left in a huff.

A little over a week later after the main rains, already late, had shown no sign of beginning, a number of local elders, among them Solomon, went to the spirit-medium and asked why the rains delayed.
The possessed medium was well aware of the dispute. Through him, the spirit-guardian told them during the seance that he was annoyed because people had quarrelled at the shrine and consequently the ritual had not been performed correctly. He ordered Solomon to pay a fine. Solomon refused, laying the blame on Isaac's brothers. In this he was supported by most of his elders. The whole issue of the unpaid bridewealth and the afflicting *ngozi* was then brought out. The medium then ordered that all parties to the dispute be summoned to attend another seance a few days later.
At the next seance, when all the parties to the dispute and prominent elders of the neighbourhood were assembled, the possessing spirit-guardian asked why the case of the afflicting *ngozi* had not been raised with him before. 'Am I not here to arrange the affairs of the spirits?' he asked. Isaac's brothers were somewhat truculent at first until one elder, a man considerably respected in the neighbourhood, pointed out to them, quite sharply, that they were endangering the whole community, for unless the matter were settled, the rains would not come and children would keep on dying. The spirit-guardian through the possessed medium, took up this theme at great length and dwelt upon the powers of the spirit-guardians and their ability to strike down with lightning all those who failed to obey them, citing several examples of this having happened in the past. After further discussion Isaac's brothers agreed to pay a portion of the outstanding bridewealth. This compromise was agreed upon and publicly acknowledged by Solomon after he had been assured that the remainder would be forthcoming after Ruth's daughter was properly married.
The matter of the quarrel at the shrine was then considered. Solomon was reluctant to accept responsibility but eventually gave way and agreed that he as well as Isaac's brothers should give a piece of black cloth to the spirit-guardian.
Finally the medium prescribed medicines and outlined a ritual designed to exorcise the afflicting spirit of Solomon's father.

Normally a case of unpaid bridewealth would be handled at the chief's court, but in Solomon's case the matter was complicated because of the deaths of all the original parties to the contract. The medium, as a member of the local community, was well aware of the issues involved. Like most mediums he made a point of keeping himself well informed. When reaching his decision (represented as that of the spirit-guardian) he was really following very closely the general feeling in the community that Isaac's brothers were the cause of all the misfortunes. It was the pressure of public opinion voiced through the elders, and supported by the veiled threat of the medium that mystical sanctions might be invoked against them personally, which caused Isaac's brothers to shift from their previous rigid position and agree to compromise. If they had not accepted the compromise, the only alternative for them would have been to leave the neighbourhood. There were strong social and economic reasons why they did not wish to do this.

Once aroused, public opinion is channelled through the mediums and becomes sharpened and clarified. The medium becomes the mouthpiece of the community, as it were, and emphasizes the moral values which all men ought to uphold. He is able to do this in a way that no ordinary person, or even a chief, can, for he speaks as only one of a whole hierarchy of remote but powerful guardian-ancestors who are ever watchful of the behaviour of men upon the earth. When he acts as a mediator in disputes, agreements reached under his aegis are considered much more binding than those reached by other means. Should an agreement be broken, mystical sanctions are believed to be invoked by the spirit-guardians not only against the parties to the dispute but also against the whole community.

As I have stated, Korekore believe that a disturbance in the moral order produces disturbances in the natural order. Consequently when natural calamities occur people immediately begin to consider their own and other people's activities in an attempt to find a cause. In the case considered, 'the cause' was readily apparent and had its roots in the dispute between Solomon and Isaac's brothers.

Not all natural disasters need be blamed upon one person or faction, however. There are a number of occurrences which are believed to anger the spirit-guardians simply because they are 'unnatural' (e.g. multiple births among cattle and humans). When a neighbourhood is not torn by dissension and there are no obvious 'causes' one of these 'unnatural' occurrences will be given as the reason why the spirit-guardian is angry and has caused the crops to fail or the rains to be late. In such cases all people can do is to go to a medium and through him seek the advice of the spirit-guardian. Whilst the whole community suffers because of this 'offence' no one individual or faction is singled out by the community as being especially blameworthy. It is only when there is dissension within a neighbourhood that the whole community, suffering under what people believe to be the penalties imposed by the spirit-guardian, is mobilized to bring about a resolution of the dispute through the mediation of the spirit-medium. The mystical sanctions operate against innocent and guilty alike: the whole community is involved. I consider this one of the most important aspects of the Korekore land-shrine neighbourhoods. The general principle of cross-cutting ties (Colson, 1962, 121) which involves each man in the affairs of others, is additionally reinforced among Korekore, by a spirit system which provides, sooner or later, a means for the formal expression, backed by ritual sanctions, of public opinion within a community. It may thus contribute to the resolution of disputes which are thought to have disturbed the natural as well as the social order.

NOTES

[1]At a private seance the medium falls possessed without the aid of drumming, singing, or playing of other musical instruments.

[2]All names are fictitious.

[3]Another example of the role of 'the stranger' in a different context. It is typical of this type of *ngozi* possession that it happens to a woman married into the offending group.

REFERENCES

ABRAHAM, D. P. 1959 'The Monomotapa dynasty', *NADA*, 59–84.

1963 'The political role of Chaminuka and the Mhondoro cult in Shona history', in: Brown, R.; Stokes, E. (eds.), *The history of the Central African peoples*. Lusaka, Rhodes-Livingstone Institute.

COLSON, E. 1960 *The social organization of the Gwembe Tonga*. Manchester University Press.

1962 *The Plateau Tonga of Northern Rhodesia*. Manchester University Press.

FIRTH, R. 1959 'Problem and assumption in an anthropological study of religion', *Journal of the Royal Anthropological Institute* 89 (2).

FRANKENBERG, R. 1957 *Village on the border*. London, Cohen and West.

GARBETT, G. K. 1963 'Religious aspects of political succession among the Valley Korekore', in: Brown, R.; Stokes, E. (eds.), *The history of the Central African peoples*, Lusaka, Rhodes-Livingstone Institute.

GELFAND, M. 1959 *Shona ritual*. Cape Town, Juta.

1962 *Shona religion*. Cape Town, Juta.

GLUCKMAN, M. 1945 'African land tenure', *Human Problems in British Central Africa* 3.

RANGER, T. O. 1963a 'The organization of the rebellions of 1896 and 1897', in: Brown, R.; Stokes, E. (eds.), *The history of the Central African peoples*, Lusaka, Rhodes-Livingstone Institute.

1963b 'The last days of the Empire of Mwenemutapa (1898–1917)', in: Brown, R.; Stokes, E. (eds.), *The history of the Central African peoples*, Lusaka, Rhodes-Livingstone Institute.

SPIRIT POSSESSION AMONG THE ZULU

© *S. G. Lee*

I

The first-hand data cited in this paper were obtained between 1951 and 1957 when I was investigating the incidence, nosology and aetiology of fits of screaming, so common among Zulu women that it is a relatively ordinary event to hear a young woman crying out '*hayi, hayi, hayi*' or uttering yelping grunts for hours, days, or even weeks. Locally the usual explanation of this behaviour is in terms of the effects of love magic, and no state of possession is involved. But in the course of my research I found myself concerned, peripherally, but in both a therapeutic and investigatory capacity, with many sufferers from different kinds of possession. In addition, when I investigated the 'cryers' (persons claiming a history of the screaming) and contrasted them with a control group of women with no such record, quantitative differences appeared between the criterion groups' responses to questionnaires, a Thematic Apperception Test, etc. (Lee 1950, 1954, 1958, 1961), which threw light on the type of personality associated with possession, and some of this evidence is cited below. Its oblique nature is a direct reflection of my original intention to concentrate upon the modern 'crying' disorder and not to carry out an intensive investigation of spirit possession.

However, various forms of supposed spirit possession are to be found among the Zulu and these still play an important part in the behaviour of many people, both those possessed (henceforth, for brevity, I will treat the conceit of possession as reality) and others who are affected by the dicta and supposed powers of spirit-mediums. While demarcation lines between types of possession are sometimes blurred by confusion in their naming, classification can usefully be attempted by asking the following questions:

(i) How long is the history of any type of possession, or of any cult activities associated therewith?
(ii) How stereotyped are the symptoms or any rituals associated with the state?
(iii) What therapies are called into play to diagnose, develop or end the possession?
(iv) What kinds of spirits are involved?
(v) Are any overt social purposes served by the possession and its consequences? What are the social functions of any associated cult activity?

All these questions can be considered, roughly, as 'social' in their emphases, but we have also to deal with another set of criterion questions, pertaining to the individual sufferer, which are essentially of psychological interest.

(vi) What purposes, if any, in terms of both conscious and unconscious wishes, are served by possession for the individual subject?
(vii) What kinds of people become possessed in the various ways? Here we must consider not only such objective variables as sex, age, or marital state, but also possible personality characteristics.
(viii) How is possession related, in the tribal frame of reference, to other disorders of individuals which are not attributed to spirit possession?
(ix) What light can Western psychopathology throw on the nosology and aetiology of possession and associated states?
(x) What, if any, is the relationship between the social epidemiology of possession and the individual characteristics of sufferers?

All these questions form the background of the account that follows: if we apply our first set of 'social' questions to the Zulu data we can see clearly that states of possession fall into two distinct main classes. The first of these, *ukuthwasa* possession, has been the more investigated by anthropologists and will be discussed in detail in Part II of this essay. For the present it is useful to note that it has a long history – as long, indeed, as recorded Zulu history itself – that it is rigid and invariant in its form, its symptoms (both physical and behavioural), its treatment within the canon of local medical practice, and in the rituals and social behaviour consequent upon both the initial stages and continuation of the possession, although on occasion the full sequence of the latter does not ensue, because of deliberate therapeutic intervention. Ancestor spirits are involved and the usual result of a complete possession is that the person involved becomes an *isangoma* diviner (plural *izangoma*), possessed of diagnostic and thaumaturgic power, and a figure of some consequence in the society. A modern modification of this cult, closely related to it in terms of questions (iii), (iv) and (v) above, is found in the appropriation of many of its elements by the syncretist, nominally Christian, separatist churches, especially the 'Zionist' forms of religion (cf. Sundkler, 1961), and this is discussed in Part III below.

The other main class of possession is much more amorphous in its characteristics. Here we have the states of, typically, *amandiki, amandawe, amabutho* and *izizwe* possession. These conditions have been very little studied, though the Junods' accounts (1927, 1934) of *Ndjao* (*amandiki*) possession among the Thonga is a relatively full description of an essentially similar condition. My own material here is almost purely descriptive, of little explanatory value, and it is for this reason that it has been included in the first part of this paper – bread and butter before cake.

These possessions are of relatively recent origin, the first reports appearing about 1910, and there is great difficulty in establishing an adequate nomenclature, ascriptions and spelling varying from district to district. Sometimes the states are confused with each other, or with pathology attributed to sorcery, and symptoms of the various 'kinds' of possession show great variation from individual to individual. The one common factor is that the naming and subjective aetiology of the states follow closely social change, particularly in culture contact situations.

Let us take some of the available accounts in a rough chronological order. According to *The Collector* (1911), *amandiki* and *amandawu* possession are practically identical, though each cult possesses its own 'language' (usually a distorted form of Zulu). *Amandawu* (frequently the same word is used for both possession and possessed) have powers of divination whereas *amandiki* have none. The word *amandiki* means a spirit, and one of *The Collector's* informants claimed to have been entered by the spirit of the Zulu King Tshaka. By oral tradition both types of possession are claimed to have originated north of the Pongola river, in Swaziland or Thongaland, and the *amandiki* claimed originally to have been despatched on a messianic mission by a woman, uSiqungana. 'They came into Zululand after Dinizulu's return from overseas' (shortly after the disastrous Bambatha rebellion against White rule). The *amandiki* bark like dogs, speaking with strange tongues, and move around the country collecting money from their relatives and doing much dancing. The *amandiki* spirits, unlike the ancestor spirits of the *isangoma* diviner, never appear in visible form. They cry out (cf. 'cryers' above) and belch like *izangoma*, and some informants claim that the possessing spirits are ancestors.

Asmus (1939) however, claims that:

> The *amandiki* are a kind of prophet and diviner, as well as being doctors of medicine, and are mostly women. They imagine themselves to be possessed by spirits which are, however, different from the *amadhlozi* (ancestral spirits) . . . . They dance and belch deeply and often, and then begin to divine . . . .
>
> The *amandawo*, itinerant doctors, are seized by a power called *ubundawo* . . . . From time to time they have seizures like epileptics. They also belch deeply and roar. They have no dealings with the *amadhlozi* . . . . (my translation).

Asmus mentions the custom of present-giving to *amandiki* and claims that, for purposes of gain, they spread their condition by the use of medicines. Here we can see a possible motive but there are also individual personality factors involved for in these cases 'which are of more recent times, we see a kind of obsessed hysterical person'.

Sundkler is worth quoting in more detail:

> A modern form of ancestor-possession is the *amandiki* or *amandawe* possession. The phenomena connected with this have been scientifically described as far as the Vandau, the Venda and the Lovedu are concerned. Quite recently – about 1910 – they appeared in Zululand. It is characteristic that the two most serious epidemics in recent times among the Zulu – 'influenza' in 1919–20 and malaria in 1933 – were among the causes of the rapid spread of this form of possession. Like the *izizwe* hysteria, the *amandawe* possession is directed at curing some illness, and initiation into the cult is regarded as a healing agency, for it is believed to be therapeutic. As with *idlozi* possession [ordinarily *ukuthwasa*], dancing is an important feature of the more modern cult. However, whereas the *isangoma* novice is most often of

a hysterical constitution, and the symptoms of the initiation (*ukwethwasa*) are quite violent, the initiates of *amandawe* possession are relatively quiet. An *amandawe* doctor is called to heal the patient. This is done by rites and dances designed to cause one of the patient's ancestral spirits to materialise. The initiate goes through many days of an exhausting dance, until at last the spirit enters her. It speaks through the initiate and expresses itself in a reputedly foreign tongue, as, for instance, a so-called 'Indian' or 'Thonga' language. In actual fact it may be only a series of meaningless sounds, which are thought by the audience to be some foreign language. Sometimes two or even as many as seven different ancestral spirits may take up their abode in the person concerned and speak in different languages (Sundkler, 1961, 23).

Of *izizwe* Sundkler writes: 'The best parallel to tongues which people in Northern Zululand know of is the so-called *izizwe* or *amabutho*. When a person is ill the Zulu doctor [herbalist] may treat him in the following way. He gives his patient a mixture to smoke which when inhaled will drive away the illness or rather replace the illness by something the Zulu call 'soldiers' (*amabutho*)' (Sundkler, 1961, 248–49). This treatment is used for some cases of psychological disturbance and the treated person will speak in 'foreign' tongues appropriate to the medicine administered.

Bryant, in an early account (1911), mentions the northern origin of the states, their epidemic nature, the possessing spirit akin to the ancestral types (*idlozi* and *umlozikana* or whistling familiar spirit), and attributes the symptoms and actions of sufferers to epilepsy and hysteria. The epileptic hypothesis is of interest, as epilepsy is common in the area, but it is equally distributed between men and women, unlike the possessions, which are almost always found in females. The Zulu have a clear idea of major epileptic seizures and while fits might be explained in terms of possession and might initiate behaviour disorder they are not, in my opinion, a major contributor to the incidence of any of the disorders discussed in this essay.

My own informants confirmed some of the above accounts and, in older women, there is less confusion with other states. These latter denied that sorcery was in any way responsible for *amandiki* and said that it was caused solely by 'the spirits of the dead'. One claimed to have been treated with her sisters, prophylactically, during the 1933 malaria epidemic, and thus spared the possession which attacked her cousins. *Izizwe* was stated to result as an integral part of cures, particularly when the patient was threatened with impending 'crying' – 'I did not actually cry out, because the herbalist caused me to have *izizwe*. These cause one to speak out like *amandiki*, but one's bodily movements are different. *Amandiki* sit like men while, in *izizwe*, you just move your body in a shaking rhythmic manner'. *Izizwe* is not regarded as always accompanied by physical distress, unlike most other forms, though psychological disturbance is often part of the syndrome.

Another informant claimed that she had suffered from *amandawe* possession but had had it converted into *ukuthwasa* by an *isangoma* diviner, as the former condition, unless treated, could lead to death.

In summary: much more intensive investigation of these states is needed and their nosology and aetiology are far from clear. However, they do seem to bear a very close resemblance to the Dancing Manias of the Middle Ages (Hecker, 1844), in their symptoms, their 'infectiousness', and in the itinerant activities of the cults. At times of national disaster they tend to occur in an explosively epidemic form and then to persist, sporadically, in individual cases. They are 'new' disorders, less indigenous to the Zulu than to neighbouring tribes, and have probably been acquired from contact with other more northerly peoples. I have come across too few cases for the evidence to be of statistical value but, essentially, these possessions are highly individual phenomena, lacking the stable socially recognized framework of either *ukuthwasa* or Zionist possession.

In *izizwe* the person possessed has no diagnostic or therapeutic powers and indeed the contribution of all these 'foreign' states to the medical practices of the Zulu is very small. To hazard a guess: the personalities of the women involved are probably not dissimilar to those of possessed Zionist converts – possession in both cases is neither as violent in its effects, both physical and psychological, nor as long-lasting, as *ukuthwasa*. Possession by spirits speaking foreign tongues is of interest, particularly as 'English' and 'Indian' are tending to supplant the more traditional 'Swazi' or 'Thonga'. Indians are not allowed to settle in Zululand, yet in the fantasies of Zulu psychotics suffering delusions of persecution it is not uncommon to find Indians as the maleficent figures. We may well have here, at a very deep level, a reflection of new culture contact stresses, worthy of more intensive investigation.

II

The word *ukuthwasa* means a 'coming out' or 'emergence', as of the appearance of the new moon or the reappearance of a planet or constellation. In the case of 'a new *umNgoma* emerging from his initiation and starting practice' (Bryant, 1906), this 'coming out' is the end result of possession by ancestor spirits – ideas of 'rebirth' as a 'new' person are involved and indeed the behaviour and symbolic acts attributed to the possessed person resemble greatly certain 'universal' birth symbols postulated by Freud (1954).

In most cases of *ukuthwasa* possession three distinct stages can be found: initial symptoms of considerable change in both physical and mental functioning; treatment, either to 'seal off' the spirit or spirits or to 'open the ways' of the victim for the ancestors; and, finally, if the second of these courses is pursued, the emergence of the possessed person as a fully qualified member of the *isangoma* cult. That these processes are relatively invariant will be seen from the following ethnographic accounts, the first being that of an *ukuthwasa* experience described in 1951. The informant was a married woman aged thirty who had been in full practice as a diviner for some eighteen months when she was interviewed by my research assistant, C. Mthembu. She was highly regarded in the area as a 'smeller-out' of sorcerers.

> I had been sick for over six months. I chiefly suffered from pains in the sides. The *izangoma* had been consulted. They said the spirits of my ancestors were angry about some unbecoming behaviour that was taking place at home, so that they were stabbing me (sharp pains in the sides). A goat was killed to propitiate them. This had no effect. A young ox was killed. I thought I was recovering after this. I could even sit up by myself. I could walk with the help of a stick. Two weeks later it came on me again, now worse than before. I was already a bag of bones. I had a very deep sleep after going several nights without. I dreamt that I saw my grandfathers and great-grandfathers [in real life she had seen a grandfather, but no great-grandfather]. I felt afraid and bowed myself down. My grandfather called me and told me: 'We are your ancestors. We have long tried to make your people understand (by illness) that we want you to be our house – to speak for us. We have decided to come ourselves as we see you in danger of death. Wake up. Dress. Go out quietly, and as soon as you

are outside the *umuzi* [homestead], run fast before your absence is discovered. We shall then guide you where we want you to go'. I woke up. It was a dream. Yet to my surprise I felt my bones strong. I felt I could walk, bag of bones as I was. I dressed quickly and slipped out of the hut. When I was out of the *umuzi* I ran. I made my unknown journey towards the east. It must have been midnight, as I reached my destination at dawn [the actual distance was 20 miles]. I came to a big *umuzi*. I felt something like a voice saying, 'Go there'. I went into one of the huts – a very big one. In it I found a number of *izangoma* sitting. Some were grinding medicines and others were smelling burnt skins and herbs. I went straight to the chief *isangoma* sitting right at the back of the hut. She simply looked at me without saying a single word. I suffered much consternation. Without asking me any questions she jumped up, howled, and began to dance. After this she burnt some medicine on burning embers and made me smell it. It made me dizzy and I felt a shiver go through my body and my heart became painful (i.e. 'I felt sad and anxious'). Then I began to cry. I cried and cried until, after a time, I was ordered to follow immediately. We went with the chief *isangoma* into the *dongas* [eroded gullies] nearby. There I was given some emetic. We then returned home. Every morning this was done until one night the spirits of my ancestors came to me and told me to rest assured that they were with me. My home people could not trace me until three weeks had passed. I stayed for months in that *umuzi*, being initiated. We used to go out with the chief *isangoma* to gatherings of the *izangoma*. After a short time I felt that I could smell things out. At meetings of the *izangoma* people hid things here and there. I could now follow the thing until I pulled it out from where it was hidden. I did not '*bula*' [divine] at great meetings connected with sicknesses, and *abathakathi* [sorcerers] smelling out – as I was not yet a full professional. I did not do so until six months after, when I was to be sent home to be given presents by my people [presents are said to be given to the spirits and not to the *isangoma*]. The giving of presents is called '*ukuhunga*'. This was a great ceremony, as all the local *izangoma* assembled at my home and danced through the whole night. I was brought in after dusk. Since I had arrived at the *umuzi* of the chief *isangoma*, I had been painted all over with ochre. It was in the morning of the following day that I went up with the others to the river to bathe. An ox and three goats were killed for the spirits. After the feast I was left at home and could work out my own cases.

This is a very typical modern account of the possession and training of an *isangoma*, though it is fairly common for the neophyte to be isolated for some months in a hut, and some of the odd subjective experiences of trainee diviners may be due to this form of 'sensory deprivation'. (Cf. Bexton, Heron and Scott, 1954; Hebb, 1958, etc.) Space precludes the citing of earlier ethnographic evidence in full but three early accounts are worth quoting at some length:

(1) Fynn (1950, 274–75), writing about 1833:

This species of witchcraft is professed by men and women which appears not to be a choice, nor could it be accomplished by choice, but as they state, commences with a fit of sickness in which case, as is general with all sick, they kill a cow, praying for a recovery from the spirits of their forefathers. They are then attacked with a delirium during which they dream dreams and run wild in the river or woods during which time the spirits appear to them with a song composed for his or her use which is the one sung by them on all occasions when called on.

He or she then plucks some plants from the riverside, part of which is eaten and the rest tied about the neck when he recovers from the trance which with the first sickness has been brought on him by the spirits of his forefathers with the intention that he should follow the profession of *inyanga*.

.... On his return he is addressed with the same respect that is given to a chief.... Having previously prepared his dress for the event [divination of the whereabouts of a concealed object], he then puts it on, differing in persons as fancy may dictate. Some the blown entrails of a bullock tied round the neck and breast, on others immense numbers of gallbladders blown. Others, pieces of hides about their necks....

(2) Shooter (1857, 191):

The seer's office, which may be filled by a female, is hereditary. It is, however (to quote the words of Mr Fynn) 'a principle understood throughout every tribe in Kafir-land that none of the children of a prophet can succeed their parent in that profession. It is believed that the requisite discernment and power are denied to them, but may frequently appear in their descendants of the second generation'. Symptoms supposed to indicate an individual's coming inspiration are mental depression, a disposition to retire from his accustomed society, severe fits of an epileptic nature, severe and numerous dreams. . . . . The neophyte talks about his marvellous visions, and 'commences running, shrieking, plunging into water, and performing wonderful feats, until his friends say he is mad; and he speaks and acts like one under the influence of a super-natural being'. He then catches live snakes (probably harmless ones) and hangs them about his neck. Thus arrayed he goes to a prophet; and presenting him with a goat, seeks to be instructed in the mysteries of the profession.

Shooter goes on to give a detailed description of such a case of possession in the father of one of his servants. An attempt was made to check the onset of possession, but this was only temporarily successful and the symptoms returned of dreams of wild animals, manic fugues, emaciation, glaring eyes and a snake draped around the victim's neck. He claimed possession by male ancestors, had visions of a 'boa-constrictor' which was captured by his people on his instructions, and wandered among rivers. But there are compensations for the discomforts of possession. 'A prophet of reputation possesses very great influence. The people reverence him not only because he is believed to enjoy the peculiar favour of the spirits; but because he enjoys the tremendous power of charging a person with so-called "witchcraft"' (Shooter 1857, 195).

(3) Callaway (1870, 259–60):

The condition of a man who is about to be an *inyanga* is this: At first he is apparently robust, but in process of time he begins to be delicate, not having any real disease, but being very delicate. He begins to be particular about food, and abstains from some kinds, and requests his friends not to give him that food, because it makes him ill. He habitually avoids certain kinds of food, choosing what he likes, and he does not eat much of that: and he is continually complaining of pains in different parts of his body. And he tells them that he has dreamt that he was being carried away by a river. He dreams of many things, and his body is muddled (*dungeka* – stirred up or made turbid – like a river) and he becomes a house of dreams. And he dreams constantly of many things, and on awaking says to his friends 'My body is muddled today. I dreamt many men were killing me; I escaped I know not how. And on waking one part of my body felt different from other parts; it was no longer alike all over'. At last the man is very ill, and they go to the diviners to enquire. The diviners do not at once see that he is about to have a soft head. (Note: a soft head, that is, impressible; diviners are said to have soft heads) . . . .

So the man may be ill two years without getting better; perhaps even longer than that. He may leave the house for a few days, and the people begin to think he will get well. But no, he is confined to the house again. This continues until his hair falls off. And his body is dry and scurfy; and he does not like to anoint himself. People wonder at the progress of the disease. But his head gives signs of what is about to happen. He shows that he is about to be a diviner by yawning again and again, and by sneezing again and again. And men say 'No! Truly it seems as though this man was about to be possessed by a spirit'. This is also apparent from his being very fond of snuff; not allowing any long time to pass without taking some . . . .

Callaway goes on to describe further symptoms, including the shedding of tears, crying aloud, and the composing of the special song – 'In this state of things they daily expect his death; he is now but skin and bones, and they think that tomorrow's sun will not leave him alive . . . .' The possessed person sleeps badly, leaps around, disturbing others, and he sings constantly. 'At length another ancient *inyanga* [diviner] is pointed out to him [that is, by the *itongo* (ancestral spirit) in a dream]. At night whilst asleep he is commanded by the *itongo,* who says to him, "Go to so-and-so, go to him, and he will churn for you emetic *ubulawo* [medicine], that you may be an *inyanga* altogether". Then he is quiet for a few days, having gone to the *inyanga* to have ubulawo churned for him; and he comes back quite a different man, being now cleaned, and an *inyanga* indeed.'

Of more modern descriptions, probably the most comprehensive are to be found in the accounts given by Bryant (1917), *The Collector* (1911), Asmus (1939), and Kohler (1941). *The Collector* gives a clear account of initial symptoms of *ukuthwasa,* the commonest signs being excessive belching and yawning and 'having a certain creeping or nervous sensation, especially in the region of the shoulders'. In the 'sealing off' of ancestral spirits river symbolism recurs. If a woman is

Plate 8 Young male neophyte in Zulu ancestral spirit cult. The goatskin strips crossed on the chest indicate the presence of the ancestors

Plate 9 Young male neophyte in Zulu ancestral spirit cult, in female attire. There is a transvestite stage in initiation

Plate 10 (*below*) Female *is angoma* medium (Zulu) dancing in dissociated state

affected it is particularly difficult for the diviner consulted to find out whether the possessing spirits are those of her husband's or her own ancestors. Any determined spirit can prevail against the husband's efforts to have his wife 'closed' to its influence. More than one spirit may be involved in the possession but there is always a leading spirit and the initial symptoms of possession will be the same as those which accompanied the death of the ancestor who has this role. [In my own experience all possessing spirits have been male, though Kohler reports spirits of both sexes as casual among the Bhaca]. Finally, *The Collector* states that the crying fits (*umbayiso*) – see below – rarely precede the *ukuthwasa* state. When this does happen the subject is regarded as lucky, as she will escape the more serious consequences to her health of possession, and will simply cry out and go into a fugue state, finding herself at the dwelling place of her senior training diviner.

Asmus (1939) shows, as do the other writers cited, that becoming an *isangoma* cannot be achieved through any apprenticeship, unlike the situation with herbalists (*izinyanga zokwelapha*) in Zulu society, and stresses that the calling is open to any person of whatever sex, age or status. His account is precise and describes the placing of the crossed strips of magical goatskin over the shoulders of the novice, the plaiting of the hair into separate strings, and 'amongst other things he is ordered [by the spirits] to fetch a snake from a deep pool. He runs to the stream and throws himself into the water. The people, who come running, see him emerge from the river painted all over with different coloured clay – the work of the ancestor spirits – which they have performed down there in the depths of the waters. Around the neck of the *isangoma* coils a python, or perhaps a mamba, one of the deadly snakes to be found here'. [My translation].

I feel that there may be some symbolic connection here between the python theme so common in accounts of *ukuthwasa* and the fact that the *inkata*, the central and most important sacred object of the Zulu (see Asmus, 1939), was covered in the skin of a python. In most accounts the power-giving snake is a female python – an intriguing parallel with the Delphic pythoness of the ancient world.

Asmus also suggests that heightened states of sensibility may well be engendered by the rigorous training of *izangoma* and, from my own field work, I think that this is very probable. Bryant (1917), found that 90 per cent of all diviners, in the early part of this century, were married women (this is still the case), and that an even higher proportion of all diviners used the 'twenty questions' method of divination: [To every statement made by the diviner the surrounding people, including the petitioner, answer 'We agree'. Sometimes the diviner requires them to clap their hands or beat two sticks together as they give the response. Slight nuances of emphasis in response are picked up by the diviner who thus arrives at a satisfactory diagnosis. The procedure bears a remarkable resemblance to that devised by the Russian psychologist, Luria (1932), to accompany the use of word association tests]; the remainder, though the *ukuthwasa* process and training are much the same, divined directly, the spirits speaking in a high whistling tone through the possessed medium.

Finally, from one of my own informants, it emerged that *ukuthwasa* could be deliberately induced as a therapeutic procedure:

> I have never had the crying ailment, but I had *ukuthwasa*. My forehead used to ache. Then my heart would ache. I had many dreams. This happened after I was married and had three children. There are two main causes of *ukuthwasa*: firstly if you are continually bewitched (ensorcelled) with earth from the graves of your ancestors, you may get ill even to the extent of dying. If you are treated in good time this may be converted to *ukuthwasa*. Secondly, it may happen that you are born with the spirits of your ancestors. These cause you to *thwasa* and they are always benevolent towards you. You may have the crying ailment, but this is not a necessary condition.

So much then for the ethnography of *ukuthwasa* possession. Again and again we find: physical symptoms which include avoidance of food and consequent emaciation, behavioural symptoms of fugue states, belching and yawning; and psychological events which include hallucinations and the dreaming of stereotyped dreams of rivers, snakes, etc. All these coincide with the Zulu social expectation and are built into the local explanations in terms of the behests of the possessing ancestor spirits. Women are the chief sufferers and the whole *izangoma* cult is female centred, male neophytes being transvestite and copying the ways of women. Social power is gained by the possessed person whose 'ways are clear'. The great stereotyping of the processes is very evident and, psychologically, it is odd that there has not been more distortion, by the errors intrinsic to 'serial reproduction' (Bartlett, 1932), through the centuries of the cult's existence. Doubtless the closed society and 'apostolic succession' of the *izangoma* contribute to this invariance.

Why do certain people become possessed? Certain very simple explanations have been offered by social anthropologists in terms of stresses in the social order and the acquisition of greater status through possession, while psychiatrists have tended to regard the state as simply the culturally coloured manifestation, in behaviour, of psychopathological states well known to Western medicine, frequently of a hereditary character. Of the first group Gluckman (1950), Hoernle (1937), Sundkler (1961), Kuper (1947) and Ashton (1943) (the last two of these were dealing with essentially similar states among the Swazi and Sotho, respectively) are, to all intents and purposes, agreed that 'to become diviners is for pagan Zulu women the only socially recognized way of escape from an impossible situation in family life; it is also the only way an outstanding woman can win general social prestige' (Gluckman, 1950).

Ashton's Sotho informants themselves stressed the gainful nature, in psychological terms, of ancestor possession and becoming a diviner, and thus accounted for the seven to one preponderance of women diviners. Their possessions, they say, 'are a reaction to neglect or to the dullness of women's lives; by becoming the centre of these ritual dances, and by forcing their relatives to give them occasional feasts, they hope to attract attention and to liven their existence. Women, they say, have duller lives than men, and being as they are the passive element in social and sexual relations, they are more liable to neglect; consequently they are more attracted to this institution than men. This is a plausible theory, but one which I have not sufficient data to prove' (Ashton, 1943, 32).

A very different type of explanation is offered by Laubscher (1937: 229), working with predominantly Thembu patients in a mental hospital, who plumps firmly for the essentially biogenetic and psychotic nature of the phenomena:

> The psychopathological antecedents in the forebears and relatives of the hospital patients are clearly in evidence in these family histories and support the inference that *ukuthwasa*, as it is popularly conceived, as well as *ukupambana* [stuporous states], are recognized psychopathological conditions well known to psychiatry. The hereditary bases of the biogenetic psychoses are thus further multiplied in this culture by the custom of second and third cousin marriage.

Incidentally, as Zulu do not marry close kin, the last sentence would not hold for them and weak strains should, theoretically, be 'bred out'. Laubscher's argument runs, in effect: biogenetic psychoses run in families – the relatives or friends of patients in my mental hospital state that *ukuthwasa* has appeared among the relatives of patients – therefore *ukuthwasa* states are biogenetic psychoses. Not only is the logic faulty but Laubscher's 'facts' were derived from a brief postal questionnaire to relatives or friends of patients whose replies might, in the extended polygynous family system, refer to individuals from a reference group of scores of 'relatives' and, in the absence of any control groups, little real proof of his hypothesis is adduced. It is not my intention to argue that there is no hereditary factor in *ukuthwasa* possession, but simply that any one to one equation, either in nosology or aetiology, with Western patterns of psychosis, is a gross over-simplification.

However, later in the same volume, we find: 'It is possible that the psychotics of the past have left their impressions on the memory of the race and these impressions have ultimately become the recognized form of behaviour and belief for most of those claiming mediumistic powers'. The psychological implications of this statement are not clear and any such Lamarckian or Jungian hypothesis is not, at present, testable.

Far more useful, at this stage, are the possibilities considered by Hammond-Tooke (1962) to explain *ukuthwasa* among the Bhaca.

(a) Possibly sufferers are neurotic and neurosis initiates the possession.

(b) Possibly the initial illness is organic and the traditional interpretation in terms of *ukuthwasa* is sufficient to lead to the rest of the process.

(c) Possibly such female functions as menstruation, pregnancy and the menopause may contribute to the high female incidence.

(d) Possibly 'a strong minded and intelligent' woman may find freedom from her common roles and the restraints of her husband.

(e) Possibly, as Hammond-Tooke found female diviners to be well-integrated individuals, intelligent and friendly, as against male diviners who appeared 'psychopathic', moody and probably homosexual, the causes might operate differentially between the sexes.

All these seem to me to be highly probable, in the light of my own research, and useful in that both social and individual causes are envisaged.

My own research was directed at elucidating the crying fits mentioned above. Three separate investigations were carried out, using questionnaires, interviews, and a form of the Thematic Apperception Test, designed specifically for the culture and the salient points of the investigation. Half of each of three large samples of Zulu women were found to report a history of the crying – a new disorder of this century. The crying is accompanied by an intense subjective feeling of fear, localized between the shoulder-blades, and a common precipitating cause is a feeling of pent-up anger. All women reporting having sufferred from the crying will be called 'cryers' throughout the rest of this essay; all others with no such history, 'controls'. For each of these categories definite and enduring patterns of personality were found. A woman who has cried once shares a great many characteristics with a woman with a lifetime of it, which she does not share with controls.

This topic is essentially peripheral to that of possession. Nevertheless, as I was investigating a 'Bantu Disorder' (in western terms, often possession or other psychogenic disorder – cf. Lee, 1950), against the background of a mission hospital in the Nqutu district of Zululand, it was inevitable that I should come into contact with the *izangoma* cult. Among my patients I had women with *ukuthwasa,* as well as others with other types of possession, and eventually it was common for patients with a wide range of behavioural disorders to be referred to me by the local *izangoma* they had consulted.

Within this context, then, I wish to examine certain of the statements and hypotheses that have been set down by previous enquirers in this field.

(1) *Possession is most commonly found in women.*

In my experience *ukuthwasa* is almost entirely confined to women, though males are occasionally encountered. The latter are almost certainly of homosexual bent and are usually young and unmarried at the initiation of their possession. I recall the news of the marriage of one male *isangoma* being greeted with Rabelaisian comment throughout the district. The possessed male will probably be trained by a female diviner, will adopt female dress and will speak in high-pitched tones. I found severe anxiety neurosis in roughly five per cent of all males of a hospital population, over two years, and in many of these cases the homosexual nature of their dreams was very clear (usually the dreamer was passive and was being attacked, sexually, or aggressively, by another male, sometimes his own male ancestors) (Lee, 1958). In general, I would agree with Hammond-Tooke that grosser pathology is to be expected in cases of male *ukuthwasa*.

In an extensive survey, based on 416 women and 148 men, I found a much higher incidence of 'Bantu disease' among women, roughly fifteen per cent of women claiming a history of minor possession, as against some five per cent of men. Disease attributed to sorcery was equally distributed, seventeen per cent and eighteen per cent, between women and men respectively. One specifically male disorder reported by Kohler (1941), *iqondo*, was rare in the area, found in about one male in a hundred, and, in any case, has none of the attributes of possession. Similarly, in dreaming, women showed, statistically significantly, a much higher reported incidence of unpleasant dreams (Lee 1958), so that, psychologically they would appear to be the sex more prone to overt behavioural disorder – the more vulnerable group. These rough figures should be cautiously regarded as the ages of the samples differed between the sexes. Although the sample was representative of the district, many more women appeared in the twenty-one to thirty age group. This is a function of the migrant labour situation, most of the men of working age being away in the towns.

Incidentally, the possibility that tertiary syphilis was causal in these psychopathological states was not confirmed, for positive Wassermann reactions were equally distributed between the sexes and though 'Bantu disease' was slightly more common among the twenty-four women with syphilis than in women free from the disease, no such relationship showed itself among the men. It would seem more likely that this slight tendency among women is not directly due to any causal role of syphilis (although this may contribute to infertility – frequently a precipitating cause of breakdown), but rather to the fact that a disordered sex life may lead to both venereal infection and neurosis (Lee, 1954).

(2) *Does ukuthwasa possession run in families? If so, is the incidence genetically or socially determined?*

Here my evidence is essentially oblique, as I have not specifically studied the family relationships of *izangoma*. And results showed the 'cryers' were no more prone to *ukuthwasa* possession than were the 'controls', the ethnographic evidence implying a relative immunity for cryers (*The Collector* 1911, cf. also Nadel 1946). As I found that the crying attacks were not so much hysterical as a very direct discharge of anxiety (Lee, 1954, 1961), with possible beneficial cathartic effects, this view may well be tenable, despite the fact that nearly all diviners are women and the crying fits are found in fifty per cent of women as against ten per cent of men.

But I had asked the question: 'have any of your blood relatives had *ukuthwasa?*' and the 'cryers', themselves possibly protected against *ukuthwasa* by their own condition or 'crying personality', showed many more such relationships than did the controls:

	YES	NO	
Cryers	21	18	$p = < .01$
Controls	26	46	

A rather neat 'control situation' exists here. In Zululand there is another kind of medical practitioner, whose training involves no unusual psychological experience. This is the herbalist, essentially a therapist rather than a diagnostician. In relationship to herbalists there were no significant differences between my criterion groups.

	YES	NO	
Cryers	21	17	$p = .41$
Controls	32	36	

In a recent predictive study, not yet published, of a random sample of 200 Zulu women, a rather similar result appeared in that, although 'cryers' were significantly more often related to both diviners and herbalists than were 'controls', *within* the crying group relationship to diviners was far more frequently found than relationship to herbalists. Space precludes any detailed discussion of the actual relationships established in this predictive study, but nearly all relatives cited as *ukuthwasa* sufferers were female, and the majority – from earlier generations – were related to the subjects through their fathers. Both 'cryers' and 'controls' reported, in a number of instances, sisters and half-sisters as *ukuthwasa* cases. One subject who had herself had *ukuthwasa* reported that her mother had also done so; another *isangoma* reported that her daughter had *ukuthwasa,* and these instances do not bear out Shooter's hypothesis (1857).

In both these studies we have the 'indigenousness' of the situation controlled. Both types of practitioners are equally ancient and traditional. Yet the 'cryers' are related, at a high level of statistical significance, to a psychopathological group from whose symptoms they are themselves relatively immune. In these circumstances it is unlikely that mere 'social infection' or imitation is responsible. A genetic weakness, capable of manifesting itself in either of the two ways, is much the more likely explanation, and Linton's (1956) hypothesis: 'data regarding mental disorders in other societies tend to suggest that there is a definite, though often not easily detectable, foundation in the organic realm for whatever psychiatric illnesses may become manifest on the behavioural levels', receives partial confirmation.

(3) *Given that there is a hereditary element in ukuthwasa, which might indeed have been suspected from the accounts cited earlier, are we dealing with frank 'organic' psychosis common in the West?* (cf. Laubscher, 1957).

Several facts seem to me to be against this explanation: (a) The *isangoma* diviner is a highly efficient person, intelligent and alert, and a remarkably high rate of spontaneous remission of psychosis would be needed to account for the emergence of such people from, say, a schizophrenically withdrawn condition. (b) In my research I found that visual and auditory hallucinations were very common among Zulu women. Over twenty per cent of women reported a history thereof. None of these showed any signs of psychosis, though many were anxiety cases. Hallucinations (common in *ukuthwasa*) do not carry the grave prognosis that they would in our society. Visions of 'the ancestors', 'angels', or 'babies' are legitimate expectations within the belief systems of this society as, indeed, is the dreaming of certain stereotyped dreams (Lee, 1958). (c) The symptoms that I have observed as preceding or accompanying the *ukuthwasa* state are usually those of an anxiety state, sometimes those of conversion hysteria. One of my patients, admitted to hospital with hysterical paraplegia, first persuaded me to 'seal off' her dreams with barbiturates (in a double blind trial with these I found that their efficacy was roughly half attributable to the tablets, half to suggestion!) then to 're-open her ways' with *nux vomica*. Eventually she became possessed by the spirit of her paternal grandfather, a very potent personage as he had been killed at the battle of Isandhlwana in 1879. She was then trained by a senior diviner, a process which included six months' isolation in a hut, and set up a lucrative practice in my back-yard. A fairly typical case, certainly not psychotic. (d) It is unnecessary to call in psychosis in hereditary disorder. A hereditary lability of autonomic function would be sufficient cause to explain most of the symptoms (cf. Jost and Sontag, 1944). (e) Severe neurosis would seem to be a more apt description of the state. A severe anxiety state is here followed by *anorexia nervosa* and the symptoms may be precipitated or exacerbated by *post partum* disturbance or glandular dysfunction. One additional fact which may be of significance is the excessive yawning of *ukuthwasa*. In my own work it appeared that 'cryers' shared this action with diviners, being much more prone to yawning attacks than were the controls. It is possible that we have to consider here ensuing hyperventilation tetany as contributory to both the physical and behavioural anomalies of both syndromes (cf. Wallace, 1961, in his treatment of 'Arctic Hysteria').

(5) *Can the 'anorexia nervosa' hypothesis serve to clarify the aetiology of 'ukuthwasa'?*

Let us first examine Western accounts of *anorexia* and follow this with some examination of the social and psychological position of the Zulu woman.

Mayer-Gross *et al.* (1955, 138–39) state:

> This (*anorexia nervosa*) is a condition almost confined to women in the years of adolescence and early adult life, although it also occurs rarely in young men .... The *constitutional factors* in aetiology are important. The patient will have shown signs in earlier years of hysterical tendencies, sometimes also minor obsessional traits, and there may be a family history of psychopathy or nervous illness .... *Physically* the patient is invariably thin and sometimes has lost so much weight that the skin seems to be lying loosely over bones only just beneath the surface .... The skin itself is dry and papery, without normal suppleness or elasticity .... There is amenorrhoea [common among Zulu women] .... Psychogenic factors also play an important part. The illness nearly always arises out of a *conflict situation*, e.g. an engagement to marry which the patient secretly does not feel willing to carry out, impaired relations with the parents ....
>
> The *anorexia* is profound. The patient has *no desire for food* of any kind, and most foods, especially the more nutritious, are regarded with repulsion .... Despite her physically reduced state, the patient

> nearly always shows a remarkable degree of *energy, alertness and initiative* . . . . She herself does not feel ill, and her *anorexia* is hardly so much a symptom to her as a guiding principle of her life . . . . There is no depression, nor any symptom of a schizophrenic kind; and it is hardly possible to mistake the condition for a psychotic state [italics in original].

Here we have a description almost identical with that of the condition of a diviner; the emaciation, scurfiness of the skin, etc. While it does not help us with the underlying aetiology of the *anorexia* (applying it to the Zulu) some hints may emerge from the causes cited. The family history is present in both disorders, and conflict situations, for the Zulu woman, abound (Lee, 1950, 1954, 1958, 1961).

Consider, also, the Freudian background to anorexia offered by Saul (1944, 274):

> In these cases it has been found that certain impulses which are rejected by the rest of the personality as intolerable because of guilt and shame are so closely associated with eating that food cannot be taken. In many cases these rejected impulses are of a sexual nature, for example, unconscious wishes to fellatio or cunnilingus or wishes for pregnancy . . . . In other cases not libidinal but aggressive impulses are in the foreground – grasping, envious, attacking desires. These are unconscious and are associated with biting and eating, which are inhibited because of guilt and shame.

Whatever the validity of such largely untestable 'depth' hypotheses, the purely descriptive fit is a close one, and it may be profitable to examine in greater detail the stresses inevitable in the life of Zulu women and some of their reactions to them. Anthropological implication is often that *ukuthwasa* is almost a matter of deliberate choice by the possessed person. But it is dreaded. I have had to try to treat women in hospitals and health centres who felt themselves threatened by impending ancestral possession and who were desperately seeking any way to avoid it. I asked 114 women: 'Do you think that diviners have a profitable life?' and 'Would you like to be one?'. Only 6 thought the life profitable, though in purely economic terms I found that the average Zulu tended to have consulted *izangoma* on at least two occasions in his or her life. Nobody wished to be a diviner – 'No. Possession by the ancestors is an unpleasant life'.

So that the choice whether to become a diviner, if there is a psychological choice involved, is almost certainly at an unconscious level. It seems to me likely that the basis of the condition is neurosis and that the degree of conscious willingness to become a diviner varies inversely with the severity of the neurosis. The relatively healthy, active and intelligent woman may indeed gain authority and prestige from the process and be able to enact a more 'male' role, all formal authority and religious observance being entirely the prerogative of Zulu men; and she is the less likely to fear the condition the more she resents, consciously, any stresses or deprivations in her everyday existence. (It is noteworthy that all *izangoma* reported by my informants continued living with their husbands after their initiation, so that their independence is psychological rather than spatial.) On the other hand, the neurotic will be pushed – willy nilly – into *ukuthwasa* by her neurosis and, in her case, predisposition will be more important than immediately exciting causes attributable to socially induced stress.

There is a possible parallel to be drawn here with the *nomkumbulwana* ceremony, where male and female roles are reversed for one day, which anthropologists (cf. Gluckman, 1954) tend to take as a catharsis of the tensions of Zulu women's subservient roles. In investigating crying I had to try to assess the chief conflict and stress situations of their life. Initially I had expected that the 'new' disorder of crying would be linked with rapid social change, the absence of migrant labour husbands, etc. In this I was disappointed. The crying tended to take place when their husbands were at home (Lee, 1961), and nightmares of a sexual nature were more common in women with non-migrant husbands. Sex in marriage – as contrasted with premarital sexual activity – was not enjoyed and often dreaded. Conflicts existed between lack of children and poverty, and in the confusion of goals at menopause (Lee, 1958). The 'cryers' were apparently affected more by rather *less* dislodgment from their traditional rut than had been experienced by the controls. Their goals, while often Western in nature, could not be achieved because they were the less trained group. They had new aims but no means to secure them.

But the 'cryers' seem comparatively immune to *ukuthwasa*. How is one to explain the fact that many women, despite Government ban, still suffer *ukuthwasa* and become diviners when they may well (in terms of crying at least) come from the 'healthier' half of the population of Zulu women?

Of my two groups I asked three other questions: Firstly: 'What time of your life was the most happy?' Here it appeared that pre-adolescence or very early adolescence was regarded as the happiest time of life. Attitudes to marriage were commonly negative – 'Before I married' – 'When I was nine years old I was healthy and had no worries'. The bearing of children had, however, been the happiest time to some fifteen per cent of informants.

This last was reflected in the answers to the second question: 'If you had your choice, what would you like best in the whole world?' The 'cryers' tended to want babies, as did many of the controls. Health and money were also desired, but 'cryers' wished much more often for traditionally *feminine* gratifications, passively, while controls wished for independent success: 'To get a job and earn my own living', 'A business stand near a town', 'To be a Western doctor', 'To get a job as an industrial worker'. This ambitious group was far the more out-looking and adventurous and it would not be surprising, in personality terms, if diviners were drawn from their ranks. On the other hand, one 'cryer' did wish to become 'a Zionist diviner and healer' (see below).

This greater 'masculinity of wish' (on the part of the controls) appeared in answer to the third question: 'Have you ever wished that you were a man?' 'If so, when?' More than half the 'cryers' had wished to be male, as against just over a quarter of the controls, but for very different reasons. The former wished to avoid the painful lot of women – 'Always, I would not suffer childlessness', 'When I meet difficulties – I w ould be able to stand them better', 'When annoyed – I would be ableto fight'; the latter's motives were far more activist: 'When I see my brothers failing to control the home well – I would do better', 'Always – being an intelligent woman, I could improve the living of my family', 'When worried – I would be independent'. In the first instances, we have male powers desired to *avoid*, in the second we have a courting of experience, largely the prerogative of males.

So the passivity of 'cryers' probably precludes their making a success, in psychological terms, of *ukuthwasa*, and it *is* the more active and 'masculine' half of Zulu women who will be motivated to the status accruing to the diviner – though more modern outlets may be available to any highly trained in Western skills. To quote Gluckman (1954) 'The symbol of a successful initiation was the right to carry a shield and spear, those badges of manhood'. Today the equivalent might well be the owning of a small business, but such outlets, through Government legislation, are usually closed to rural Zulu women.

Further confirmation of the more active attitude of the controls was gained, obliquely, by the use of a Thematic Apperception Test picture stimulus depicting an *isangoma* stirring her medicines. All subjects showed a considerable knowledge of the practices of the cult, but only two out of eighty-four subjects described her as 'happy'. There was considerable difference between the groups in the full descriptions of the actions of the diviner in the picture. The 'cryers' tended to see her merely as stirring emetic or making medicine to 'clear her ways', the controls on the other hand introduced clients into their stories, and showed themselves as the group more capable of envisaging constructive action and dominance in a social situation of divination.

From all this we have, obliquely, possible evidence of statistical links between *ukuthwasa* and individual personality, but there are also some general 'anecdotal' considerations worth taking into account, if the early condition in *ukuthwasa* is regarded as *anorexia nervosa* (cf. Saul, 1944). We have seen that conflict is common concerning sex and aggression, that masculinity of role is desired, and we have aggressive and phallic symbols recurring in the state of *ukuthwasa.* Also, meat and beer, masculine prerogatives in everyday life and rarely available to pre-menopausal women, are freely enjoyed by *izangoma.* Husbands who have been bitten by their wives are often admitted to hospital. These last two sentences seem slightly dissociated, until one reflects that the Zulu language is filled with 'oral' terms. Hundreds of words in Zulu refer to the feel of substances in the mouth (Bryant, 1906; Doke and Vilakazi, 1948) – apprehension of outside stimuli is, in linguistic terms, predominantly oral rather than visual or tactile, and a possible corollary is given by the fact that the hundreds of words for 'oral aggression' (backbiting, slander, vilification, etc.) greatly outnumber the mere handful of words connected with physical aggression. This in a warrior nation. A possible connection may exist between this facet of the culture and the fact that the most serious and important form of possession is accompanied by disturbances in eating.

But all this is largely speculation and needs empirical verification. All that can legitimately be claimed at present is that it might be possible, along these lines, to illuminate the psychological background of ancestral possession.

III

I wish now to examine a modern modification of *ukuthwasa* possession, brought about by the conflicts of cultures, but probably fulfilling much the same purposes, both social and psychological.

This arises within the framework of the so-called separatist churches, of which over two thousand exist in South Africa. These are breakaways from orthodox Christianity and, roughly speaking, may be divided into two types, 'Ethiopian' (more consciously nationalistic and adapted to modern culture contact conditions), and the 'Zionist' type of sect, in which Christian tenets have been adapted to indigenous patterns of thought. There is no space to discuss either these syncretist sects or the possessions found therein in great detail, but a very good and full account can be found in Sundkler (1961).

In the Zionist churches possession is apt to be ascribed to the presence of *umoya,* possibly best translated as 'spirit' which – in my experience – is a transmutation of a collective ancestral spirit, although it is, naturally enough, within these nominally Christian sects, linked with ideas of the Holy Spirit of Christianity. To cite one of Sundkler's informants, a Zionist prayer-woman: 'The diviners [*izangoma*] defile the Christian faith, claiming that they too have the Holy Spirit'. Patients of mine who claimed, as good Zionists, to dream often of '*ingelosi*' – angels, on being pressed further, described these angels as ancestors wearing long white robes and, occasionally, wings!

So that despite all the Christian trappings and symbols involved, what we have here is essentially the old divination cult in a new form. The dreams of those possessed by The Spirit are very similar in content to *ukuthwasa* cases, water and snake symbols abounding, and the dress of the future diviner will be influenced by dreamed instructions. The crooks or staves carried by Zionist women may well be the counterpart of the spear and gnu's tail of the *izangoma*. Briefly, other parallels exist in the sacred dancing of Zionists, immersion in pools, either in baptismal or other rites [though pools are regarded as being inhabited by essentially maleficent monsters – cf. Sundkler, 1961], belching is common as an accompaniment to 'speaking with tongues' and prophesying by the Zionist diviner. Divination tends to be by direct speech of The Spirit, though 'amen' can serve the same purpose as 'we agree' when the audience's participation is required. Food taboos operate, pork and stimulants often being prescribed. Diagnoses of the causes of illness, a most important function in both cults because of the prevailing ill-health of the people, are likely to be couched in terms of sorcery, but therapy in the separatist churches would never consist in the 'replacement' of 'The Spirit' by foreign spirits such as *amandiki* or *izizwe*, as these latter are regarded as of the devil. Ancestral visitation is regarded as morally tolerable for it can suffer an easy change into angelic influence or 'The Spirit' and, as in the older cult, misfortune is readily ascribed by the Zionist diviner to the displeasure of the ancestral shades. I have come across several cases of *izangoma* who have become respected Zionist practitioners.

Generally, Zionist possession and divination cult activities would seem to be the less strenuous form, both physically and psychologically. There is seldom serious illness involved and I have found no record of sensory deprivation during training – the emphasis lies rather on baptismal rites and purification. Drumming in church services tends to be less protracted, and as a result dissociation is not so extreme, and cataleptic states – often found among *izangoma* – are rare. Separatist ritual and belief are much less stereotyped and great local variation can be found within an area ten miles square.

It should not be thought, however, that all women who join the separatist Churches will become diviners therein. In the 'crying' study cited above, thirty-eight out of one hundred and fourteen women had belonged to a 'Bantu Church' – sometimes to more than one, as fission and segmentation are very common in these sects, but of these only four had talked with tongues, and five claimed to have had '*Umoya*' – The Spirit. There was a slight tendency, not statistically significant, for the 'Bantu Churches' to be found more among the denominations claimed by 'cryers' than among the controls, but reports of any possession by 'The Spirit' were evenly distributed between the two groups.

However, we can again look for any association between *ukuthwasa* and membership of separatist churches, in genetic terms. In the later predictive study, which included a random sample of 176 Zulu women, the following figures emerged:

Question: Have any of your blood relatives had *ukuthwasa?*

CONTROLS (no history of crying: N: 88)		
Denomination:	YES	NO
Western Churches	12	38
Separatist sects (including Zionists)	8	11
(Zionists	5	2)
Pagans	10	9
CRYERS (a history of the crying fits: N: 88)		
Western Churches	23	27
Separatist sects (including Zionists)	11	5
(Zionists	6	3)
Pagans	14	8

While again it is obvious that 'cryers' are more likely to be related to sufferers from *ukuthwasa* than are the controls, irrespective of religious affiliation, it appears that *within* both groups, 'cryers' and controls, the members of separatist churches, *particularly the Zionists,* tend to be related to *ukuthwasa* cases. It would seem to be a most tenable hypothesis that any genetic weakness, giving a predisposition to neurotic disorder, may be accommodated by at least three types of behavioural reaction: (1) *ukuthwasa* and becoming a diviner (if the subject is of an active and aggressive personality), (2) crying out (if the subject is 'feminine' and passive), and (3) joining one of the 'Zionist'-type sects (possibly for women of an intermediate position as regards these personality characteristics).

Just as practically all 'cryers' and *izangoma* are female, so there is a great preponderance of women within the Zionist sects. Traditionally-minded chiefs often complain, 'These damned Zionists steal our women', and with good cause. Becoming a Zionist gives a Zulu woman considerably more independence – whether or no she becomes a diviner she can hold authority, preach and be respected in her own right. Should she become a diviner she is not isolated in her practice as is the *isangoma*, but will be sustained by the presence and support of her congregation. She will not have had to endure the stringent suffering and training of the older cult and she will not be under the same economic pressure to produce results – only token payments are made to *izangoma* for 'unsuccessful' divination. (Equally she is not as likely to make as much money for her own use.) In effect, the Zionist diviner's burden is the lighter.

However, it seems very likely that, in motivational terms, *ukuthwasa* and Zionist possession have many common elements – membership of both cults, in different ways, tending to act as a 'therapy' for both constitutional neurosis and immediate social deprivation. In both cases the guilts aroused by the omnipresent ancestors can be coped with and assuaged. In both cults – indeed in all the syndromes that we have discussed – the unconscious life of the individual woman may shape, formally, her actions in her society.

REFERENCES

ASHTON, E. H. 1943 *Medicine, magic and sorcery among the Southern Sotho.* Communications from the School of African Studies, No. 10, Cape Town, University of Cape Town.

ASMUS, G. 1939 *Die Zulu, Welt und Weltbild eines bauerlichen Negerstammes.* Essen, Essener Verlagsanstalt.

BARTLETT, F. C. 1932 *Remembering.* Cambridge, Cambridge University Press.

BEXTON, W. H., HERON, W., and SCOTT, T. H. 1954 'Effects of Decreased Variation in the Sensory Environment', *Journal of Canadian Psychology*, 8.

BRYANT, A. T. 1906 *Zulu-English Dictionary*, Pinetown, Marianhill Mission Press.

1911 'Zulu medicine and medicine men', *Annals of the Natal Museum*, 2.

1917 'The Zulu cult of the dead', *Man*, 95.

CALLAWAY, CANON 1870 *The religious system of the Amazulu.* Springvale, John A. Blair.

The Collector 1911 Pinetown, Marianhill Mission Press.

DOKE, C. M., and VILAKAZI, B. W. 1948 *Zulu-English Dictionary.* Johannesburg, Witwatersrand University Press.

FREUD, S. 1954 *The Interpretation of Dreams*, London, Allen & Unwin.

FYNN, H. F. (ed. D. McK. Malcolm). 1950 *The Diary of Henry Francis Fynn.* Pietermaritzburg, Shuter & Shooter.

GLUCKMAN, M. 1950 'Kinship and marriage among the Lozi of Northern Rhodesia and the Zulu of Natal', in: Radcliffe Brown, A. R. and Forde, D. (eds.) *African systems of kinship and marriage*, London, Oxford University Press.

1954 *Rituals of rebellion in South-east Africa.* Manchester, Manchester University Press.

HAMMOND-TOOKE, W. 1962 *Bhaca Society.* Cape Town, Oxford University Press.

HEBB, D. O. 1958 *A textbook of psychology.* Philadelphia, Saunders.

HECKER, J. F. C. 1844 *Epidemics of the Middle Ages.* London, G. Woodfall & Sons.

HOERNLE, MRS A. 1937 in: *The Bantu-speaking tribes of South Africa* (ed. I. Schapera), London, Routledge.

JOST, H., and SONTAG, L. W. 1944 'The genetic factor in autonomic nervous-system function', *Psychosomatic Medicine*, 6.

JUNOD, H. A. 1927 *The life of a South African tribe*. London, Macmillan.

JUNOD, H. Ph. 1934 'Les cas de possession chez les Va Ndau', *Africa*, 4.

KOHLER, M. 1941 *The Izangoma diviners*. Ethnological Publications, 9. Department of Native Affairs, Pretoria.

KUPER, H. 1947 *An African aristocracy*. London, Oxford University Press.

LAUBSCHER, B. J. F. 1937 *Sex, custom, and psychopathology*, London, Routledge.

LEE, S. G. 1950 'Some Zulu concepts of psychogenic disorder', *Journal of Social Research*, 1.

1954 *A study of crying hysteria and dreaming in Zulu women*. Unpublished thesis submitted for the Degree of Doctor of Philosophy in the University of London.

1958 'Social influences in Zulu dreaming', *Journal of Social Psychology*, 47.

1961 *Stress and adaptation*, Leicester, Leicester University Press.

LINTON, R. 1956 *Culture and mental disorders*, Springfield, Thomas.

LURIA, A. R. 1932 *The nature of human conflicts, or emotions, conflict and will*, New York, Liveright.

MAYER-GROSS, W., SLATER, E., and ROTH, M. 1955 *Clinical psychiatry*, London, Cassell.

NADEL, S. F. 1946 'A study of shamanism in the Nuba mountains', *Journal of the Royal Anthropological Institute*. 76.

SAUL, L. J. 1944 'Physiological effects of emotional tension', in: J. McV. Hunt (ed.) *Personality and the Behaviour Disorders*, New York, Ronald Press.

SHOOTER, J. 1857 *The Kafirs of Natal and Zulu country*, London, Stanford.

SUNDKLER, B. 1961 *Bantu prophets in South Africa* (2nd edition), London, Oxford University Press.

WALLACE, A. F. C. 1961 'Mental illness, biology and culture', in: *Psychological Anthropology* (ed. F. L. K. Hsu), Homewood, Dorsey Press.

EAST AFRICA

SPIRIT MEDIUMSHIP IN BUNYORO

© *John Beattie*

Elsewhere I have given some account of initiation into the spirit mediumship cult of the Banyoro, a Bantu people of western Uganda, and have discussed some of the cult's social aspects, and some individual possession ceremonies (Beattie, 1957, 1961, 1964b, 1966). Here I present a general account of the cult and of its social and cultural significance.

If, following Raymond Firth, we distinguish between spirit possession, spirit mediumship and shamanism, Nyoro culture can be said to exhibit all three, but spirit mediumship, that form of possession in which the possessed person 'is conceived as serving as an intermediary between spirits and men', is the most strongly institutionalized, and I deal chiefly with it here.

First I consider some of the kinds of spirits which, Banyoro believe, can affect living people, why and how they are thought to do so, and how their activity is diagnosed. I then describe how and by whom spirit activity can be dealt with. And finally I discuss the cultural and social context of spirit mediumship in Bunyoro: why do people still practise it so widely, and what are its more important social implications?

Nyoro traditional religion does not centre on an ancestral cult, like that of many Bantu peoples, though ancestral ghosts may be important. It is concerned with the worship of a pantheon of hero-gods called the Cwezi. In Nyoro traditional history these were a wonderful race of people who came to Bunyoro many generations ago, ruled the country for a few years, and then mysteriously disappeared, some say into Lake Albert. They are said to have been fair-skinned (a Nyoro historian suggests that they may have been Portuguese) and to have possessed marvellous wisdom and miraculous powers. It is said that when they vanished from the country they left behind them the spirit mediumship (*mbandwa*) cult, of which they themselves are the objects, through which the Nyoro people still retain access to the magical power and wisdom which they represented.

There are said to be nineteen of these Cwezi spirits (nineteen is an auspicious number for Banyoro). Even today almost all are believed to be potent forces in everyday affairs, and the names of most of them are known to everybody. As well as being linked as quasi-historical figures with the early beginnings of Nyoro society and culture, some of them are also associated with certain elemental aspects of the environment, like the early Greek gods. Thus Rubanga is associated with thunder, Kagoro with lightning, Kalisa with cattle; Kazoba and Kiro respectively with the sun and night (the ordinary terms for which are *izoba* and *ekiro*). It has been suggested that the Cwezi gods are in fact no more than personifications of certain natural forces, and it is evident enough that whatever else they are, at least some of them are this.

Particular Cwezi are loosely associated with the small, more or less localized agnatic descent groups in which the Nyoro community was traditionally organized. Banyoro say that in former times these groups were very much larger than they are now, and every such group was associated with one, perhaps two, of the Cwezi spirits, depending on the clan to which its male members belonged. This spirit was called the 'household spirit' (*mbandwa* or *mcwezi w'eka*), or sometimes 'the trusted thing of the household' (*omwesigo gw'eka*), and one member of the group concerned was its initiated and accredited medium.

These Cwezi *mbandwa*, in their role as 'household' spirits, were supposed to be concerned primarily with the well-being, health, prosperity and, especially, fertility of the agnatically centred groups with which they were associated. It was believed that if they were neglected they might bring illness or other misfortune on the members of the group. Even today diviners sometimes attribute such a misfortune as a woman's miscarriage to the neglect of her traditional 'family' or group spirits, especially in the case of mission-educated Banyoro. But so long as possession ritual is performed periodically in the spirit's honour, appropriate sacrifices made, and a spirit hut or shrine maintained, the household spirit's influence is thought to be wholly beneficial. These Cwezi *mbandwa* are distinguished from all other spirits as 'white' *mbandwa* (*embandwa ezera*); for Banyoro the colour white symbolizes purity, virtue and auspiciousness, as it does for other peoples. These white *mbandwa*, they say, come to purify (or 'whiten'; the verb is the same, *okweza*) the homestead and to give it blessing, so that its members may be healthy, prosperous and fertile. The auspicious aspect of the traditional cult is also evident from the requirement that the household medium should be a gentle and well-behaved person (*muculezi*), preferably initiated into cult membership as a young girl (or less often a boy), and he or she is treated with deference by all the other members of the household, even by the household head (*nyineka*), who traditionally wields supreme authority in the home.

Though the number of 'white' Cwezi spirits, mediated through the traditional Nyoro 'group' cult, remains constant, there is in addition a large and increasing number of 'black' *mbandwa* (*embandwa eziragura*), which are not the objects of the traditional cult, but which are rather thought of as 'catching' individuals more or less haphazard. These are thought on the whole to be inimical rather than beneficial. All of these 'black' spirits are said to be of foreign origin. Some of the older ones, like Irungu, the spirit of wild animals and the bush, are believed to have come from the regions north of the Nile; others, like Kapumpuli or Kaumpuli, the spirit of plague, from neighbouring Buganda. But an even larger number derive from the context of social change and culture contact, which during the past three-quarters of a century or so Banyoro have undergone with more rigour than most African peoples. Such modern spirits include Kifaru, the *mbandwa* of military tanks (*kifaru* is the Kiswahili word for rhinoceros); Ndege, the *mbandwa* of aeroplanes; Njungu, the *mbandwa* of 'Europeanness'; Mpolandi, the *mbandwa* of 'Polishness', and many others (for a fuller list see Beattie, 1961). The last is of particular interest: during the last World War a considerable number of expatriate Poles were accommodated for a time in a large camp near Masindi in Bunyoro. So large a concourse of Europeans was a new and alarming phenomenon to Banyoro (who like other East African peoples feared that the Europeans' ultimate object was to eliminate them and take their land for themselves), and it was not long before it became assimilated to the traditional *mbandwa* cult.

It is worth stressing that the words Mpolandi and Njungu denote abstract concepts ('Polishness', 'Europeanness') and not actual Poles or Europeans, the terms for whom are *Mupolandi* and *Mujungu*.

Mediums possessed by these *mbandwa* are not thought to be possessed by actual individuals; *mbandwa* spirits are not people, though they are imbued with quasi-human attributes. What they are possessed by is the generalized force or power by virtue of which Poles, or other Europeans, are thought to be what they are.

But as well as *mbandwa* spirits, both black and (decreasingly) white, the ghosts (*mizimu*, sing. *muzimu*) of dead people may, Banyoro believe, affect the living, and they too can only be dealt with through spirit possession and mediumship. Like most other spirit agencies, the activity of ghosts is thought to be generally inimical (though there are exceptions: see Beattie 1964b, 128). It would be surprising if it were otherwise: for Banyoro, as for most people, recourse to the supernatural is usual only when things go wrong. Strictly, Banyoro cannot be said to have an ancestral cult (though the father's ghost is regarded as especially important); few commoners can remember the names of their forebears for more than two or three generations back. Ghostly activity is generally diagnosed on the basis of known or presumed social relationship, and if a person dies with a grudge against someone whom he believes to have wronged or neglected him, a percipient diviner may well attribute any misfortune which subsequently befalls the latter to the offended ghost.

It is natural that in most cases where ghostly activity is diagnosed the ghost should be a dead kinsman, or less often an affine, of the victim, for kinship obligations are onerous and highly regarded – though decreasingly honoured in recent times – and few people can be sure that they have not at some time or other neglected or offended a deceased kinsman. But the ghosts of 'outsiders' are also much feared. Thus it is said that a sister's son's ghost can 'finish off a whole household' – in Bunyoro 'sisters' sons' (*baihwa*) are regarded as both 'outsiders' and kin (Beattie, 1958). In traditional times, also, the ghosts of household slaves, who were usually war captives, were regarded as especially dangerous. Here as in other contexts Nyoro culture seems to invest with ritual power categories of people who in everyday affairs occupy inferior and subordinate social status.

As in the case of the *mbandwa* spirits, the relationship between ghosts and people is thought to be a reciprocating one. Ghosts are dependent on humans for the services they need, just as humans' well-being is dependent on the ghosts' goodwill, or at least upon the withholding of their ill-will. Thus a ghost, like an *mbandwa* spirit, is said periodically to be 'hungry', and 'to want meat', in which case the blood sacrifice of a ghost or chicken may have to be made to it. Or it may require one of the household goats (it must be a black one) to be dedicated to it. It will almost certainly require the building of a small spirit hut. And without a medium as its vehicle it cannot speak with the living and convey its needs to them. But unlike the traditional *mbandwa* spirits some (though not all) kinds of ghosts can be destroyed by men: I describe below how this can be done.

There are other kinds of spirits which can 'possess' people and communicate through mediums. Thus the ghosts of certain animals slain by hunters, such as hippos, may sometimes possess their killers (Beattie 1963b), and it is said that certain powerful medicines used in sorcery and associated with animal horns (*mahembe*) can assume a kind of personality and afflict their victims by entering into them. But by far the most important kinds of possessing spirits are the various types of *mbandwa* and the ghosts of the dead, and in what follows I deal only with them. What they all have in common is that they are thought of as powerful, extra-human agencies, representing potentially dangerous forces which men have no ordinary, empirical, means of controlling. By spiritualizing and so in some degree 'personalizing' these forces men may hope to come to terms with them, sometimes even to control them.

As already noted, spirits, whether *mbandwa* or *mizimu*, usually manifest themselves in situations of misfortune. A man becomes ill, his children sicken and die, his crops fail, he loses his money or his job; a woman has repeated miscarriages or loses her babies in infancy (both all too frequent, alas, in Bunyoro): all these misfortunes and many more still bring Nyoro peasants to the diviners to find out what malevolent agency is responsible. Divining in Bunyoro is a part-time occupation (for a fuller account of it see Beattie, 1964a); most diviners are also small-scale peasant cultivators like their neighbours, and although they vary greatly in skill and prestige there are several in every Nyoro community. Most are also initiated members of the spirit cult, being mediums of one or more of the traditional Cwezi *mbandwa* (whose activities are not restricted to the clans with which they are particularly associated), and usually of a number of the newer 'black' *mbandwa* spirits as well. There are many different techniques of divination, but the most popular is by throwing nine cowry shells on a goatskin mat and interpreting the ensuing pattern. Also popular, but more expensive, is divination through spirit mediumship itself; some spirits (though not the traditional 'white' Cwezi ones) can divine for clients when 'on the head' of their mediums.

Whatever the mode of divination, the diviner is likely to attribute his client's troubles to one of three broad types of agencies; sorcery, some kind of *mbandwa* spirit, or a ghost. If sorcery is diagnosed, as nowadays is very likely, the question of spirit mediumship does not arise; sorcerers are people as their victims are, and they can be dealt with as such (for a brief account of sorcery in Bunyoro see Beattie, 1963a). But if the activity of either a *mbandwa* spirit or a ghost is diagnosed, it can only be dealt with through the possession cult. The sufferer, or sometimes, as when the patient is a small child, his mother or other appropriate representative, must be, or appear to be, possessed by the offending spirit, and must generally, also, act as the spirit's medium and mouthpiece. Only when the spirit has been persuaded or otherwise induced to manifest itself through possession can it be properly dealt with, and its harmful effects on its victim ended.

This 'cure' can be achieved in either of two ways. Either the attacking spirit can be induced to leave its victim's head and then be destroyed, or it can be persuaded to say what it wants through its medium, who thereby enters into a more or less permanent relationship with it. Only a few kinds of lesser spirits and ghosts can be destroyed, and even then the operation is said to be a highly dangerous one. The powerful Cwezi *mbandwa* are, of course, immortal, and the other major *mbandwa* spirits, including most modern ones, are similarly indestructible; the only course open to their victims is to enter into an enduring relationship with them as their mediums. Of ghosts, only those of persons unrelated or only very distantly related to their victims, strangers, household slaves (*bairu rubale*), blood partners (*banywani*), and some affines, can be 'captured' and destroyed. Like the major *mbandwa*, the ghosts of close relatives or spouses can only be dealt with by entering into a lasting mediumistic relationship with them.

Doctor-diviners (*abafumu*, sing. *mufumu*) practise various techniques to induce a 'destructible' ghost to leave its victim, which it often does under considerable protest, uttered, through its victim as medium, in a falsetto voice and in a special 'ghost' vocabulary. Once extracted, it may be deftly imprisoned in a pot or other receptacle, and buried, left far away in the bush, or burned. If the last course is chosen the fire must be a strong one, for if it is not the ghost may escape as the ropes which bind the pot are burnt, and if it does so it may avenge itself terribly on its would-be destroyers (for detailed accounts of such ghost-disposal activities see Beattie, 1964b).

But generally the patient or his representative must enter into an enduring mediumistic relationship with the spirit concerned. This usually involves a lengthy and expensive course of initiation, in which several established mediums participate, and which culminates in manifestations of possession and mediumship by the novice. After this, he is himself an accredited medium, and he may if he wishes participate profitably in the initiation of others, and (if he has been initiated into the cult of a 'divining' *mbandwa*) he may even set up as a part-time diviner himself. It seems that in pre-European times initiated mediums formed what were virtually corporate groups or guilds, stressing their difference from ordinary people, and conscious of strong mutual loyalties. But nowadays mediumship is a much more individualistic and clandestine affair, partly owing, no doubt, to half a century's rigorous repression by both Government and missions. Nevertheless its group aspects are still strongly stressed in initiation ritual.

This ritual (there is a fuller account of it in Beattie, 1957) may continue for several days, and it expresses a number of themes, of which the following seem to be the most important. First, there is the *rite de passage* aspect; the initiate's acquisition of a new status is marked by the dramatic enactment of death and rebirth, by his being given a new name, and by his being presented with a special headdress and other cult objects. Secondly, and associated with the foregoing, the ritual has a didactic or 'learning' aspect. The initiated has to acquire an unfamiliar vocabulary, different from ordinary Runyoro, which is said to be used by ghosts and *mbandwa* spirits. Also, and most important, he receives detailed instructions on how to simulate possession by the spirit or spirits whose medium he is to be. Third, complete secrecy is strongly stressed, and its importance is impressed on initiates by a severe formal cursing and 'uncursing'. Fourth, as already mentioned, the initiate's obligations to and fellowship with his co-mediums are strongly emphasized. And finally there are rituals designed to relieve the initiate from the dangerous ritual condition in which initiation (some of the procedures in which are abnormal and shameful by ordinary Nyoro standards) is believed to have placed him.

Once the novice has been properly initiated, and has undergone a mediumistic possession in the approved form, he (or more likely she) has achieved full status as a *mubandwa* or spirit medium. If she is a medium in the traditional Cwezi cult she would, traditionally, have been required to undergo further possessions periodically, involving mediumship, invocation, sacrifice and feasting, for the benefit of the local domestic group whose medium she is. If she is a medium for another *mbandwa*, or for several, she will likewise be required to undergo possession ritual from time to time, though for her private good (or for that of the member of her family on whose behalf she is performing the ritual), rather than for that of any kind of kin group. She will also be able to participate in other possession ceremonies and initiations, and to share in the feasts, and fees, which these involve. And if she – or he – is a medium for a 'divining' *mbandwa*, she can, as already noted, set up if she wishes as a part-time diviner.

Spirit possession and mediumship, then, are strongly institutionalized in Bunyoro, in a wide range of connected social contexts. Almost everyone knows that spirits of different kinds can be induced, by the usual techniques of singing, the rhythmic shaking of gourd rattles, drumming, etc., to 'mount into the heads' of their mediums; that they will indicate their presence in expected ways (by the use of particular regalia, a falsetto voice, a special vocabulary); that they will bless those present once their good-will is secured, ask for meat and drink, perhaps for an animal to be dedicated to them or for a spirit hut to be built; that they may make other requests, for example that kinsfolk live in amity, that a neglected obligation be discharged; and that some *mbandwa* spirits, when 'on the heads' of their mediums, may practise divination.

It follows from this that aspiring mediums are well aware of what is expected of them, and in any case they undergo a rigorous course of instruction during initiation. Can we say, then, that mediumship in Bunyoro is a fraud? Are mediums, who unanimously represent themselves to their clients as being wholly unconscious of what has transpired during their possessions, really so, or do they, as they put it, really 'see'? The evidence from Bunyoro shows that very often they do; as most Banyoro themselves are well aware much so-called possession is merely assumed. Banyoro also recognize that mediumistic diviners can make substantial profits – initiation into the cult of some *mbandwa* can cost up to £30 or more.

But even though Nyoro mediums are not always in a state of genuine dissociation when they appear to be so, it does not follow that they never are. And it may be suggested, further, that there are degrees of dissociation, of the extent to which an actor may be 'carried away' by the role he plays. Certainly the fire-lit darkness of the hut, the noise and steady rhythm of the rattles and drums, the singing, and (sometimes) the use of inhalants such as tobacco and other herbs, may well induce in the suggestible an abnormal psychic state. Even where it does not do so, or where it does so only in limited measure, it would be an over-simplification simply to assert without qualification that mediumship is a fraud. A Nyoro ex-medium informant perhaps provided the clue. She knew, she said, that *kubandwa* was deception. 'But', she went on, 'I thought that all the same it would be good for the patient if I did what I was required to do' (she was being initiated on behalf of her small child who was ill). What she saw herself as performing was, it might be said, a religious ritual or drama, and such a rite may be thought to be pleasing to the spirits and an effective means of influencing them, even when it is recognized (except, perhaps, by the very simple-minded) to be a dramatic performance, and not taken to be literally 'true'. This at any rate appears to be the way in which the matter is regarded in twentieth century Bunyoro. Perhaps the first beginnings of the drama in ancient Greece were not dissimilar.

I turn now to consider a little more fully the social and cultural contexts of Nyoro mediumship. First I ask, in terms of Nyoro values themselves, why after more than half a century of vigorous Mission and Government opposition the cult is still widely practised, though increasingly in its modern individualistic form rather than in its traditional 'group' context. Some of the answers have already been given. The old group cult, which was explicitly directed to the well-being and especially the fertility of the agnatically based local group, is now in decline, but most peasant Banyoro still live hard and uncomfortable lives, in which illness and sudden death are frequent, infant mortality rates are high, and modern medical facilities are few and far between. Most Nyoro peasants still lack the scientific education which might enable them to face these hazards and deprivations with resignation;

they continue to believe as firmly as their ancestors did that their lives and fortunes are constantly subject to the interruptions of powerful spiritual forces from outside themselves. But though these powers are sometimes capricious, they are not beyond human influence: being in some sense 'persons' they can be entered into relations with through the mediumship cult, and so dealt with in the familiar idiom of inter-personal social relationship.

Through the cult, also, Banyoro can cope in ritual and dramatic if not in 'practical' terms, with the new and alarming forces of social change. Thus (to revert to an example already quoted) during the colonial period every Munyoro knew that the highest power and prestige were vested in the intrusive Europeans, whom they both feared and respected. But there was little likelihood that the ordinary Nyoro peasant could ever become acquainted with a member of this dangerous and unfamiliar race, much less exert any kind of influence on them. But through the mediumship cult he could: 'Njungu', 'Europeanness', could be manifested in the familiar idiom of the traditional culture, and so could be accommodated and come to terms with. Had the cult's adaptive aspect been more fully understood by administrators and missionaries, their attitude to it might perhaps have been less repressive.

Another reason for the cult's popularity undoubtedly was simply that it was fun, at least sometimes. The mysteries of initiation were no doubt always secret, but possession ritual had its public aspect, at least in traditional times. People still talk of the great *mbandwa* ceremonies and feasts of the past, which often continued for days, and the dramatic and public representations of the various distinctive powers which were believed to influence human affairs may, as I have suggested elsewhere, almost be said to constitute a Nyoro traditional theatre. Banyoro are not alone in wishing to enliven a drab and monotonous existence (the life of a subsistence peasant agriculturalist is not a glamorous one) by occasionally dressing up in weird costume, dancing and making music, and performing dramatic, often exciting and even fearful rituals.

As elsewhere, also, participation in the Nyoro mediumship cult is largely, though by no means exclusively, something that women do. Of nine ex-mediums (converts to the revivalist and fundamentalist *Balokole* branch of the Native Anglican Church) whom I interviewed in

1953, eight were women. The social status of women in Bunyoro is low, as it is elsewhere in East Africa, and subservience and deference towards men is traditionally expected of them – an expectation decreasingly satisfied in modern times. But as mediums (and in Bunyoro women may and do mediate male as well as female spirits) they can command attention and respect, as well as providing themselves, if they practise divination, with a substantial source of income.

Even for men, mediumship may be associated with low social status in other contexts. The medium whom I knew best had high prestige as a diviner (he had served a prison sentence for practising the proscribed *mbandwa* ritual), but outside this role he was a weak and ineffectual person, looked down on by his neighbours because he lived as a dependent in his wife's father's homestead, and had not, as a respectable Nyoro husband should, paid full bridewealth and taken his wife to live in his own village.

I have noted that divination can be a source of substantial profit to those who show aptitude for it, and this, too, may well be a reason for sharp-witted men and women to take up the cult professionally; it is certain that medium-diviners in Bunyoro do not lack clients. And there is, lastly, one other reason – or at least Banyoro believe so – for taking up mediumship, and this is in connection with sorcery. If a man wishes to injure or kill another, he can do so either by paying a medium-diviner to send a spirit to inflict his enemy, or by himself becoming a shaman, through initiation into the cult, and doing so himself. This, however, is believed to be a recent use, or abuse, of the mediumship cult, and the 'white' Cwezi spirits have no part in sorcery; only such new and dangerous spirits as Kifaru can be used in this way.

These then are some of the grounds on which Banyoro still practise and have recourse to the *mbandwa* cult. I now ask, finally, what are the actual implications of cult activity, both psychological and cultural, whether Banyoro are aware of them or not? Since manifest and latent function may sometimes coincide (and Banyoro themselves are by no means naive sociologically) some of these implications have been dealt with in preceding paragraphs. Though most of us would say that spirits do not exist, at least in the forms in which Nyoro peasants conceive them, and so they cannot have the powers attributed to them, none the less it is true that cult beliefs and practices do provide a kind of security; they do provide a means of coping with adversity and with the stresses of social change where practical techniques for doing so are inadequate or non-existent; possession does afford a kind of catharsis or (in Nyoro terms) 'purifying'; and the cult does provide drama and entertainment, as well as, for some, financial profit.

Less obvious, perhaps, is the cult's importance as a powerful force for social conformity. Some of its sanctioning aspects were noted earlier: the ghosts of dead kin seek to uphold kinship values of mutual co-operation and solidarity; the 'white' *mbandwa* are concerned to maintain the social cohesion of the groups which are dependent on them. As in many cultures, illnesses or other misfortunes are generally thought to be due to someone's fault. Through divination the fault may be identified, and, sometimes at least, restitution can be made. While they are in the heads of their mediums, spirits may admonish the living and may require them to fulfil neglected obligations. And to disobey the injunctions of a spirit to which a present misfortune is attributed would be to invite disaster.

Turning, lastly, to the cult's aspect as a system of belief, in traditional terms at least it makes sense. Banyoro are not metaphysicians, and their cosmology is not the result of scientific 'model-building' on the Western pattern. But their traditional world view is nevertheless a consistent one in its own terms. Their universe has a spiritual as well as a material aspect; it is a world of forces which although their effects are manifest are not themselves tangible. Force is in the last resort spirit, and in terms of the *mbandwa* cult, men, themselves spirits, can enter into and, sometimes, participate effectively in the unseen world of extra-human powers.

REFERENCES

BEATTIE, J. H. M. 1957 'Initiation into the Cwezi spirit possession cult in Bunyoro', *African Studies*, 16, 3.

1958 'Nyoro marriage and affinity', *Africa*, 28, 1.

1961 'Group aspects of the Nyoro spirit mediumship cult', *Rhodes-Livingstone Journal*, 30.

1963a 'Sorcery in Bunyoro', in: *Witchcraft and Sorcery in East Africa*, eds. J. Middleton & E. H. Winter, London, Routledge & Kegan Paul.

1963b 'Spirit mediumship and hunting in Bunyoro', *Man*, 63, 241.

1964a 'Divination in Bunyoro, Uganda', *Sociologus*, 14, 1.

1964b 'The ghost cult in Bunyoro', *Ethnology*, 3, 2.

1966 'Consulting a diviner in Bunyoro: a Text', *Ethnology*, 5, 2.

THE SHETANI CULT AMONG THE SEGEJU OF TANZANIA

Robert F. Gray

The East African coast as it extends along most of Kenya and Tanzania is occupied by a dozen or so tribal groups which are often spoken of collectively as Swahili peoples (Prins, 1961). One of these is the Segeju of Tanzania. Among the Segeju a cult of spirit possession occupies a prominent place in the native medical system and in the magico-religious life of the society. It is my impression from travelling through different parts of the coastal area that similar cults are found in most of the other Swahili tribes, but to my knowledge no description of the cult has previously been published. Therefore the primary purpose of this essay is to give a preliminary account of the cult as it appears among the Segeju.

The main features of the cult are as follows. The region is represented as abundantly inhabited by spirits known as *shetani* who are divided into eight or ten 'tribes' having different characteristics. Each spirit has a name and also a distinctive personality. Most are capricious or mischievous, and some are downright malignant. A spirit is capable of possessing a person in such a way as to cause mental disturbance and physical sickness. The victims of spirit possession are usually women, and this is regarded as the most common cause of sickness in women. If it is suspected that a person has been possessed by a spirit the diagnosis must be confirmed by divination. After that the spirit must be exorcised by forcing or cajoling it to vacate the victim. There are several methods for expelling the spirit, but the most popular is a ritual dance. A woman who has been cured of spirit possession thereby gains membership in a society of other former victims. This group of women takes a prominent part in the dancing and other ritual connected with an exorcism. These women enjoy considerable prestige in their own village, the more so as the ritual is a costly affair, beyond the reach of most of the village women, and their superior status is even recognized in other villages.

The Segeju live in some 25 villages strung along the coast between the port of Tanga and the Kenya border. The tax register in 1956 listed 2,000 tax payers, and the total population was estimated by the government-appointed chief – the Jumbe Kuu – at 8,000. All but two or three of the villages are located on or very near the shore of the Indian Ocean, and the principal occupation is fishing. The Segeju are keenly aware of their tribal identity. Marriages outside the tribe are uncommon and few people of other tribes are to be found in Segeju villages. As an index of their solidarity, the Segeju have elaborated a tribal history, mostly legendary, going back to ancient origins in Arabia (Baker, 1949). According to Portuguese records, the Segeju, under the same name, were living on the East African coast as early as the sixteenth century (J. Gray, 1950). The largest village and the administrative headquarters for the tribe is Moa, with about 400 houses, four mosques, five shops, and a modern cement-floored fish market. The smallest villages are hamlets of ten or twelve houses. My observations were made mostly at three villages – Moa, Sibutuni, a medium-sized village, and Bomandani, a small village of thirty houses, which is the home of one of the leading medicine men of the tribe.

About half the men at Moa are directly engaged in fishing, and most of the others work at some related occupation such as boat-building, preparing fishing equipment, or marketing and transporting fish. At the smaller villages an even higher proportion of the population are fishermen. In addition to fishing, the Segeju also plant subsistence crops – maize, sorghum, millet, rice, and cassava – and cultivate and harvest coconuts, both for domestic consumption and as a cash crop. These crops, however, do not provide sufficient vegetable food to last the whole year; they must be supplemented with food purchased with money obtained from the sale of fish.

The entire population of the tribe is Muslim. At the time of my visit, the only Christian family in the tribal area was that of the medical dresser at the Moa dispensary, and his presence was resented by the villagers. Although they think of themselves as orthodox in their faith, abstaining strictly from alcohol, for example, some of their Islamic practices, as we shall see later, are mixed with pagan elements, more noticeably in the smaller villages. Every village has a mosque where the people pray on Friday under the leadership of a *mwalimu* (pl. *walimu*, 'teacher'), who is also usually the teacher at the village Koranic school; but only at Moa is the full weekly programme of ritual carried out: there each day the five calls to prayer are chanted from the main mosque by the *mnadi sala* ('caller to prayers'). When I was there about twenty pious men attended this mosque for prayers daily without fail, and a hard core of five or six older men frequented the place almost constantly. On Thursday night there is a long service for the young people, called *Maulidi* – a chanted liturgy under the direction of a religious official with the title of *Imamau*. Most of the people, however, limit their observances to Friday, which is a day of rest for the fishermen.

Most of the Segeju men and a few women can read and write a little Arabic, which they closely identify with Islam, but only two or three men at Moa really understood Arabic. Every Segeju child is supposed to study at Koranic school, and a fair number actually finish the course, which lasts from two to four years depending on how apt the pupil is. Moa has two schools where the children sit cross-legged on the ground for an hour or two every morning and afternoon, reciting passages from the Koran and copying Arabic letters and words on a board with pot-black. Some of the students learn to adapt Arabic script to the writing of Swahili, and these people are literate in a limited sense. All the villages have their own Koranic schools, but in the smaller villages the teachers are less competent and the instruction more cursory.

The *shetani* spirits, with which we are concerned in this paper, are thought to be creatures recognized in orthodox Islamic doctrine. The learned men of Moa pointed out to me that the name *shetani* is derived from Arabic *sheitan* – the name of a host of demons ruled by Iblis the Devil. According to the *Shorter Encyclopedia of Islam* the demons known as Shaitan and Djinn are mentioned in the Koran in such contradictory ways that Muslim scholars have never been able to agree on their nature and powers. Thus it is not surprising that different Segeju informants gave somewhat different accounts of *shetani*. On several points there was fundamental disagreement. For example, many of the people believe that a *shetani*, particularly one acting in the service of a sorcerer, can cause the death of its victim; whereas the *walimu* and other learned men deny this, affirming that life and death are solely in the hand of God.

Shetani are thought to be divided into tribes (*kabila*, pl. *makabila*) which are usually named according to the region or human tribe of their origin. The lists of tribes differ slightly from village to village. Bomandani is frequented by the following eight tribes of *shetani*: Jini (spirits of the sea), Nyare (a tribe of local origin), Kipemba (from the island of Pemba), Kimasai (left behind when the Masai of the interior raided the coastal villages), Mafira, Kibwengo, Ovyo, and Kigala.

Jini (from Arabic, Djinn), also known as Ruhani, inhabit the sea and are quite different in character from all other *shetani*. They are of the utmost importance in the lives of fishermen, regulating the catches of fish and determining the safety of the fishermen at sea. Some informants deny that Jini are *shetani* at all, stressing the contrasting characteristics of the two groups of spirits. Jini, for instance, although invisible, have human form, while other *shetani* are formless like the wind. Jini are circumcised Muslims, while other *shetani* are described as pagans or children of the devil, depending on the context. However, there are good and bad Jini, malicious and benevolent. All misfortunes and disasters at sea, and also good luck, are attributed to Jini. When a fisherman dives into thirty feet of water for his fish trap, around which may be lurking sharks, he fortifies himself with the thought that sharks are under the control of Jini: if the Jini are favourably disposed towards him he will be safe; if unfavourable, no discretion or effort on his part can save him from his fate.

Fishermen make frequent offerings to Jini, usually bread, rice, or bananas, at points in the sea where something has happened, good or bad, indicating the presence of Jini. One day while I was sailing with two Moa fisherman in an *ngalawa* (outrigger dugout canoe) the captain of the vessel dropped a half loaf of bread into the sea at a certain point. He explained that in the previous year a fisherman while dozing on the outrigger crosspole had lost his balance and fallen into the sea. He went down and was never seen again. It is believed that he was seized by Jini who inhabit that portion of the sea and made to join their colony; for Jini sometimes recruit human beings and transform them into Jini. There is an immense amount of lore concerning Jini, including eye-witness accounts of people who have seen and dealt with them. However, Jini do not enter the bodies of their victims and possess them in the manner of other *shetani*, and therefore this lore falls outside our present topic of spirit possession.

Ordinary land *shetani* are also referred to as *pepo*, which is a common Bantu word for 'spirit' or 'wind'. These *shetani* may lurk anywhere, but are specially fond of large trees, streams, and the sea shore. In general, *shetani* should be avoided, for they can cause sickness, accidents, and almost any kind of misfortune. They can also be helpful to a person by causing his crops to flourish, bringing him success in love, or harming his enemies; but such help is considered to be unwholesome and is never publicly solicited, as this would make people think one was a witch. Notions of witchcraft and sorcery have been mostly assimilated to the *shetani* cult among the Segeju. A sorcerer is a person who knows how to conjure a *shetani* for his own service, usually for the purpose of destroying a personal enemy, who, in the eyes of the community, may be a blameless person. People known to possess the evil eye are called witches (*mchawi*, pl. *wachawi*), but they are feared mainly for their control over *shetani*. The only person whose intimacy with a *shetani* is socially approved is the medicine man or *mganga*. His powers of exorcising demons depends largely upon the co-operation of his tutelary spirit.

Since *shetani* are creatures of Iblis, who is a rebel against God, they dislike and fear the Koran, which is the symbol of obedience to God. People avail themselves of this symbol for protection against the inroads of *shetani*. Thus, nearly all children, and also many adults, wear an amulet tied around the neck. It is a passage from the Koran copied on paper and sewed up in a little leather pouch. The other principal method of using the Koran is to write a verse on a board and then wash the ink off into a vessel. This fluid is thought to contain the essence of the written passage and may be drunk as medicine or sprinkled on a person endangered by a *shetani*.

A person possessed by a *shetani* is often thrown down at the onset as if by an invisible force. In other cases the presence of a *shetani* is first suspected with the gradual emergence of symptoms of sickness or mental abnormality. But in every case the diagnosis must be confirmed by divination before any measures are taken to expel the demon. I was able to learn the names of twelve diviners recognized by the Segeju. They all held the Islamic office of *sheikh* or *mwalimu*. Most diviners also teach at Koranic schools, though not all teachers are diviners. The diviner must first of all be told the exact day and hour of onset. He then consults a set of tables which provide him with a reference to a verse in the Koran. This text, if correctly interpreted, indicates whether the patient has indeed been possessed by a *shetani*, and if so to what 'tribe' the *shetani* belongs. It may also reveal other information about the *shetani*, but not its name: this can only be divulged voluntarily by the *shetani* itself. The elders state that in former times an astrological method of divination was used, which was superior to the present method; this involved direct observation of the stars. Although in 1956 no-one in the tribe was competent to practise the astrological method, one highly esteemed diviner at Sibutuni, Gunda Makame, with whom I discussed the technique of divination at length, had taken some preliminary instruction and hoped sometime to complete his course under a famous astrologer at Tanga.

The diviner writes his diagnosis in the form of a prescription which leaves several alternative courses of action open to the patient. He may apply to a *mwalimu* – usually a different one from the diviner who diagnosed the case – to have his *shetani* exorcised. This method, preferred by the more dignified elders of the community, is thought to conform to Islamic doctrine. It is a private ritual which involves religious chanting, the use of symbolic Islamic objects, and the mystical number seven. During my stay with the Segeju no actual case of this kind of exorcism came under my observation, and therefore I cannot describe it in detail.

More likely the victim of spirit-possession will take his prescription to a *mganga* who, though personally a Muslim, plays an essentially pagan role in his office as *mganga*. A Segeju *mganga* must serve a long apprenticeship before he can practise his art independently. Besides spirit exorcism he is taught herbalism and the preparation of charms. The term *mganga*, or some obvious cognate, is found in many Bantu languages as a designation for 'medicine man'. In most Bantu tribes the *mganga* is also a diviner, but among the Segeju divination is regarded as an Islamic art, practised exclusively by *walimu*. The *mganga* of Bomandani, Mwaiti Mwanjavyo, and also several other leading *waganga*, had spent some time on Pemba in advanced studies. That island is highly respected by the Segeju as the home of the most skilful medicine men as well as the most ruthless witches.

Whereas a *mwalimu* compels a spirit to leave its victim through wielding the spiritual power of Islam, a *mganga* effects a cure by establishing communication with the spirit and persuading or enticing it to remove itself. A *mganga* acts, in a strict sense, as a spirit medium. As was mentioned earlier, every *mganga* has a tutelary spirit through which he makes contact with other spirits. His own *shetani* is associated with his principal medicine calabash, the stopper of which is carved crudely in the form of a head; this figure in anointed with blood from time to time as an offering to the spirit, and thus it is covered with a gummy patina.

The simplest method for expelling a demon, and usually the first to be tried, is called *kusemea* (literally, 'to talk to'). The *mganga* conducts a private seance with the patient, summons the spirit in question, attempts to establish rapport and then persuades the spirit to stop harassing the victim. The charge for this seance is four shillings. Although quite often successful, the seance method does not inspire complete confidence. The cure is not regarded as permanent; it is obtained too easily and cheaply; the *shetani* will come to realize that it was tricked and sooner or later will repossess its victim. When that happens the patient will probably return to the *mganga* to be treated with another seance, for that is all most people can afford. An ordinary Segeju who is prone to spirit possession does not expect to escape completely from the clutch of his *shetani;* the most he can hope for is to hold it at bay through inexpensive methods of exorcism which bring only temporary relief.

We come now to the major form of exorcism, referred to by the special term *kupunga*. It is regarded as the most effective method and preferred by most people, especially women, whenever possible. The idea of *kupunga* is to entertain the *shetani* with a ritual dance (*ngoma*) and feast, in return for which it agrees to release its hold on the victim. The procedure, which involves considerable expense to the family of the patient, lasts a full week. The *mganga*, assisted by an apprentice, directs the ritual and presides over the dance. The principal dancers are women who have previously been exorcised in a *shetani* dance. These women are lay experts on the ritual of *kupunga*, and having themselves once played the role of principal character, they are thought to understand the mystical experiences which the patient goes through. Drummers are hired for the whole week. On both the sixth and seventh days a goat is sacrificed. Blood from the sacrifice is fed to the patient and the women participating in the ritual; at this time some of the women are temporarily possessed by their former *shetani* and may behave in an unrestrained and aggressive manner. This ritual dance is based on the theory that a *shetani* is inordinately fond of noise, dancing, blood, and frenzy, all of which are provided in abundance. The climax occurs on the sixth day when the *shetani* publicly reveals its name. On the last day it is supposed to withdraw from the victim, and this concludes the ritual.

Shetani dances are strictly forbidden during Ramadhan, the Islamic month of fasting. In the weeks immediately preceding Ramadhan the *mganga* tries to clear the slate of accumulated cases. There is continuous dancing, especially in the smaller villages, which creates an atmosphere of gaiety similar to that of the carnival season as celebrated in some Catholic communities just before Lent. The active participants in the dancing are mainly, though not exclusively, women; however, nearly all the villagers – men, women, and children – attend the dances as spectators when their work allows them to. Against the background of this general description of the *shetani* cult, I shall now present two case histories illustrating some of the main features.

The first case is that of Mwenshika binti Bakari, a vigorous woman of about thirty, living at Bomandani. When she was ten years old Mwenshika suffered from a severe ear-ache. Her father took her for divination to a *mwalimu* at Sibutuni, and it was disclosed that she had been possessed by a *shetani* of the local Nyari tribe, who was causing her ear-ache. She was then taken to a *mganga* at the village of Manza who conducted a seance and established contact with the *shetani*. The *shetani* was persuaded to leave the girl and she recovered from her illness. Mwenshika subsequently was married and bore five children, two of them dying in infancy. During all that time she enjoyed good health until two weeks before the dance to be described. Then suddenly one day, while returning from the beach where she had gone to relieve herself, she was thrown down by some invisible force, and afterwards she was mentally abnormal.

Mwenshika took to wandering through the bush in a state of trance, and there was danger that she might get lost or injure herself. So she was confined at home under the watchful eye of an attendant, and as soon as possible she was taken to a diviner. The diviner confirmed what her friends already suspected, that she was possessed by the same *shetani* that had seized her in childhood. This was only to be expected, the villagers explained, because she had been treated originally by the simple method of *kusemea*, which usually results in repossession at a later date. A *shetani* dance was decided upon and Mwaiti, the *mganga* of Bomandani, was engaged to conduct it.

Mwaiti gave an estimate of 400 shillings as the total cost of the exorcism. This sum was raised by her family: her father paid about half of the total, her husband the next largest share, then a prosperous brother of her mother, and so on down to more distant relatives who contributed small sums of one or two shillings. A day was set for the dance to start, four drummers were hired, and the society of women who had previously been cured by a ritual dance was informed of the plans. The ritual went on the full seven days. The dancing schedule called for two sessions a day – from two to four in the afternoon and from eight to ten at night. Two of the afternoon sessions were omitted altogether because the *mganga* was called away on more important business. When the dancing went with a proper swing and the people were enjoying themselves the evening session continued till midnight or later.

During the whole course of the dance and for several days afterwards Mwenshika lived at the *mganga's* house attended by her mother and another kinswoman. She was enjoined to strict silence for the entire period. The society of past *shetani* victims also spent a good deal of time at the house. When the time came for a session to start, the dancers gathered inside the house with Mwenshika while the *mganga* chanted an invocation. This was the signal for the drummers to tune up their drums by warming the heads with handfuls of blazing grass. There were three drums, so that the four drummers were able to take turns resting during the dance. Two of the drums were played by being struck with the open hand – a short, squat, upright drum with a single head, and a long narrow lap drum closed at both ends. The third drum consisted of an upright cylinder of wood covered with a loose brass plate. This was played with two pieces of heavy plaited rope bound on the ends to form knobs. It was capable of creating a terrific din and would not join in until a dance was reaching its climax. The drummers also sang songs from time to time with themes of praise for the *shetani*. The chanting of the *mganga* and some of the singing was in an esoteric tongue not understood by ordinary people.

The dance took place in an open-sided thatched shelter attached to the *mganga's* house and in the open space in front of that. From ten to fifteen women were usually dancing at any one time. Occasionally some men joined the dancers for short periods. The *mganga* himself would lead the group in starting each new dance; then he dropped out and his assistant took over – an apprentice medicine man, fully as old as his master. Mwenshika danced constantly. The *mganga* gave her various insignia to carry – first a spear, then a club or an ebony staff. She wore bells on both ankles, as did some of the other women. A dance, lasting for fifteen to twenty minutes, would start with small shuffling steps, which became more energetic as the drums quickened; it sometimes ended with frenzied stamping and posturing of the body. Mwenshika carried a stick in her mouth as a symbol and reminder of her muteness. She was completely absorbed in her dancing and seemed to enjoy every minute of it.

Everyone in the village not otherwise occupied came to watch the dancing. There were forty to sixty spectators at the afternoon sessions and more at night. The final days brought a larger crowd. This audience was critical of the drumming and dancing, sometimes praising it and sometimes censuring it. They talked freely and laughed at humorous episodes, as when Mwenshika's ankle bell came loose and one of the other dancers followed her around trying to tie it back while she was still dancing. The *mganga* himself was not overly solemn, but the dancers were serious in their demeanour throughout.

The high point of the dance came on the sixth day with the rite of *kutoa jina* – inducing the *shetani* to reveal its name. That day, before the afternoon session started, the participants danced through the village. At the head of the procession marched the *mganga* leading a sacrificial goat whose horns were decorated with coloured ribbons. The drummers followed, and then Mwenshika and a double file of dancing women. When the procession reached the dancing place the goat was tied to a front post of the shelter to await its fate. The dancers entered the house, and there Mwenshika submitted to having her head shaved. Incense was wafted into her mouth, nose, and ears, and she was given a new costume to wear – a wide pleated skirt made of many folded coloured cloths tied round her waist and a wide-topped turban-like headdress. After the *mganga's* invocation the dancing started as usual, but there was more excitement than on previous days. Midway through the session two offering tables were set in the open space before the shelter. These were made by placing wide brass trays on pedestals which were overturned grain-pounding mortars. A ritual feast was laid out on each table, consisting of seven coconuts, seven bananas, a large rice cake, and a bottle of honey.

The goat was now led away to be ritually slaughtered. Mwenshika was placed on a stool; the women dancers surrounded her and held cloths over and around her so that she was completely tented. The *mganga* recited an imprecation and there was a minute or two of tense silence. Then a squeaky voice began speaking from inside the tent. This was the voice of the *shetani* for which everyone had been waiting. It went on speaking for about five minutes. The substance of its remarks, as explained to me by people who professed to understand its language, were in praise of the dance with which it had been entertained. It was completely satisfied, so it stated, and promised to evacuate Mwenshika's head at the completion of the dance and leave her mind unencumbered. Then it told its name and genealogy, which was extremely long, going back many generations.

The cloths were whisked away and the drums started again. Mwenshika was hoisted on the *mganga's* back and he danced about with her pickaback for a couple of minutes while the whole company broke into a frenzied dance. The dancing stopped and people gathered round Mwenshika to offer her tidbits of cake from the offering table, which they popped into her open mouth. Then all the dancers sat down and rested while portions of the food were passed around. The *mganga* brought a bowl of blood from the slaughtered goat, which he mixed with honey and fed to the dancers. On tasting the blood several of the women behaved wildly and danced madly about, whirling and cavorting. These women had been temporarily possessed by their old *shetani*, who were unseen attendants at the dance. They spoke with 'tongues' and ran up to some of the spectators, including my wife and myself, and made threatening gestures. When this excitement subsided the afternoon session was finished.

The seventh and final day of the dance was rather an anticlimax. The events were much as on the previous day except that the *shetani* did not speak. The ritual feast was laid out as before, and people offered Mwenshika tidbits and also small coins. This rite was called *kutunza* (to 'pamper') *shetani*, i.e., to give it presents – hopefully, farewell ones. A second goat was slaughtered, the blood was fed to the dancers, and some of the women again acted wildly. That evening a session of solid dancing brought the programme to an end. The next day I was taken to see Mwenshika at the *mganga's* house, the first time I had been permitted to speak to her. She was still not allowed to talk and carried a stick in her mouth. She stood quietly while I complimented her on the dance. Another girl afflicted with a *shetani* had just moved into the *mganga's* house in preparation for her dance, which was to start the following day. Now she came running up to me speaking in 'tongues'. Mwenshika got excited and started stamping her feet in the dance rhythm. It seemed obvious that the *shetani* was still with her, and I mentioned this to her father. But he was not worried, for with his own ears he had heard the *shetani* accept the dance and sacrifice and promise to leave his daughter.

The second case I wish to present ended in the death of the patient, Chuma Kukuma, a man of about forty, also of Bomandani. As in the case of Mwenshika, the history starts with a previous possession by a *shetani* several years earlier. At that time Chuma had had an episode of mental disturbance. He became irrational and violent and, as his brother described it, would throw men about with the strength of an ox. Finally he was subdued and kept tied up in his house for a whole week. He had the reputation of being a philanderer; therefore his relatives suspected that his seizure had something to do with his philandering.

When there is a possibility that spirit possession may involve a sorcerer of the same village it is customary to consult a diviner of another village. Chuma's brothers went to Tawalani and found out through divination that his trouble was caused by a *shetani* that had been sent to annoy him by the outraged husband of a woman to whom he had been paying attention. The name of the sorcerer was not disclosed, but under the circumstances no moral blame was attached to him anyway. The deranged man was exorcised by the same *mwalimu* at Tawalani, who used the mystical Islamic method. Seven loaves of bread and seven coconuts were arranged on a table which was held over Chuma's head by his brothers, their hands joining to form a circle around him. A cock was slaughtered by the *mwalimu* and the blood applied to the patient. Then parts of the Koran with special mystical meanings were read aloud. The rite accomplished its purpose; Chuma recovered completely and went back to his occupation of fishing.

He remained well until the onset of his final sickness two months before his death. Then he started complaining of pain in his eyes, chest, and abdomen, and was no longer fit for work. His brothers went to the same diviner at Tawalani, but this time he was not able to fathom the cause of the sickness. They then went to other diviners – four in all – and the nature of the trouble gradually transpired. Some man who held a grudge against Chuma was causing his sickness by means of sorcery. Again the identity of the sorcerer could not be determined by divination, though a good deal of other information was obtained. First the sorcerer had poisoned his victim's food with magical medicine; then he had made a pact with a *shetani* to bring about the patient's death. He had gone secretly to one of the trees known to be frequented by spirits and made a deal with a vicious *shetani*, promising to bring a goat there and sacrifice it when the victim died. As Chuma's enemy was practising sorcery with intent to kill, it was decided that exorcism would be ineffective. Only the sorcerer himself could save Chuma by withdrawing the *shetani* he had employed.

Suspicion fell upon a man named Rashidi Mohamed with whom Chuma had quarrelled a few months previously over the rent of some coconut trees. Rashidi was a quarrelsome character who lived next door to the *mganga* and was thought to possess the evil eye. When Chuma's condition became serious his brothers went to Sheikh Edrisa of Sibutuni, the highest ranking Muslim in the area, and requested him to try Rashidi for guilt by a mystical ordeal. Sheikh Edrisa refused and offered his pious opinion that Chuma would recover if God so willed in spite of *shetani* and sorcery; and as for Rashidi, if he should be responsible for Chuma's death, his just punishment would come when he met God.

Although I had heard about Chuma's sickness from one of his brothers who was giving me lessons in the art of sailing a *mtumbwi* (canoe without outriggers), I had not realized how serious his condition was; nor did I know that the case involved *shetani* and sorcery until the day of his death. His family took little interest in the physiological aspects of his sickness and did not seek modern medical treatment for him. Chuma finally went into coma, and then for the first time I was requested to see him. The patient was lying in a darkened room of his house, obviously in a state of extremity, attended by his wife and mother. His breathing was stertorous, his pulse weak and thready, his reflexes unresponsive. An hour later he died. The findings were insufficient to make a diagnosis: possibilities that suggested themselves were sleeping sickness, cerebral malaria, syphilis of the central nervous system, poliomyelitis, and helminthic infestation of the brain.

Chuma was buried the next morning with an orthodox funeral attended by 200 men and women from Bomandani and other neighbouring villages. The considerable expense of the funeral was borne chiefly by the father-in-law of the deceased who was the *tajiri* or rich man of the village, an irascible old man who went around to all the relatives, who included most of the funeral guests, demanding contributions. Rashidi Mohamed was present in the crowd looking as sympathetic as anyone. The women wailed when the bier was carried from the house to the mosque, but in a subdued and dignified manner. There was a short prayer service at the mosque, then the bier was carried to the grave. The body was laid on its right side, head facing east, in a narrow trench at the bottom of the grave, and covered with a board. Several visiting *walimu* took turns in reading aloud from the Koran during the burial. The grave was filled in to ground level and two dippers of water were poured over the head. The remaining earth was piled over the grave in a neat bevelled mound. The whole group stood round the grave for a while reciting prayers in unison. Then the group broke up and strolled back to the village, except for three men who stayed on by the grave reading selected passages from the Koran from small booklets. As it was the month of Ramadhan, the funeral feast, which otherwise would have lasted two days, was omitted.

In the days following I discreetly asked a number of people for their opinions. Most of the people were noncommittal on the question of sorcery, not wishing to become involved in a quarrel which did not concern them. Two extremes of opinion were expressed by the fish buyer Juma Bakari and the village *mwalimu* Salim Bakari (not brothers). Juma, who personally disliked Rashidi, believed that the evidence convicting him of sorcery was conclusive and that something should be done about it. Salim, on the other hand, scoffed at this notion as being nothing but malicious gossip. In my conversations with Salim I got the curious double impression that he was both a pillar of the church and at the same time the iconoclastic village atheist. This was because he was an uncompromising monotheist and had no belief whatsoever in *shetani*. He was afflicted with asthma which everybody else in the village believed was caused by a *shetani*, but Salim laughed at the idea and steadfastly refused to go to a diviner or *mganga*. His scepticism about so many village beliefs made him sound like an unbeliever, but in fact he was highly respected as a devout Muslim. A few of the elders at Moa shared his views, but not many. Salim believed firmly in Western medicine despite the experience of his one visit to the Tanga hospital, during which he was dealt with in a cursory manner and discharged without explanation or effective treatment of his ailment.

The interpretative conclusions that can be safely drawn from this short account of the *shetani* cult are very limited. One simple conclusion, obvious to anyone who has observed the communal life of the Segeju villages, is that the *shetani* dance furnishes the village with its major form of public entertainment and recreation, and for the participants it offers a means of dramatic and artistic expression. When a dance is in progress, the accompanying noise and excitement dominate the village. The people come as connoisseurs to watch the performance, savouring critically the skill of the dancers and drummers, the *mganga* who directs them, and even the recitation of the *shetani* itself. There is little other amusement in the lives of Segeju fishermen and their families. This entertainment factor accounts, in some measure, I think, for the vigour and popularity of the cult and for its persistence in the face of some disapproval on the part of the highest religious authorities in the society.

Since much of the sickness in a village is attributed with more or less certainty to the action of *shetani*, the cult occupies a central position in the native system of medicine. The interpretation I would suggest here is similar to that offered by Evans-Pritchard for witchcraft and sorcery in general. The ideas and beliefs about *shetani* provide acceptable explanations for the sickness and other misfortunes which inevitably befall every family from time to time. Moreover, there is something they can do about these misfortunes other than wringing their hands and worrying. They can busy themselves with consulting diviners and arranging to have the offending *shetani* exorcised.

The *shetani* cult, like most important institutions in any society, is interwoven with the social structure of the village. The *shetani* dance in a socio-economic context is an example of conspicuous consumption. Only the wealthier families can afford this form of exorcism; participation in the dance is a means of publicly displaying their superior economic status. Tensions and antagonisms between individuals and family groups find overt expression in accusations of sorcery, which are all part of the cult. The social position of the *mganga*, with the prestige and respect which it commands, depends almost entirely on his role in the cult.

The *mganga*, however, has a rival for prestige in the village *mwalimu*, and, in a few villages, the *sheikh*. The *mganga* is generally more prosperous than the *mwalimu* (traditionally a poor man), but the *mwalimu* has moral ascendancy over the *mganga*. There is no doubt that tension exists between these two characters, not necessarily between them as individual personalities, but between the roles they occupy and between the cultural and ideological systems they represent. The *mganga* finds his roots and his strength in pagan African culture, the *mwalimu* in Islam – a cultural complex originally alien to societies like the Segeju which has now been largely absorbed into their culture without entirely displacing all the contradictory elements in the original pagan culture. Or, to look at it from a different viewpoint, the Segeju in embracing Islam, an international and intertribal institution whose basic tenets they could not change, found some of their own customs and institutions incompatible with those tenets. These had to be either abandoned, if openly in conflict with Islamic law, as in the case of beer-drinking customs or divination by pagan means, or altered. The spirit-possession cult, it would seem, was adapted to the new code with a minimum of change so as to become barely tolerable to Islam, leaving tension at those points on which Islamic doctrine does not give a clear, peremptory ruling.

In this interpretation and in several other places in the paper I have assumed that a spirit-possession cult existed among the Segeju before they were converted to Islam. Now in conclusion I would like to cite briefly some comparative evidence supporting this assumption. The basic pattern of the Segeju cult, but without the Islamic traits, appears in a number of societies of eastern Africa, for example, the Taita (Harris 1957), the Kamba (Lindblom 1920), the Giriama (Noble 1961), and in northern Ethiopia (Messing 1958). It appears as far south as Mozambique, where Junod (1962, II, 479 ff.) described it among the Thonga. In the societies mentioned above the spirits connected with the possession cult are distinct from ancestral spirits. Usually they are divided into several types or 'tribes' as among the Segeju. However, the Ndembu of Zambia have a spirit-possession cult with most of the features of the Segeju pattern, but in this instance the spirits are those of dead ancestors (Turner, 1957, 292 ff.). Here there seems to have been a merging of two different sets of spirits into a single cult. The Segeju at present have no ancestral cult involving sacrifices and propitiation. If they ever had one, then it must have atrophied through neglect as the Segeju adopted Islamic funeral practices and ideas about death.

The basic pattern of the Segeju possession cult would appear to have had its origin in pre-Islamic African culture. Among them the pagan cult was adapted to Islamic usages and doctrines with surprising success, leaving the original pattern essentially intact. This process of syncretism, however, has left a small residue of unresolved contradictions and tensions.

REFERENCES

BAKER, E. C. 1949 'History of the Wasegeju', *Tanganyika Notes and Records*, 27.

GRAY, SIR J. 1950 'Portuguese records relating to the Wasegeju', *Tanganyika Notes and Records* 29.

HARRIS, GRACE 1957 'Possession "hysteria" in a Kenya tribe', *American Anthropologist* 59.

JUNOD, H. 1962 *The life of a South African tribe*. Hyde Park, University Books (reprint of 1927 edition).

LINDBLOM, G. 1920 *The Akamba*. Uppsala.

MESSING, S. 1958 'Group therapy and social status in the Zar Cult of Ethiopia', *American Anthropologist* 60.

NOBLE, D. A. 1961 'Demoniacal possession among the Giryama', *Man* 61.

PRINS, A. H. J. 1961 *The Swahili-speaking peoples of Zanzibar and the East African Coast*. London, International African Institute.

TURNER, V. W. 1957 *Schism and continuity in an African society*. Manchester, Manchester University Press.

SPIRIT POSSESSION IN NORTHERN SOMALILAND

© *I. M. Lewis*

INTRODUCTION

As Muslims participating in the world culture of Islam, the Somali lack much of that immediacy in the mystical evaluation of human affairs which is so characteristic of many tribal religious systems. This is partly explicable in terms of orthodox Muslim eschatology, according to which, as Somali believe, the final evaluation of man's conduct is not experienced in this life but in the hereafter. Thus the unjust and those whose religious observance and moral conduct leave much to be desired may enjoy greater worldly fortune and success than those who scrupulously honour the tenets of their faith. Only on the day of reckoning will the account be finally settled and the righteous rewarded for their devotion and effort. This separation between the mundane social order and divine retribution is, I believe, further strengthened by the ease with which so many conflicts are resolved by a direct appeal to physical force. Petty disputes are readily blown up into serious issues involving large numbers of people, and feud and fighting are widespread and frequent.

Nevertheless although God's ultimate judgment will only be revealed and experienced in the after-life, God is regularly approached in prayer and sacrifice, through the mediation of the Prophet Muhammad, to intervene in human suffering. Indeed, men turn equally to Him in despair and thanksgiving. And since Somali hold that man is inherently sinful and far removed from God's grace, powerful advocates are needed to plead with God through the Prophet if their prayers are to be answered. Here men turn for help to those holy men (sg. *wadaad*) and saints (sg. *weli*) whose religious devotion to God has been rewarded by enabling them to perform miraculous works. It is through the blessing (*baraka*) of these saints particularly, and this includes all lineage ancestors as well as men remembered for their personal piety, that the Prophet is petitioned to intercede with God.

Living holy men and saints are by definition excluded from full participation in the secular warrior life of Somali pastoral society. Their role is that of non-combatant mediators, and their mystical influence which includes the power of applying the curse (*habaar*) or sorcery (*sibir*) to uphold their authority appears as, in effect, a compensation for their lack of direct secular power. It is possible indeed to discern a well-defined polarity in Somali notions of power such that those who lack secular strength – either in general, or sometimes only in special situations – are considered to be correspondingly mystically endowed (cf. Lewis 1963). This mystical coverage is extended to include destitute old women whom it is dangerous to treat with contempt and rewarding to treat with kindness; and the position is much the same with such traditionally despised minority communities of craftsmen as the Yibir soothsayers who wander from camp to camp, blessing newly married couples and newly-born children.

There is thus a fairly wide spectrum of categories of persons who, while of very different social status, and lacking effective secular force, at least in certain situations share the property of mystical power. At one end of the scale lie those such as saints whose special mystical powers unequivocally emanate directly from God; at the other pole, there are those such as the Yibirs whose mystical force derives from sources which are closely connected with the devil (*shaydaan*). Spirit-possession is also associated with the devil, or with devils, and in this paper I shall argue that this phenomenon is invoked to account for physical and mental distress (rather than misfortune) in situations where those afflicted are in some sense deprived of secular efficacy. I shall also argue that spirit-possession in this cultural context is closely associated with sex and with relations between the sexes. Persons who are thus deprived are not sources of mystical danger to others so much as themselves endangered, and it is only in the institutionalized means of treatment for spirit-possession afflictions that the victims obtain a measure of redress and thus, obliquely, put pressure on others whom they cannot otherwise influence. My argument is thus that, in conformity with the general notions outlined above, spirit-possession diagnosed in cases of mental and physical disturbance, is a refuge of the weak and injured: it is utilized by those who seek redress but find other means of effective action blocked or culturally inappropriate. Again, it has to be emphasized that to a variable extent the persons concerned are not necessarily weak and helpless in a total sense, but sometimes only in a particular context.

Along with cursing, sorcery, and the evil eye, spirit-possession thus features as one explanation of physical and mental illness. But all sickness is not explained in such terms. Like health and good fortune, illness generally is ultimately in God's power to withhold or bestow, and in my experience it is usually in such fatalistic terms that most afflictions are accepted and endured. The afflicted seek relief through prayers and offerings to God, while Muslim prophylactics are freely employed and full use is made of such resources of modern medical treatment as may be available. It should be added that, in addition to some expertise in bone-setting and such surgical operations as trepanning,[1] Somali possess a considerable diagnostic medical lore,[2] including knowledge of the carrying of malaria by mosquitoes, although the therapeutic value of traditional pharmaceutical and other treatment (cupping, blood-letting, and cauterization) can scarcely have been great.[3]

In interpreting and treating sickness, consequently, it is the contexts of its occurrence, rather than its actual physical symptoms, that decide which cause is sought and accepted and what treatment is followed. And, as will be seen, there is often dispute as to the cause of illness. Spirit possession, or 'entering' as it is generally described, figures as such a cause only in a limited and fairly clearly defined range of contexts. In my experience, four such contexts can be distinguished where illness is ascribed to possession, and these I follow here. The symptoms, it may be as well to add at this stage, include such diverse elements as fainting, falling down, vomiting, feebleness, bodily aches and pains, and general malaise and depression, as well as such classical features as violent bodily agitation and epilepsy. Madness also is often attributed to spirit-possession. Of the four contexts which I recorded and examine here, the first concerns the possession of a man by a woman he has jilted, or by a woman whom he desires but cannot marry. The second is concerned with the possession of young camel-herders in circumstances of deprivation and sexual frustration. The third involves the possession of married women when they experience hardship and frustration. The fourth concerns men, again generally in circumstances of personal affliction and distress. It is thus not merely illness as such which evokes spirit-possession as its cause, but illness, real or imagined, in these contexts.

In the first case there is a direct and obvious nexus of personal feeling (as with the contexts in which the evil eye is thought to operate) and the person possessed is said to be 'entered' by the person he has thwarted, or who is the cause of his frustration. In the other three contexts this nexus is less obvious and clearly defined, and is less directly referred to, since the possessed person's affliction is not directly related to the human source of antagonism and injury but treated obliquely as a sickness caused by a spirit. And consistently with this indirect relationship between the victim and the source of antagonism, the spirit involved here is not as in the first case that of a person, but a nature sprite belonging to that mysterious host of mischievous powers which as Muslims the Somali know under the name of jinns.

These sprites, which are anthropomorphic in character, being said to be 'just like people', are thought to frequent deserted houses, and old camp sites, caves, forests, particular trees, and all dark, empty places. During the day, particularly, they live in the shade, often underground, but appear at night and can sometimes be seen by man. The form they then assume may be no more substantial than that of a will-o'-the-wisp. Uncanny and mysterious appearances of light at night may be attributed to them, and a shooting star is picturesquely said to be one struck down by an angel. Like men, they own livestock, live in their own houses, marry, and engage in trade and commerce and have their own shops and markets. Like mankind too, as Somalis know from their own experience of society, some are learned in the Quran and may quote back chapter and verse of the sacred book when passages from the Quran are invoked against them. Some, following orthodox Muslim theology, are regarded as believers.

These sprites are particularly closely connected in Somali thought with wild animals. Thus they need no zaribas to defend their flocks from attack by wild animals as men do, for all the wild animals are their friends. The hyena, which owing to the anatomical peculiarities of its genital organs Somalis regard as a hermaphrodite, and which takes a considerable toll of livestock as well as sometimes attacking the unwary shepherd as he sleeps at night, is considered to be particularly closely connected with jinns. Some indeed say that it is a jinn. More specifically, a species of large lizard (*maso 'agalay*), and a smaller fat-tailed lizard, both harmless to man, should not be killed since they are believed to be the wives of jinns.

These devils, as they are often described by Somali, are essentially malign and dangerous to man. Although some are Muslims, as a whole they stand opposed to God and seek to subvert his moral order: yet ultimately God is believed to have control over them, as over every other creature. These contradictions, which to some extent reflect the ambiguous character of the divinity as at once the source of blessing and of suffering, are evident in conflicting opinions as to the power directing jinns when they molest man. Of those which are considered to be Muslims and learned and which I refer to as 'learned sprites' (*wadaaddo*),[4] it is sometimes said that they are sent by God, though this is by no means the generally accepted view. Despite these obscurities and ambiguities concerning their relationship to God, their most general attribution is to the Devil and they are seen as his agents or 'soldiers', parallel with the ranks of angels who support and execute the commands of God. As there is a struggle within man between right and wrong, good and bad, so the forces of light and those of darkness are similarly pictured as locked in continuous conflict. These sprites consequently become endowed with the envy and covetousness, and the corresponding malice, which are part of human experience and of which they serve as objectifications. It is believed that there are men who are also jinns, and that these may unleash their devils on those they envy. Envy and desire are likewise held to provide the animus for the generality of these demons which have no human familiars to enter and trouble men. No living thing except the date palm is immune from their unwelcome attentions.

Since they lurk everywhere, care must always be taken lest these malignant sprites enter a person's body and harm him. Plates and dishes containing food are covered at night to prevent jinns getting into them and so entering the body; and milking vessels are treated on the inside with smoke from burning incense, not merely to make the milk especially palatable, but also to protect it from contamination. Incense, which is invested with religious power, and the leaves and bark of all pleasantly smelling trees and plants, are regarded as affording protection against these noxious powers, and employed in exorcising them. Thus on all occasions when the presence of jinns is feared men burn incense to drive them away; and at dusk as men gather round the fires in the camps it is usual to sprinkle a little incense among the flames with the pious words: 'God deliver us from the devils, In the Name of God, the Compassionate, the Merciful'.

It is important to emphasize that although certain individuals are believed to have an 'agreement' with a jinn, these sprites are essentially free-ranging and autonomous, they are not regularly linked to individuals or to groups; and the only respect in which they can be said to 'mirror' the social structure is in their division into the unlearned and learned, paralleling the division of human society between those who are warriors (*waranleh*) and those who are holy men of God (*wadaaddo*). There is no conception of their being grouped in descent groups corresponding to the basic social divisions of society. They are believed, moreover, to operate entirely arbitrarily and capriciously and there is no connection between them and the souls of the dead, or the ancestors of either individuals or groups. Thus the relationship which Firth has cautiously noted between social structure and spirit hierarchies in his comparison of Tikopia and Malay spirit beliefs is not found here (see Firth, 1959, 142). It is essential to recognize that what is involved here is not shamanism, nor a cult of benevolent, or partly benevolent powers, the possession of which confers oracular or other supernatural gifts on those possessed, as amongst the Nuba or Dinka (Nadel, 1946; Lienhardt, 1961). Northern Somali spirit-possession is on the contrary concerned with the exorcism of malign influences which are seen as one cause among many of sickness.

Spirit-possession for the Somali is thus an illness, an unwanted undesirable state associated with affliction and suffering: spirits cause disease, they do not cure it. To understand how the four contexts in which illness is so ascribed to possession relate directly to personal deprivation we have to consider briefly some of the salient aspects of Somali social structure, particularly those concerning the position of women and the character of the traditional etiquette governing relations between the sexes.

THE ROLES OF MEN AND WOMEN IN PASTORAL SOCIETY

The Northern Somali are essentially a pastoral people living for the most part as nomads in an arid and uncertain environment in which their principal wealth consists of flocks of sheep and goats, some cattle, and herds of camels. In a fluid setting of frequent movement from pasture to pasture where ties to locality count for little, social relations are primarily based upon agnatic descent; and this principle of social cohesion is so pervasive that ultimately the entire Somali nation of at least three million persons could be represented in a single all-encompassing genealogy. In day-to-day affairs, people's loyalties are more narrowly circumscribed by their membership of small contractually defined lineage groups whose members in concert pay and receive blood-compensation (Arabic *diya*, Somali *mag*) for injury and death. These groups are rapidly mobilized in the disputes and feuds in which Somalis are so regularly embroiled through the incessant friction which prevails over access to the sparse water and grazing resources of their country.[5]

Although their members are often scattered geographically, and they are not thus strictly localized, these units are clearly defined groups and marriage within them is forbidden by strong and explicit legal sanctions. Women pass at marriage from the *diya*-paying group of their natal family to that of their husband, in return for the receipt of considerable marriage payments, and there are no patterns of preferential marriage. The well-known Arab practice of preferential marriage with the father's brother's daughter, though known to be a feature of many Muslim societies, is not followed by the Northern Somali. Yet, although a wife is subject to the authority of her husband, she continues to retain strong jural ties with her own natal *diya*-paying group; and it is they rather than the husband and his agnates who bear the brunt of responsibility in paying or receiving blood-money incurred in respect of her life. Thus, if a man's wife is murdered, he has no full title to her blood-wealth, but only a claim to a sororatic replacement from her kin (cf. Lewis, 1962).

Whether as daughters or as wives, women are subject to strong and direct jural control by their menfolk. A man may, within limits which are only vaguely defined, beat an erring wife and can expect the support of her kin in any corrective action he takes as long as they are interested in the maintenance of the marriage. Indeed, the perfect image of the husband, as of the father, is the stern *pater familias* with full authority to compel obedience and submission. On his wedding night, the husband is required by custom to chastise his wife with a small ceremonial whip, the public display of which is the sign of his newly married position. These powers vested in men are firmly upheld by the Muslim legal courts, although a woman can, at least in theory, appeal against excessive physical chastisement. Husbands, moreover, can divorce their wives very easily, and in fact do, while women cannot directly gain divorce and can only have their marriages annulled, on such grounds as the physical incapacity of their husband, on recourse to a Muslim court. They can of course resort to other remedies – such as simply absconding. But as long as the wife's kin are concerned for the continuance of her marriage every effort will be made by them to find the run-away wife, and, if caught, she will be beaten and returned to her husband. In the end such desperate tactics, when repeated sufficiently, are likely to force even the most reluctant of husbands to concede divorce. Yet the position nevertheless remains, that society greatly strengthens the husband's hand and weakens that of the wife. So that even where a wife does thus force divorce upon her husband, she is likely to forfeit the Islamic personal dower which her husband undertook to give her when he married her and to which she is entitled on the termination of her marriage.

Throughout their lives women remain, in effect, second-class citizens. A woman's blood-wealth is generally rated at half that of a man (i.e. fifty instead of one hundred camels), and women's rights to inherit property under Islamic law are rarely fully honoured, particularly where such capital assets as camels are concerned. The obverse of these disabilities is that in all public transactions a woman has the right to call upon the support and help of her menfolk. It is their duty to supply her with adequate subsistence, to protect her interests generally, and to carry out all those tasks which it is unseemly for a woman directly to execute herself. Women, like young children, are conceived traditionally as being weak and defenceless and ideally they should provide a submissive and passive foil to the aggressive dominance and masculinity of their husbands and male kin. A woman who displays independent initiative, courage, and fortitude will be described with grudging praise as a 'man'; while on other occasions men will readily complain how feeble, demanding, and unreliable their womenfolk are.

In the same vein, a man should ideally be complete and self-reliant, and it is unmanly and dishonourable, traditionally, for men to display open affection for their wives. Men should address their wives brusquely, and the latter reply in an appropriately submissive tone, at least in public. At the level of actual behaviour as distinct from ideals of conduct between the sexes, the exigencies of the nomadic life demand that men must be ready to leave their wives and homes at a moment's notice to see to the needs of their herds in distant pastures, to join in their watering at the wells, or to engage in other activities connected with clan politics which may take them far from home for unspecified periods. No man whose conduct reveals that he is emotionally dependent upon his wife, or wives, can hope to enjoy a reputation for male hardihood. Indeed, those who betray such a lack of independence are unfailingly stigmatized as being little better than women. In the same tight-lipped puritanical tradition, the ideal of pre-marital chastity in women is strongly held, and the practice of female infibulation is seen as a device to ensure virginity at marriage. Traditionally, there is very little open courting prior to matrimony and arranged matches are common. Only engaged couples are sometimes allowed some degree of licence in indulging in a limited degree of sexual play.

Young men, in any case, are by the nature of their herding duties with the camels removed for weeks and sometimes months on end from contact with the girls who look after the sheep and goats in the camps. The camps composed of the wives and children of closely related men (often brothers) – who themselves are often away – and the flocks of sheep and goats upon which they depend for subsistence, move largely independently of the grazing camels in the charge of young herders. The camels are far more mobile and wide-ranging in their movements than the flocks which are so much more demanding in their water requirements. The former, consequently, can be taken out to areas of lush pasture far from the families and sheep and goats which, in the dry seasons especially, have always to keep close to the wells. These two herding units, the one in the care of boys and unmarried men, and the other in the charge of women and marriageable girls and young children, tend to move closer, or to camp together, after the rains when there is plenty of fresh pasture. It is in these seasons that the young camel-herders have an opportunity of contact with girls of marriageable age and there is a general expansion in the range and intensity of social life.

From an early age the distinction and separation of the sexes are stressed. Girls, who wear clothing which always discreetly conceals their pudenda, are taught to look after the sheep and goats, to milk them, and to weave ropes and cords from bark fibre. At the same time, they help in the preparation and cooking of food and the care of their younger siblings. Boys, who are often less modestly clothed, also help with the management of the sheep and goats until the age of about seven when they are sent out with their elder brothers and cousins to learn the rudiments of camel husbandry. This involves them in long and lonely treks with the camels and introduces them to a hard and exacting life in which they enjoy few comforts. Normally they have no cooking utensils with them and have to subsist on the milk of the camels in their charge. In the dry seasons particularly, when milk is scarce and there is little water to satisfy their thirst, their lot is not an enviable one. This is the severe training school in which they learn to endure the rigours of hunger and thirst and to cultivate those attitudes of alertness and suspicion which are so strongly engrained in the Somali character.

After marriage, men spend less time out with the camels, except when they lack younger agnatic kin, or servants, to supervise their herds. They retain, however, overall responsibility for the management of their herds (and flocks), and play an important part in regulating watering movements and in preparing the wells which often have to be dug out seasonally. Their other main tasks and interests lie in the field of clan politics: and they are often away from their tents and wives, pursuing these interests, visiting their herds, or making expeditions to trading centres to buy provisions. Married women are less mobile. Though they may take milk or clarified butter to sell in neighbouring markets, and also lead caravans of camels to the wells to bring back drinking water for the household, they play an essentially domestic role concerned with child care and cooking. They are associated only with the burden camels which they load with their collapsible huts or tents and all their effects when they move camp. The milking camels are the concern of men, and only men milk them.

The differentiating effects of this sexual division of labour are reinforced by a partial application of Muslim notions of purdah. Women, amongst the nomads, are not veiled or strictly secluded; but the woman's part of the tent may not be entered by men other than her husband or kin, except at the risk of incurring charges of adultery. Women, likewise, eat separately from their menfolk. The head of the family and his guests are served first, while women eat afterwards with the children.

This almost total domestic involvement of women, in contrast to the men's monopoly of public affairs, is also strongly emphasized in religious worship. Although like men, women are frequent visitors at the shrines of saints to which they go to seek relief from affliction as well as in search of fecundity, they are almost totally excluded from full participation in the public Muslim cult. They are not admitted to the mosques where men regularly pray; they do not participate effectively in the highly developed activities and regular ceremonies of the mystical religious orders or 'brotherhoods' which play such a vital part in men's religious life; and at all large-scale public Muslim feasts and festivals they gather only on the periphery of the all-male crowd, trilling at appropriate points in the rites. While a considerable number of men succeed in going on pilgrimage to Mecca, few women accomplish this highly prestige-giving act of devotion. Thus, in religious life also, women play an essentially passive role. They are not expected to be ostensibly devout, as men are, and the fact that they very rarely observe the obligatory daily prayers excites little adverse comment. In sum, it is not going too far, I think, to suggest that men consider that their own active public devotions sufficiently sustain the religiosity of their womenfolk. It is this background of confinement and constriction in the relations between the sexes and in the overall position of women which illuminates most of the contexts in which spirit-possession occurs amongst the Northern Somali.

YOUNG MEN'S POSSESSION

The most general term in Somali for possession by a spirit is *gelid*, meaning literally 'entering' (from the verb *gal*, to enter), and the victim is said to have 'caught' (*qab*)[6] the spirit in the same way that other illnesses and diseases are 'caught', and to be in turn held in its thrall to the extent that he speaks with its voice and voices its demands. The victim is also described as having 'yielded', 'succumbed' or 'agreed' to the spirit, so that the notions involved, at least grammatically, include active behaviour on the part of the victim as well as of the invading spirit. The accompanying physical symptoms, ranging from mild hysteria to acute physical illness, are very varied as we have seen.

The most personalized and direct notions of spirit-possession come into play when a young man exhibits any or all of these symptoms in a context which young Western-educated Somalis describe, as we would describe it, as that of unrequited or frustrated love.[7] The standard situation here is where the youth has jilted a girl. A man may, for example, be troubled by a girl who loves him and whom he promised to marry but did not. If a young man falls sick in these circumstances, it is suspected that the girl who desires him and whom he has abandoned has possessed him. She will not let him go. The actual agency and mechanism by which this form of possession occurs is not explained very precisely. The girl is said simply to have 'entered' the man. It is obvious that this statement is intended to be understood in a metaphorical rather than a literal sense, and further enquiry reveals that Somalis are not much concerned by their difficulties in explaining the process which occurs. If pressed, however, it will be suggested that the girl has sent a jinn to trouble the man. This, indeed, is the only explanation Somalis can offer since any suggestion that the girl's soul (*naf*) is the agency of possession is excluded. The soul, the immortal essence of man, leaves the human body only at death, which it survives as the sensate entity to experience God's rewards and punishments.

Here, as in other cases of possession, the standard treatment consists in the exorcism of the invading agency. This is administered by a holy man who intones passages from the Quran (particularly the sixty-sixth Sura, known as Yaasiin) against the spirit while the victim is shrouded in blankets, and incense is burned on a fire, producing dense choking fumes. This atmosphere is, of course, well calculated to stimulate dissociation in the patient, but I am doubtful if dissociation actually occurs in the majority of cases. Whether it does or not, however, the patient is well prepared from his own cultural training to make the stock responses which the situation requires. At the beginning of the treatment, the invading spirit identifies herself according to the following formula: 'I am a girl named . . . , and I desire this man. He promised to marry me, but did not'. As the treatment proceeds, the spirit is alternately cajoled and threatened by the might of God's word to quit its victim, the cleric conducting the treatment incessantly muttering, 'If you don't come out, I will burn you'. Burning here refers to the fiery power of the verses from the Quran and the cleansing efficacy of the smouldering incense. The spirit, in successful treatments, responds to these threats by a series of stereotyped formulae indicating the line of its retreat. It promises to withdraw from the body of the victim through his chin, through his nose, his ears, and other points on his frame. But not until the spirit says that it is coming out by 'the little finger of the left hand' is the exorcism considered complete and the patient discharged as cured. As far as I am aware, this stereotyped phrase is not used in other contexts, but for the Somali, as for other Muslims, the left hand is inauspicious, almost unclean; and the little finger is regarded as weak and puny and as the least useful of the fingers.

Sceptical observers who are not intimately concerned for the well-being of the victim point out that in seances of this kind the voice of the 'spirit' is indentical with that of its host. Those directly involved view the matter differently. In one instance which I heard of but did not witness, a holy man was said to have attributed the death of a wife and daughter to this type of possession. When he later married another woman she in turn fell sick, experiencing fainting fits in which she uttered the name of another woman. This woman, whom his wife knew to covet her husband, was diagnosed as the cause of the malady, and the man was advised to sacrifice a ram and to offer its blood to appease the spirit. When this was drunk by his sick wife (being consumed by the invading spirit) she gradually recovered; or so I was told.

What is clear in such cases is the basis of personal antagonism, directing the attack of the invading spirit, and generally stemming from unrequited love between men and women. That frustrated desire should find expression in this pattern of mystical retaliation is consistent with the fact that in situations of this kind no formal legal redress is possible for the woman. Breach of promise between private individuals is not a recognized tort, and it is only where a formal engagement exists and preliminary marriage payments have been made that court proceedings can be pursued involving not merely the individuals directly concerned, but also their kinsmen. Private understandings, where they exist, cannot be subject to litigation and passionate feelings between the sexes cannot traditionally be directly vented in public.

Where young men's desires are frustrated the position is very similar since, as we have seen, for a man to express openly any attachment to a woman is shameful in the extreme. Thus it is perfectly understandable that the same malady is sometimes diagnosed in the case of a man who falls sick when he is prevented from marrying the girl of his choice by the opposition of his father and elder kinsmen. For a man who thus rejects the ignoble expedient of elopement and accepts the decision of his elders must conceal his feelings. Thus possession of a man by a woman here is seen by young educated Somalis today, very much as we would see it, as simply a case of disappointed love in circumstances where the idea of a love-match simply could not be entertained. Spirit-possession provided the only acceptable idiom in which such instances of frustrated desire could be presented without shame. Illness brings no dishonour.

This line of interpretation applies equally to a kindred type of possession which often manifests itself in young camel-herders when they return from their hard life of solitude and isolation to the warmth and excitement of the family camps and the girls who await them there. On these occasions some young herders often evince signs of hysteria which are interpreted as a form of spirit-possession. The smitten youths are not considered to be suffering from an illness, but rather to be temporarily mentally disturbed, being described as 'mad', a word which in Somali as in English connotes many degrees of perturbation, ranging from wrath to extreme insanity. Here it is not the spirit of a particular person which causes this state, but a nature sprite called *saar*, this term denoting both the spirit and the condition of the person possessed. The word *saar* calls for some explanation in view of its connection with the Ethiopian Shamanistic *zar* cult, but I defer this to a later section, merely noting here that whatever its origin, *saar* has peculiar semantic appropriateness since in other contexts it signifies something that is placed on top of something else (for example, a parasitic creeper), and is also used to describe the position of the adopted stranger client – one who comes inside from without.

When a youth in these circumstances becomes hysterical, his companions mount a dance, known as 'beating the sprite', for his relief. The intention is clearly and explicitly cathartic, and it is essential that girls should participate in the dance if it is to be effective. The dancers form a loose circle round the possessed boy and begin dancing slowly to the accompaniment of hand-clapping and the singing of a standardized chorus, an example of which I give below. The tempo mounts and the afflicted youth begins gyrating in the centre of the circle, his movements becoming wilder and wilder as he sings his solo song, again of a standardized form, commanding general attention, and then breaking into a song composed for the occasion in which he announces his plight. This of course is said to be the sprite singing in him; and, as the tension mounts, the youth frequently seizes a stick or sword, threatening those gathered round him with hysterical and exaggerated gestures. As he does this, with, at any rate on the few occasions when I have witnessed the scene, a truly frenzied expression, the sprite possessing him shouts 'Catch me; do not catch me' as he darts towards and then away from his companions. At last, after a short space of time which may be no more than an hour, he drops sweating and exhausted on the ground, apparently in a trance-like state. From this he eventually rises muttering the Muslim creed: 'There is no God but Allah and Muhammad is His Prophet' and recovers his normal state. The explicit significance of this gesture is that he was alienated from normal human society and from God and has now returned to his senses and to Islam. Also explicit is the notion of the opposition between God and his works and the capricious and malevolent world of jinns which we have noted earlier.

The introductory chorus sung as the party begin to 'beat the *saar*' takes the following form:

The spirit and the seas have grown small (? receded)
LaLaLa . . .
You don't invite the devil,
Take shelter from it by reciting 'In the name of God,
  The Compassionate, the Merciful',
Pour water over it (to stop its fire)

Then the smitten boy commands attention with some such lines as:

All you saints and men of God,
All you white-haired boys,[8]
And all you women,
Until I say the word,
Keep your mouths shut for me!

This is repeated three times and when the youth sings his own, or some other *saar* sprite song describing his condition. Four typical examples are the following:

i Like the winged hornbill in flight,
  I am herded with the stars,
  I drink from the rain-shower as it falls from heaven,

I don't accept cool clapping,
Loud and rumbustious is the rhythm I know,
I drink blood,
Then I recover my senses.

In the following song, the singer is less concerned with his own state of alienation and exhaltation and refers more directly to the intention of the dance:

ii Oh girls, abuse and praise,
Are stored in my stomach,
Which do you prefer?
Which shall I spread my blanket for?

In the next song the singer announces his complete dedication to the *saar:*

iii Birds flock in trees,
Each has its own call,
No one understands the others,
Let the administrative officer imprison me for years on end,
Let him cut off my nose and ears,
Let him force me to give up my religion,
Let him chain my legs,
Whatever I suffer, I will never give up the *saar*.

In the final example, the possessed youth simply boasts of the superiority of his own kinsmen's interpretation of this dance:

iv Did I not tell you so?
Oh Rubo (a girl's name) apart from our own people,
Oh Rubo, all other people,
The way they beat the *saar* is unaccomplished.

In the puritanical traditional ethic of the pastoralists which condemns overt courting and discourages mixed dancing, this context of possession is little more than a special type of dance which permits and encourages men to give vent to erotic feelings in a culturally acceptable mode. For the camel-herders returned from their world of isolation and hardship it represents a welcome release and indeed a sublimation, since there is no question of the *saar* dancers indulging in actual sexual intercourse. Yet the erotic intention is almost explicit in many of the songs sung on these occasions, and it is significant that the phrase 'to beat the *saar*' is a colloquialism for sexual intercourse.

Thus this dance is characterized as a form of play (*ayaar*) or game, rather than as a serious ritual designed to remove illness, although it is recognized that certain youths are more than usually prone to this type of hysteria and may, when so possessed, be a danger to themselves and others.[9] It is also recognized that in many cases a boy may sham possession in order to have the opportunity of displaying his desire, through this dance, for a particular girl, or that he may adopt this device to attract the attention of a girl he loves and to impress her with the strength of his desire. Today, with the growth of more liberal attitudes towards relations between the sexes, the dance seems increasingly to have these latter functions, particularly where it is performed in towns. It has also been adopted under the name of *baahilaawe* or *baar'adde* in certain rituals associated with the ceremonies performed in honour of a number of local saints, particularly in that connected with the cult of Shaikh Husseyn Baliale, whose tomb in southern Ethiopia is one of the most widely frequented shrines in North East Africa (cf. Lewis, 1959). It has thus found a precarious niche in the general cult of saints, but one which orthodox holy men regard as heterodox, and the ceremonies of which it forms part have consequently been officially banned throughout the Somali Republic.

WOMEN'S POSSESSION AFFLICTIONS

By far the most common form of possession in Somaliland is that affecting women and generally attributed to the malign influence of the same category of sprites as the preceding (i.e. *saar*) type. Here, however, possession is regarded (especially by women) as a disease which is often serious. A number of distinct, named *saar* sprites are recognized as the agents responsible (I noted a dozen such individually named demons), and treatment, which is costly though often only temporarily successful, is always by a woman specialist or shaman (*alaaqad*) who is described as having 'authority' over the spirits. Such experts are almost invariably widows, childless women, or divorcees, and not infrequently managers of brothels or dens where men meet to chew the stimulant leaves of the Khat plant (*Catha edulis*, the succulent leaves of which contain drugs of the benzedrine family). All are women who have in the past been, or are recurrently subject to *saar* possession, and who generally fail in some important respect to conform to the ideal of Somali womanhood which is that of the married woman with children.

Those mediums who are most widely respected claim to have been initiated into the appropriate propitiation mysteries and to have secured authority to conduct their seances from similar experts in Ethiopia where the *saar* (*zar*) cult is highly developed amongst Christians, Muslims and pagans (for recent accounts of *zar* there, see Leiris, 1958, and Messing, 1958). In keeping with this association, the most serious sprite afflictions are often ascribed to 'Ethiopian sprites' (*saar habashi*, also known as *menghis*), and in the prevailing context of Somali-Ethiopian tension and animosity, this is sometimes explained by Somali as a kind of retaliatory mystical scourge sent against them by the Ethiopians. Although the actual date of the introduction of the belief in these *saar* sprites is unknown, there is thus, I think, little doubt as to its ultimate origin in Ethiopia, whence the belief has also spread to Arabia, the Northern Sudan, and Egypt (see Cerulli, 1936; and for a recent account of *zar* in Khartoum, Barclay, 1964, 196–209). This, however, is not to say that the Somali interpretation of the *zar* complex contains all the elements which are found in Ethiopia or in these other countries into which it has spread. The emphasis in Somaliland is, as I have said, on exorcism, rather than on shamanism as it operates in Ethiopia; nor does the cult as it functions there and in Khartoum here provide an actual corporate organization through which the members of depressed classes can enhance their security and status. Thus the Somali mediums normally claim no particular gifts as seers or fortune-tellers and have no special standing in contexts other than the treatment of the afflicted.

Treatment, conducted by the medium, ranges from elaborate seances akin to those regularly practised in Ethiopia to simpler ceremonies involving only the patient and her doctor. Whatever the form of therapy, the medium is handsomely rewarded for her services and the essence of treatment consists in the appeasement of the possessing sprite by the presentation of luxurious gifts to the patient. These, provided by the patient's husband or other relatives, include such acceptable articles as perfume, silks, other clothes and finery, as well as such especially delectable foods as sweetmeats, dates, coffee, and tea. This theme of luxurious presents and sociability, contrasting sharply with the rigours of the nomadic life, is strongly emphasized. The *saar* sprites are always described as liking and coveting 'all good things', all the things in fact which every Somali wife hankers after. And there is an ambivalent aspect since the sprites may attack a woman when she is got up in all her finery, and consequently is sensitive to the envy of others, as much as when she herself is reduced to wearing rags and envies other better dressed women.

Thus one woman described how she had first become possessed many years before:

> I was staying at Berbera, and one dark night, wearing good clothes, I walked along a deserted alley between two houses. Suddenly something caught me and flung me to the ground. I was carried home and found that I had broken out in boils. This was because I had walked over a sprite which bit me and caused me to fall ill. The *saar* sprite attacked me because I was wearing good clothes and perfume. I was ill for three years and then cured by a medium. I was afflicted by an Ethiopian sprite called 'Mamme'. Sometimes when I am not wearing good clothes the sprite still beats me.

The ambiguity expressed here provides an effective rationale for the commonly expressed women's view that these sprites attack both the rich and the poor and that no woman is immune from them. Sometimes this is stated more precisely, women maintaining that certain specific sprites attack only the poor, while others confine their attentions to the well-to-do.

In the most elaborate cathartic seances (which I have not myself seen, men being rigorously excluded) the spirit medium is said to wear black clothes while her female attendants are dressed in red and the patient herself is clad in her oldest clothes. When cured at the end of the rite, she too is expected to put on red clothing. These sprites are definitely connected symbolically with the colour red and are sometimes identified with a 'red wind'; they are also said to take a person's blood, and the offering of blood to them is an important element in many of the cathartic rites. In the seance, the afflicted woman is placed on top of an ox while the other women sing *saar* songs conjuring up the sprite, or 'beating the *saar*' as it is again described, and rousing the patient to a pitch of hysterical frenzy as in the camel-herder's dance. Drums or paraffin tins are beaten in an increasingly fast tempo and the women attendants uncover and dishevel their hair in various gestures of abandonment. Married women normally wear their hair modestly coiffed by a coloured handkerchief. The presiding medium stands in the centre, often wielding a sword, while the victim is led round on the ox's back wriggling her body and shoulders in time with the rhythm. After some time the subject of the rite falls swooning on the ground, the dance is then stopped, and the ox is killed. When the patient recovers, she is helped upright and steps over the ox's blood. The medium and her acolytes and the patient and her women friends then cook and eat the meat of the slaughtered beast. All the expense incurred and the medium's personal fee are borne by the patient. In the less elaborate ceremonies which are more commonly held, a cock, sheep or goat is killed for the sprite, and the party feasts on this meat and on boiled rice or grain. Tea and coffee are also prepared and dates and other delicacies are passed round and perfume (as in a religious ceremony involving men) is liberally sprinkled on the participants.

No matter how simple the ceremony, the exorcism always entails considerable expense; generous amounts of food and other luxury articles are required 'for the sprite' (i.e. for the patient) and for the medium who administers the treatment. One man claimed, for instance, that in addition to the medium's cash fee of forty-five shillings for the treatment of his wife, the latter had been instructed to buy five bottles of perfume, twenty pounds of dates, and ample quantities of sugar, grain, tea, garlic, onions, and potatoes, all of which were expended at a small party of women organized by the medium. Such outlays, I believe, are not unusual even when the process of treatment is at its most informal. Since the treatment may not be successful, or only temporarily alleviate the patient's affliction (the possessing sprite being then said to be 'too strong' for the medium to control), repeated recourse to a succession of mediums inevitably involves considerable expenditure. In the case of married women, these unwelcome responsibilities fall upon their husbands, and it is scarcely surprising therefore that these sprites are said generally to hate men. For this reason men must be excluded completely from the ceremonies.

Men, in their turn, are uniformly unsympathetic to these female ailments and the standard male reaction is to regard them as feigned or trivial complaints assumed by their wives to extort unnecessary luxuries and attentions from their menfolk, with complete disregard for the expense involved. I have heard it suggested by men that a jealous wife might thus deliberately seek to dissipate her husband's wealth in order to prevent his seeking a second wife. And this is not merely an example of extravagant male fantasy, since I have heard of cases where young wives were afflicted by *saar* possession when their husbands began to initiate proceedings to marry a second wife. In this vein men invariably describe the onset of the supposed affliction in some such terms as the following: One's wife feels poorly, or depressed, and may actually be at the same time suffering from a 'real' illness, when an old crone comes along and tells the impressionable woman that she is indeed ill and is afflicted by *saar* possession. She can easily be cured, however, the malicious old woman continues, as long as her husband can be persuaded to pay the necessary expenses. On no account should a report be made to a hospital, for that would certainly prove fatal, and men must have nothing to do with the treatment. This provision, it will be noticed, opposes *saar* affliction and its treatment to the world of men, to their religious practice which would otherwise be invoked in the treatment of illness, and to modern western medicine. The two last, as we have seen, are not considered by Somali to be in any way incompatible and are regularly combined in the treatment of disease.

In this fashion men see the seeds of discontent and envy developed in the minds of their wives by the over-solicitous attentions of malicious old women. And it is significant that this is thought to be a lucrative pursuit to which old women in straitened circumstances turn, selecting their candidates carefully from those who are not their own kinsmen. Thus men generally are highly sceptical of women's sprite afflictions which they regard at best as malingering, and at worst as a pernicious extortion racket through which men are led to indulge their wives' insatiable demands for new clothes and delicate foods. Men support this view of the matter by pointing out how much more frequently the wives of the rich are smitten than those in poorer circumstances, a conclusion which is countered, as we have seen, by women's claims that there are two sorts of sprite – one for the rich and another for the poor.

These points of view are illustrated in the following case. A man whose wife was away in the interior with his flocks and young children was sent word that she was ill, that sprite-possession had been diagnosed, and that she needed money for a cure. The husband grudgingly sent some money only to be met with further demands as the treatment proceeded. Quickly tiring of these repeated requests and anxious for his wife's health, the husband set out to find out for himself what was happening. When he arrived at his wife's camp in the interior, he found that both she and his daughter were ill from what he regarded as pneumonia and urged them both to go to the hospital. The wife, egged on by the medium treating her, refused on the grounds that doctors could not cure her. The husband impatiently removed his daughter forcibly, ignoring his wife's protests, and carried her off to the hospital where she was treated for pneumonia and began to improve after a few days of injections. His wife still refused to follow the same course until, in desperation, her husband threatened her with divorce and told her that she must choose between him and her 'sprite'.

In another instance, the new young bride of a highly respected elder complained of *saar* sickness. The husband who was a trader of substantial means soon found himself faced with a bill for £40 for treatment which he accepted with marked reluctance. However, as the medium who had treated the woman told her that she must hold a spirit seance every year at the same time or she would again succumb to the affliction, her husband soon realized that this was not the end of the matter. As he was very fond of the new bride he put up with this for some time, but after a few years he felt that he had had enough and decided that he must settle his wife's complaint once and for all. He adopted the brusque, but as I was told, successful expedient of locking his wife in a room in his house and beating her soundly. After that, apparently, there was no further trouble.

These examples indicate how most men view *saar* sprite possession when their own wives are afflicted, even though the majority firmly believe that such sprites do actually exist and are a potential hazard to health. Where, however, there is a direct connection with the profitable role of spirit medium, attitudes tend naturally to be more sympathetic. Thus one of the most prominent mediums in Northern Somaliland in 1956 was the wife of a well-known elder, and the couple – who were childless – had both been on pilgrimage to Mecca and enjoyed considerable public esteem. The wife's authority over these sprites was, she claimed, revealed to her one night in a dream, and since then she has practised with increasing success as a medium. Such qualms as her pious husband felt were stilled when he consulted leading members of the religious establishment and was told that indeed the Quran testified to the existence of the sprites which his wife claimed to be able to control.

Yet, in general, men show little patience when their own wives are subject to this costly affliction. Scepticism centres not only on the fact that it is generally rich women who are most often possessed, but also on the fact that the affliction is almost solely restricted to women (the *saar* possession of the camel-herders is, as we have seen, not considered seriously as an illness – nor does it involve financial outlays). For women are considered weak and foolish and easily swayed. The more general interpretation advanced here, namely, that the phenomenon must be seen as an aspect of the excluded social life of women, the constriction of the married woman's position, and her lack of other means for venting grievances, is also consistent with this emphasis on the 'weakness' of women. For it is their weakness in relation to the dominant males which makes them especially susceptible to mystical dangers. A quarrelsome and flighty wife is more liable to speedy divorce than one who takes refuge in sprite-possession, although, as has been seen, even this device must be used with moderation if it is not to provoke the same result.

The association of *saar*-spirit possession with women as a counterpart to men's involvement in the official cult of Islam, which is another aspect of this male-female dichotomy in Somali society, is very evident in the following story. The wife of a rich official in the Public Works Department of the government was feeling out of sorts one morning and sitting alone in her house in which there happened to be £50 in cash of her husband's money. An old woman came and told her that she was possessed by a *saar* sprite and would need a lot of money to pay a medium to 'beat the *saar*' for her if she was to recover. The wife readily fell in with these suggestions, and a lavish party was quickly mounted under the direction of a medium and the old crone and her friends. When the husband returned from his work at midday for lunch, he was amazed to find the door of the house tightly barred and a great hubbub audible inside. The medium ordered his wife not to let him in, on pain of serious illness, and after knocking angrily for some time the husband went away and bought his lunch in a coffee shop.

When he returned in the evening the party was over and his wife met him and explained that she had been very ill, that *saar* had been diagnosed, and that, alas, she had had to spend all the money in the house on a cure. The husband accepted this unpalatable news with remarkable restraint. However, on the following day, which was a holiday, while his wife was out, the husband took all her gold jewelry and her cherished sewing machine to a money lender from whom he received an advance of cash. With this money he assembled a large party of holy men and feasted them royally in his house. When his wife returned later in the day she found the door of the house shut and barred and heard sounds of hymn-singing from within. After trying unsuccessfully to get in, she went off disconsolately to consult with her neighbours. When she returned later, she found her husband sitting quietly inside the house and asked him what he had been doing. 'Oh', said the man, 'I was suddenly taken very ill, and to get better I had to summon a party of holy men to say prayers and sing hymns for my recovery. Mercifully I am now better, but unfortunately since there was no cash left at home I had to pawn all your gold jewelry and even your sewing machine in order to entertain my guests'. At these words, the woman raised a loud lament; but after a little reflection her anger subsided as she perceived the reason for her husband's action, and promised never again to 'beat the *saar*'. The husband, in his turn, said that he would never again entertain holy men at her expense. With his wages he later redeemed his wife's riches.

However fictional this tale may sound, it faithfully expresses prevailing attitudes towards spirit affliction and highlights the contrasting interest of women in *saar* and of men in the official cult of Islam. It is not inconsistent with this distinction that in the rare cases where illness in adult men is ascribed to spirit possession, the sprites involved should be those who are regarded as the learned shaikhs amongst jinns which I refer to as 'learned' sprites (*wadaaddo*).[10]

POSSESSION BY 'LEARNED' SPRITES

These sprites, it is believed, strike men rather than women, causing possession with the same range of symptoms noted earlier, and in keeping with this distinction it is appropriate that they should be considered more deadly and dangerous than *saar* sprites since the threshold of resistance to mystical malignancy in such weak creatures as women is considered to be low. Here, as with *saar*, possession by these powerful demons is not attributed directly to any context of personal hostility between individuals or groups, although there is thought to be some danger of contagion which may be increased by hostility and bad feeling on the part of those already afflicted. Thus not only can a man catch the disease from someone who is already suffering from it, but such transmission is likely to be encouraged if the two men quarrel or fight. Several people afflicted with this malady whom I encountered told me that they had 'caught' it from others suffering from it with whom they had fought, and it is believed to be particularly dangerous both to the possessed and to his assailant to strike an afflicted person on the shoulders.

It is clear, however, from the way in which this affliction is discussed and from the instances which I saw or heard of, that the precipitant leading to a diagnosis of possession by these sprites is always some particular hardship or deprivation or a deeply felt personal difficulty such as impotence. While I doubt if all the cases which I know of involved real psychological disturbance or serious deficiencies of character (in terms of Somali values), such deviations, particularly where they are striking, are I think also likely to be referred to *wadaaddo* possession, and incline those so handicapped to resort to this affliction when they encounter insuperable difficulties. But in the absence of adequate information on the epidemiology of mental illness in Somaliland it is difficult to pursue this theme further.

The element of deprivation which underlies all these cases is well represented in the following instance. A man I met told me that he was recurrently subject to possession by four 'learned' sprites (such multiple possession by *saar* in women is also encountered). They had originally attacked him when he was a boy ten years old and was starving and hungry. Now, whenever he lacked food and help, they spoke to him, asking why he was starving them and why he did not give them tea and perfume. They also threatened him that if he did not give them perfume they would kill him. When this happens, if he has no money, he begs for help and buys perfume and food, then the sprites leave him. However, they also come back, he told me, whenever he is angry and begins quarrelling and fighting. Then they say to him, 'Why are you fighting? We could kill you'. That these sprites should thus figure as in effect opposed to fighting is consistent with Somali conceptions of the pacific role of the holy men, of which they are the spiritual counterparts. And the implied connection between deprivation and fighting is very obvious to Somalis, however tenuous it may seem to us. For they see war, desolation, and drought as intimately related. It is lack of water and pasture for their herds which makes men hungry and bellicose and regularly leads them in desperation to seek those necessities by force; and war itself, in turn, brings further desolation and misery. Thus war and drought are aptly contrasted in proverbs with peace and milk.

As with *saar* possession in women, this affliction is most effectively treated by those who have at one time suffered from it and who now hold 'authority' over it. This power, however, is limited appropriately enough to holy men who are the human equivalents of the sprites involved. The procedure usually followed is similar to that applied in the treatment of men who are possessed by a woman they have jilted. Thus the patient is swathed in blankets in a room with a fire on which incense is burnt, and verses from the Quran are recited against the possessing demon which is exhorted to quit its victim. Again there is the dialogue between the spirit and the exorcist, and in this case especial difficulty may be encountered since this type of sprite is, as we have seen, credited with considerable knowledge of the Quran. In reality, of course, this can only be manifest when the patient himself is a shaikh or one unusually well-educated in religion (which is not always the case). The inhalation of perfume is also (as with *saar*) considered helpful: and again like *saar*, 'learned' sprites are sometimes said to favour red clothes, although I do not think that this is universally attributed to them or considered very important. Again, and in distinction to the treatment by holy men of diseases other than *wadaaddo*, recourse to a hospital is believed to be extremely dangerous. Thus, in a number of cases, patients suffering from pneumonia have been removed from hospital by their relatives on the advice of a holy man claiming power over the sprites, sometimes with fatal results.

While *saar* possession is a well-established phenomenon in Northern Somaliland (although its precise antiquity is unknown), *wadaaddo* seems to be a more recent importation: generally, indeed, it is said to have entered the centre and west of the country from the east within the last forty years or so. This process is described in such a way as to suggest that the affliction is pictured as an infection gradually spreading westwards from the east, and its origin is universally attributed to the Maajeerteyn province where it is connected with Sultan 'Isman, the redoubtable clan-head of the Maajeerteyn clan who was deposed by the Italians in 1927 when they assumed forcible control of this part of their former colony.

The stories which attest this attribution vary considerably in details but all versions emphasize two themes. These are first that these sprites were formerly the spirit familiars of the Sultan (they are often described as his 'soldiers') and on his deposition were released to trouble mankind generally; and secondly, that they are also in some way directly connected with a small Maajeerteyn lineage of sheikhs and holy men called the Fiqi Buuraaleh. This is a priestly group which has a very high reputation for mystical powers, corresponding to its weakness in numbers and secular power. Cerulli, for example, writing apparently of the situation in the late nineteen twenties, reports that this lineage is credited with the power of protecting crops from devastation by sparrows – a miraculous power attributed to other, unrelated, priestly lineages amongst the southern Somali cultivators (Cerulli, 1964, 158). Thus, in the centre and west, far from any zone of actual contact with, or direct knowledge of this lineage, *wadaaddo* sprites are sometimes referred to as Reer riqi Buuraaleh, as though they represented a mystical line of holy men which maliciously, and capriciously, visited men with sickness: and sometimes the human Reer Fiqi Buuraaleh are referred to as possessing the greatest power in controlling and curing the disease ascribed to them.

It is important to emphasize that this 'learned' sprites disease is never ascribed to any other priestly group, or to the activities of holy men in general who, as we have seen, are generally credited with using the curse and sorcery to protect their persons and property from attack by warriors. It thus appears that the Reer Fiqi Buuraaleh, having acquired a wide reputation for their mystical efficacy reinforced by their association with Sultan 'Isman, his conquests, and fierce resistance to the Italians, have in an inter-clan context of hostility between the Maajeerteyn and their neighbours come to be regarded as a source of generalized malign influence. This interpretation, at least, is supported by the ascription of responsibility for the most deadly form of *saar* possession ('Ethiopian *saar*') to the Ethiopians in the context of Somali-Ethiopian hostility.

CONCLUSIONS

Although spirit-possession in Northern Somaliland is seen traditionally by many as a specific type of malady on a par with other known diseases and ultimately most closely related to madness,[11] it is, as I have argued here, rather an explanation which is invoked to interpret real, or assumed, physical and psychological symptoms in a number of fairly clearly defined contexts. To understand these contexts it is necessary to appreciate that Muslim theology, as the Somali interpret it, presents the problem of a divinity who is responsible both for happiness and affliction and whose rewards and punishments fall due in the after-life rather than in this. The gulf in the moral evaluation of human interaction which this creates is partly filled by the readiness with which antagonisms and tensions are ventilated by direct recourse to physical combat. But not everyone can be secularly powerful and secure; envy and covetousness, consequently, cannot be excluded, and there remains a general notion of mystical influence as the ultimate resource of the downtrodden and weak. This assumes a variety of forms – the curse, sorcery, the evil eye, and spirit-possession – each associated with different cultural contexts and structural situations. The last, however, is only mobilized in a limited number of culturally defined circumstances which involve the underlying element of deprivation and which, for the most part, are concerned with relations between the sexes. To a large extent these are analogous to the situations in which the more elaborate *zar* cult operates in Ethiopia and the Sudan and to the social nexus of such similar phenomena as the Hausa *bori* cult (Greenberg, 1946), or the more limited *saka* possession cult amongst Taita women (Harris, 1957).

It is in this sense rather than in any holistic one that these beliefs, which ethnographically are part of Somali religion, are, as it were, tailored to the social structure and system of values. The characteristics attributed to the spirit entities involved cannot themselves be seen as exactly mirroring the social structure in which they serve as objectifications of fear and envy, for spirit-possession is very far from being at the centre of the official cult. And in any case many of their attributes derive directly from the religious heritage of Islam, although they are not identical in all respects with those found in the beliefs of other Muslim peoples (see, e.g., Westermarck, 1926). It is in this sense that the correlations which Firth has tentatively noted between the secular social order and the characteristics of spirits in Tikopia and Malaya, or which Lienhardt has so carefully explored for the Dinka, or, nearer home, which Messing records in Ethiopian *zars*, cannot be fully parallelled here (cf. Firth, 1959, 142–144; Lienhardt, 1961, passim; Messing, 1958). Ultimately, however, it seems to me that the problem which deprivation poses is one which is inherent in the Somali system of values and presents what might be described as a loophole through which new beliefs (such, for example, as *wadaaddo*) may readily be absorbed to explain, and in some cases actually to remedy, afflictions of this kind. Unfortunately, of course, we do not know what happened before *wadaaddo* or *saar* made their appearance, and there is little point in speculating.

In the absence of adequate psychological evidence it is likewise difficult to assess the extent to which those who seek these remedies in the culturally appropriate situations are in fact subject to real mental disturbance or illness. But it appears, at least in my experience, that those who are specially susceptible to possession are those who are congenitally, or who feel they are, least able to cope adequately with the pressures and ideal standards of the pastoral life which is their lot. Thus not only women in general, who in relation to men are considered to be intrinsically weak, but women with particular burdens or personality problems seem those most prone recurrently to seek this solution to the difficulties experienced by them in such a male-dominated society. This is particularly clear in the case of those women who regularly succumb to possession and find security as professional mediums. I think also that those men who regularly succumb to the affliction attributed to clerical sprites probably show similar characteristics. It is consequently tempting to compare the epidemiology of *saar* possession in Somali women with the incidence of depression and other mental illnesses in women of depressed circumstances elsewhere. Certainly there is much to suggest that the Somali woman often finds herself trapped in circumstances from which there seems to be no easy line of escape except through what men unsympathetically assume to be a form of malingering. This, at any rate, is thoroughly consistent with the character of the relations between the sexes in traditional Somali society. And it is therefore scarcely surprising that spirit possession should so often be linked with the covert and indirect expression of emotion (whether of love or hate) between men and women.

Today this old pastoral order is changing. In towns particularly the relations between men and women are freer than formerly and such questions as the general enfranchisement of women, freedom to contract love-matches, and the direct expression of love and its acknowledgement as an honourable sentiment are all hotly debated, not least in the press and on the radio.[12] At the same time, the modern 'pop' song (*heelo*) which has evolved in the last two decades or so to become widely listened to on the radio in both town and interior treats freely and directly of love and passion in a manner which many of the guardians of the old order find shameful and disgusting (c.f. the poem 'The evils of the Balwo', Andrzejewski and Lewis, 1964, 151–152). It is highly significant for our analysis, moreover, that in these modern songs, men and women are described as smitten and held in thrall by love in precisely that terminology which is traditionally employed in the corresponding contexts of spirit possession.

Despite these developments, belief in *saar* sprites, although waning, has not disappeared, and they continue to be invoked in cases of personal difficulty. The accompanying dance is also, I think, increasingly acquiring popularity as a form of spectacle in town, although it can now only be performed clandestinely since it has been banned by the Government as unorthodox and superstitious.

NOTES

[1]Dr R. E. Drake-Brockman, a medical officer with long experience in Northern Somaliland, describes these and other procedures – including the insertion of animal bones in shattered bone structures – in his book (1912, 156–162).

[2]For some indication of the range of traditional diagnostic knowledge and the wealth of terms in Somali for locally occurring diseases and medical processes, see M. Maino (1953).

[3]Thus as early as 1854, Richard Burton noted sceptically that Somalis associated malaria with the bite of the mosquito, and attributed this 'superstition' to the fact that 'mosquitoes and fevers become formidable about the same time' (Burton, 1943, 33).

[4]*Wadaaddo* is the plural of *wadaad*, the Somali equivalent of the Arabic shaikh or *fiqi*, meaning a holy man, one learned in religion. The singular form is *not* used of these 'learned' sprites.

[5]For a fuller analysis of Northern Somali social structure, see Lewis 1961.
[6]Other related meanings of the verb *qab* are to marry (man speaking), and more generally to have, hold, or do.
[7]Thus the theme of a recent play by Abdi Rodol and broadcast on the Somali Service of the BBC is the unhappy plight of a love-sick girl whose father refuses to allow her to marry the man of her choice. She falls sick and is treated for spirit possession, but this brings no relief. At last her true condition is correctly diagnosed by a learned sheikh who persuades her father to agree to the marriage she desires.
[8]This refers to the practice common among young men of bleaching their hair. 'White-haired boys' is, however, also a synonym for the *saar* dance.
[9]In 1953 one such youth attending a boys' boarding school in Northern Somaliland, when stimulated to a pitch of frenzy by *saar* songs sung to him by his school-fellows, seized an axe and killed one of his companions. The boy was tried for homicide in a court and a plea of temporary insanity was accepted on the evidence of a medical witness who testified that the accused was suffering from a form of epilepsy. The boy explained that he was safe as long as he was wearing a protective amulet containing verses from the Quran. He had not been wearing this at the time of the murder. (C.f. Ross, 1956).
[10]This is also sometimes called '*ardooyin*, from '*ardo*, a student of religion. This particular plural, however, unlike the word *wadaaddo*, is only applied to these sprites and never to their human counterparts.
[11]Madness may also be caused, it is believed, by excessive absorption in religious devotion. Thus there are many clerics, often disparagingly called 'Sufis' (i.e. mystics), who exhibit similar hysterical symptoms at religious ceremonies to those of the *saar*-possessed camel-herders. These are seldom treated with much respect, but regarded rather as crazy fanatics.
[12]For an interesting, revealing, and remarkably frank correspondence on the subject of 'love', see *The Somali News*, 1964, all weekly issues for July-September, especially that of August 21.

REFERENCES

B. W. ANDRZEJEWSKI and LEWIS, I. M. 1964 *Somali poetry*, London, Oxford University Press.

BARCLAY, H. B. 1964 *Buuri al-Lamaab*, Ithaca, New York, Cornell University Press.

BURTON, R. F. 1943 *First footsteps in East Africa*, London, Everyman.

CERULLI, E. 1936 'Zar', *Encyclopaedia of Islam*, IV, p.1217. Leiden.

1957 *Somalia. Studi editi ed inediti* I. Rome.

1964 *Somalia. Studi editi ed inediti* III. Rome.

DRAKE-BROCKMAN, R. E. 1912 *British Somaliland.* London, Hurst and Blackett.

FIRTH, R. 1959 'Problem and assumption in an anthropological study of religion', *Journal of the Royal Anthropological Institute* 89: 129–148.

GREENBERG, J. 1946 *The influence of Islam on a Sudanese religion,* Monographs of the American Ethnological Society, 10, New York.

HARRIS, G. 1957 'Possession "hysteria" in a Kenyan tribe', *American Anthropologist,* 59: 1946–1066.

LEIRIS, M. 1958 *La possession et ses aspects théâtraux chez les Ethiopiens de Gondar,* Paris.

LEWIS, I. M. 1959 'The names of God in Northern Somaliland', *Bulletin of the School of Oriental and African Studies,* 22: 134–140.

1961 *A pastoral democracy,* London, Oxford University Press.

1962 *Marriage and the family in Northern Somaliland,* East African Studies 15. Kampala.

1963 'Dualism in Somali notions of power', *Journal of the Royal Anthropological Institute* 93: 109–116.

LIENHARDT, G. 1961 *Divinity and experience: the religion of the Dinka,* Oxford, Clarendon Press.

MAINO, M. 1953 *Terminologia medica e sue voci nella lingua Somala,* Alexandria.

MESSING, S. D. 1958 'Group therapy and social status in the Zar cult of Ethiopia', *American Anthropologist,* 60: 1120–1127.

NADEL, S. F. 1946 'A study of shamanism in the Nuba Hills', *Journal of the Royal Anthropological Institute* 76: 25–37.

ROSS, A. D. 1956 'Epileptiform attacks promoted by music', *British Journal of Delinquency* 7: 60–63.

WESTERMARCK, E. 1926 *Ritual and belief in Morocco,* London, Macmillan.

SPIRIT POSSESSION AMONG THE LUGBARA

John Middleton

I

The casual observer in Lugbara will see little of spirit possession in the everyday life of the people; yet it is of very considerable importance to them and in some ways central to their entire system of religion. In this paper I describe spirit possession among the Lugbara and indicate its principal significance, in both religious and political situations.

The Lugbara are Sudanic-speaking farmers living on the high plateau of the Nile-Congo divide. They lack centralized political authority, being organized traditionally in a number of politically autonomous territorial groups, the average population of which is about five thousand. I call these sub-tribes. Each is based upon a patrilineal sub-clan, of which the genealogically senior man is a rain-maker. Though he holds some rudimentary political authority, his position is primarily a ritual one. Sub-tribes are linked by personal ties of intermarriage and neighbourhood, and by having a common culture and language. But traditionally there was no overall political linkage, and in fact the cultural variation between sub-tribes was considerable. Sub-tribes are divided into from three to six levels of territorial section, each based on a core provided by a patrilineal lineage. The smallest group is the basic residential unit, the family cluster, based on a three to five generation lineage. The head of this lineage, whom I call the elder, is head of the cluster. Besides elders and rainmakers the only other traditional holders of any political authority are the 'men whose names are known' (*'ba rukuza*), whose position is not hereditary and depends on personal qualities of leadership and wealth. Since the advent of colonial rule in 1900 government chiefs have been appointed, but they stand in most respects outside the traditional system.[1]

The Lugbara highlands are fertile and at the same time remote from centres of large populations. These facts have enabled the Lugbara to escape many of the disasters that destroyed or weakened most of the neighbouring peoples of the Southern Sudan culture area: famine has been rare, and they were not seriously affected by the depredations of Arab slavers during the 19th century. None the less, they have faced recurrent epidemics of human and cattle sickness, and were affected to some extent by the Mahdi rebellion in the Sudan and, of course, by the setting up of colonial rule and the establishment of Christian missions. A small-scale fragmented society of this type is very fragile and vulnerable to external events of these kinds. In addition, like other people, Lugbara are subject to the continual hazards of local crop failures, death and sickness of men and livestock; also local feuds and wars were traditional and continual. The Lugbara maintain that ideally their society and its culture should not alter; but they have to recognize that in actuality they do so. An important part of their religious system, and especially certain processes and persons concerned with forms of spirit mediumship, are concerned with understanding and accommodating various kinds of social and cultural change.

II

The central feature of the religious system of the Lugbara is the distinction between two kinds of 'spiritual being', the ghosts of the dead on the one hand and the various manifestations, aspects or refractions of Divine Spirit on the other. I have described these elsewhere and here need present only an outline account.[2] Lugbara conceive of the universe as being divided into two main spheres, that of order and that of disorder. The sphere of order is the cosmos, set at the centre of a universe of chaos. Spirit the Creator (*Adroa 'ba o'bapiri*) created the first human beings and animals, who were not members of a society. Society, defined by social and moral order, was formed by the two Hero-ancestors of the Lugbara. Before the Heroes is the time of myth, since them the time of genealogy, if we use Western temporal concepts. The social order, the sphere of 'society', is characterized by people living in clans and lineages, recognizing the authority of elders, rainmakers, and the ancestors, an authority that is validated by genealogy. Outside it – Lugbara use the word *amve* ('outside') – is the sphere of disorder, a sphere of asocial, amoral power, validated by myth and controlled by Spirit.

This basic distinction is found at three levels or realms of experience or existence. There is that of the total universe, in which the main distinction is between the world of men living in society, on the earth on the one hand, and the heavens, the place of *Adroa,* Spirit in its role of Creator, omnipotent, everlasting, invisible, beyond the control of men and ultimately responsible for everything, on the other. The second level or realm is that of the surface of the earth, in which the main distinction is between the settlements and cultivated fields, occupied by men and women, both the living in their compounds and the ancestors buried beneath them, on the one hand, and the grass and bush land beyond the settlements, occupied by wild beasts and the aspect of Spirit known as *Adro,* an anthropomorphic figure, white and cut in half lengthways, on the other. The third level or realm is that of the individual organism, in which are two distinct elements, the soul (*orindi*), and the individual spirit (*adro*); at death they separate, the soul becoming a ghost living in its shrine in its descendants' compound, and the spirit going to the bushland when it becomes part of a collectivity of *adroanzi* ('Spirit-children').

I have described these notions at length elsewhere.[3] The total concept may be summarized:

Adroa, the Creator	Men and women, society
Adro in the bushland	The settlements
Adro in the individual	The soul

The left-hand column represents power, change, creation, unpredictability, myth, ultimate continuity, and 'evil'; the right-hand column represents authority, stability, order, genealogy, the brief life-span of people and their communities, and 'good'. Men have to live their lives as best they can, hoping to maintain social and moral order by the proper respect for authority, while continually threatened by the impingement of the outside sphere of disorder, which is the sphere of all-powerful Spirit, beyond the control or accurate knowledge of men. Change and evil occur when the two spheres in any way impinge too closely on each other or when the classificatory distinction is in any way disturbed. Lugbara would like the two spheres to be kept separate, but this never happens for very long, as their own experience of forces beyond their control tells them. If they cannot control the power of Spirit, they can at least try to accommodate it by understanding it.

III

Men can try to understand Spirit by various means: by divination, by observing omens, by sacrifice and prayer, by temporarily sending certain persons as it were into the other sphere, and by listening to persons who come from it.

These various persons are, therefore, to one extent or other and in various ways, mediums between the two cosmological spheres. And possession is one important way by which mediums may do this.

There are several situations in which change, which Lugbara see as a consequence or concomitant of what may be called cosmological confusion, is of concern to them. Some are recurrent and periodical, others not. They include birth, at which Spirit indirectly creates a new individual and places his *adro* (spirit) in him at some time between conception and the actual birth; death, at which the spiritual elements of a person separate and enter the sphere of Spirit; the activities of witches and sorcerers, whose powers are believed to be associated with those of the individual's spirit which is temporarily stronger than his sense of responsibility (which comes from his soul); the activities of certain specialists, in particular smiths, who in a sense perform the spiritual act of creation or re-creation; the activities of hunters, who have to enter the sphere of Spirit in the bushland to hunt wild animals; the entry of Spirit, even though peripherally, into the rite of sacrifice to the dead; the sending of certain sicknesses to individuals who wander, literally, into the bushland and there encounter Spirit in one form or other; the sending of epidemics, famines or similar disasters; the appearance of Arabs and Europeans at the turn of the century; more recently, the appearance of various kinds of evangelists and Christian preachers; and lastly, the possession by Spirit of women who thereby are given the powers of divination and of mystical curing.

All these situations have in common the contact or intermingling of the spheres of order/men and power/Spirit. All are regarded, to a greater or lesser extent, as evil, dangerous and even polluting. And in all of them a human being acts as a mediating agent to understand and so in some measure to control the contact. These mediators include several kinds of person. Sacrifice to the dead is made by elders; control of famine and epidemics is the concern of rainmakers; the impact of Arabs and Europeans was controlled by prophets; and in all the other situations the mediation is by diviners. We need not be concerned further here with all these kinds of mediums. But one or two points need consideration. One is that all of them are, either permanently or temporarily, given asexual attributes as a sign of their liminal roles; the second is that only diviners and prophets act while possessed by Spirit, elders and rainmakers not being under possession; the third is that among those who are possessed there is a distinction, in their political roles, between those who are men and those who are women.

The first point is that these liminal persons are regarded as being asexual. The men are said occasionally to be impotent or homosexual, and those that are not, the elders and rainmakers, act when under the observance of sexual taboos which make them temporarily 'like women' (*okule*). The women are either barren, or pre-pubertal, or post-menopausal, or temporarily not having intercourse with their husbands or other men; they are regarded as 'like men' (*agule*). Among the Lugbara this permanent or temporary asexuality is an essential characteristic of their being able to act as a medium between the social and the Spirit spheres. It is a symbolic attribute, and has nothing to do with their other, normal, social roles.

I turn now to the other points I have mentioned.

IV

The spirit mediums in Lugbara who act while in a state of possession are diviners, prophets, and evangelist preachers. The most common and, we may assume, the most 'traditional', are diviners. Diviners are known as *ojou*, which is etymologically related to the word *ojo*, the bulb of a gladiolus or gladiolus-like flower that grows wild in many parts of highland Lugbaraland along the Nilo-Congo watershed.[4]

Divination is a power given to a person, usually a woman, by possession by *Adro*, the aspect of Spirit that is thought to dwell in the bushland and near river-beds; it has the form of a tall white-skinned man, cut in half down its body and hopping about on one leg. *Adro* is greatly feared and is known as *Adro onzi* ('evil Spirit'). The possession typically occurs about the onset of puberty. The girl wanders naked into the bushland and is 'seized' by *Adro*. She is initiated on her return into the status of diviner, and sets up a shrine for *Adro* in her compound. She may practise during her marriage, but if so she should not at that time be having sexual intercourse with her husband. And she may practise after the menopause. Many diviners are also doctors (known by the same term, *ojou*), who remove objects from the bodies of people who are sick from witchcraft or sorcery attacks or who have been given sickness because they wandered into the sphere of *Adro* in the bushland. They withdraw the objects (small stones and pieces of organic matter) either by sucking by mouth or by pretending to remove them in a twist of grass held in the hand. Some diviner-doctors are men, and these are usually also the operators of oracles (women oracle-operators are very rare).

Diviners have as their central role the identification of certain mystical agents who have sent sickness to their clients. They 'know the words' of Spirit, in all its forms, and of witches and sorcerers (the 'words' of the ancestors are known by oracles, and need not concern us here). They act as midwives; at the mortuary rites for a dead person a diviner is called to contact the soul (*orindi*) which leaves the body at death and flies into the sky to be with Spirit (*Adroa*), until a diviner contacts it to bring it back to its new shrine, so that it becomes a ghost (*ori*); diviners purify returning hunters and men who have killed others in war and feud. But their main everyday role is to identify manifestations of Spiritual power. They do this, in the darkness of a hut, with the use of a divining-gourd (*weke* or *koyo*), which is used as a rattle. And they divine while in a state of possession.

Possession while divining is induced by various means. Traditionally it is by the chewing or consumption in water of pieces of the bulbs called *ojo*, or of their thick fleshy leaves. And pieces of the bulb are among the commonest objects withdrawn from a patient's body by a doctor. In addition, the shaking of the divining-gourd may help to induce a trance or trance-like state. I do not know enough about the medical and physical aspects of possession to know to what extent this possession is 'real' or 'simulated'. Certainly the followers of the prophet Rembe, whom I discuss below, became berserk after consuming the bulb. But from my own somewhat inexpert observation I should judge that few Lugbara diviners can be said even to enter a state of deep 'trance' or 'possession'. I think that for Lugbara the question is really a somewhat meaningless one. Lugbara diviners are putting on a dramatic performance of some skill, and this would seem to be as important, if not more so, than being 'really' possessed, so that it is irrelevant whether they are fully conscious of what they do when possessed or not. This is the reason that I have written 'real' and 'simulated' in quotation marks: in Lugbara perhaps no possession is 'real' in any medical sense, yet is perfectly 'real' in the context of divination. One or two diviners told me that of course they only pretended to draw out objects from a patient's body: they first secreted the objects in their mouth or hand. But this did not mean that by 'withdrawing' these objects they were either cheating or failing to withdraw the sickness. They could 'hold' or 'seize' the sickness in the object, and that was the most important aspect of the whole process. The object chosen would seem to symbolize the believed aspect or manifestation of Spirit responsible: small pieces of granite represent the fireflies which are the corporeal vehicles for the *adroanzi* ('the children of Spirit'); a piece of gristle or meat represents the growing piece of placenta that a sorceress is thought to cause to enter into the body of her rival co-wife's child; and so on.

Not all doctors, as distinct from diviners who are also doctors, go into possession. Possession is an adjunct of divination and not of curing. It is also performed by women. We must therefore ask what is the function of possession, and why should it be essentially an aspect of some form of femininity?

Lugbara say that Spirit 'seizes' or 'catches' a person in order to possess him or her. It is thus Spirit who enters the sphere of order from the 'outside'. This is not the only manner or occasion in which Spirit may do this. Spirit may send lightning or omens such as leopards, hyenas, snakes and various water creatures; it sends a spirit to each person after conception, as I have mentioned; it may possess a girl so as to make her into a diviner; and Spirit may send prophets to the Lugbara, as I mention below. In all these situations a human agent is considered to be able to act as a medium, and is possessed by Spirit as an essential part of the role of spirit medium. In other situations I have mentioned the diviner is still in a state of possession, but it comes as a consequence of the diviner herself 'calling' or 'speaking words' to Spirit and herself inducing possession in the ways I have described. The only situation in which possession is clearly not induced and which comes as it were out of a clear sky is that of the initial possession of the young girl: she is then initiated so that she knows when and how to become possessed when she wishes to act as a spirit medium. On other occasions, those in which she acts as a curing doctor, she does not usually become possessed, although she may still put on an immensely dramatic performance. Many diviners dress in rags, often with long uncut hair, and usually present an extremely bizarre appearance.

V

Some diviner-doctors (*ojou*) are men, but they are not important or numerous, and but rarely act as though possessed (I have heard that possession occurs in men, but I have never seen it). Some of those who can make at least indirect contact with the outside sphere of Spirit are also men; these are elders when they sacrifice, rainmakers dealing with rain or famine, and of course hunters, but these last are in a somewhat different category. As I have mentioned elsewhere,[5] all these must observe sexual taboos on these occasions, to give themselves temporary asexuality. But none are possessed: they are not acting as mediums interpreting the ways of Spirit but are merely making some kind of offering, material or immaterial.

There is, however, one exception. This is the case of the prophets. I have written an account of the famous prophet Rembe elsewhere,[6] and here need summarize only those few facts of his career that are relevant to this paper.

Rembe was not a Lugbara, but a Kakwa, from the north of Lugbara-land. He was approached by certain Lugbara 'men whose names are known' about 1895, and he gave them magic water with which to ward off the recent outbreaks of meningitis and rinderpest, and also the Arabs and Europeans who had just appeared at that time. These men, who had the mystical means to deal with these various external powers, were made chiefs by the Belgians in 1900, and re-appointed by the British in 1914. In the years of the first world war, as a consequence of more epidemics and of the general unsettlement of the period, the Lugbara sent for Rembe, who came and himself established the cult of *Yakan* or *Dede*, based on the drinking of the magic water. He introduced new forms of social grouping into Lugbara, and after threats of disturbance attributed to him he was taken to Yei in the Sudan and there hanged. The movement led to a revolt in 1919. Since then the cult of *Yakan* has changed its form and aims, and it is today one of several spirit cults, which I discuss below.

Besides being a prophet, Rembe was also a diviner. He is said to have kept an oracle in a pool, with the body of a giant rainbow-coloured lizard and with a man's head; and he was the first person in Lugbara experience to have used a divining-gourd. He drank the water of *Yakan* and dispensed it to his adherents, and both he and they would be possessed, become frenzied, and show other symptoms of dissociation. I do not know the exact nature of any substances which he put into the water, but certainly after his departure from Lugbaraland his followers consumed *ojo* bulb, and when about to fight against government police and troops they ate the variety called *kamiojo* ('lion-*ojo*'), which sent them into battle berserk and believing in the power of the *Yakan* water to turn bullets into water.

I need not describe Rembe's cult at greater length here. But there remains one important point. Rembe was a prophet and he was also a political leader and reformer. The organization of his cult was an attempt to rid the Lugbara of their traditional form of social organization, that of the segmentary lineage system, and also of the cult of the dead associated with it. In its place he introduced a series of grades. He was at the top; beneath him were his chief followers, who included many of his original disciples who had been made chiefs by the government, as I have mentioned – these were the *opi* ('chiefs') of the cult; beneath them were the many dispensers of the water; and at the base were the ordinary adherents, both men and women equally, and irrespective of age and clan affiliation. The drinking of *Yakan* water was thought to have certain consequences, among which were everlasting life and the return of the ancestors and the cattle that had died in the recent epidemics. These consequences would clearly have destroyed the basis for the cult of the dead, which was to be replaced by the cult of *Yakan*. *Yakan*, the name of the cult, referred essentially to a form or aspect of Spirit; it was outside the sphere of men, and manifest to them only by the actions of Rembe and the drinking of *Yakan* water.

VI

Today the prophets of the *Yakan* cult have gone. The cult is one of several spirit cults, in which possession is a central part of the members' behaviour. *Yakan* is today the name of a distinct spirit entity rather than its original form of an aspect of Spirit: the distinction is by no means clear but is expressed by Lugbara who attribute to it a greater individuality and autonomy than they did at its first appearance at the time of Rembe. It possesses people, both men and women, who are believed to have wandered from the compounds and cultivated lands into the bushland near the river beds. They are overcome with shaking and trembling, and maintain shrines, known as *Yakanijo* ('*Yakan*-houses') in which they place small offerings of grain.

Another cult, which I have also described elsewhere, is that of *Balokole*. This is a Bantu word meaning 'the Saved', and is the name of a breakaway group from the Anglican Church in Buganda and Rwanda whose members follow the tenets of the Moral Rearmament Movement. Ganda evangelists for the movement entered Lugbaraland in the late 1940s, and met with mixed success. The strict adherents are connected with the Anglican mission church in Lugbaraland: they occasionally enter into trance and speak with tongues, and accept Pentecostalist ideas with enthusiasm. The idea has spread out across the country, with loosely organized adherents who are typically related by kinship and neighbourhood to the families of Christian evangelists and teachers. Possession and trance are signs of the attention of the spirit *Balokole*, whose powers come from Spirit and from the Christian God; the cult members equate the two deities.

There are lastly certain wandering evangelists, prophets, self-styled messiahs, healers, and so forth, who were in various parts of Lugbaraland during my stay. They were not important in the sense of having a numerous following, and I must admit that at the time I paid them little attention, regarding them merely as quaint figures who stood outside the general pattern of Lugbara life. But I did not understand their historical significance. None stayed for very long, and many were not Lugbara; all were for the most part scorned by the ordinary people. Those whom I met considered themselves sent from God, and they equated the Christian God, Allah, and *Adroa* the Creator Spirit. One maintained that he was Rembe, returned from the Sudan and strengthened by the power of Islam: one of the names given to Rembe's original cult was *Ola,* a variant of Allah. Rembe appeared partly in response to the raiding of the southern Sudan by Arab and other Muslim slavers, and part of his role was presumably to cope with and to accommodate this new manifestation of outside power, which in this case took on, among others, the guise of Muslims.

These recent evangelists try to organize their followers into churches and sects, in which, as in the original *Yakan* cult, traditional lineage ties are irrelevant and members are given cult status *qua* members. Again, they are trying to introduce a new form of organization so as to cope with the new manifestations of Spirit.

VII

It would appear fairly obvious that among the Lugbara both diviners and prophets deal with confusion between the spheres of what I have called order and disorder. The main distinctions are that while both are possessed by Spirit they are possessed in different situations, and that usually diviners are women and prophets (including the evangelists) are men, although both are given attributes of permanent or temporary asexuality. Diviners operate within a traditional context of cosmological confusion; prophets deal with radically new intrusions of Spirit that demand an attempt to re-form the basic principles of social organization. Once their efforts to achieve this fail (as they have all done so far), then the spiritual powers that they have dealt with, and are believed to a greater or lesser degree to have been able to control, become as it were 'traditional' and are taken over by diviners, who must still go into possession to contact them.

Finally, there are many other spirits in Lugbara that can possess people, usually by 'seizing' them and making them shake and tremble. Some of these are fairly common, such as the spirit known as *ajualiri*, which sends a lung sickness; *oyakiya* or *ajukuja*, a spirit manifest in earth-tremors; *ogbei*, which sends dysentery. There are also other spirits which send various sicknesses of which trembling is a symptom and which are said to be 'of long ago' and 'far away'. An example known and feared throughout western Lugbaraland is the spirit known as *Mmua*, which is sometimes said to be a spirit and sometimes said to be a clan in the far north-west of the region. Whereas the sicknesses of *ajualiri*, *oyakiya*, *ogbei* and so on are treated by diviners, a person who is 'seized' by *Mmua* is said not to be so treated, and indeed it is said that nowadays *Mmua* has virtually ceased seizing people at all. It seems a fair conjecture – and can really be little more – that all these various possessing spirits are aspects and reifications of various powers – both natural and human – which at one time or another have affected the Lugbara. At first they are dealt with by prophets; then accepted and controlled by diviners; and finally de-spiritualized and no longer important enough to be dealt with by diviners at all. We can probably now never know what 'external' power was spiritualized as *Mmua*, but the hypothesis that it was a conceptualization of some such power seems a likely one.

NOTES

[1]The social organization of the Lugbara has been described at greater length in Middleton, 1958, 1960b, and 1965.

[2]See Middleton, 1960a.

[3]See Middleton, 1968.

[4]I regret that I do not know the botanical names for these plants. They include several plants with bulb- and onion-like tubers, and the leaves of some of them are used to make string.

[5]See Middleton, 1968.

[6]See Middleton, 1963.

REFERENCES

JOHN MIDDLETON 1958 'The political system of the Lugbara of the Nile-Congo divide', in: J. Middleton and D. Tait (editors), *Tribes without Rulers*, London, Routledge & Kegan Paul. pp. 203–229.

1960a *Lugbara Religion*. London, Oxford University Press.

1960b 'The Lugbara', in: A. I. Richards (editor), *East African Chiefs*, London, Faber & Faber. pp. 326–343.

1963 'The Yakan or Allah Water cult among the Lugbara', *Journal of the Royal Anthropological Institute* 93 (1): 80–108.

1965 *The Lugbara of Uganda*. New York, Holt, Rinehart and Winston.

1968 'Some categories of dual classification among the Lugbara of Uganda', *History of Religions*. Vol. 7, No. 3. Chicago, Univ. of Chicago Press. 187–208.

SPIRIT POSSESSION AND MEDIUMSHIP AMONG THE ALUR

© *Aidan Southall*

CASE STUDIES OF SPIRIT POSSESSION

The Alur are a Nilotic people, some two hundred thousand strong, living west of Lake Albert and the Albert Nile, partly in northwestern Uganda and partly in the adjacent parts of the eastern Congo. The Nilotic Acholi are their close neighbours and relatives to the east, the Bantu Nyoro to the southeast, across Lake Albert. The Madi to the north and the Lendu (Bale) and Okebo (Ndo) to the west, are all Moru-Madi speaking Sudanic peoples upon many sections of whom the Alur had a profound political influence, while themselves being culturally influenced in many other respects.

It goes without saying that the field-worker, however successful his rapport, can never really expect to attend a sufficient number of spirit possession seances to be confident that he has been witness of a representative sample. This is one of the ineluctable limitations of field work on esoteric aspects of culture which simply have to be accepted. He is perhaps fortunate if he has attended any as a reasonably undisturbing participant, to check on his otherwise hearsay information.

Although the manifestations of spirit still appear protean, even within their cultural channelling, none the less, actual participation in a seance immediately gives the investigator a far more profound and confident basis for the interpretation and understanding of the more conventional and attenuated accounts of such experiences which informants can give him. On the other hand, it must be admitted that there seem to be some definite advantages in the accounts which are based on informants who have turned King's evidence, as is shown by the wealth of ritual detail and interpretation in the accounts of Beattie (1961) and of Bamunoba and Welbourn (1965). Obviously both sources are necessary, yet I think Cory's (1955) combination of participation and hearsay gives a misleading and exaggerated picture of the elaboration, coherence and consistency of rites. I have to confess that I have not yet adequately completed my data by going through them systematically with skilled informants.

Towards the end of my main period of field work, in the village where I had first started and where the people knew me best, I had the chance of rather full participation at a spirit possession seance in June 1951. It was after the time of the evening meal, when people sit round and talk, with the darkness lit by glowing embers and crude little kerosene lamps made of tin cans, that the unmistakable rhythm of the spirit (*jok*) drums suddenly beat out very near by.

Anything which breaks into the somewhat limited daily round of regular activities arouses interest and provides entertainment. Several small boys took off in the direction of the sound, but most school-age boys and girls did not. Maria said she would have to pay a shilling to the padre if she went, so it would mean paying for nothing. I went off eventually with Petero, although he was somewhat reluctant at first:

> Won't they be cross with me for taking you? We are converts [*jukusomo,* literally 'readers'], I 'read' Catholicism, we are people of Jesus. However, Jesus died long ago, it was you who killed him, not us, you red people killed him, we did not know about it, that is why we still go on with things like this. But actually long ago it [*Jok* possession] was not like this, nowadays it is on the increase. The spirits of the soldiers who fought and died in the First World War [and presumably also in the Second] became like angels [*malaika*] and began to possess people. When I was in the King's African Rifles at Tororo [a town in Eastern Uganda, with a railway junction through which many soldiers from North Uganda would have had to pass, so that it also had a military depot] in the last war I too was possessed by *Jok.* I slaughtered a sheep and a white chicken and built the shrine of *Jok.* We danced *Jok* with a drum only, and the clapping of hands, [cf. Evans-Pritchard, 1956, 98] not with rattles, and *Jok* departed from me forthwith. But the cults of *Jok Udude* and *Jok Rubanga* have added the use of rattles and other elaborations.

So we came to the hut, in a pause when the drum had stopped, and entered. The two important diviners, who had been summoned from neighbouring lineage settlements, were sitting at ease on chairs at the far side of the room. They were middle-aged men. Eight or ten women of the village were there. They included some wives of the village lineage and also some daughters of the lineage, married into other villages who had probably come specially to participate. (The beating of the drum began again.) Two of these were kneeling, shaking violently. Two or three babies were passed from woman to woman as one or the other of them became violently possessed and was liable to drop them. One woman began to be very violently taken, jumping about the floor on her knees and approaching the fire, her whole torso shaking, her shoulders flexed forward and shuddering, her head lolling madly round and round and side to side as if head and neck were a ball on a piece of string. As her knees were on the edge of the red-hot embers and her head practically knocking into them, another woman fended her off from them. Then the other who had been shaking on her knees seemed suddenly and forcefully propelled from inside and in a moment the two possessed women were in a fierce grapple with their arms, as if wrestling, while still on their knees. Both would again have been in the fire but for the other woman fending them off. Others shouted at them 'You have killed one another enough!' (*wunegurwu oromo*) and they seemed to recover their normal senses enough to stand up and violently abuse one another: 'You are a Lendu![1] Shit! Arsehole!' and so on. The 'dancing' continued. The same one again became violently possessed, jumping round on her knees, and then it was as if some sudden inner force propelled her straight through the door outside, threw her on the ground full length and rolled her over and over on the bare earth of the compound, up the slope to the edge of the grass. There she lay still, then walked quivering back to the hut and stood inside the door quivering uncontrollably from head to foot.

This continued for some hours through the night. When any of the women was taken so violently that she could not recover after her performance, water was brought in a calabash, spat over her and also given her to drink. Or else she would go and kneel between the legs of one of the diviners, with her back to him, and he would blow water over her, pressing her body behind the shoulders with his fingers. Also, either one of the diviners or the dancer of the moment, might be handed the calabash of water and spray water out of their mouths over the company in general. (Spraying water, beer, or other liquid out of the mouth over other persons is a standard mode of blessing.) Early on in the proceedings, several women danced on their knees up to the woman who was holding the sick baby for whose cure the seance was being held. They sprayed water over him, saying '*Wafoyo Wafoyo!*' (we are glad! we are glad!) This was welcoming the *Jok* spirit which had come to the baby and caused its illness, but which when properly received in this manner should leave the baby well again. One of the possessed women, while standing by the wall of the hut, quivering slightly, cried out in an unnatural, staccato voice, '*Ju-idho ku kec ongo!*' (One does not 'dance' *Jok* hungry!) – rapidly repeated. This was a hint that beer should be provided, but none was brought.

The range of performance may be characterized thus. Sometimes it comes on people as a gradual enhancing of their voluntary rhythmic shoulder movements to the drumming. Sometimes it really seems to break out as it were from inside them, head drooping, eyes closing, and general quivering increasing to the fierce climax in which the devotee is leaping up and down on her knees without apparent effort of the legs, breasts wildly flying up and down, clapping and slapping against the chest, head rolling madly. Sometimes the arms are raised in contortions above the head.

The other form of dancing is on the feet, with strings of iron bells tied round the ankles. This characterized the later phase of the seance and was more under voluntary control although one woman had to hold on to the door post to stop reeling over. Those dancing with bells do not sing – it seems to be too hard work – and after it their breath comes out of their lungs almost in a whistle. Those dancing on their knees sing until they become possessed with violence and then fall silent.

There were no prophetic utterances, and apart from that already mentioned no indication that the performance was directed at the sick baby. As on many other such occasions on which I participated, it seemed to combine the enjoyment of a spontaneous concert party, the service of a spirit or deity and the thrill of occult powers. My companion, who had at first hesitated to take me there, later seemed to treat the proceedings almost as a joke, talking raucously, bantering with the others and almost burlesquing the songs. When he got tired and wanted to go to bed he came to take fire, but the diviners said that fire could not be taken. The seance ended with dances of mere entertainment, my Alur clerk being one of those who responded to the invitation to perform. There was mild and unheeded protest at this from one of the women with bells, who complained at having to get them out again, asking 'does one "dance" *Jok* for nothing?' In these formal dances some respect is shown to *Jok* in the way of dress. A woman with an old flowered skirt on was given a white one to put over it when she danced, and one who was wearing only the traditional pubic leaves was given a cloth to put round her. The young mother of the sick baby, though sitting there took no part and seemed quite withdrawn. She was a fairly devout Roman Catholic. For the more serious part of the proceedings, the drum was beaten by one diviner and the calabash rattle shaken by the other, but towards the end they were handed over to the woman. Eventually my companion said 'come on, let us go, the *Jok* is over' and the diviner said 'we also are tired'.

The next day was Sunday and by coincidence a priest – in this case an Acholi from east of the Nile – was on his periodic visit to the nearby church, which like all bush churches was most of the time in charge of a lay church teacher. The local faithful had been going to the priest since Thursday for confession and absolution, preparatory to attending mass on Sunday. My clerk went to him at dawn and later to mass. But few if any men, or wives, went from the village. On the other hand, the nubile girls put on a staggering turn-out of massed white skirts and new cloths to flaunt before the padre and the local boys on their way there and back. The conjunction of two types of religious observance was thus quite striking.

At 10.30 a.m. the *Jok* drum sounded again and I went down with some of the women. Inside the hut we now found a wooden box with a cloth spread on top and two bottles with flowers in them, all in obvious imitation of a Christian altar. Behind the altar was a mat on which the young mother sat with her sick baby in her lap and bells tied round her ankles. The drum was now beaten by one of the village elders who had himself been possessed by several *Jok* spirits and was by way of being an expert. The two diviners in charge sat on chairs beside. It all appeared distasteful and embarrassing to the young mother who made no effort to enter into the spirit of the thing.

After several *Jok* songs the drummer began to complain: 'My children, what shall we do? If she just ties *Jok* up in this way what can we do?' They all began to take up this strain of complaint against the young mother for being so slow in letting *Jok* possess her so that they could get on with their task. An older woman leaned forward smiling and told her kindly that she should let *Jok* possess her with joy. But the drummer said 'Well, that is all very fine but this is a matter of disease and death, not a matter of rejoicing. After all, who would go seeking for *Jok*?' And one of the diviners asked 'Well then shall we be sleeping here for ten days over your affair?' And he exhorted her to allow *Jok* to possess her, so that she could seize the goat and rush out of the hut. The young he-goat was tied on the right of the door and a sheep on the left as we looked out.

The young mother remained impassive and none of the methods of stimulus and suggestion seemed to have any effect. One diviner stepped to the door and took out of the roof a sprig of the coarse, yellow flowered, lupin-like shrub and drew it over mother and child as if switching something off them and out of the door. The rattle was shaken near her back with hand clapping over her head, as they struggled on with the drum rhythm and singing. One of the senior elders of the village appeared in the doorway complaining 'here has *Jok* appeared right at my doorway, a matter of death, a matter of *Jok* – let there be no rites of *Jok* in my village here. You are breeding misfortune'. Evidently he felt that the rites should have been held at the mother's natal home.

Suddenly the young mother was shaking convulsively and the baby had to be taken from her. But she was not accepting it graciously. She was weeping and seemed under great duress. Then she leaped up and rushed at the door, knocking the flower bottles off the 'altar', seizing the goat's rope and so outside. There was a crush at the door as the others rushed after, trying to loose the sheep also on the way. The drum was still beating inside. Then we were all outside in the grass. The mother was sat on the mat, with the altar brought beside her and the baby returned to her arms. The bells were removed from her legs and put on the altar. The drum was in the grass.

A clean earth space was hoed for the shrines of *Jok*, one for the mother and one for the baby. The miniature huts were soon constructed. A white chicken was waved round the space anti-clockwise. The goat and then the sheep were suffocated by holding the mouth shut and compressing the wind pipe with the thumb. Then their throats were cut and the blood collected. The chicken's head was cut off and with a prayer to *Jok* it was brushed against the foreheads, shoulders and chests of mother and child and the blood on the knife was touched against the diviner's lips.

The meat was cooked by early evening, distributed and eaten. The diviners and their assisting participants then washed their hands in a bowl of water and blew the water over the baby and its grandmother. White chalk solution was poured over the *Jok* shrines. Roasted chicken meat had already been offered at them and *Jok* informed that everything had now been done for him, he had been fed, and should now go somewhere else far away and not come back.

The women then began to dance again to the drum in the courtyard before the hut. This appeared to be purely for pleasure and entertainment, though in a way it expressed rejoicing that *Jok* had been seen off. The diviners were in another hut. A final session of drumming and dancing was held at night.

In this case, the reason for the seance was the baby's illness, which I, as a fellow villager, had on a common sense basis diagnosed as bronchitis and had been treating with sulphonamide pills, so that by the time the seance was held – to me quite unexpectedly – I was sure that the baby was well on the way to recovery. Fortunately for all concerned, the baby did get well. The mother had obviously wanted to have nothing to do with a cure through *Jok*, but her hand had been forced by her own mother's insistence and the general weight of public opinion. It was also said that she herself had been possessed by a *Jok* called *Memba* while she was still a girl. This gives further relevance to the seance as well as emphasizing her ambivalence as a Christian convert.

In April 1950 I participated in a *Jok* seance near the village of the Chief of Ukuru, though it lasted several days and I was unable to remain at it continuously. I heard the drums early in the morning and was taken there by an Alur whose confidence I had. The seance had in fact been going on all night. Although I did not know the principals, I was well known in the area and so to them. The drumming stopped at my approach, but when I invited them in *dhu Alur* to carry on, they did so. Eventually I was invited inside the hut and to partake of the beer.

The songs of several different *Jok* spirits were sung, to discover which one was responsible for the illness of the patient being treated on this occasion. When the songs of *Jok Adranga* were sung, the green creeper *Bombo*, – used in many rituals and prominent in those for twins, – was brought and tied round the head and legs of the patient. The male diviner and a woman assistant took a potsherd containing beer, sesame and other grains, and a whole egg, to put in the path and other places around the hut. A special mark was made on the patient's chest between her breasts with a powder of various leaves and roots. It is possible that the latter produce some narcotic effect through inhalation, but I cannot be sure. The front of her body had also been painted white with chalky water. In the case of another seance, which I could not attend, I was told that the diviner put hot embers of *Nyilia* root in a potsherd and made the patient inhale the fumes, sitting by it.

Most of the time the patient sat very still, her legs straight out on the floor before her, facing the door, with a set expression. A three foot stick encrusted at one end with cowry shells was pressed by the diviner against the patient's body, behind the shoulders near the armpits, then the woman assistant circled it round the patient's head three times thrice repeated and placed it in front of her resting on her left shoulder. Part of the time the diviner knelt behind her with the palm of his hand flat on her head while he shook his rattle over it and sang the songs of *Jok*, with a great light and joy of exhilaration in his eyes. Several of the 'acolytes' became possessed, shaking violently and 'dancing' on their knees. By about midday when I had to leave they all decided to stop, as they were tired after being at it all night, and wanted to rest during the day.

I returned at nine o'clock the same evening and stayed till one o'clock in the morning by which time they were getting sleepy. A goat had just had its throat cut on the threshold and the blood poured out over it, for the patient and her husband to cross, four times for the woman and three for the man. Portions of the goat were roasted, resting on twigs over the fire. When this was finished the first round of eating the meat with millet porridge began for us all. The fire was burning up brightly; a little flickering tin lamp hung crookedly on the wall, and my hurricane lamp seemed to be welcomed for its extra light rather than feared as a revealer of secrets. So the darkness of the proceedings seems to be a result of activity at night in a culture traditionally without lamps, rather than a requisite accompaniment. No doubt, however, there are a number of senses in which night is appropriate to major aspects of a *Jok* seance. It is also easy to see how houses go up in flames. At times the fire was flaming up to the thatched roof, and the woman hanging the tin lamp flaming against the shiny, smoke-blackened elephant grass was told that she would burn the house down. Later in the evening there were rows of women's bodies sleeping on the floor not so much like sardines as like some huge fish laid in curved folds together. The half-flexed legs of one woman fitted into those of the next, and one had her arm put lightly round the shoulders of the other.

Wherever women are there are also babies and these bizarre experiences must form an indelible part of the impressionable childhood of every Alur. One mother was curled up asleep with twins a few months old lying about on her so that in the flickering light you could not tell whose head was which. Small children and babies were allowed in and out of the hut at all times. During the daytime a small girl about five years old was herself acting as nurse to a baby strapped on her back, bounding up and down to the rhythm of *Jok* and patting its bottom to the time. Thus the rhythm of *Jok* is ingrained from infancy.

While such matters are both subjective and culture-bound, the rhythms, the drumming, the dancing and the songs of *Jok* must appear to the European observer as the most impressive manifestations of their kind in Alur culture. On this occasion the rhythm was terrific and very compelling, though in fact the manifestations of possession were no more violent than on the previous occasion described. In this case four drums were used and eight rattles: two single skin cylindrical drums (*thimbo*) of Nyoro type, which are used only in the rituals of *Jok* and of chiefship, and two conical kettle drums or 'Uganda drums' (*akili*) (Trowell and Wachsmann, 1953; 366 ff.)

I returned to the seance again from six till eight o'clock the next evening. As in the first case described, the dancing was now mainly of the voluntary type, on the feet, with the heavy bells tied round the legs. One of the keenest woman acolytes and the husband of the patient were dancing thus with tremendous vigour, but no sign of hysteria or trance. In deference to *Jok*, she was wearing a clean white outer skirt and he a cape of barkcloth. But later, when they were both streaming with sweat, they removed these, leaving her in her dirty underskirt and he in his shorts. His wife the patient sat still near the hearth in the dark. It was said that she was too ill to dance. Anyone can join in and dance in this way, without necessarily becoming possessed, and it is said that some of the best dancers never have been. Again my clerk was prevailed upon to dance, and I only escaped by promising to do so next time. The songs of *Jok Memba* were played for him, as the more recent ones which he would most likely know.

I have no details of the subsequent course of this seance, or the fate of the patient. The drums could not be brought out of the hut until the following day, which they counted the fourth – the ritual number for women. Among most Nilotic peoples ritual stresses the number three as symbolically associated with masculinity and the number four similarly with femininity. The principle is quite clearly stated, but it is not always so clear which symbolic number is required, nor actually to observe that practice has conformed to principle (cf. Lienhardt, 1961; 143, 290).

The seances so far described both occurred in Uganda. In October, 1950, I had been living for some months in a large Alur village of the Jupiyo chiefdom in the then Belgian Congo. I heard accounts of many *Jok* seances but only participated in one. It was held in the village without any specialist diviner being summoned from outside, to try out whether the wife of one of its members was ill because of *Jok*, and if so which one. Just before nine at night two or three small boys came rushing up, gasping '*dhanu pong' i ot jok*' (people are crammed full in the house of *Jok*). It was no special house, but that of the woman and her husband, which by virtue of the occasion had become the house of *Jok*. It was indeed full of the parents and children properly belonging to it, some dozen other women, a few men and some more children.

They were drumming and singing the songs of *Jok Memba* and the patient herself and another woman, with two younger girls, were on their knees shaking violently. The patient and the other woman held rods in their hands and were groaning 'hiinu! hiino! hiiyu! hiiyo!' Then the other woman got onto her feet in a corner, still shaking violently. Space was made in the middle and she danced on her feet without stopping for more than an hour. She remained all the evening the best and most vigorous dancer. She could only gasp out notes of the melody and incoherent renderings of some of the words. The patient's husband was the main drummer, though anyone else who knew how could take over from time to time. When *Jok Aligu* was drummed and sung the dancing woman called for a stick, which she brandished with both hands, supposedly representing a spear, for *Aligu* is a hunter's spirit.

Bands of *ubiya* (thatching) grass are tied round the upper and fore-arms of the possessed dancers, as it is said that otherwise the *Jok* will never leave them (Cf. Field, 1960, pp. 223). The kneeling women, at the onset of possession, often proffer both hands to those singing and clapping close to them. Their hands are clasped with cries of '*Wafoyo! Wafoyi! dit!*' (We give thanks, we give thanks to you greatly) evidently in welcome to the *Jok* spirit which has entered into them. On this occasion one woman sitting with her baby strapped to her back, shaking her rattle with great enthusiasm, suddenly became convulsively possessed, whole trunk and limbs shaking violently, head and neck lolling all around. The rattle fell from her hand and she seemed unable to hear shouts warning her to mind the baby. When questioned next day she insisted she could hear, yet refused. She said you feel the *Jok* spirit fall first upon your liver (*cwiny*) but later you feel it in your whole body. (Literally and anatomically *cwiny* means 'liver' but it is the word always used in reference to the seat of the emotions and thus metaphorically equivalent to the English 'heart'.)

My Muganda servant, who was also present, and on very friendly terms with the Alur, at once equated the spirit possession and 'dancing' of *Jok* with that of *Mukasa, Kibuka* and the other great deities of the old Buganda pantheon. This was made illegal under missionary influence early in this century. A parish chief who finds it now is said to confiscate all the property of the dancer. In the Belgian Congo also the dancing of *Jok* had been made illegal. This had led to some improvisation. They really could not beat the drums properly, and once before they had held a seance without any drumming, so that I should not hear. None the less a great deal of spirit possession was occurring. One of the villagers had visited a neighbouring village and found them treating *Jok* possession there. When he returned he found *Jok* still on him and so he brought the possession back with him. About two years before, very many people had been possessed in this village, including even young children before their teens. Two diviners were called 'to take *jok* into the grass'. One of them treated for *Jok Memba* and others closely associated, the other treated for *Jok Riba*.

It was said that the patient of this seance, when not actually made ill by *Jok*, could become strongly possessed and speak with other tongues that they could not understand. Thus, she was said to have spoken in Luganda, although she had never learned it or been to Buganda, and Lendu which no Alur round about knew. She could also prophesy, and in this manner had once instructed them to go and bury an egg under a tree for somebody who was ill.

In the same village, one of the chief's wives had been possessed on a number of occasions. *Jok* speaking through her announced that her sickness would depart if a new house were built for her. She was a senior wife, respected but perhaps somewhat neglected, living in a tumble-down hut on the edge of the village. During my stay the chief did summon his people and they built her a new house.

DIVINER, PATIENT AND CONGREGATION

In these seances, which have become the commonest variety in contemporary Alurland, the diviner-mediums in charge always seemed to be men, although there was no rule to this effect, nor is it possible to make any generalization about their social or personality characteristics. They come from both noble and commoner lineages. I never saw the diviners in charge of these seances go into trance, or prophesy or even dance. They were occupied in drumming, singing, treating the patient and unobtrusively organizing the proceedings. However, they had all reached the status of diviner (*ajoga*) or *won jok* (master of *jok*) mainly through having been possessed by many spirits of *Jok* themselves. On the other hand, a majority of the acolytes or congregation were usually women. These are the *mon abende* or *nyithi jogi*. Most of them have been possessed, initiated and cured, perhaps of a number of spirits, and now they enjoy every opportunity of going through the motions again. The performance depends greatly on them, for theirs are the most lively singing, clapping and dancing and the most violent bouts of possession.

Dancing and trance alike are highly stylized, even at their most violent, following a pattern to which all have been mentally and physically conditioned from infancy, so that to become possessed is itself to give oneself up to a pre-ordained pattern. Unfortunately, I cannot define the psychic and somatic states of the patients and acolytes whom I watched. Obviously, certain somatic infections cannot be cured by these means as Alur believe. But it is likely that the mental state of many is eased and supported by the collective acceptance of this theory of causation and its impressively dramatic cure.

I have had to employ the term and concept of dancing, but the Alur do not use the term *myel* (dance) of the rhythmic movements of spirit possession, just as they refuse to call a 'funeral dance' *myel*. What I have translated as 'dancing *jok*' is *idho jok*. *Idho* is the ordinary word for 'climb' and refers particularly to the shaking of the body when the medium is in a sitting posture. Hence the derivation of the word *ja'idho* (medium). The phrase *yengo jok* (to shake *jok*) is also used, and *yengere* (to shake oneself). *Teng'o* is in general 'to knock' and in particular 'to clap the hands' and hence *teng'o jok* is a common phrase used of a spirit possession seance. *Jok* is commonly said to 'fall upon' a person, or to 'fall upon his head', but it is also said *Jok epor*. This verb *por* means 'to jump', 'to mate' (of animals) and 'to elope' (of a girl who goes with her suitor without waiting for the marriage payments to be made).

As to the precise aetiology of Alur spirit possession, it is impossible to give a scientific account. It may be that herbs with some narcotic effect are used, but they are certainly not singled out in any distinctive way from the other herbs which have purely symbolic significance. The Alur do not seem to be greatly addicted to narcotics. Although illegal, it is very easy to grow hashish in their country, but it is not very commonly grown or smoked. Nor can it be said that patients or acolytes are predisposed towards dissociation by prolonged lack of food or violent physical effort. Food is often available during seances and both the most violent and the most profound manifestations of possession usually occur before, rather than after, energetic dancing, which in any case is practised more by the acolytes than by the patient. Beer may also be drunk, but not enough to make intoxication a very significant factor. The cumulative power of suggestion would seem to be the main mechanism involved, arising from the prolonged, infectious rhythm of bodily movements, drumming and singing. It is quite possible that the diviner has some hypnotic effect upon the patient, but this is not elaborated into a recognised and formal technique as far as I could observe.

It is difficult to resist the conclusion that many of the acolytes, especially the women, and no doubt the diviners themselves, find release in seances from the frustrations of ordinary life. This certainly conforms with well recognized experience elsewhere, and we cannot enlarge upon it here. Married women usually have to live away from their own kin, among people who are relative strangers. Their status is inferior, their work monotonous and their diversions few. If in addition they fail to produce healthy children, in a society still subject to very high infant mortality rates, they fail in the chief matter which can compensate for their general disabilities and their prospects are correspondingly dim. It is hardly surprising that some women become keen devotees of spirit possession. If actual sexual activity is included, as in some cults, the attraction may be that much stronger, but this is not the main motivation. Systematic analysis of the life and family circumstances of devotees would surely explain the latent functions of spirit possession for many individuals.

We have to remember that experienced mediums who become the recognized practitioners who are called to organize spirit possession seances as curative mechanisms are also themselves diviners, both male and female. The word diviner and the word *ajoga* alike cover a number of distinct activities which may be under the charge of distinct practitioners. But a diviner's competence often extends over many of these and, in any case, diviners collectively are responsible for diagnosis, interpretation of causation and its allocation between the major alternatives of failure to observe or perform ritual requirements, witchcraft, sorcery and spirit possession. Park (1963) has shown very well how divination, especially in the form of spirit possession, can assist in personal decision-making precisely by removing it and raising it above the level of personal involvements and tensions, conferring external and superior authority upon it by convincing drama, and so relieving the patient of all anxiety as to the source of his trouble, successfully concentrating his attention upon one line of solution and hence very likely facilitating the cure.

Diviners have to be well entertained, or the spirits will be less instead of more well disposed towards the client. They are well compensated, in the modern form of cash, or the more traditional form of domestic animals. The experience and treatment of spirit possession is at the same time part of the cure of disease and potentially part of the training and initiation of a divining medium. For this latter further payments are made, but none of these transactions reaches the huge sums mentioned in Ashanti (Field, 1960, 73). Also unlike Ashanti, the diviners of these seances have no fixed shrines or headquarters, but go to hold seances wherever clients call them.

THE MEDIUMS OF DEPARTED CHIEFS

Having described some experiences of the commonest form of spirit possession among the Alur, I wish to give an account of possession by the spirits of dead chiefs, which approaches more closely to a formal cult of spirit mediums. The extent to which it is perceived as institutional is limited by various factors. Since it is attached to the descent lines of hereditary rulers, and in particular to the chief most recently deceased, it is at any one time unique in any single traditional polity. The degree to which it is standardized cannot easily be studied through space, and through time is subject to the limitations of oral tradition. The reluctance of Alur to speak of such matters makes reliable information very scarce. There is not only the reluctance to reveal secret information to outsiders, but the fact that the cult is really esoteric and it is wrong for Alur themselves to be inquisitive about it unless their status entitles them. The number of Alur who have accurate knowledge of it in any one chiefdom is probably quite few. The rest know of its existence only vaguely, as one of the ineffable mysteries of chiefship, surrounding with awe those known to be in some way involved in it. I conclude that such cults are part of the common heritage of Alur culture, yet differing only in degree from those of even non-Nilotic neighbours such as the Nyoro; that they are probably widespread among the numerous ruling lines of Alur chiefs, yet subject to considerable regional variation of detail. These variations cannot be defined or interpreted with confidence, because they cannot be studied over time and therefore it is hard to distinguish the truly protean possibilities in the manifestation of spirit on the one hand from the distinctive regularities imposed by cultural tradition on the other.

Ukuru is the largest Alur chiefdom and I worked in it more than in any other, but I only happened upon the special significance of possession by the ghosts of dead chiefs and secured any coherent information about it towards the end of my time there. During the last four generations at least, and perhaps for much longer, even throughout the existence of Ukuru and beyond, the spirit of the previous chief has taken possession of a person who has thereby become his medium. It is spoken of as an essentially voluntary act on the part of the spirit, an act which may or may not occur, which cannot be known until it does occur, and which cannot therefore be regarded by the Alur as predetermined, institutional, or regular. Yet it is definitely said to have occurred for the last three generations, less circumstantially for several more and very probably in every generation. Therefore to the observer, once discovered, it appears 'regular' and 'institutional' as an important feature of Alur chiefship, which is central to Alur society. It is analogous to the behaviour of the spirits of commoners, whose possession of their living descendants is regarded as essentially contingent rather than automatic, as if it were not only unknown upon whom the ancestral spirit would fall, but whether it would fall at all; whereas to the observer it appears that a departed elder's spirit invariably falls upon one of his sons, most usually the eldest; for otherwise his shrine could not be built, which is unthinkable. A similar ambiguity characterizes the *emandwa* cult in Ankole, (Bamunoba and Welbourn, 1965, 21). Possession by any spirit always shows itself first in illness. But where possession by the spirit of a chief differs radically from any other is that, whereas most ancestral spirit possession essentially follows the system of patrilineal descent within a lineage and is a major expression of it, the spirit of a deceased chief always falls upon non-kin. From my rather slender evidence, it appears to fall either on a wife of the reigning chief, or on one of his most trusted commoner elders.

Intimacy with the reigning chief, whether as wife or trusted elder, is thus a characteristic of this mediumship. In the case of the elder, he seems invariably to be a member of one of the very ancient commoner clans which seem to have surrounded and attended upon the chiefs of Ukuru from time immemorial. Their elders act in a generalized way as courtiers and counsellors, companions and confidants, ambassadors and priestly assistants of the chief. Once again, the air of secrecy and unobtrusiveness which surrounds them prevents their roles from being seen as strictly formalized, although one suspects that objectively they may in a sense be more so than they seem.

When I visited the medium of Chief Amula, who had died in 1942, I found in his homestead a new hut built with the finesse associated with chiefs' huts and ancestor shrines. On the wall by the door was chalked '*Ot pa Jok madwong' manda wi ng'om cyeke*' (house of the *Jok* who is great indeed over all the land) with the date '14 – 1950'. The medium said he built this hut for the *Jok* of Chief Amula. During Amula's life he always stayed with him, he was the Chief's *japir* (envoy) and sat on the royal mat (*Kolopakic*) at Amula's feet. Before Amula died, the medium built him a hut in his own village – which is still there, though dilapidated – and Amula used to come there every day from his village, returning home in the evening. Then when he fell sick he stayed at home and died there. Seven years after Amula's death the medium fell very ill and was about to die, but recovered again. A year later he fell ill again and Amula's *tipu* (shadow, spirit), began to speak to him and he sent word to the reigning chief. Then 'all sorts of things which had been lost were revealed', – especially odd belongings of Amula. Any time the medium goes into the house which he built for the *Jok* of Amula it will speak to him. The spirits of other brothers of Amula also stay there and the spirit of any chief can be summoned by them.

The medium had not been an *ajoga* (diviner) before Amula's spirit came upon him, but now he is called *wo' Jok* (Son of *Jok*) and also commonly *ajoga*. He can consult Amula's spirit about anything, and thus others can consult the oracle through him for a fee. He had recently been to Paidha, a neighbouring Alur chiefdom, at the request of the Chief of Paidha. For the spirit of the latter's father, Chief Ng'ukadho, had wandered away to Ukuru, whence his mother had come. She had been the daughter of Chief Nziri of Ukuru, the grandfather of Amula. To take Ng'ukadho's spirit back to Paidha a special path had to be made and all the regalia taken to accompany him. In the case of Ng'ukadho's spirit, also, the *Jok* had revealed 'all things that had been lost' and also spoke of all the bad things which had happened to Ng'ukadho during his life. The spirit of Chief Nziri fell not upon a man but upon a woman, Nyarayi, one of the wives of Chief Alworung'a, Nziri's son.

These mediums can also cure people, like diviners, through the instructions of the chief's spirit and so they too are called *ajoga*. The medium may go to the patient with drums as an ordinary diviner does, his body shakes with *Jok* in the form of the chief's spirit. If the spirits refuse they do not come to shake the patient at all, saying, 'let that man die and follow us'. Or else the 'Son of *Jok*' may just tell the patient to do this or that to remedy the omission which has brought illness on him and which the 'Son of *Jok*' has diagnosed through the chief's spirit.

The somewhat irregular incidence of mediums for the spirits of departed chiefs is illustrated by the case of Anyuna and his son. Anyuna, who is no longer alive, was medium of Chief Alworung'a, the father of Amula. His son, Awong'a Wod Anyuna (Awong'a the son of Anyuna), seems to have inherited his father's qualities and become a more general medium of the spirits of chiefs. He is particularly spoken of in connection with the spirit of Chief Abook Ucweda, the father of Nziri, and with the shrine of Rukidi, which is almost the premier shrine of Ukuru. He cannot have had the kind of personal relationship with Chief Abook Ucweda that the medium of Chief Amula's spirit had with Amula or that his own father had with Chief Alworung'a, since Abook Ucweda had died long before. The shrine of Rukidi is not associated with any particular chief but is rather the state shrine of Ukuru chiefdom as such. If Wod Anyuna goes with offerings to the shrines of Abook Ucweda, or of Rukidi, it is said that he speaks in one place, but his voice, *the voice of Jok*, is heard by the people all around. The spirits speak through him, and everyone hears all round, but Wod Anyuna's mouth does not move.

This information was obtained in 1950 and 1951. In 1962 I was able to pay a short return visit to Alurland. There was a big funeral dance for one of the most important and senior members of the chiefly lineage. On such occasions thousands of people attend and all important members of the chief's lineage sit in conclave. The reigning chief dominated the circle, but a close second to him was Wod Anyuna, sitting in a seat of honour, with a twin-bladed rain spear planted before him. I asked who he was, not knowing at the time, and the answer was 'the Son of Jok, whom the Chief fears, medium of the spirits of the chiefs'. Unfortunately I did not discover whether the medium of Amula's spirit was there, or even whether he was still alive.

One other example of possession by the spirits of dead chiefs may be given. Down by the Nile in Junam to the east of Ukuru there is a small lineage of chiefly descent called Pacego. They came from Acholi many generations ago, but the more powerful Junam chiefdom of Ragem 'took their drum', that is, deprived them of political chiefship. But the rituals of chiefship continued and *Jok Muswa,* the special *Jok* of their chiefdom, continued to possess the principal wife of the chief in every generation. She is called 'the wife of *Jok*', and after *Jok* falls upon her, sexual relations between her and her husband must cease, nor can she ever leave him, or be divorced, however much they quarrel. *Jok Muswa* has twin children. Pots with two necks are usually prominent in the rituals of twins, but actually it is a pot with three necks which *Jok Muswa* has in his shrine. He has many other children too, some of whom possess only women, but others men. *Jok Muswa* has leopard skins like a chief, which his medium (the chief's wife) wears when she attends a *Jok* seance. He also had a twin-bladed spear. Junam is geographically and culturally half way between Alur and Acholi. This case gives some indication of the common elements found in chiefly spirit possession even in marginal parts of the country where there are variations in many cultural features.

THE NATURE SHRINE OF JOK RIBA

On a high cliff above Lake Albert on the Congo side is the shrine of *Jok Riba*. It is peculiar among the great Alur shrines in being primarily linked to a natural phenomenon, rather than to a political personage, unit, or event. Riba is dedicated to the force which is said to produce large shoals of dead fish, which float to the surface towards the end of each year and make a rich haul for fishermen. The area is probably subject to some kind of seismic disturbance. On the shore there is a slowly flowing spring of mineral oil. All these features, together with the cliff above, are associated with Riba. Before the coming of the Alur it was venerated by the Lendu.

It was some six or seven generations ago, while many groups of Alur were still moving about and establishing themselves in different parts of the country, that Chief Keno came from Ukuru and established himself among the Lendu at Riba. It was a long way from the effective sphere of Ukuru power, but Keno seems to have been a great traveller. He must already have been an old man, for many of his sons had established semi-autonomous ruling lines of their own. He came with wives and companions. The Lendu Androsi received him among them and told him that Riba was the key to the country.

Keno took over the service of the spirit and the shrine, making the offerings of first fruits in eleusine, maize, beer, fish and termites. Riba was also a rain shrine, for which a black goat was offered with beer and eleusine.

However, Keno did not stay at Riba. He left the small group of Alur there, like a tiny theocracy surrounded by Lendu and by other Alur chiefdoms. Keno was eventually killed by the Lendu and according to tradition eaten by them. His son Ukelo remained in charge of Riba as *Jalambila* (priest). This position became hereditary and four other priests have succeeded Ukelo in the direct male line down to the present. The spirit of Riba first fell upon Ukelo's brother Mukama, who thus became the medium (*ja'idho*) of Riba, and this also became a hereditary position. Eventually a third hereditary line, beginning with one of Ukelo's grandsons, became in charge of secular affairs as headmen. There were thus the priest (*jalambila*), the medium (*ja'idho*) and the headman (*jego*), all from the lineage of Keno. There was also a hereditary commoner line of ritual firedrillers who had come with Keno. The priest had a hereditary assistant to help him in taking the offerings to Riba, who was from another line of commoners. The people of Riba seem to have lived peacefully. They made no expansive political claims, nor were they subject to attack (except that they had a quarrel with the Chief of Mukambo), for they and their shrine were greatly revered. The neighbouring Alur chiefs of Panyikang'o and Mukambo on the lakeshore and Jupiyo and Ruvinga in the mountains had a specially close relation to them and were supposed to send regular offerings. They even claim that Kiyabambi, the king of Bunyoro in Ukelo's time, sent Riba a ritual billhook and a cow with two tails as an offering.

At the time of my visit the medium had recently died and Riba had not yet fallen upon a successor. The medium is buried like a chief, with leopardskin, cow skin, colobus monkey skin, wildcat skin, barkcloth, and beads round his neck, wrists and ankles and in his mouth. The chiefs of Panyikang'o, Mukambo and Ruvinga are informed, but the death is not made public and indeed must not be mentioned except in circumlocution. The people gather in the village of the medium, but there is no wailing. He is buried at dead of night by his children, the priest of Riba and the mediums of other manifestations of *Jok*, when the rest of the people are all at home asleep. A hut is built over the grave, with a fence of elephant grass and fig trees planted round it, such as is only done for chiefs and for *Jok*. At the next harvest, when the eleusine is ripening, the hut is broken down and taken into the grass, where it will all burn when the grass is burnt, and fresh beer is taken to Riba to inform him of the news.

As in the case of the state *Jok* of Pacego, Riba only catches the *Ja'idho* (medium) and no one else. But Riba has 'children' some of whom catch only men, some only women. The *Ja'idho* is also called Son of *Jok* like the mediums of chiefs in Ukuru. *Min Riba* (the mother of Riba) once possessed the wife of a *Ja'idho*. *Won Riba* (the father of Riba) never possessed anyone here, his village is far away in Nyakole (i.e. Ankole). *Min Riba's* village is Kaveta in Pongo, a part of Panyikang'o behind Mahagi Port on Lake Albert. Riba himself gave all these names and information when he spoke through his medium, praising himself in the Alur style of giving the name and origin of his mother and father.

No rules or regularities determine when or upon whom Riba falls in order to choose the new *Ja'idho,* except that he must be an agnatic descendant of Mukama, the first medium. In this case, Mukama was a personal name, but it is well known as the title of the kings of Bunyoro, Karagwe and many other kingdoms of the Interlacustrine Bantu. As soon as Riba falls, even if it is at night, the possessed runs roaring like a lion to the priest (*jalambila*) of Riba. The priest receives him and he hides behind the partition of the hut saying, 'Today I am owner of the country, I have come', still in a loud voice like a lion. The priest throws down a skin for him and he sits on the skin in the priest's hut, dressed in a kob skin, which none can wear without the priest's permission. They begin to blow flutes (*osegu*) and the *Ja'idho* remains silent in the hut for two weeks. He cannot go out and he appears to see nothing. The descendants of Ukelo, the first priest, can go there and they sing and dance and drink, blowing the flutes and beating the drums of Riba in great rejoicing 'that the Chief has returned'.

During the fortnight the lineage of the medium (JupaMukama) builds him a new house in their village. But they are not allowed to see him and are fined if they do. He has to be taken there at dead of night when they are all asleep, conducted by the lineage of the priests (Jup Ukelo) quietly but accompanied by his regalia. JupaMukama have given a goat to be slaughtered at the entrance to the homestead as the new *Ja'idho* approaches, and after this they are allowed to look upon him. Three days later (the male ritual number) he is taken into the grass, shaved and has white chalky liquid painted on him. The Chief of Panyikang'o is supposed to have brought secretly to the new hut a new regalia of beads, cowry shells, barkcloth, stool and skins of leopard, colobus monkey, kob antelope, wildcat and goat. The *Ja'idho* is dressed in these and 'dances' for the first time outside his new hut there. But after this he returns to his former old hut. The new hut is likened to the special temporary *ambaza* hut used in Lendu wedding ceremonies and borrowed from them by the Alur. The *Ja'idho* wears kob skin on ordinary days and only puts on leopard skin when he 'dances'.

I could not discover any very significant utterances by *Jok Riba* through his medium, except when he 'praises himself', or when he falls upon a new medium he may say 'I had gone back to my country, but now I am returning to improve your country, to ripen your food, give you health and prosperity, etc'. A great deal of what he says is in *dhuthugi* ('the language of their own country' – i.e. that of *Jok*) and cannot be understood, for it sounds like meaningless groans. The *Ja'idho* 'dances' regularly twice every moon, once three days after it begins (*lak dwi*) and once when it is full (*mudho*). On such occasions the flutes are played and the priest washes him in an infusion of 'leaves of *Jok*', then dresses him in his regalia and also ties plaited grass round him (here called *rukete*), perhaps with the same purpose as in Ukuru. Lunar symbolism is not particularly prominent or explicit among the Alur and in this case the moon may be mainly of chronological importance, or there may be a link with ritual practices in Bunyoro where the moon is of great ritual importance (Roscoe, 1923, 107 ff). It is interesting that the Nyima shaman among the Nuba (Nadel, 1946, 28), like the medium of Riba, is secluded in his hut for two weeks at his major installation. Such a period is presumably based on reckoning half a lunar month. The Nuba shaman and the medium of Riba also both have to be buried at night.

SPIRIT POSSESSION IN THE CONTEXT OF ALUR RELIGION

Phenomena of spirit possession and mediumship in Alur culture seem to be exclusively associated with the service of *Jok*. This is no very precise definition since practically all spiritual manifestations, good and bad, are attributed in some way to *Jok*. These cannot be dealt with here, but to make clear the place of spirit possession in Alur culture it is necessary to indicate briefly where it stands in the range of *Jok* manifestations. These can be ordered in many perspectives, some of which converge: the spiritual perspective, the temporal perspective, the spatial perspective; the particular perspective of a chiefdom, of its ruling line, or of its ordinary folk.

It seems that to the Alur the highest spiritual connotation of *Jok* is spiritual power in general, perhaps Great Spirit is appropriate, perhaps Divinity as in the Dinka case (Lienhardt, 1961). There may now be no possibility of refining this further. Alur grammar and syntax enforce no specification as to sex or as to personal or impersonal quality. Yet, mirroring the human family, major manifestations of *Jok* are often treated in a way which implies the attribute of Father, while a secondary, associated manifestation is Mother and more subordinate ones are children. This justifies me in using 'he', 'him' and 'his' of *Jok* where convenient, since English provides no uncommitted pronoun. *Jok* in essence and in general has no direct dealings with men, but only in a particular, named form.

The concept of *Jok* embraces nearly all spiritual phenomena among the Alur, except for some beliefs and practices adopted from neighbouring peoples, and even these have in most cases been assimilated or approximated to it. Though singular in form, it is composite in character, as in the case of *Jok Matar* which embraces all the ancestral spirits. *Jok Matar* is recognized in many chiefdoms, as also is *Jok Rubanga*. But at the same time chiefdoms frequently recognize their own particular *Jok* under a distinctive name. This unity and multiplicity has been similarly noted in many contexts among the Dinka (Lienhardt, 1961, 56, 96). As among the Dinka there are many occasions on which the particular identity of *Jok* cannot be known until it is announced in some way by the spirit itself (Lienhardt, 1961).

The plural form *Jogi* is only used of less important multiple manifestations such as minor local spirits, or by grammatical agreement when several persons are collectively identified with *Jok*, as with the initiates or acolytes at spirit possession seances, who are called *Nyithi jogi*, 'children of *Jok*'. They are also called *mon abende*, which seems to be related to the Nyoro and Interlacustrine Bantu root *bandwa* for spirit possession in the Cwezi cult. Indeed, one of my Alur informants specifically volunteered this identification, saying '*gibandwa, ginabende*' (they are *bandwa*, they are *abende*). Diviners of many varieties (*ajoga*) are also linked to the concept of *Jok*, as are manifestations of spirit which are definitely regarded as evil perversions, notably in the case of the witch (s. *Jajok*, pl. *jojogi*) whose attributes include detestable practices such as cannibalism, necrophagy, incest, sodomy and bestiality.

The great communal festivals devoted to *Jok* are normally occasions of joy and thanksgiving, but it is a rejoicing that the people have been spared and that normal good fortune in health and harvest has been vouchsafed. There is no wish for a closer personal approach to or visitation from Jok, whose coming to the individual seems always to take the form of sickness or other misfortune. It is consistent that most diseases are seen as manifestations of *Jok* and therefore natural that his visitations are greatly feared. Yet celebration and rejoicing to receive him are the only answer to his coming. Once he comes, resistance or escape is impossible. The only hope is to receive him fully and with gladness, so that he may, as it were, pass through and out 'into the grass' where he can again be externalized in his shrine and dealt with at a safer distance in prayer and sacrifice. This ambivalence and paradox is reflected also in the fact that while nobody in his right mind wishes to become a servant of *Jok* in a personal sense, those who have been forced to do so seize the opportunity to gather and re-enact his coming in the seances held for the possession of his subsequent victims, and these occasions have great attraction as entertainment.

The major manifestations of *Jok* are to be found in the cult of ancestral spirits, the service of the special shrines of a chiefdom, reception of the spirits of certain chiefs by their own individual mediums and the possession of ordinary people by other spirits of diverse origin. These manifestations not only differ in frequency and importance, but the relation between them varies somewhat from one chiefdom to another, but according to a consistent pattern, and is also held by the Alur to have changed significantly over time. For the sake of clarity I shall illustrate this in the case of the chiefdom of Ukuru and relate other regional differences to it.

To the ordinary person in Ukuru, the highest aspect is that in which *Jok* is the collectivity of all departed spirits. But in this all-embracing capacity he is never dealt with direct. For in every intervention of *Jok* in human affairs it is necessary first by appropriate means to discover who he is and then to deal with him accordingly. As the collectivity of departed spirits in Ukuru he is *Jok Matar*, or White *Jok*. We have seen that white chalk is painted on his worshippers. But departed spirits are no more equal than the living and we have seen that special manifestations of *Jok* attach to the spirits of departed chiefs. Furthermore, each Alur chiefdom has its own special *Jok* which is its spiritual essence and embodiment. In the case of Ukuru, and perhaps all Alur chiefdoms, this is believed to take the material form of earth brought from the original Alur homeland. That is, while the ancestors of Ukuru chiefs were migrating, this earth was carried with them in a pot, tended by a special guardian lineage. The pot is said to have been a pot with two necks, such as is used in the rituals of twins. This is linked to the Ukuru myth of Alur origins which commences with the birth of twins. Some would even believe that the umbilical cords of the twins were also in the pot. The rain stones of the Ukuru chiefs are sometimes said to be derived from the bones of Ucak, the father of the twins. The Bito dynasty of Bunyoro also begins with the birth of the twins Isingoma Mpuga Rukidi and Kato Kimera. (We cannot here explore the importance of twins for myth, symbol and belief in their intricate further ramifications.) This *Jok* is the ancient and pristine *Jok* of Ukuru, an essential embodiment of the chiefdom in a political sense, as *Jok Matar* is in a human sense. Indeed this *Jok* is also *Jok Matar*. *Jok Matar* in every way stands for the primary spiritual essence of Ukuru. Yet the *Jok* of the chiefdom, who travelled materially in the earth, contained in the 'twin' pots symbolizing its territorial jurisdiction and origin, is also sometimes called *Rubanga*. He is never openly referred to as *Jok Rubanga*, but if I pressed the experts as to who he was they would sometimes whisper, *Rubanga*. It is impossible to define this with greater precision, and I have tried to represent it as it is. We are dealing with overlapping concepts.

Rubanga is certainly not a Nilotic Lwo word, and is usually taken to be of Runyoro derivation. It is also the case that the presence of *Jok Rubanga* in Alurland is much clearer and stronger in those parts whose proximity and links to Bunyoro are greatest. Alur think of *Jok Rubanga* in his highest capacity as the Creator, *Racwic* (here the metaphor of creation is from pottery) but the odd thing is that the name of the Creator in Bunyoro is *Rubanga* (Roscoe, 1923, 21). In Ankole he is also *Ruhanga* and in Buganda, by phonetic change, takes the form *Muwanga*. Furthermore, 'it seems probable that *Muwanga* is, indeed, the *lubaale* (divinity) most generally used by diviners' (Kaggwa and Welbourn, 1964, 220). The question arises as to whether it is also by phonetic change that *Ruhanga* appears as *Rubanga* in Alur, and also in Acholi. It is strange, however, that one of the Acholi chiefdoms whose *Jok* is *Nya Rubanga* (Girling, 1960, 226) is Palabek, which is one of those most distant from Bunyoro and whose founder is actually said to have come from Anuak, several hundred miles further north. However, not so far west of Palabek are the northern Madi, who are separated from the Alur by the Lugbara and a distance of about a hundred miles. Among the Madi, *Rabanga* is the name both of their principal divinity and of the earth (Williams, 1949, 203). Stranger still is the fact that, while the ethnography of Bunyoro tells us very little about *Rubanga,* Miss Davis' Dictionary (1938 and 1952, 147, 149) gives *Rubanga* as 'The *omucwezi* of twins'. More recently this has been confirmed by Beattie (1962, 2) who refers to 'the *mbandwa* spirit Rubanga, one of the most powerful of the traditional Cwezi spirits, and especially concerned with twin birth'. In two other entries the same dictionary gives 'Ruhanga, n., God' and 'ruhanga, o–, n., skull' followed by 'ruhanga, o–, n., NK (Sc. in Runyankore) valley'. These divergences, convergences, or coincidences cannot be further explored here, but the question of Bunyoro influence upon Alur religious belief and practice cannot be altogether avoided, although it is obviously part of a much wider question.

The *Jok* of the Ukuru chiefdom is enshrined in three important localities which mark stages in the westward migration of the Ukuru chiefs and their people up from the Nile into the highlands. While they were still at a place now called Kalowang', the *Jok* went into an ant-hill in the hut of one of the chief's wives and refused to travel any further. So the lineages of Pathedi and Paleu, who had taken it in turns to carry the *Jok,* were left behind to look after him at Kalowang'. This was some eleven generations ago. A little further up into the highlands the same thing happened again at a place now called Rateng. But again the Ukuru Alur travelled on, till they reached their present country. Each time the *Jok* stopped, guardians were left with him in that place, but a continuous embodiment of him was nonetheless carried on. He came to rest at Rukidi near one of the major villages of the present Ukuru chief. Rukidi, as we have seen, was also the Runyoro name of the founder of the Bito dynasty in Bunyoro. He is supposed to have been a Lwo, whose brothers were ancestors of other Lwo tribal groups such as the Alur and Acholi. The Chief of Ukuru goes with his retainers and in full regalia to sacrifice and take first fruits to the shrine of Rukidi every year after harvest. This must be considered the most important regular festival in Ukuru and comparable rituals occur in other chiefdoms.

Jok Matar as he is manifested in the ancestor cult, and *Jok Matar* or

Rubanga as he travelled with the chiefs and people and now resides in the principal shrines of Ukuru, is the most revered manifestation of *Jok* to the Ukuru Alur and certainly the most ancient. In this aspect, *Jok* is part and parcel of the Ukuru Alur identity itself, and for the chiefs and their kin goes back beyond this to the intrinsic essence of the Lwo. Manifestations of spirit possession and mediumship are strikingly absent except in the case of the mediums of fairly recently departed chiefs and the probable association of possession and prophecy with notable events such as the Ukuru *Jok* going into the ant-hill at Kalowang, and subsequently at Rateng'. When *Jok Matar* comes to ordinary folk they may 'shake 'a little but do not seem to go into deep or violent bouts of possession.

Frequently and importantly, spirit possession and mediumship are associated with the new cults of Jok which seem to have appeared increasingly among the Alur since pressure of outside influences became intensified about eighty years ago. The widespread incidence of such phenomena in Ukuru may indeed be even more recent. It is impossible to trace the exact sequence in which the new forms of Jok appeared. The first *Jok* of the new type in Ukuru was probably the one we shall have to call *New Rubanga,* as distinct from the ancient *Jok Rubanga* of Ukuru chiefdom. Then came *Jok Memba* and subsequently a host of others, some of which were really new, but many others were simply the *Jok* of some other Alur chiefdom on the move. There was thus a tendency for the Joks (*Jogi*) of a number of chiefdoms to become mobile, so that several chiefdoms seemed to exchange one another's while still retaining their own original version. *Jok Matar* of Ukuru spread to the other highland chiefdom of Ang'al further south, *Jok Riba* spread to Jupiyo. *New Rubanga* came to Ukuru from some chiefdoms in the Nile Valley, while from others *Jok Anyodu* also spread up to Ukuru. Most obviously, this reflects the increasing mobility of the Alur themselves and the breaking down of the autonomy, isolation and exclusiveness of each chiefdom. But religious observances are not always recognized as being such sensitive indicators of social change.

SPIRIT POSSESSION AND RELIGIOUS CHANGE

There is a universal feeling among the Alur that the regime of the spiritual has got out of hand in modern times, corresponding to the colonial period and their first awareness of the outside world. No doubt they are most aggrieved in their feeling that witches are seriously on the increase and that nothing effective is done to control them, now that the powers of the chief are curtailed and former ordeals and punishments banned. But their concern is also great for the fact that manifestations of *Jok* are more diverse, numerous, violent and unregulated, so few of them falling into the properly co-ordinated channels of orthodox expression which were adequate in the past. It seems as though new and hitherto unknown spirits can fall violently upon anyone at any time. Formerly the regular, communal worship of chiefs, elders and people was sufficient to maintain harmony between spirit, man and nature. (Compare the analogous assertions of change and proliferation in the supernatural world by the Nilotic Nuer (Evans-Pritchard, 1956, 29, 104) and Dinka (Lienhardt, 1961, 104–5, 138).)

In some parts of Alurland the harmful proliferation of *Jok* is directly attributed to the defeat and death of Kabarega, king of Bunyoro, and the subsequent neglect of the shrines there. I was given the most detailed interpretation of this by the Chief of Ang'al Jupiyo in Congo Alurland, an old man notably steeped in Alur tradition, in whose village I lived for five months in 1950. According to him Kabarega and his priests took care of the spirits of Jok which were responsible for all kinds of diseases (*tho rimu, ang'yewo, undyer, tho adundu, tho rimu makayo ic, tho manego dhanu pil, twal, ucendi, tho pyer, aling'ling', barwic, moko ecobo kor dhanu, moko egoyo tok dhanu, moko kayo i ng'ut dhanu . . .*). It is difficult to translate these terms and descriptions with any accuracy or to be certain to which diseases they apply, but they seem to include smallpox, chicken-pox, headaches, an infection of the eyes making them bloodshot and discharging pus, various diseases causing internal bleeding visible in the excreta and with accompanying pains in the stomach, pains in the chest and pains of the joints and muscles affecting the hips, the back and the neck.

According to the Chief of Jupiyo shrines were built in Bunyoro to the spirits presiding over all these diseases. If their guardians went to the king he gave them people to sacrifice, especially people with umbilical hernia. It was *Rubanga* who called for this sacrifice. People with umbilical hernia appear as special sacrifices to *Jok* in the traditions of the Junam Alur of the Nile Valley just to the north of Bunyoro. As recently as 1950 there was a notorious case over such a sacrifice

(Southall, 1956, 299). Roscoe's account (1923, chapter III) is generally consistent with this in respect of the regime of spirits, sickness, shrines, priests and their relation to the king of Bunyoro.

My informant continued:

> When the Europeans defeated and captured Kabarega and broke up all the shrines of *Rubanga* (he) began to walk everywhere, crossed the water (Lake Albert and the Albert Nile) and caught people this side and when the diviners inquired into it they found that it was Rubanga, and also *Udude*, the wife of *Rubanga*. Some of the Magungu (the people of northwest Bunyoro, nearest to the Alur) got medicine (*yath*, that is, herbs, bark, or roots) with which they could treat people for this and they held spirit possession seances for *Jok Rubanga*.

There was obvious fear and dislike of these manifestations of what I have called '*New Rubanga*', yet his basic identity with '*Old Rubanga*' is neither explained nor denied. Thus he said '*Rubanga* is like our ancestor, if he had not created men the world would have been empty, so they rejoice that he created them'.

While avoiding unsubstantiated distinctions and clarifications of what is essentially and subtly indistinct, amorphous, overlapping, interpenetrating and shrouded in mystery and a cloud of ignorance we may justifiably say that *Rubanga* is a very superior immanence of *Jok*, manifested in the creation of men (though Alur are really very vague about this) and also in life force both in its harmonious aspect of general fertility and in its perverted aspect of disease. It is thus that some Alur may put *Rubanga* at the head of a genealogy from *Jok*. Indeed, the inclusion of *Rubanga* is probably a minor piece of modern sophistication, but none the less significant. In Ang'al, the *Jok* of the chiefdom and the *Jok* of the ancestors are both alike recognised as being *Rubanga*. In Ukuru, *Jok Matar* is vaguely recognised as having the same identity.

From the mountains of Ang'al it is possible to look eastward straight across Lake Albert to Bunyoro fifty miles and more away. Older Alur such as my informant in Jupiyo have vivid memories of Kabarega's wars, for, although they were safely insulated from major physical involvement by the waters of the lake, they heard the guns firing on the other side, and were deeply affected by the defeat of what had been to them the greatest political power in the previously known world. To the extent, therefore, that we entertain as a working hypothesis that the most disturbing events in the world of affairs are reflected in the world of the spirit, it is entirely reasonable that the Alur should attribute the proliferation of *Jok* and the spread of violent spirit possession (which in their eyes is closely identified with the attacks of epidemics and diseases) to the defeat of Bunyoro and the breakdown of the system of spirit mangement and control maintained by the Bunyoro state until that time.

Kabarega's battles with the Europeans began in 1872 with the Battle of Masindi between him and Sir Samuel Baker, and he was fighting a good deal during the next two decades against Buganda to the southeast and Toro to the south. But what the Alur remember is most likely the final campaign against Kabarega which began in 1894 with the British invasion of Bunyoro, which drove Kabarega into the northern forests where guerrilla warfare continued until Kabarega was captured in South Lang'o in April 1899 together with King Mwanga of Buganda, by then also a fugitive. The fighting in north Bunyoro would certainly have attracted the attention of the Alur across Lake Albert, and it is to this area that they point when describing the outbreaks of spirit possession following the breakdown of Bunyoro guardianship. They point particularly to the landmark of Mount Igisi which is easily visible from across the lake. Not only is this the area associated with Kabarega's desperate and unsuccessful struggle, but it is the area of the Palwo, the Nilotic Palwo subjects of Kabarega who had a special relationship with the Lwo-derived Bito dynasty of Nyoro kings and perhaps even with some aspects of the system of spirit guardianship. Furthermore, the Palwo were, of course, very close to the Alur in language, culture and identification.

Another significant stage in the spread of spirit possession is marked by the story that Chief Amula of Ukuru became possessed by *Jok Hala* in 1917. The story is still told in Ukuru, but it is said to have been a slander spread about Amula by 'Adhere Kaman' (Abdulrahman) a Munyoro who had been made administrator of part of Amula's country and who would almost inevitably have been on bad terms with him. According to the slander, Amula was possessed by *Hala* so that the spirit should bring him guns out of the hill and he was hiding the guns on Usi hill. This was certainly a very inflammatory story at a time when the first British administrator had only reached Ukuru three years before and had remained in the District almost single handed.

The District Records do not specifically mention *Jok Hala* but undoubtedly the entry in March 1917 must refer to the same incident: 'Evidence that he twice made witchcraft to kill District Officers and bring guns to drive out the Government'. Already in 1915 Amula was reported as 'too steeped in beer and old ways, and too old to become really progressive'. In 1916 he was 'not improved – made no effort to recruit for the King's African Rifles' (!) So in 1917 he was deported to Masindi in Bunyoro and his son ruled in his place.

The identification of *Hala* with Allah is quite clearly made by the Alur. Among their Lugbara neighbours to the north Allah assumed the form of *Ola* (Driberg, 1931, 418). It is difficult not to associate the incident with the Yakany or Allah Water Cult which had led to many outbreaks further north. According to the District records the cult began as a cure for cerebrospinal meningitis and appearing successful, the claims for its virtues increased until eventually it was going to preserve from death, bring ancestors to life, bring dead cattle to life, permit Government orders to be flouted with impunity, provide immunity from rifles, which would be made to fire only water, and bring rifles to clear the Europeans out. The Lugbara especially took to it, but the Alur were rather on the fringe, and it was seen that it would fit easily into the complex of *Jok* beliefs and practices. In Lugbara it gave rise to shrines with flag poles attached, very similar to those of *Jok* in Alur. It is interesting that the spread of the cult in this part of Uganda has been officially regarded as derived from the outbreak among the Kakwa, on the southern margin of the Sudan, at Yei in January 1919. Yet its possession of Amula cannot have been later than 1917 when he was deported to Masindi.

However, Driberg (1931) and Middleton (1963) have traced the course of the movement more thoroughly. Although it was active among the Dinka and Bari in the 1880s and reached the Lugbara by about 1892, the Alur were insulated against this by the southern Madi living between them and the Lugbara of Terego. It then subsided and did not break out violently among the Lugbara again until 1918 and 1919. Even then it was mainly in north-east Lugbara and little in the south. The episode of Chief Amula and *Jok Hala* therefore appears rather isolated and no such outbreaks of any kind have ever been reported among the highland Alur, though Middleton (1963) mentions later occurrences among the Junam (riverain Alur) on the Nile at Panyango and Panyiguru in 1924.

Spirit possession is not so frequently attributed to *Jok Hala* today, but the name is sometimes used interchangeably with that of *Jok Memba*. *Memba* is just the English word 'member' adopted as another sign of the modernity of this cult. Perhaps it may also express the joyful and gregarious release from everyday frustrations and inhibitions, which we have noted as one characteristic of the congregation of acolytes in these seances. Another occasional synonym (even in the French speaking Congo) is *Jok Sore* (sorry). *Jok Memba* is derived from the spirits of the Alur soldiers who died in the First World War. It is thus a very symbol of change, mobility and external influence.

In principle each *Jok* spirit has its own cult and its own practitioners and devotees. Certainly each has its own distinctive repertoire of songs and associated drum rhythms. Indeed, many of the most popular songs are in origin songs of *Jok*. But in practice a diviner of standing is competent with respect to a number of different spirits of *Jok*, while on the other hand many people have been possessed by half a dozen or more different ones. However, a person who has been possessed by many spirits is likely himself to be a diviner qualified to deal with many spirits. The line of distinction is a fine one, but rests on whether or not he has paid the necessary fees to a master diviner (*won Jok*) and acquired the medicines and other secret apparatus. The medicines may well include herbal preparations which help to bring on states of dissociation (Cory, 1955, 931). The different possessing spirits are to some extent distinguished by their accompanying symbolism and practices, though a good deal of this seems common to many. When a person has been exorcised for possession by *Jok Memba* a shrine is built and a tall pole, often of bamboo, is erected with a small piece of white cotton fluttering from the top. This is in line with the general white colour symbolism of Jok, while the 'Flag' may possibly have associations with the army, like the spirits of the departed soldiers from whom *Memba* takes its origin. The shrines of the Allah Water Cult among the Lugbara had a similar symbol. But this has its counterpart in traditional Alur symbolism also. A pole is also set up, with a bunch of medicines attached to the top, to accompany a new ancestor shrine. It is not obligatory, and is in fact a feature borrowed from Lendu culture, as its name *Lyeza*, or in some parts *kyenzra*, implies. Similarly in the Alur dance a 'maypole' is erected with medicines at the top. Each medicine has its own detailed meaning and purpose, but the general significance of all these poles is that the wind should blow propitiously (*yamu kudhu ber*) which always signifies good health to the Alur.

The new *Jok Rubanga* is often accused of having orgiastic elements, though I cannot claim to have witnessed them. Some diviners in charge of seances for *Jok Rubanga* are said to pair off the males and females who attend. This would be likely to add to the attractions for many, while also provoking disapproval and criticism. The existence of similar practices in the *mbandwa* cult of Bunyoro, Buha (Scherer, 1959, 890–2) and the *Buswezi* cult of Sukuma – Nyamwezi strengthens the link of Rubanga with Bunyoro and the Interlacustrine Kingdoms. Older Alur definitely regard the possession cults of *Jok Memba* and *Jok Rubanga* as a deviation from traditional Alur culture, saying that they and other new possessing spirits came from Bunyoro and Palwo, or from the lake shore and Nile valley which lies in between.

There is no doubt that, despite the ubiquity and frequency of their activity, the status accorded to these new cults of spirit possession is lower than that of the time honoured *Jok Matar* and old *Jok Rubanga* of the ancestor cult, the state *Jok* of each major chiefdom and the Jok of major chiefs who have each acquired their own individual mediums as recounted for Ukuru. *Jok Riba* is an almost unique case of *Jok* manifested in an extraordinary natural phenomenon which has also acquired its own priesthood, mediumship and petty theocratic state. Besides this there are the legion spirits of hills and rocks, rivers and trees, the classical field of animism as popularly conceived. These are mostly low in the scale of importance. Some of them are regarded as *Jok*, but most are not, because like Riba they antedate Alur occupation, but unlike him have not been important enough to declare and name themselves through Alur mediums. Many therefore remain Lendu in character, like the former inhabitants of much of Alurland, though now incorporated in the general practice of Alur religion and ritual.

For example, Alur sometimes refer to malicious spirits of the streams as *Jok Adraga*. For a patient suffering from *Jok Adraga*, a goat may be sacrificed at the stream and the patient is washed with medicine. But this *Jok* also makes himself known in seances and one song I recorded runs 'Adraga with thick hair, Adraga of the river, let us go home and look for beer that he may drink, Adraga with thick hair, Adraga of the river'. Crazzolara (1960, 181) describes the Lugbara river spirit as 'Having a large head with long hair' among other variable characteristics. No certain etymological comparison is possible because of the tonal complexity of Lugbara and the related Okebo and Lendu languages, from which the Alur have borrowed. Middleton (1963, 97) gives Adro and Adrogua as Lugbara names of the river spirit. The analogy is close, for Adro is the very spirit which catches Lugbara adolescent girls and causes them sickness, turning them into diviners through the process of cure.

Perhaps the most important feature of the new manifestations of *Jok* in spirit possession is that they provide a metaphorical representation of the most fundamental changes which have shaken Alur society. Although the traditional society had important aspects of mobility and was always evolving, it was none the less a closed society in orientation. The ordinary Alur was bound to the corporate lineage into which he was born and its collective territory in which his ancestors were buried. He was also bound to the chief whom he served and on whose efficacy his security, health and prosperity were seen to depend. All these things were expressed in his service to the ancestors through the cult of *Jok Matar* and his contribution to and participation in the more important corporate worship of *Jok* in the shape of the hero ancestors and chiefs of his tribe. This worship in theory was, at least in intention, in fixed forms, at fixed times and places. By contrast with this, the new *Jok Rubanga*, *Memba* and the other recently invading spirits are as mobile as modern man. They may attack anyone at any time in any place. As they are seen to be in some respects intruders from outside, although distinctively clothed in much Alur cultural dress, they can certainly catch an Alur away from home, as he fights distant wars on foreign soil, or earns his living working for strange employers. Where large numbers of Alur go abroad on labour migration, the new spirits of *Jok* can also be served, because diviners, mediums and acolytes are all likely to be present. Alur abroad may even find converging correspondences between their own new spirits and those of other tribesfolk, leading to further interpenetration, deviation and syncretism. But orthodox traditional Alur religion cannot possibly be maintained abroad. It is foreign soil and the spirits concerned do not belong and cannot be accommodated there. Neither the shrines themselves, nor their special guardians and officiants, nor the proper regalia nor the correct medicines are there.

Whether the new spirits of *Jok* are a premonition of change or simply an inevitable reaction to it cannot be proved. Perhaps no historical analysis, however long term and detailed, could establish the point satisfactorily, for the interweaving is too subtle and esoteric. But the possibility that they are to some extent a premonition certainly cannot be ruled out. The fighting in Bunyoro, the closing in of the Arab slave traders from north and east, the remote echoes of the Mahdist upheaval reverberating from the Sudan, the coming of fire-arms, ivory poachers and new trade goods, of Christian missionaries and finally of colonial rule, can all be pointed to as antecedent events producing cultural shock and vibrating through the field of religion. But the rapid spread of the new spirits seems likely to have carried this spiritual dimension of change very often beyond the effective range of the new forces in their secular form. The new cults were both symptom and cure, representing the new problems and anxieties of a changing world at the dimension of spirit and also providing a new technique of treatment.

The story of the Allah Water Cult among the immediate Lugbara neighbours of the Alur brings out some striking differences, despite the important common elements already mentioned. The cult had arisen and spread characteristically among acephalous peoples such as the Dinka and Bari, threatened by Mahdist and Dervish raiders, among small groups revolting against Azande power further west and among the equally acephalous Kakwa and Lugbara. Besides this it appeared in military camps and towns (Masindi, Entebbe), where members of the same tribes were present in army units or civilian employment. Among the Lugbara, while Middleton assumes that it was persons of traditional consequence who acquired and spread the cult, it seems almost to have transformed the society, leading to new possibilities of political integration and co-ordination, so that in a number of cases it was the leaders of the cult who were made government chiefs by the first colonial administration.

Nothing of this kind happened among the Alur. The Allah Water Cult in its characteristic form never gained a significant foothold among them, despite its proximity on many sides. It was only one of several external currents of influence playing upon them at the time and although as we have seen important changes did occur in Alur religious behaviour, they were very effectively internalized and so firmly grafted onto what was there before that, despite disapproval, criticism and awareness of foreign influences, they appeared essentially as reinterpretations and re-emphases in the basic continuity of Alur religious tradition.

Indeed, this appears like a particular case of a much more general law, according to which the incidence of autonomous and revolutionary or millenarian outbreaks of religious expression is closely associated with the degree of psycho-cultural threat (often accompanied by physical deprivation and oppression) which is present on the one hand, and the efficacy of social institutions to meet and accommodate it on the other. Small, acephalous societies are particularly vulnerable in this regard, as is indicated by the numerous separatist movements in the North Nyanza area of Kenya, with its 'galaxy of missions' (Welbourn, 1961, 114), the Cargo Cults in New Guinea (Worsley, 1957) or the Ghost Dance throughout western North America (Mooney, 1965). By contrast, although Alur political specialization was modest, it proved adequate to their needs in this respect during the period of colonial Indirect Rule, particularly at the ideological level. The much stronger structure of specialized authority in Buganda has likewise been associated with the absence of effective outbreaks of religious separatism, and it is important to note that this is not a mere question of the availability of suppressive political force. On the other hand, where the severity of psycho-cultural threat is extreme, and combined with direct economic and political discrimination, as in South Africa, or Rhodesia (Gelfand, 1962, 48–9), autonomous religious movements spring up even among those from highly centralized traditional societies, granted the fact that the threat is intensified by their absence from home in the towns and on the European farms (Sundkler, 1961, 33–4, 85 ff, 93). The most impressive account of the successful internalization of spiritual change, through the grafting of new spirit possession cults on to an older continuous tradition, is Field's (1960) study of the shrines which sprang up 'like a crop of mushrooms' in Ashanti.

COMPARATIVE ASPECTS OF ALUR SPIRIT POSSESSION

We may finally attempt a brief assessment of the similarities and differences between the form of spirit mediumship among the Alur and some of their neighbouring peoples. Similarities may in some cases be due to direct cultural links, borrowing and common derivation, while in others they may only reflect the similar structuring of situations which arise from similar needs and serve similar purposes among peoples at comparable levels of development.

There can be no doubt that, in this aspect of their culture, the Nilotic Alur are marginal members of the *Cwezi* complex which spreads from Bunyoro in the north to Nyamwezi in the south and from Rwanda and Burundi in the west (and probably further) to Busoga and Bugwere in the east. The *Cwezi* cult shows considerable variation over this wide region, but the overlap of common elements from one area to the next is very great throughout. The Alur are far from possessing the *Cwezi* cult in its entirety and are not even aware of the *Cwezi* by that name, but the presence of *Rubanga* amongst them, together with many specific aspects of their belief and practice, clearly identify them as marginal members of the complex. In this respect the Alur show more resemblance to the Banyoro across Lake Albert than they do to their much closer northern neighbours the Lugbara. This is part of the empirical meaning of the claim by Alur chiefs to fraternal ancestry with the Nyoro kings and of the Nyoro tradition that the Bito dynasty derives from a Nilotic source.

In Alur, Nyoro and Sumbwa (Cory, 1955) alike, spirit possession is manifested first in sickness and diagnosed by divination, but this is part of the structuring of such situations which is extremely widespread. In all three areas there is the suggestion that, in the past, possession was managed within the descent group and it is likely to be a more recent development that spirits have fallen upon people quite indiscriminately, without regard to descent. There has been a corresponding increase in the number of possessing spirits present in any community and similarly in the number by which an individual medium is possessed. While in Alur the older form of possession was channelled mainly through the ancestor cult, and violent physical possession did not figure largely in it, in Nyoro and Sumbwa the possession cult was linked to specific clans or lineages, the lineages being accredited to particular Cwezi spirits in the case of the Nyoro, with a regular mechanism of succession to the position of lineage medium. It is only the Alur chief's cults and that of *Jok Riba* which approximate to this formal pattern. These variations reflect differences between these peoples in their systems of descent and residence, as well as the greater centralization of the Nyoro.

All share the white symbolism of the most revered and traditional spirits, and this of course is enormously widespread as a mark of respect for elders and ancestors (cf. Turner, 1957, 107, 120). But the Nyoro symbol of black for the newer and less respected spirits is not reported as general and black is more significant to the Alur in rain rituals. The Alur kneeling of the initiate between the legs of the diviner-medium is probably equivalent to the sitting on the lap reported for the Nyoro, but lacks the multiple symbolic associations with marriage ritual which characterize the latter. However, the marriage metaphor does appear in the installation of the medium of Riba, where the temporary hut is likened to the *Ambaza* or wedding hut of the Lendu. Both Alur and Nyoro initiate an adult proxy for a sick child. Their general techniques of inducing possession by dancing, drumming, rattling and singing seem similar and in both cases there are complaints from the experts if the patient's submission and reception of the spirit is delayed, so that distinctions between degrees of loss of consciousness, or between personal states of trance and conformity with culturally patterned behaviour equated with spirit possession and inculcated from infancy, are hard to draw and probably meaningless. In all three, infusions figure in the rituals and may assist processes of dissociation, but are clearly not regarded or relied upon as automatic inducements. There is a similar ambivalence in that both Alur and Nyoro seances must be defined as joyful occasions of welcoming the spirit, yet in fact they are occasions of dread and suffering for the patient and it is surely with relief that the spirit is eventually taken out into the grass where he can be entertained in a material shrine. But Alur seances are lacking in formal elaboration and especially in the ritually induced terror which is used to ensure secrecy in the Nyoro and Sumbwa rites. All employ garbled speech but in Alur again, it is not formalized into a secret 'language' as in the other two areas. However, Alur stick much more consistently to their numerical symbolism of three for male and four for female, whereas in Bunyoro it is somewhat confused and also combined with other ritual numbers and in Sumbwa there is only a certain ritual stress on three. The tying of grass onto the persons of initiates figures in Alur and Nyoro but it is not clear whether the significance is the same. Both Nyoro and Sumbwa emphasize the mutual sexual rights and obligations of cult members, but in Alur this only appears as a rather unformalized aspect of the new *Rubanga* cult in some areas.

The spiritual regime of the Lugbara is very different. We have already seen that the Allah Water Cult played a much more revolutionary part among them than in its faint appearance in Alurland. The ancestors were conceptually divided from God in a marked dichotomy (Middleton, 1960, 249) and it is only the possession of girls by river spirits and their eventual initiation as diviners that can be at all compared to spirit possession among the Alur. However, apart from the syncretism of *Jok Adraga* already mentioned, the river spirits among the Alur do not usually give rise to spirit possession or mediumship. They occupy a lowly place in the hierarchy, are harmful and feared, but adequately dealt with by formal ritual observances. The Lugbara identification of major epidemic diseases with spirit possession suggests a further counterpart with Alur and Nyoro, which would be interesting if there was evidence for a historical connection, but it is evidently rather ill defined and its source impossible to trace.

Comparison with a quite different culture area such as that of Shona (Gelfand, 1962) brings out the extent of similarity which arises from structural-functional likeness rather than common genetic origin. The Shona have a somewhat similar spirit hierarchy, with a distant, otiose, directly unapproachable divinity and nearer, more immanent spirits linked to chiefdoms and descent groups. Each chiefdom has a major guardian spirit with its own medium, somewhat resembling the mediums of Alur chiefs' spirits. The spirits which appear in kin groups do not cause possession or have mediums (except in the case of aggrieved spirits who died with an unrighted wrong). Formal worship is sufficient, rather as in the case of the old *Jok Matar* of the Alur. Although this aspect is not fully explored, it is plain that the *shave* spirits of the Shona (Gelfand, 1962, 177–8) correspond closely to the spiritual dimension of change as found among the Alur. The *shave* are numerous though of low status, and new ones are always appearing. They are not tied to chiefdoms or descent groups. While the older *shave* represent baboons, Matabele who died as foreigners in Mashonaland, or Shona who died away from home (as in the case of the Alur *Jok Memba*), the newer ones may even represent Europeans. The older ones conferred mainly skill in hunting and healing, but the newer ones may assist in understanding Europeans and even in behaving like them, speaking English or 'Kitchen Kaffir' and so directly helping initiates in their search for modern employment outside tribal society. It is perhaps to be attributed to the common stock of symbolic referents offered by similar natural environments that the Shona tribal spirit 'roars like a lion' on possessing his medium, just as *Jok Riba* does in his, and as the leading medium in the Buswezi is said to be eaten by a lion.

NOTE

[1]One of the tribes formerly under partial Alur domination and therefore regarded as of low status.

REFERENCES

BAMUNOBA, Y. K.; WELBOURN, F. B. 1965 'Emandwa initiation in Ankole', *Uganda Journal* 29 (1), 13–25.

BEATTIE, J. H. M. 1961 'Group aspects of the Nyoro spirit mediumship cult', *Rhodes-Livingstone Journal* 30, 11–38.

1957 'Initiation into the Cwezi spirit possession cult in Bunyor*Aor*', *ican Studies* 16 (3).

CORY, H. 1955 'The Buswezi', *American Anthropologist* 57, 923–952.

CRAZZOLARA, J. P. 1960 *A study of the Logbara (Ma'di) language*. London, Oxford University Press.

DAVIS, M. B. 1952 *A Lunyoro-Lunyankole-English and English-Lunyoro-Lunyankole dictionary*. London, Macmillan.

DRIBERG, J. H. 1931 'Yakan', *Journal of the Royal Anthropological Institute* 61, 413.

EVANS-PRITCHARD, E. E. 1956 *Nuer religion*. Oxford, Clarendon Press.

FIELD, M. J. 1960 *Search for security*. London, Faber.

GELFAND, M. 1962 *Shona religion*. Cape Town, Juta.

GIRLING, F. K. 1960 *The Acholi of Uganda*. London, HMSO.

KAGGWA, L. B.; WELBOURN, F. B. 1964 '*Lubaale* initiation in Buganda', *Uganda Journal* 28 (2), 218–220.

LIENHARDT, G. 1961 *Divinity and experience*. Oxford, Clarendon Press.

MIDDLETON, J. 1960 *Lugbara religion*. London, Oxford University Press.

1963 'The Yakan or Allah Water Cult among the Lugbara', *Journal of the Royal Anthropological Institute* 93 (1), 80.

MOONEY, J. 1965 *The Ghost Dance religion*. Chicago, University of Chicago Press.

NADEL, S. F. 1947 'A study of shamanism in the Nuba mountains', *Journal of the Royal Anthropological Institute* 76 (1), 25.

PARK, G. K. 1963 'Divination and its social contexts', *Journal of the Royal Anthropological Institute* 93 (2), 195.

ROSCOE, J. 1923a *The Bakitara*. Cambridge University Press.

1923b *The Banyankole*. Cambridge University Press.

SCHERER, J. H. 1959 'The Ha of Tanganyika', *Anthropos* 54, 841–904.

SOUTHALL, A. W. 1956 *Alur society*. Cambridge, Heffer.

SUNDKLER, B. G. M. 1961 *Bantu prophets in South Africa*. London, Oxford University Press.

TROWELL, M.; WACHSMANN, K. P. 1953 *Tribal crafts of Uganda*. London, Oxford University Press.

TURNER, V. W. 1957 *Schism and continuity in an African society*. Manchester University Press.

WELBOURN, F. B. 1961 *East African rebels*. London, SCM Press.

WILLIAMS, F. R. J. 1949 'The pagan religion of the Madi', *Uganda Journal* 12 (2), 202.

WORSLEY, P. 1957 *The trumpet shall sound*. London, MacGibbon and Kee.

THE THEORY AND PRACTICE OF SUKUMA SPIRIT MEDIUMSHIP

R. E. S. Tanner

The Sukuma, a Bantu people numbering more than a million, occupy a large area of the cultivation steppe south of Lake Victoria and, with their allied tribe, the Nyamwezi, of largely similar customs and language, spread south to the central railway line.

This is an area of low rainfall, heavier near to the lake and drying out to the south and east, averaging about thirty inches per year, and of limited fertility. The people are widely spaced to take advantage of surface water and grazing, in small agnatic groups and single households where, in the past, the normal social unit was structured around the father with his married sons. Although life has improved economically with a huge increase in cotton growing, this has probably taken place at the expense of food crops and by using up vacant land; the life of Sukuma tribesmen is generally still hard and uncertain. Their culture is based on stock-keeping and on cultivation, and their interest in the former has changed from an interest which had a strong religious basis to the present economic and social considerations in which their numbers, for most owners, continue to be more important than their quality. Also the wide spacing of their homes has contributed to the difficulties of providing even primary education and to the comparatively small influence of Christianity and Islam except in the areas near to the lake and in the small towns and trading centres; they are a conservative people. Each chiefdom has a different origin and there are considerable differences between, as well as within, chiefdoms in social and magico-religious practice.

The Sukuma believe in God as having supreme power. He has a large number of aspects and names which vary in popularity and use from one locality to another; for example, near to Lake Victoria, God is often referred to as Ngassa, while to the south this name is little used and then only in association with water. Although they are monotheistic, there is no overall cult directed to one God and no direct worship of God other than the use of his local name as a part of invocations spoken by a spirit medium in ancestor propitiation ceremonies or in everyday phrases. They believe, however, that their God is not a positive force intending that they should benefit from life, and in their invocations and in the use of his name in conversation, they hope that he will be instrumental in neutralizing the forces of evil acting against them so that they will be left alone in a neutral environment which will enable them to prosper (Tanner, 1956).

Inferior to this God in overall power but individually active, usually malignant and powerful, are the bilaterally ascended ancestors of every Sukuma, who have to be propitiated to ensure their neutrality, either because they have been irritated in the spirit world by their descendants' neglect, or because they were angered in life by acts alleged to have been committed by their relatives. This neutrality is understood by the Sukuma to be benevolent. God and the ancestors are good, not because they arrange or insure good, but because they leave the Sukuma alone to prosper. Typical examples are dying away from home, which requires the symbolic reunification of the dead ancestor with his descendants' home, or mistreatment of a woman during a famine, resulting in her death, for which propitiation has to be made. The Sukuma, whether practising his traditional religion or not, sees his ancestors and descendants as a continuous chain in which he is a link. In addition to the indifference of God and the potential malevolence of his ancestors, he can also be affected by the evil acts of his agnates and neighbours, expressed through witchcraft.

It is necessary to stress that the Sukuma in his magico-religious practices wishes to be left alone and that he seeks to neutralize the evil influences which are preventing him from gaining in wealth through the fertility of his wife and children, cattle and fields. In order to return to this state of neutrality, he has to know what to neutralize and he is not able, unaided, to find this out. He has to go to a medium-diviner who will endeavour to diagnose the cause of his misfortune by a process of elimination.

These spirit mediums, who are usually men, practise because they have been possessed by one at least of their own ancestors, through whose power they are able to diagnose the cause of the misfortunes of others (Tanner, 1957a). They themselves have become sick, lost cattle, babies have died or rain has not fallen and, on consulting a spirit medium, they have been told that one of their own ancestors wishes them to practise as a medium. It is impossible to find out whether this is a *post-hoc* rationalization of spirit mediumship but certainly they are emphatic that it is impossible to practise successfully without the benevolence of their ancestors. But there is no direct obligation to practise inherited from father to son or from mother to daughter; very often they have never heard of the ancestor causing their misfortune, much less that he or she was a medium. There is no relationship to mental abnormality or epilepsy nor do mediums appear to be social deviants. The need to take up mediumship is not associated with dreams, nightmares or omens. In this sense, spirit mediums are helped by their ancestors and the withdrawal of this help must mean the loss of their powers, so those who are practising mediums can be assumed to be successful. There are no non-human spirits known to the Sukuma and there has been no development of new spirits in recent years. There has been, however, some blurring with the Islamic concept of the evil spirit, *Shetani*, the term which is usually used now in the vernacular for any spirit activity.

Spirit mediumship is not an organized and clearly defined cult in which particular mediums are confined to particular spirits. Everyone in Usukuma is permeated by the influence of his ancestors, which can be used for mediumship, but is also essential for the successful practice of leechcraft and the organization of local social and magico-religious groups. Each mediumship has been initiated by the activities of a particular spirit but the medium is not in exclusive control of or apparently wholly dependent on this initiating spirit – his invocations are addressed to all his ancestors and this particular spirit may not be mentioned. This is ascribed to the need to avoid making all the ancestors jealous of the one who is being propitiated. Further misfortune or the inability to practise after training would be attributed to other ancestors needing attention, rather than to the continuing malevolence of the original one.

In its present form propitiation does not involve any continuous acts or thoughts directed towards a particular ancestor; thus a medium states that a sick man should change his name but it is only necessary for this to be changed formally and used once for the propitiation to be successful; he does not have to use the name every day. Thus the medium who practises has to be constantly on guard to ensure the benevolence of other ancestors.

This typifies the limited powers of the ancestors in their cognisance of their descendants' affairs and the interdependence of the living and the dead. The latter can only survive as entities if their descendants remember them and the former can only prosper if their ancestors are propitiated and so withhold their malevolence; their personalities are essentially human and except that they function immaterially rather than materially, they have not taken on any characteristics which they did not possess in life. The Sukuma belief that the dead can influence the living is a logical extension of their conception of family and lineage unity as involving the past, present, and future. In this it seems that the cult of ancestor worship has changed from a regular cycle of remembrance from the household to chiefdom level to the present situation, in which propitiation is only initiated after their malevolence has been shown in personally experienced misfortune. It is probably not possible to find anyone now who carried out these regular neutralizing rites and they probably ceased to be practised prior to 1939. So the present practice of spirit mediumship is, in theory, only related to the personal counteracting of misfortune.

Once the man or woman has been told that he has to take up spirit mediumship, he becomes the pupil of a practising medium for whom he works until he has acquired enough knowledge to start practising himself. Living with the medium, he acquires a visual knowledge of the technique and, while working for him, he learns the medicinal and magico-religious herbal lore of his master. Certainly, nothing is imparted without the medium profiting from his pupil's work, or the knowledge being bought. Each medium's knowledge of techniques and the magical or medicinal ingredients of his medicines are personal to himself alone, acquired by trial and error, purchase and experiment. It is his economic capital, which he will not release without an equivalent economic return. Apart from the cash profit from dealing with patients, his pupils must also be accounted as a visible profit of his calling, doing the heavier work and advertising his abilities.

This training may take years to complete, during which time the pupil comes and goes, depending on his ability to leave home and work. Sometimes his master is practising and he learns by observation; at other times no one comes for consultations or lives with the medium in order to undergo a lengthy cure, so that the apprentice is little more than a house servant, as a distant relative might be, who must carry out his share of domestic and agricultural tasks if he wishes to remain attached to that particular medium. There is no formal consecration ceremony before the medium starts to practise, although there would be an initiation if he wished to join the mediums' cult group.

The medium practises in the open air within his own house compound or in a special area immediately outside. This place is usually near to the small conical shrines of sticks, stones and thatch put up for particular ancestors. Sometimes this place is encircled with aloe plants and stones and kept well swept. Sometimes, however, it is enough for the medium to sit beside his ritual staff, which is decorated with strips of skin from the propitiatory sacrifices which he has carried out, and from which hang the small gourds containing his medicines. He himself, when he carries out a consultation, will be dressed in hides, necklaces and bangles and use a number of articles such as decorated fly-whisks, Maasai swords, iron spears, bells and gourds which are associated with various ancestors. They are necessary for proper consultations, and are acquired often at some cost in money and in time spent in searching, and they are imitatively treated as the actual articles used by these ancestors. They are sacred to his particular mediumship and will decay from use in time just as the original articles used by his ancestors have decayed and disappeared.

THE MEDIUM'S ROLE

The medium, once he has started practising, will not be accorded any special position by his own community; until he has proved himself successful he will only be a stock-keeper and cultivator with a sideline, and even after he succeeds he will not be excused communal tasks, nor will he feel that he no longer needs his neighbours' help. Above all, his social position will depend on whether he is dealing with occasional patients coming to him for consultation or whether he is an office-holder in an active group cult, which may be of social, economic, and magico-religious importance to a part of the local community. Mediums do not appear to make claims about what they are able to achieve, and in conversation with other Sukuma, they are noticeably reticent about their powers.

Few, if any, of the people who come to a medium for consultations will come from their own neighbourhoods. Most consult a medium some distance from their homes with whom there is no existing relationship and whose reputation has been enhanced by gossip. Much travelling is done by persons in trouble seeking a successful medium.

Since the person consulting a medium is not his neighbour and is often unknown to him, the medium has to use his cunning to extract possible causes from the patient, and he uses his assistants and pupils between consultations to find out the local pressures and problems which might be at the root of his client's troubles. The medium himself often travels widely seeking for better herbal and magic medicines, and he is able to apply the knowledge gained in other parts of Usukuma to his client's problems.

The typical medium is semi-literate at the most, but seemingly above the average in intelligence. His role may still be a way to social significance for the intelligent person of limited education, who can find no other way of advancing himself in his own locality. Although there is clearly an economic incentive to practising, this cannot be the only reason. The time spent in acquiring esoteric knowledge and practising is time away from trying to make money from stock-keeping, cotton growing and food cultivation to support his family and to fulfil and expand his social obligations to his neighbours and those who may come and consult him. Few mediums practise full time and those who do so do not appear to benefit materially from their practice because success will result in greater obligations to sacrifice, which in turn will mean greater expense. An important part of sacrifice is the entertainment of neighbours so that they will not become jealous of a medium's success and he himself fall victim to their animosity. Success brings social importance which he has to maintain through a web of reciprocities: he cannot benefit materially except in secret or by subterfuge.

The spirit medium has several roles – to diagnose, to propitiate and to cure – all or any of which may be played in a particular case. It cannot be said that the cult and the medium's role are clandestine, or that they have been affected by government disapproval or Christian propaganda. The Government's Witchcraft Ordinance was never used against mediums, and up to the present the Christian missions have only influenced a small number of Sukuma.

Consultations take place during the daytime, preferably in the early morning, when the ancestor spirits are considered to be more readily contacted. They are not hurried affairs and the propitiation ceremonies which may result from them are lengthy and quite openly performed – the absence of neighbours, when there is no meat or beer to be had from a sacrifice, may be due to their indifference and to their awareness that it will not be different from others which they have seen. Anyone can watch, and the children come and go; there is a sense of purpose in the performance but only a few of the persons there are actively involved. The only recent change in these practices seems to be that the majority of literate persons would regard the cult as out-of-date and they would be ashamed to attend openly, so consultations for them take place privately, perhaps in the evening.

When he diagnoses, the medium either induces in himself a state of auto-hysteria with the aid of gourds or tin rattles held in both hands and shaken near to his head, or he does the same to his consultant (Tanner, 1955a). The magician sits on a stool in the circle dressed in a number of lion, leopard, or goat-skins, wearing also a mass of stone and shell necklaces and bangles and a head-dress of coloured beads and holding in his hands rattles and a ceremonial fly-whisk. The person consulting him squats on the ground in front of him, and between them on the ground lies the fee for the consultation in coin, which remains there until the person is satisfied with the diagnosis and the cure is provided.

The patient brings with him a twig from a euphorbia bush on which he himself has spat; if, however, the sick person is too ill to come himself, he spits on a twig of the same bush and his representative takes it to the magician. This twig is passed to the magician without comment, although the patient goes over the necessary details in his heart as he does so. The name of the sick person is not even mentioned. The magician sniffs the twig and ruminates over it for a few minutes before starting the seance. (This connection by spitting is also used by those magicians (*nchemba ngoko*) who diagnose through examining the entrails of a young chicken after the consultor has spat into its beak. They are also possessed by ancestor spirits in order to practise but they work without any initiating hysteria.)

The magician settles himself well on to his stool and proceeds to twirl his rattles slowly in front of him. The rattles consist of gourds filled with small stones and sand and are shaken close to the head. This rattling noise is supposed to trouble the spirits invoked, who readily assist in the seances in order that the noise may stop. Soon the magician hiccoughs a little and mutters to himself in a rising crescendo, often accompanied by piercing whistling resembling the Maasai cattle-calls. The muttering then becomes clearer and resolves itself into a jumble of words and sounds uttered in falsetto voice. Suddenly the magician stops rattling and starts to pronounce as his diagnosis what he had been told by the ancestor spirit while he was in his trance. The stopping of the rattling is said to be done by the ancestor spirit and not under the direct volition of the magician.

Informants state that the language of this delirium is Kinaturu, which is regarded as the tongue of the ancestors of all magicians, since they are all thought to have descended from the Naturu tribe. This, however, is unlikely, as the sounds seem to be merely a repetitious jumble of monosyllables, used because of their phonetic simplicity rather than because they might make connected phrases, and indeed no one was able to interpret any of the words or phrases used. The connection with Naturu, a small hunting tribe to the south-east, seems to be mythical; there is certainly no present connection between mediums and this tribe. There does not appear to be a distinct vocabulary as with the Buchwezi cult in Usukuma, possibly because mediumship no longer involves any group activities or initiation in which such a vocabulary could have been learnt and passed on.

Just as much of the equipment used or worn by the medium at consultations is thought to be rare and to have come from elsewhere, so the alleged use of another and little-known language may be due to the same need to take the medium's observable acts out of the Sukuma's normal social world. The medium's behaviour in consultations and in other cult practices is noticeably un-Sukuma; where they are restrained and unexpressive, he is flamboyant and voluble; while they dress monotonously alike, he becomes a bizarre figure covered with strange or out-of-date objects. In his practice he is the antithesis of normal Sukuma behaviour; but as well as being atypical his performance is also dramatic, so that for both the medium and his patient possession may be a form of catharsis of short duration. There may be an interval of weeks at least between the diagnosis and the time when the person concerned is able to carry out the obligation imposed upon him.

The process of possession may take a few minutes or hours of prolonged rattling, and its onset can be seen in the mounting physical movements and verbal ramblings, until the medium drops the rattle and begins to give his diagnosis in the form of a dialogue in which he develops his theme to the accompaniment of affirmative grunts or silence from the patient.

If the patient is possessed, the medium will question him while the former is hysterical, in order to find out which ancestor is the cause of the trouble and why he is angry, and he will then gradually permit his real personality to take over again. The consultation should not be terminated abruptly or the ancestor concerned would be further angered. It is difficult to judge the depth of this dissociation but consciousness is certainly affected, although mediums do react to sudden movement. Clinically the symptoms observed on several occasions made the condition classifiable medically as hysteria (Batchelor, 1953). The possessed person does not move from the sitting position assumed at the beginning of the session and although his behaviour above the waist may appear to be completely out of control, no attempt is made to restrain him. The medium is usually in early middle age while most possessed patients are post-puberty women of all ages up to well beyond the menopause. The possessed person is not treated with any particular care or reverence, and the attitudes of the onlookers seem to show that this is a commonplace happening. There is no spreading of hysteria to the onlookers and the medium allegedly sits at an angle to his patient during the session to prevent himself from also becoming possessed. Also there are no spontaneous trances of mediums in everyday life, nor do persons who are not mediums experience trances which are thought to be indicative of the need to take up mediumship.

In one of the seances witnessed, an old woman, who had been intermittently ill for some time, sat on a sheep-skin on the ground, sideways to the magician who was seated on a small stool; first of all he drew a line of chalk across her chest and back and crumbled some of the chalk on the top of her head. He then whistled irregularly a few times to call up the spirits and then, having tapped the handles of his rattles together as another sign, started to rattle slowly, with a gradually increasing tempo, holding the rattles on either side of her head. The magician himself, although very vigorous during the rattling, appeared to be under complete control throughout. After a few minutes the woman started whimpering and crying, quivering and working her shoulders up and down. As soon as this happened the magician started to shout questions at her in a loud and aggressive voice. As the woman became more hysterical her eyes rolled upwards and she started to mutter and babble; the magician repeatedly shouted at her, 'Who are you, who are you?' until at last she spoke in a restrained and inexpressive voice and, in a series of isolated phrases, said that she was an old woman who had been chased away from her home because of suspected witchcraft and had died of starvation in the forest. Another spate of rattling followed until the woman started to speak again and said that she wanted her great-grand-daughter to sleep in a round house (i.e. not one of modern design) and to wear a necklace of ostrich-egg beads. The seance was then broken off; the magician wiped the chalk marks from the woman's body, and she was helped to her feet, and, still moaning, was taken into the house to recover.

In another seance the son of the magician assisted in the work by using a third rattle behind the patient's head. In this case, the patient was a young woman who had failed to conceive after several years of marriage, and hysterical reactions did not start until some twenty minutes of rattling had elapsed. There is no time limit to such a session, and if the patient is unusually resistant he or she may be given some ground herbs to smoke as a narcotic, in order to subdue conscious actions and induce greater receptivity.

The distinctive whistling used to call up the spirits is alleged to be answered in the hysterical state by whistling, if the troublesome spirit is a man, and by laughter if it is a woman, but these were not heard in these two cases. The slow crescendo of the rattling allows for the gradual arrival of the spirit concerned, since if it arrived too quickly it would have a harmful effect on the patient. The seance involves sustained effort for both the magician and the patient, and the charge is usually about five shillings in silver, or sometimes a goat for especially good results. It can take place at any time of day, for it does not depend upon the voluntary appearance of the spirits, as is the case with propitiation ceremonies at the family shrines, or when a magician requires the presence of his own ancestors in order to make a diagnosis for a patient.

In other seances it is normal for the patient to be washed down with

Plate 11 Part of the ritual of initiation into the Buchwezi mediumship cult, Sukuma, Tanzania. A young initiate steps over the prone body of the initiator and a slaughtered sheep

Plate 12 Initiation into the Buchwezi mediumship cult, Sukuma, Tanzania. The group of young initiates is about to enter the water for ritual washing

Plate 13 (below) Group of initiates into the Buchwezi mediumship cult, Sukuma, Tanzania: ceremony of ritual washing

leaves dipped in magic medicines, after which both the leaves and remaining water are taken out of the compound and left at a cross-roads, so that any evil which may have come out of the seance will be picked up and carried far away by any stranger who passes over the debris.

The medium, allegedly through the assistance of his ancestors, is also able to cure his patients by providing medicines which are both herbal and magical in content. The medium is aware of the active elements in his prescriptions and reduces their strength to a very low level because of the fear of poisoning. The medium's wide botanical knowledge is used to deal with the external symptoms with some success where they are not symptomatic of deeper infections – cuts, sores, coughs, colds, fevers, swellings and pain can all have Sukuma botanical remedies (Tanner, 1959). A medium does not refuse to attempt to cure the incurable; to do so would be to lose an opportunity and there is comfort for the sick person in his activity, even if there is no cure. Rumours of cures seem to spread more quickly and successfully than rumours of failure. The magical element comes with the mixing purely on herbal medicines with ingredients based on such analogical beliefs as that elephantiasis is curable by the use of the baobab tree, whose shape resembles the infected limb. This magical element becomes dominant in the medium's preparation of protective, aggressive, creative and assertive medicine (Cory, 1949) where the ingredients are mostly chosen for their analogous properties, such as dust from the chief's house for strength, leper's excreta for killing, lion's fat for bravery. There is no direct connection between mediumship and witchcraft; a medium may be capable of working evil but there is no assumption that, as he deals in protective magic medicines, he will also be able to create injurious ones; certainly such aggressive activity is thought to be very much less than his protective and other actions.

The medium also propitiates. He may carry out further sacrifices to his own ancestors or assist at the sacrifices of others in their compounds, or publicly on behalf of a parish suffering from drought. He may participate and play an important part in the organization and practice of cults such as the Buchwezi, partially or wholly dependent on magical elements, regardless of their social and economic functions. These categories are not exact, as the medium will deviate into whatever speciality brings success, while others practise in several categories at the same time.

It is obvious to most Sukuma, and they do not deny it, that mediums have not the power which they allege they have; if they had they would be more successful than they are. The mediums themselves are aware of their own failings; some feel that they would indeed be able to do what they profess to do if they were able to get into better relationships with their ancestors and were able to carry out their practice without any interference from an indifferent God. It is not credulity alone which makes the Sukuma use these mediums – these ones may be bogus but there may be others who are not so – indeed some clients play tricks on them to show that they are charlatans. But they do this for their own private satisfaction; they would be unlikely to tell their neighbours for fear of incurring the medium's enmity and so perhaps becoming the object of his witchcraft.

The medium has not made many changes to adjust himself to current life – most of the ancestors who have to be propitiated are still thought to belong to the long distant past, although there have been cases of soldiers dying overseas in the 1939–45 war whose spirits have had to be propitiated. There have been no developments of new spirit forms and the medium's techniques and equipment are still essentially traditional. Though ranking in the cult shows European influence dating from the early days of the colonial administration, so that mediums may be graded as kings, queens, judges, and police, there do not appear to have been any more recent adjustments.

The system survives no matter how many corrupt mediums practise, because the Sukuma are worried by life, possibly now more than ever before; the old political organization, which was already in decay, has been abolished by the new government, but it has not yet been replaced by a system useful and intelligible to the common man. The breakdown of their traditional religion as a part of their total social system has meant that they can no longer seek and find single causes for illness and misfortune deriving from their environment. They can no longer see them as due to Sukuma causes alone, although they are compelled by the circumstances of their lives to try and deal with them in Sukuma terms. Now they may consider misfortune as a combination of enmities – the Indian shop-keeper, the secretary of the local co-operative, the headman, neighbours and relatives – and they see no incompatibility in trying several methods at once, including Western medicine, in the hope of chancing on the cause; at least they can hope to eliminate some of the possible factors through consultation with a medium.

CULT ORGANIZATION

Each medium endeavours to be the centre of a specific spirit cult, either by initiating one or by becoming the leader of an existing cult so that he rises in economic and social importance as well as in magico-religious significance.

It seems that in the last century the medium's role, and the consequent organization of the cult, has gone through three stages. In the first stage, prior to the colonial period, mediums were few in number and closely integrated into the political as well as the religious life of each chiefdom. They were an essential element in the balance of the chiefdom, for the chief required their support if he was to remain in power, while at the same time they prevented him from becoming dominantly powerful. The chief had to be chosen by a group of elders appointed by the former chiefs as advisers, and by the heads of clans and lineages in the chiefdom. This process functioned much as an American presidential or party convention, except that with intermittent deadlocks resolved by the divination of a medium's caucus (Cory, 1951), who must have been canvassed in advance to support a particular candidate.

The ceremonies of installing the chief included various rites involving magical ritual and medicines, without which he could not function validly. The mediums concerned could thwart this success by not carrying out the rites correctly, so their support was necessary from the start (Tanner, 1957b). The chief had subsequently to recognize these obligations to his initial supporters, or the possibly delicate balance of power in his favour within the chiefdom might be upset by innuendo or witchcraft imputations.

Similarly, the chief, as the embodiment of the chiefdom's welfare, had to carry out a continual series of rites for the control of the agricultural cycle and to provide rain, as well as to prevent epidemics and to promote successful warfare (Cory, 1954). He was unable to carry out these rites alone so that, throughout his reign, he was obliged to use mediums whom he had to support while they were working in his interests. Many of these mediums from the past are still remembered by name, indeed so important were they that it is sometimes difficult to say which was the medium and which the chief. In myth they are represented as workers of miracles, and this gives traditional support to the modern medium's claim to eminence.

In the second stage the medium joins and attempts to become the centre of a cult which may depend, to a greater or lesser extent, on a magico-religious component. These cults may vary from dancing groups, in which this magical element is very small (their main activity being competitive dancing between two opposed groups such as the Bugika and Bugaru, in which the dance leaders use magic medicines to attract away the members of the other group), to professional organizations of mediums, sorcerers, hunters, fishermen and village elders. Lastly, there are societies in which mediums predominate but which attract a lay following, such as the Buchwezi group. It appears that these forms of corporate groups are undergoing change and they are unlikely to survive when other forms of entertainment are provided, when education is extended, and when the social life of the people becomes more individualized.

Nevertheless these groups, in one form or another, still have great influence in Usukuma. Although they are formed in small local chapters, which may be within a chiefdom or parish, the wider organization covers the whole of Usukuma, so that it can provide a member with contacts in areas other than his own which would otherwise be lacking, since clan structure is weak and implies no corporate activities and few and diminishing obligations. Although so widely dispersed, the framework is still Sukuma and the existence and viability of local chapters depends entirely on dominant individuals who have successfully combined the satisfaction of a local need with their own advantage. Also, the organization in local chapters is compatible with the spread-out nature of Sukuma homesteads and fields. There have, however, been infrequent gatherings of chapters from much wider areas, as in the last mediums' group meeting in Geita in 1949, and in some Bugika and Bugaru dancing society sessions in recent years in Bukumbi and Kissessa. The feeding and accommodation of such large groups is too difficult for many large meetings in a countryside where the settlement is sparse and dispersed.

Within each group there is a hierarchical structure of grades and specific positions, which can be gained by a combination of social skill, expenditure on entertaining and, certainly in the societies depending on magical powers, skill in mediumship. The head of a Buchwezi chapter would be called 'kingi' in his own area but he could not automatically claim that position in another chapter in a nearby chiefdom. Certainly no position is acquired without paying in food and money to those in the group above and to the chapter in general, and payment alone would not be enough if a man were not socially acceptable. Although these initiations were carried out by the group of rank-holding mediums, they certainly could not be considered as a means of private enrichment, as such presentations were made publicly and applauded by the chapter as a whole.

Joining the chapter of such a group as the Buchwezi involves the diagnosis by a medium that the patient's ancestors require him or her to go through the necessary initiation as an act of propitiation; the group appears to have no mythological charter and members go no further back in their explanations than to say that they had ancestors who were members. The patient-client need take no further part in their functions unless he is advised to do so as a result of further divination, or unless he wishes to do so because the chapter provides satisfactions unobtainable elsewhere. This cult has no mythological connection with the Cwezi cult of Bunyoro; in Usukuma it is connected with Lake Victoria and in the southern areas with water-holes, and initiation involves walking backwards into water. The rituals included the burying of protective medicines at cross-roads and on the lake shore, the removal of the spleen from a live sheep at the gateway to the compound, the painting of the initiates with white clay, walking backwards and forwards three times over the sheep and prostrate medium, asperging the initiates and making them drink protective medicines.

The Buchwezi chapter, whose initiations were observed in 1953 (Tanner, 1955b), and in 1964, do not appear to have changed the rituals, but the ages of those being initiated seemed to be decidedly higher. The majority of those being initiated in 1953 were below puberty and mainly boys, while the 1964 initiates were spread over all age groups and both sexes, with some predominance of divorced women. Although the rituals were long and complicated, as in the

Buyeye snake charmers' society (Cory, 1946), it seemed that the chapter observed had a strong sense of group identity to which the ritual was subsidiary. They liked being together, watching and participating in ritual, singing Buchwezi songs and keeping other people away for the period of the meeting in the 'kingi's' house, which lasted several days. Although politically the Sukuma have acquiesced in a unitary government and a one-party state, nevertheless socially they seem to thrive on competition between rival groups and chapters.

The third stage, which is developing currently with the decline of the cult groups, consists of individual mediums practising without much of the traditional training and equipment, in order to deal with the problems of the urban and industrialized communities in Usukama. The number of mediums around Mwanza, the main town of Usukama, is very much greater than in the rural areas, and they practise more on Sundays than on other days, to deal with the problems of employed persons. In many cases they have nothing in their compounds to show their occupation and wear no special costume for consultation, because this fits them better in their secular environment.

SUMMARY

To sum up – mediumship is taken up by both men and women as a result of personal misfortune, attributed by a diviner to an ancestor, who is not, however, thought to remain in permanent association with the medium. Mediums either practise intermittently as consultants to the sick and unhappy, which brings little increase in their social status, or they become rank holders in cults which are dependent on magico-religious activity, and membership in which may bring increased social prestige. As part of an organized cult mediumship appears to have gone through three stages in the last century. In the first there were few mediums, but they were closely integrated into the political and social life of the chiefdom. Second, they proliferated into widespread cults, divided into chapters, associated with magico-religious activity. And lastly, mediums are today catering for the urban and industrial workers.

REFERENCES

BATCHELOR, I. R. C. 1953 'Hysteria', *British Medical Journal*, May 9, 1953, 1041–1043.

CORY, H. 1946 'The Buyeye, a secret society of snake charmers in Sukumaland', *Africa*, 16.

1949 'The ingredients of magic medicines,' *Africa*, 19.

1951 *The Ntemi*, London, Macmillan.

1954 *The indigenous political system of the Sukuma*. Kampala, East African Institute of Social Research.

TANNER, R. E. S. 1955a 'Hysteria in Sukuma medical practice', *Africa*, 25.

1955b 'The initiation rites of the Buchwezi secret society', *Illustrated London News*, 226, April 19, 1955.

1956 'Introduction to the Northern Sukuma's idea of the Supreme Being', *Anthropological Quarterly*, 29, (3).

1957a 'The magician in Northern Sukumaland'. *Southwestern Journal of Anthropology* 13, (4).

1957b 'Installation of Sukuma chiefs in Mwanza district', *African Studies*, 16, (4).

1959 'Sukuma leechcraft – an analysis of their medical and surgical system', *East African Medical Journal*, 36.

SPIRIT INITIATION IN ANKOLE AND A CHRISTIAN SPIRIT MOVEMENT IN WESTERN KENYA

© *F. B. Welbourn*

I have described elsewhere 'Emandwa Initiation in Ankole' and the 'African Israel Church Nineveh' (Welbourn, 1965, 1966). Both are group spirit cults. Although the former notably stops short of possession, the phenomenon is clearly hinted at; and the cult is sufficiently close to those described by Beattie (1957, 1961) and Cory (1955) to fall into the general class of spirit mediumship. The latter, as a group cult– – and quite apart from its strongly Christian reference – appears to be of a type previously unknown to Luyia and Luo among whom it is chiefly found. The purpose of this essay is to place the two side by side and to ask whether either can help towards an understanding of the other. Individual mediumship cults will be mentioned only in passing.

ANKOLE

The modern kingdom of Ankole is an amalgamation, under British influence, of a number of Hima chiefdoms (Morris, 1962), each of which was divided into the ruling pastoral Hima and agricultural Iru. Material in this essay comes from an Iru community in the central chiefdom of Nkore, whose hereditary chief is 'king' of the new political unit. But, apart from slightly differing myths of origin, there is little difference in cult or myth between the two ethnic groups, who speak the same language and are loosely organized into patrilineal, exogamic clans. These observe the same totems, but use different eponymous names across the ethnic boundary (cf. Taylor, 1962, 101 ff.). Ruhanga (the Creator) is associated with the sun and wholly benign. Although daily morning prayers might be said to him by the chief wife of each household, and his attention is called before a ritual for lower spirits, he is generally thought to be inactive. The king is said to be descended from a legendary Cwezi dynasty, common in one form or another to all the Hima chiefdoms, and themselves descended ultimately from Ruhanga. He has special powers, as the mediator of blessings; and his successor is a reincarnation of the undying kingship. But his corpse is allowed to rot; and there is no cult of the royal tombs. The king had his private diviners borrowed from neighbouring Bunyoro (Bamunoba, 1965); and he was subject, in private, to the spirit initiation to be described.

Evil could be accounted for by sorcery, curses, the evil eye, the breaking of taboos and the violation of a totem. The latter led inevitably to death. Certain spirits, of unknown origin, are traditionally associated with specific diseases (e.g. Kahumpuri with plague), others with particular professions (e.g. Ryangombe and Rushoma with hunters). Others are used by diviners; and contemporarily the most powerful are Nyabingi and Mungu, who are recent immigrants. The latter is particularly interesting, since he entered Ankole along the Arab trade route. Unlike other spirits, he insists on being the sole possessor of his mediums. In origin his name is the Swahili form for the God of Christians and Muslims who, in his 'jealous' aspect, appears to have entered Ankole more effectively through direct assimilation to the traditional culture than through the efforts of missionaries.

Traditionally Iru lived in clan villages; but social and ritual co-operation at this level was slight (cf. Taylor, 1962, 100). More important were the lineages, which were not arranged in a segmentary series, and of which several might be represented in a village. It was common for four generations to live within one homestead. When a son had many wives he might form his own homestead in the same village, remaining within the same lineage. In case of a quarrel, one member might move to form his own lineage among his clansmen elsewhere. The head of a lineage or a homestead appointed his successor from among his agnates.

Within this kinship grouping the eldest son was responsible for making regular offerings to his father's ghost. Ghosts were wholly malevolent and included those not only of all related adults but of children and of strangers who died in the homestead. But it seems likely that, until it was suppressed by government and mission alike, the most important cult was one which affected the whole lineage rather than individual homesteads within it. This was the cult of the

Cwezi spirits, of whom six are named (Kagoro, Kyomya, Mugasha, Murindwa, Ndahura and Wamara). The legendary Cwezi dynasty was fair-skinned. It ruled for a short time and then mysteriously disappeared. An initiate is introduced to the spirits of his father, his mother and his father's mother and acts in effect as priest on behalf of the whole homestead. Different lineages within the same clan have, in principle, the same patrilineal spirit. In practice they may be different, thus demonstrating the very loose way in which the clan and lineage systems are related. Particular spirits may be antipathetic to one another; and, if any of the three spirits of one homestead is at odds with any of the three spirits of another homestead, marriage between members of the two groups is followed by quarrelling and other difficulties. The sociological implications of this belief require further investigation. The immediate practical effect is that marriage is prohibited not only within patrilineal clans but with members of specific lineages in other clans. But the same antipathies are not necessarily found in different parts of the country.

Although the overt actions attributed to Cwezi spirits are almost wholly malevolent, it is believed that, if they are given their dues, they are guardians of the well-being of the homestead and ward off other Cwezi spirits who may wish it harm. But they require regular offerings; and, if these are not made, the spirits may show their displeasure by causing sickness to people and animals, failure of crops or misunderstandings within the homestead. Each third day was dedicated to them. Women might do pottery and weaving. But there was no work in the fields. Iru men attended beer parties. Hima men would sing, drink, roast beef and wrestle. The Nkore day of rest appears to have been not only more frequent, but less puritanical, than that of the Jews. On additional special occasions the members of the homestead were led several times round the central house in a litany of blessing. If an enemy army was approaching a village, or on starting a journey, vows of an offering might be made in return for a safe outcome. On such occasions a man might entrust (*okusiga*) his family to the spirits. At seed-time the spirits were invited to accompany their wards to the fields. Otherwise they might destroy the crops. At harvest an offering of the first-fruits was dedicated. Otherwise death or sickness would follow. A goat of the homestead was given to the spirits and must be replaced if it died. If any sickness or trouble was diagnosed by a diviner as being caused by a Cwezi spirit, a special offering, with prayer, was made at its shrine. In more severe cases, the spirit might demand the initiation of the patient himself. This might happen even when the patient was very young or very ill. A symbolic initiation might then be performed to be followed by the full rite at a later date.

Traditionally, each homestead must have one initiate, who was not necessarily its social head. Care might be taken, after consultation with a diviner, to arrange for the initiation of a successor before the death of the incumbent. But, at least within living memory, spirits have demanded the initiation of additional members of the homestead. They might show their will by causing trouble either to the chosen one or to any of his immediate relations. Initiates might be either male or female. There is no evidence of any special characteristics to direct the choice as mediated by the diviner.

Initiation itself was an unpleasant experience and, at least overtly, was avoided if at all possible. An agnatic relative (himself initiate) was indicated by the diviner as sponsor. The latter's first duty was to instruct the candidate in the obligation of absolute obedience to those already initiated, in the points of the rite where his response must be accurate, and in some of the secret spirit vocabulary known only to initiates. But it was integral to the rite that the candidate should not know what was going to happen next, so that the detailed instructions which he received during its course genuinely aroused fear or shame. On the eve of the ceremony, the sponsor arrived at the candidate's home, wearing the three headdresses appropriate to his own spirits and bearing those which had been prepared for the candidate. With him were a group of initiates, of any lineage, also ritually attired. Along with relatives of the candidate there was feasting, dancing and singing. But the centre of the occasion was striking fear into the candidate, teasing him and making him behave like a baby. On the following morning he was led off into the bush with every appearance that he, instead of a cow, was to be slaughtered in sacrifice. He was symbolically redeemed; and two days were spent, along with dancing, the shaking of rattles and singing of spirit songs, in horseplay, of which the candidate was the constant butt. He was set impossible tasks, severely beaten for failure, and laughed to scorn when a bystander showed how to simulate their accomplishment. He was told to do shameful acts (to choose any person of the opposite sex with whom to have intercourse in public; to abuse his mother and father). Refusal was met with punishment for disobedience, compliance with the same punishment for acting shamefully.

The first day ended with the candidate being given the head-dress of his father's spirit and later that of his paternal grandmother. At the end of the second day he was given that of his mother; and he was then expected to fall to the ground as though possessed. (Throughout the two days the participants feigned possession. In the rites described by Beattie (1957) and Cory (1955) genuine possession was expected to occur and to be feigned only in cases of natural failure. But in Ankole 'possession' during group initiation ceremonies was expected to be a deliberate artifact. Its actual occurrence appears to have been reserved to individual mediums working as diviners.) On being raised, he was made to swallow a stone signifying that he must never reveal the secrets of initiation. He was given a ritual name, which must never be used outside the society of initiates. (This was usually of a scurrilous character – 'The Dog that Steals', 'The Thief Whose Penis Has No Foreskin', 'Cunning and Greedy'.) Finally, he was tested in his knowledge of the spirit vocabulary, punished for ignorance, and reminded, in a final symbolic action, not to reveal his secret knowledge.

Late in the day the company returned to the candidate's home. For several days he was expected to behave like a child and had unfettered right to beg and steal. After this, his sponsor instructed him how to build a shrine for each of his three spirits. He was now responsible for regular offering at these shrines on behalf of the whole homestead – offerings which appear to have been frequently neglected. If any trouble in the homestead was diagnosed by a diviner as due to one of the three spirits, the initiate led the members in the appropriate offering; and he took part in the initiation of further candidates from any lineage. As the spirits are called *emandwa*, so all initiates are themselves *emandwa* – not, as in some other cultures, when they are possessed (for possession is no part of their office) but at all times. It has to be understood from the context whether the word, as used in conversation, refers to a Cwezi spirit or to an initiate.

Owing to the great secrecy imposed not only by the rite itself but by its suppression at the hands of government and mission, it is impossible to obtain information except from initiates who ride loose to the traditional implications of the cult. One educated Nkore was unable to find a sponsor when he wished to experience the rite. But it seems that, through intense fear, shame and physical brutality, both men and women (at times, boys and girls) were admitted to membership of a secret society which gave frequent opportunity, at each new initiation, for release of aggression and offered a new status in society as a whole. This was not necessarily a higher status, for technically it was not necessary for the head of the homestead to be himself initiated. His paternal rights were safeguarded not only by empirical sanctions but by the ancestor cult. It would be sufficient for his wife or one of his children to mediate between the homestead and its spirits. It is, however, noticeable that women and children were admitted on the same terms as men; and the cult may have provided an outlet from the rigid restraints on their behaviour at normal times. At the same time, it provided an opportunity for corporate ritual, at a level which transcended clan and lineage organization.

WESTERN KENYA

The Luyia and Luo of Western Kenya are respectively Bantu and Nilotic tribes. The former practise male circumcision and traditionally despise their uncircumcised neighbours. Wagner (1939) and Lonsdale (1964) have described the breakdown of traditional social units, under the impact of missions and British government. The influence of both has been relatively benign. But disturbance of traditional life has been effected by the demands of British administration, emigration of workers to settler farms in the neighbouring areas and their subsequent return, the growth of a dense agricultural population and the incidence of large numbers of missions, many of them congregational in polity. At least since the late 1920s there has been a proliferation of independent churches so that an administrator remarked, 'Among the Luyia we expect a new religion every month'. The East African Revival has had considerable success among both tribes (Welbourn, 1966). Spirit possession was known in individual cases and was used by diviners. But the only report of anything approaching a group cult is by Owuor (n.d.), who describes what amounts to group therapy for cases of hysteria attributed to spirits who entered Luo country during the war with the Nandi in the years immediately preceding colonial rule.

The introduction of a group cult was left to the Canadian Pentecostal Mission, which in 1919 settled at Nyang'ori in the south-east of Luyia country bordering on the Luo. Pentecostalists preach a simple message of individual salvation, which expects not only the traditional revival moment of conversion, but a second moment (sometimes postponed for years) of 'receiving the Holy Spirit'; and this may be characterized by glossolalia and catalepsy. Thus gifted, the individual enters a group which is set apart from the world by the special experience of each individual member and practises a corporate cult distinguished not only for the fervour of its preaching, but for the rhythmic and repetitive character of its singing. A congregation 'singing in the Spirit' is said to be wholly different from a congregation not so moved; and it is hardly surprising if, in conditions so favourable to dissociation, individuals receive the Spirit most commonly at such times. 'Spiritual healing' is practised.

The American Friends Africa Mission was a much more staid body. But its boys' school at Kaimosi further to the north was in tribal land threatened by the discovery of gold with the fear of alienation. Against the background of this anxiety, one deviant Friends missionary promoted a wholesale 'outpouring of the Spirit' at the school. It was disapproved by the missionary leaders; and numbers of Africans left the mission either to join the Pentocostalists or to form independent groups such as *Dini ya Roho* ('Religion of the Spirit'). One group, known as *Lisanga*, is remembered as 'making horrible noises to show their closeness to God'.

Against this general background, though not as a direct result of the incident at Kaimosi, the African Israel Church Nineveh was formed in 1942. Zakayo Kivuli, born about 1896, had gone to school at Nyang'ori in order to avoid conscription during the first World War. After work on settlers' farms and marriage in 1921, he eventually returned to school in 1925, was baptised and sent, with his wife and children, to the Jeanes School at Kabete. This had been established as a result of the visit of the Phelps Stokes Commission in 1924. It stressed the importance of character training combined with the teaching of practical subjects to meet the need of rural communities. Kivuli returned to become mission supervisor of schools and started to ask himself, 'Does the word of God preached by Europeans really come from God or is it merely something concocted by them to deceive Africans?' Late in 1931 he had what he describes as liver trouble. On February 6, 1932, he became convinced that he was a sinner; and on February 12 he received the Spirit. The experience was closely assimilated to that of Saint Paul (Acts 9: 4–9), whose name he now took. He started to preach widely in the villages, urging public confession and praying (he claims successfully) for the sick. He was supported by the missionary but disliked by many African Pentecostalists.

During this time, a group of Luo Anglicans in the neighbouring area also received the Spirit. Kivuli met their leader; and the two have remained close friends and associates. In 1942 Kivuli was elected liaison officer between the missionaries and the African church; but, owing to widespread jealousy of Kivuli, the head of the mission was unable to confirm the appointment and gave his blessing to Kivuli who wished to start an independent church from his own home. He was joined by the Luo group. By 1958 there were 40 registered congregations in Luyia country and 16 in Luo country. Elsewhere there were 37 congregations founded by migrant Luyia and Luo – eastwards to Nairobi and Mombasa, westwards into north-east Tanzania. The total membership, recorded in detail, was 4,900. Kivuli is 'Founder and High Priest' and known, throughout the church, as 'Father'. The church is characterized by the essentially family atmosphere which pervades its life and by the fact that it is not merely a ritual society but a community in which religious belief is deeply involved with empirical affairs. Even if Kivuli is in the last resort an autocratic father, he is held in deep affection. There is constant coming and going, and mutual hospitality, between his headquarters and the outlying congregations. Quarrels between members are reconciled and widows are cared for. Polygamy is allowed to men who had more than one wife on becoming church members. It is forbidden to others. In the congregations women outnumber the men by two to one. They take the lead in singing hymns and may preach to mixed congregations. They have entire control of special women's meetings. Pagan fathers have been known to encourage their daughters to join the church, where their virginity will be honoured; and men from other churches may seek their wives in African Israel. The church is held in very high repute by government agricultural, medical and veterinary officers; and members are encouraged to join Community Development classes. There has been considerable pressure to form schools under church control; and in 1952 there was an unsuccessful suggestion to found a credit bank.

Politics were originally forbidden; but this had been unpopular with the younger men for some years; and in 1961 Kivuli openly allied himself with the Kenya African National Union, declaring that God had already chosen both the civil and the spiritual leader of an independent Kenya.

The normal dress is ankle-length for both men and women, though young men, and men at work, may wear shorts. Men commonly wear a turban which, like the dresses, must be monochrome. Black signifies evil, and mixed colours a mixture of motives. Clothes are, however, embroidered 'AIN'; and the same inscription appears on doors and window-frames of houses, on cups and teapots.

Church services are spontaneous in character, though they are kept under close control by the leader, and the general pattern of prayer, exhortation, singing and public confession leading to possession, is fairly clear. The most popular hymns are locally composed for leader and chorus, to a melody and rhythm which spring naturally out of the African words. As the song gathers way the congregation, who start sitting, stand one by one; megaphones are produced; drums are beaten and any old piece of metal used to give its particular tone; hands are clapped and feet are stamped with more and more excitement; the dance is continued by men and women climbing on the benches. The following account by an impartial eye-witness gives some impression of the total effect:

> The people came singing, beating drums and dancing. The man in front carried the flag and was followed by two men carrying drums. The rest of the men and women followed in line. Most of them were dressed in white; a very few had yellow and green dresses. When they reached the church they all shouted 'Halleluya' and then entered. They left the flag outside the church and continued singing, jumping and making a lot of noise. When one of the church elders stood up, the singing stopped; but the church was still noisy because some, who had 'received the Holy Spirit', went on praying and jumping about. There was then a prayer which lasted ten minutes, during which more people received the Holy Spirit. A man preached; and then about eight women stood and confessed their sins. When they were saying the final prayer, a woman fell on the ground and made a lot of noise. She had received the Holy Spirit.

Public confession is integral to the cult, though recently there has been an attempt to distinguish those sins which are better confessed in private. Services on Fridays are specially devoted to this activity;

and the practice of wearing no shoes in church derives from the experience that, in the general excitement engendered, members might dance, rather hard, on one another's toes. But possession may also spring out of hymn-singing on Sundays; and no service is properly Spirit-filled unless there are several cases of catalepsy. Sunday services are preceded by a procession round the villages, with flags and drums, in an attempt to attract new adherents.

It is perhaps theologically significant that a statement of belief, prepared in 1957 for the Christian Council of Kenya, begins, 'We believe in God the Father, God the Son and God the Holy Spirit. We live by the guidance of the Trinity and the Holy Spirit'. The Cwezi spirits of Ankole are conceived as being ultimately of human origin, while Mungu and Nyabingi are ultra-human. All are, in the last resort, created by Ruhanga but act independently of him. African Israel, on the other hand, understands Holy Spirit as the direct agent of God and attempts to expound him in New Testament terms. He is the author not only of 'possession' but of charity and other virtues (Galatians 5:22f.). The additional accent on him, which appears even in a formal theological statement, suggests that he might easily become, in popular belief, a sort of demi-god.

The statement continues, 'Our main objects are (i) To win people for Christ; (ii) To establish Christian fellowship to all races; (iii) God is love, we must love one another; (iv) To teach the world that all have sinned . . . and that Christ is the only Saviour . . . '. Within the central emphasis on spirit-possession as integral to African Israel (though not necessarily to other Christians), the theology is characteristically evangelical, with an additional emphasis on the values of hard work, cleanliness and western rural technology. This is, of course, a public language, in the sense that African Israel is essentially directed towards winning new converts. At the same time, it is a language which carries full meaning only for those who have themselves been 'filled by Holy Spirit'.

Morality is extremely puritan, based not only on the teachings of evangelical missionaries but on further reading of the Old Testament. Spiritual healing is expected to occur; and dreams are regarded as important sources of revelation, though it is probable that both phenomena occur more frequently in the newer, rather than in old-established, congregations. Some relatively well-educated schoolmasters are members, though they view even their own pneumatic experiences with some detachment.

African Israel appears to be a dynamic community set apart not for a purely ritual function but in an attempt to restore, around what it knows of Christ and of western technology, something of the solidarity of tribal life destroyed by the impact of the west. Its empirical and mythological dimensions are clearly co-ordinate and equally essential. In Beattie's (1964) terms, its instrumental and expressive activities are mutually supporting. In Jaques' (1955) terms, changes in 'phantasy structure' have kept pace with changes in 'manifest structure'. Initiation through confession induces shame; and the weekly services give ample opportunity for the expression of repressed guilt – possibly in a dissociated form. The element of fear seems to be largely absent. and aggression to be projected almost wholly on to the Devil. Women have a higher status than they would be accorded in tribal society, or even in some of the mission churches. There is a certain ambivalence towards Europeans. The church is to be led by Africans; and Europeans, if they joined, would have to accept this leadership. At the same time, there is deep respect for European technical wisdom and a ready welcome for any Europeans who are prepared to meet Africans on equal terms.

DISCUSSION

Beattie (1957) outlines four connected themes in the Nyoro cult, which he finds also in Cory's (1955) description of the Sumbwa. These should be followed up in the two cults here described.

1. *Initiation sets the cult members permanently apart from the uninitiated in respect to possession. The assumption of a new personality is enacted in symbols of birth and death. It is reinforced by special regalia, food taboos and a secret language.* In Nkore an initiate becomes *emandwa*; but he is not possessed in the dissociative sense. He is set apart rather in respect to priesthood within a particular homestead. In Israel, possession is expected, though it may not always occur. The title 'Israel' itself implies 'set apart as the people of God'. In Nkore the assumption of a new personality is enacted in the simulated sacrifice of the candidate, his redemption and behaviour as a child. (Child-like behaviour is expected both before and after the initiation; and there is no enactment of birth as such.) Re-birth in Christ is integral to the evangelical preaching adopted by

African Israel. In Nkore there are no food taboos except the fiction that *emandwa* (not their human agents) do not eat hot food. Israel has taboos not only on certain kinds of food, but on alcohol, tobacco and sexual intercourse at certain seasons. In both, the new personality is reinforced by special regalia. In Nkore there is a secret language used only within the society; and Israel uses theological terminology which makes no sense outside the context of Christian Spirit-possession.

2. *Initiation is conducted in secret, in the total absence of non-initiates. This aspect has perhaps been reinforced by prohibition on the part of both government and mission.* This certainly holds true for Nkore. It is even possible that the intense secrecy imposed by prohibition is making, out of a cult which originally had positive social value, an anti-social activity. Israel very carefully screens potential visitors to Sunday services, and probably excludes them altogether from the Friday confession services, which must be regarded as the focus of initiation. But with social approval of the church in its total aspect has gone a relaxation of security measures, a desire to have a written history, and a much greater readiness to co-operate with other bodies claiming to be Christian.

3. *An initiate acquires new social obligations and rights, symbolized by the use, to describe relationships within the society, of terms taken from kinship and marriage.* A Nkore initiate, as priest to his household, is responsible for preserving proper relations with the *emandwa*. As himself *emandwa*, he may be called on to initiate others. There is no evidence of the use of kinship terms within the society. Special obligations, both towards other members and towards the support of the church as a whole, are explicit for all members of African Israel. As a group of those who have experienced possession, they form the social matrix within which others may have the same experience. The Founder is known by all as 'Father'. This is not merely a ritual title but an affectionate expression of his charismatic power.

4. *Initiation confers a ritually dangerous condition, which has to be removed by ritual sexual intercourse.* There is no evidence of this in Nkore. The rite appears to use the suggestion of sexual impropriety as a means of moral instruction. It may be that this ritual element in the spirit cults of other Hima chiefdoms has undergone a reinterpretation in Nkore. In the early Church, there was much discussion of the ritual dangers of baptism – such that sin after baptism might be irredeemable. In

African Israel there appears to be no sin which cannot be forgiven through confession. The prohibition of sexual intercourse at certain seasons is a ritual not expected of Christians of other churches. Rules about polygamy are recognized as specific to the church. At the same time, they are regarded as moral, and not merely ritual regulations and offered as a contribution to general Christian thinking about polygamy.

It seems that the Nkore spirit cult and African Israel conform sufficiently closely to the same pattern to make comparison worth while. Pentecostal Christianity has externalizing characteristics (Lienhardt, 1960, ch. 4) additional to those found in more conventional Christian groups. Certain psycho-somatic phenomena, which the latter would regard as originating in the individual psyche, are described by Pentecostalists in terms of a personal force acting from the outside. This is sufficiently close to traditional African modes of response to have made it a ready tool for Kivuli's need to come to terms with the West. For a man who had entered fairly deeply into the technical and bureaucratic structure of the white men, there must be a corresponding adaptation to their mythology. In other parts of East Africa, Christianity has tended to become a new cult, offering some opportunity of accommodation with the invaders, but increasingly irrelevant to pressing secular concerns. Kivuli seems to have inspired a community which, consistently Christian in intention, has been able to relate its mythology very closely to its empirical needs. Perhaps this would have been impossible in more orthodox Christian terms, with their relative distance from traditional African forms. There is extremely little evidence of active anti-European feeling either in the foundation of his church or in its later history; and, even after his identification with the Kenya African National Union, he remained on excellent terms with white Christians. But he seems to have found a mythological form which was relevant to the social and economic demands of colonialism and, at the same time, could sustain the new empirical expectations of nationalism. It is, therefore, tempting to suggest that – although there are no reports of traditional group spirit cults among the Luyia – Kivuli was able to adapt western mythology to a general Bantu pattern in an accommodation which was also relevant to a rapidly changing social structure.

On the other hand, it is possible that African Israel may throw some light on the character of the Nkore cult. Kantai (Welbourn, 1964) has described in Maasai a monotheism of a distinctly Hebraic pattern, with no lower spirits and no ancestral ghosts but with occasional cataleptic incidents which in Bantu societies would almost certainly be interpreted as possession. At the other end of the scale, in the Nyoro and Sumbwa cults possession is expected to occur, even if it is known that at times it may have to be feigned. In the Nkore group cult, possession is always a dramatic act and not expected to be a dissociative experience. This might be a response of the Hima pastoral culture, like that of the Maasai ignorant of possession but desiring to accommodate to the dissociative traits of Bantu Iru. It might, on the other hand, represent the decay of a cult which was originally dissociative; and, in view of the occurrence of possession in similar cults in neighbouring Bantu-Hima societies, this seems the more likely explanation. African Israel is a response of African society to the impact of a strong invading culture, in which possession by the Spirit of that culture helps to stabilize the tensions of structural adaptation. It may be that the Cwezi cult was in its origin the means by which structural adaptation to the demands of an invading Cwezi dynasty was eased through possession by their spirits. Stenning (Taylor, 1962, 110) thought that the spirits of this cult were of Hima origin. As cultural assimilation took place, the original needs of the cult disappeared; and it remained as a cult providing mythological sanctions for a stable society and an outlet for the repressions inherent in any society. In both cults, the status of women is raised; and this may indicate that, in the task of accommodation to an invader, all the resources of society have to be mobilized, so that women – at least for the sake of that task – are released from their traditional subordination.

At the same time it has to be asked whether the 'phantasy structure' of the two cults is the same. An ancestor cult in one society may represent – as has often been suggested – repressed guilt feelings towards the departed. In another it may be the projection of more primitive persecutory phantasies. In psycho-analytic terms, it should be possible to make the beginnings of a distinction based on the primacy of restitution or of placation in the intention of gifts to ancestors. Such a study requires psycho-analytic, as well as anthropological, training. But a beginning ought to be made. It may be difficult to determine the relation between individual psychology and the structure of society. But there is sufficient evidence of cultural factors affecting psychological development; and it is at least reasonable to suppose that there is a causal relation in the other direction also. Neither can be regarded as an independent determinant. But, if a psychology is inadequate which ignores cultural factors, no purely sociological description can be complete which omits the psychological elements involved. They may be as important as past history in determining the future of contemporary institutions.

The immediate point of departure in this essay is Jaques' chapter in Klein (1955, ch. 20). He attempts to apply Klein's development of Freudian analysis to some of the phenomena of behaviour in groups. There are two fundamentally different modes of dealing with the satisfying and frustrating aspects of experience. In the first (Klein's 'paranoid-schizoid position') the two experiences are sharply separated in the imagination. The supposed source of satisfaction becomes an object of love, that of frustration an object of aggression or a persecutor who has to be *placated*. In the extreme case this splitting of experience may be transferred to the objective world. The mother's breast, which is a source of both experiences, is perceived as two wholly separate objects.

Although this psychic mechanism may become the source of certifiable psychosis in individuals, it seems probable that it is implicit in the normal experience of rearing; and there is nothing derogatory in suggesting that it is continually used by 'normal' adults. As an example of its outworking, Jaques quotes a British merchant ship in which, in order to allow the captain to be mythologically wholly benign, the first mate is mythologically a 'shit' and must remain so as long as he holds that particular executive position. Gluckman (1954), using a different vocabulary, describes how ambivalent emotions towards a Swazi king are acted out in ritual rebellion. The kingship itself is secured by allowing the possibility of ousting its present occupant. In western political societies, on the other hand, politicians become the sources of persecution, the objects of aggression. The monarchy is 'blatantly extolled'. Kings reign but do not rule; and rebellion becomes revolt – the attempt not to replace a particular sovereign but to destroy the whole institution of monarchy.

Klein's second mode (the 'depressive position') is that in which satisfaction and frustration are recognized as originating in the same object. Guilt is aroused by the desire to aggress against the loved object (paradigmatically the mother's breast, now perceived as a whole); and there is desire to make *restitution* for the wrong done even in imagination. This is what Winnicott calls the 'stage of concern' (1958, 262–277). It characterizes the conflicting emotions held in creative tension between spouses and between parents and children. It is also basic to the sense of individual responsibility which British administrators and Protestant missionaries alike have tried to instil into Africans.

In psycho-analytic terms, both modes of response are learnt in the early stages of an infant's relationship with its mother. I have suggested elsewhere that the relative emphasis placed upon them in adult behaviour may be related to cultural factors (Welbourn, 1968). It is a thesis to be investigated that the spirit cult in Ankole is a playing out of the 'paranoid-schizoid' mode, while African Israel is an expression of the 'depressive' mode.

In the Nkore cult, the aggression displayed – not only in physical bruality but in mocking laughter – suggests a paranoid origin. Spirits are felt, at different times, as sources both of succour and of persecution. They have to be placated; but it is difficult to detect any sense in which restitution has to be made to loved objects. The psyche is split in its attitude towards them. Ancestral ghosts are regarded as wholly arbitrary in their behaviour. Victims are not thought to deserve the misfortunes attributed to ghosts but rather to be suffering from 'bad luck'. In the same mode, Nkore culture lays a tremendous emphasis on shame – the fear of social persecution – as a sanction of conduct.

On the other hand, it has been suggested that African Israel is a response to an Anglo-Saxon culture in which administrators and missionaries laid considerable stress on responsibility and guilt, derivatives of the 'depressive position'. That 'schizoid' elements are still present is indicated by the projection on to the Devil of feelings of aggression and persecution. But the central rite of confession is felt as a means to restitution, issuing in an inner sense of peace. There is considerable emphasis on mutual responsibility within the society. Feelings towards Europeans seem to be of an integrated 'love-hate' character. The Founder himself is a father-figure who may be severe in his judicial capacity but can nevertheless be criticized and regarded with deep affection.

Much more analysis of this kind might be possible. But the suggestion is that fundamentally similar cultural forms – arising perhaps in response to similar external circumstances – may hide different unconscious phantasies. It is in the details of the cults, rather than in their overall forms, that evidence of these differences may be found. It may be that they have wholly different implications for their future.

REFERENCES

J. H. M. BEATTIE 1957 'Initiation into the Cwezi Spirit Possession Cult in Bunyoro', *African Studies*, 16, 150–161.

1961 'Group Aspects of the Nyoro Spirit Mediumship Cult', *Rhodes-Livingstone Journal*, 30, 11–38.

1964 *Other cultures*. London, Cohen and West, chapters 12 and 13.

J. K. BAMUNOBA 1965 'Diviners for the Abagabe', *Uganda Journal*, I, 29 (1).

H. CORY 1955 'The Buswezi', *American Anthropologist*, 57, 923–52.

M. GLUCKMAN 1954 *Rituals of rebellion in South-East Africa*, Manchester University Press.

E. JAQUES 1955 see M. Klein (1955).

M. KLEIN 1955 *et al.* (eds.) *New directions in psycho-analysis*. London, Tavistock Publications.

G. LIENHARDT 1961 *Divinity and Experience*, Oxford, Clarendon Press.

J. M. LONSDALE 1964 *A political history of Nyanza* 1883–1945. Unpublished thesis accepted for a Ph.D. of the University of Cambridge.

H. F. MORRIS 1962 *A history of Ankole*, Kampala, East African Literature Bureau.

H. A. OWUOR (n.d.) 'Spirit possession among the Luo of Central Nyanza'. Typescript in the library of the East African Institute of Social Research, Kampala.

B. K. TAYLOR 1962 *The Western Lacustrine Bantu*. London, International African Institute.

G. WAGNER 1939 'The changing family among the Bantu Kavirondo', *Africa* 12, (supplement).

F. B. WELBOURN 1964 'The idea of a High God in three East African Societies', seminar on *The High God*, held at the Institute of African Studies, University of Ife.

1965 and Y. K. Bambunoba, 'Emandwa initiation in Ankole', *Uganda Journal*, 29 (1), 13–25.

1965b 'Shame and guilt', in C. G. Baëta (editor), *Christianity in Tropical Africa*. London, Oxford University Press for International African Institute.

1966 and B. A. Ogot, *A place to feel at home*, London, Oxford University Press.

D. W. WINNICOTT 1958 *Collected papers*, London, Tavistock Publications.

INDEX